HUNTERS AND KILLERS

HUNTERS AND KILLERS

Volume 1: Anti-Submarine Warfare from 1776 to 1943

Norman Polmar
and Edward Whitman

Naval Institute Press
Annapolis, Maryland

Naval Institute Press
291 Wood Road
Annapolis, MD 21402

Library of Congress Cataloging-in-Publication Data

Polmar, Norman.
  Hunters and killers / Norman Polmar and Edward Whitman.
    pages cm
  Includes bibliographical references and index.
  ISBN 978-1-59114-689-6 (alk. paper)
  1. Anti-submarine warfare—United States—History. I. Whitman, Edward. II. Title.
  V214.P65 2015
  359.9′34—dc23
                                    2015019061

♾ Print editions meet the requirements of ANSI/NISO z39.48-1992 (Permanence of Paper).
Printed in the United States of America.

23 22 21 20 19 18 17 16 15   9 8 7 6 5 4 3 2 1
First printing

Maps created by Charles Grear.

Such is the U-boat war—hard, widespread and bitter, a war of groping and drowning, a war of ambuscade and stratagem, a war of science and seamanship.

—Winston Churchill, 1939

Contents

Personalities and Maps viii
Perspective ix
Terms, Abbreviations, and U.S. Ship Designations xi

1   Early Undersea Warfare   **1**

2   The First ASW Challenge   **17**

3   ASW in Other Areas   **47**

4   Lessons Learned, New Platforms,   **61**
          and New Technologies

5   Developing Sonar and Radar   **84**

6   Building ASW Forces   **98**

7   First Confrontations in the Atlantic   **112**

8   The Conflict Widens   **132**

9   The End of the Beginning   **157**

Appendix:
World War I Submarine Losses 183

Notes 184
General Index 197
Ship Name and Class Index 205
Submarine Name and Class Index 209

Personalities

Vice-Admiral Gordon Campbell, Royal Navy 30
Sir James Alfred Ewing 38
Admiral Sir William Reginald Hall, Royal Navy 40
Admiral Reginald Guy Henderson, Royal Navy 43
Captain Cyril Percy Ryan, Royal Navy 72
Dr. Paul Langevin 86
Dr. Robert William Boyle 88
Grossadmiral Karl Dönitz, German Navy 110
Captain Donald Macintyre, Royal Navy 134
Sir Charles Rodger Winn 136
Dr. Philip McCord Morse 174
Admiral Sir Max Kennedy Horton, Royal Navy 176

Maps

Map 1. The North Sea and British Home Waters 18
Map 2. Otranto Straits Barrage 50
Map 3. Principal North Atlantic Convoy Routes 121
Map 4. The Mediterranean Theater, World War II 147

Perspective

Winston Churchill, twice First Lord of the Admiralty and Britain's prime minister during World War II, said of the Battle of the Atlantic: "The only thing that ever really frightened me during the war was the U-boat peril. . . . I was even more anxious about this battle than I had been about the glorious air fight called the Battle of Britain."[1] And, "The U-boat attack was our worst evil. It would have been wise for the Germans to stake all upon it."[2]

The Battle of the Atlantic was the longest "battle" of World War II. It began in September 1939, and although the Allies had largely prevailed by the spring of 1943—forcing German U-boats out of the North Atlantic—the struggle did not end until the German surrender in May 1945. Indeed, days before the end of the war the German Navy sent to sea the first of what could have been one hundred Type XXI U-boats, at that time the world's most advanced submarine. It could—and did—evade many of the Allies' best anti-submarine tactics and weapons, and had it entered the war earlier, the outcome might have been different, or at least delayed.

Anti-Submarine Warfare (ASW) did not begin with World War II, as implied in many histories of warfare, nor even in World War I. Rather, it began during the American Revolution, in 1776, in response to the American submersible *Turtle*'s attack on a British ship-of-the-line anchored off New York City. The *Turtle*'s attack failed, but it alerted the British to a new danger, and they soon developed procedures to counter such underwater threats. Submarine attacks and countermeasures were again employed in the American Civil War, the first conflict in which a warship was sunk by an enemy undersea craft.

By World War I, submarines—especially the German *Unterseeboots,* or U-boats—had developed to the point that by the spring of 1917 the German U-boat campaign had almost isolated Britain from its overseas sources of food and war materials. Despite a massive Allied ASW campaign waged in the Atlantic and Mediterranean, the U-boats were never completely defeated in World War I.

In addition to the Second Battle of the Atlantic (1939–1945), submarine/anti-submarine conflicts in World War II were fought in the Norwegian-Arctic Seas, the Mediterranean, the Indian Ocean, and across the broad Pacific.

Hunters and Killers examines these ASW actions and addresses the strategic contexts, technologies, platforms, and tactics that evolved on both sides of the submarine/anti-submarine struggles since the early 20th Century. This volume carries the history of ASW through the spring of 1943—the turning point of the Battle of the Atlantic. It was at that point that *Grossadmiral* Karl Dönitz withdrew his U-boats from the North Atlantic.

Volume 2 of this history covers the final two years of the Battle of the Atlantic, the ASW campaigns in the Pacific conflict, then the 45 years of the Cold War, including the near-nuclear exchanges between Soviet submarines and U.S. ASW forces in the Cuban Missile Crisis, Argentine submarines versus British ASW forces in the Falklands, and other, less significant anti-submarine operations. Also discussed are the ASW organizations, weapons, sensors, and tactics of the period covered.

Since the early decades of the last century, several hundred non-fiction books have been written about submarines and submarine warfare. These have ranged from memoirs by submarine commanders and submarine admirals to general histories of submarine development and operations, to technical dissertations. But in that same period, except for numerous accounts of the Battle of the Atlantic, there have been only some *half-dozen* significant books about ASW in general. None of those has tried to portray the entire history of ASW, from the earliest efforts to counter underwater craft in 1776 to the end of the 20th Century, and on into the new millennium.

The authors hope that *Hunters and Killers* will remedy that shortcoming. The bibliography and acknowledgments for this book will be found in Volume 2.

Norman Polmar
Edward Whitman

Terms and Abbreviations

AAF — Army Air Forces (U.S.)

Alberich — Anechoic hull coating used for German U-boats

anechoic — coating on submarines to reduce the coating effectiveness of an enemy's active sonar by absorbing acoustic energy to reduce the reflected sound; may be a rubber-like coating or tiles

asdic — British active sonar

ASV — Air-to-Surface Vessel (radar)

ASW — Anti-Submarine Warfare

ASWORG — Anti-Submarine Warfare Operations Research Group (U.S.)

BIR — Bureau of Invention and Research (British)

CAM — Catapult Aircraft Merchant Ship

CinC — Commander-in-Chief

CNO — Chief of Naval Operations (U.S.)

displacement — U.S. and British submarine displacements in long tons (2,240 pounds); foreign submarine displacements are based on metric tons (1,000 kg, or 2,205 lb)

double hull — submarine hull configuration in which a non-pressure hull surrounds all or major portions of the inner pressure hull. The between-hull volume may be free-flooding or contain ballast tanks, fuel tanks, and possibly weapons and equipment (at ambient sea pressure).

EASTOMP — Eastern Ocean Meeting Point

FCS — Fighter Catapult Ship

Fido — Mark 24 "mine" (acoustic homing torpedo)

GHG — *Gruppenhorchgerät* (sonar)

GRT — gross registered tons

HF/DF — High-Frequency Direction-Finding ("Huff-Duff")

HUK — Hunter-Killer

Hz — Hertz

HMS — His/Her Majesty's Ship/Station

kHz — Kilohertz (1,000 Hz)

knot — one nautical mile per hour (1.15 statute miles per hour)

LUT — *Lagenunabhängiger Torpedo*

MAD — Magnetic Anomaly Detection (also Magnetic Airborne Detection)

MHz — Megahertz (1,000,000 Hz)

Mod — Modification

MOMP — Mid-Ocean Meeting Point

n.mile — nautical mile (1.15 statute miles)

NRL — Naval Research Laboratory (U.S.)

OIC — Operational Intelligence Centre (British)

PDH — Portable Detection Hydrophone

PGS — Portable General Service (hydrophone)

pressure hull — submarine hull that provides protection against sea pressure for crew, machinery, weapons, and equipment; it may be encased within an outer, non-pressure hull—i.e., in a *double-hull* configuration

radar	(orig.) Radio Detection And Ranging	snorkel	intake and exhaust tubes to permit the operation of a diesel engine in a submerged submarine (at periscope depth)
RAF	Royal Air Force (British)		
RDF	Radio Direction-Finding		
RNAS	Royal Naval Air Service	sonar	(orig.) Sound Navigation And Ranging
saddle tanks	ballast and/or fuel tanks fitted within the outer hull of a submarine		
		WESTOMP	Western Ocean Meeting Point
		VP	patrol squadron (U.S.)

U.S. Ship Designations

ACR	armored cruiser	CVE	escort aircraft carrier
AG	miscellaneous auxiliary	DD	destroyer
AO	oiler	DE	destroyer escort
AP	transport (troop ship)	DM	light minelayer
APD	high speed transport	IX	miscellaneous—unclassified
AR	repair ship	PE	Eagle patrol craft
AV	seaplane tender	PG	gunboat
AVD	destroyer seaplane tender	PY	patrol yacht
AVG	aircraft escort vessel (later CVE)	PYc	coastal patrol yacht
BB	battleship	SC	subchaser
CA	heavy cruiser	SS	submarine
CL	light cruiser	SSK	hunter-killer submarine
CV	aircraft carrier		

Early Undersea Warfare

In November 1775, Sir William Tryon, the British governor of the colony of New York, forwarded new, secret intelligence to Admiral Molyneux Shuldham, the commander-in-chief of the Royal Navy's North American station. Shuldham and his fleet were wintering in Boston:

> The great news of the day with us is to Destroy the Navy, a certain Mr. Bushnel has completed his Machine, and has been missing four weeks, returned this day week. It is conjectur'd that an attempt was made on the *Asia,* but proved unsuccessful—Return'd to New Haven in order to get a Pump of new Construction which will soon be completed,—When you may expect to see the Ships in Smoke.[1]

Governor Tryon's information about what was at first called the "Connecticut Water Machine" had been gleaned by several loyalist spies and proved to be surprisingly accurate. And, although both he and Admiral Shuldham greeted this earliest known submarine warning with indifference, if not derision, within a year, in New York Bay, "Mr. Bushnel's [*sic*] Machine" would mount the first recorded submarine attack on a hostile warship—and come close to sinking it.

Born in Westbrook, Connecticut, David Bushnell (1740–1824) was a mathematics student at Yale in 1772 when he carried out several experiments to demonstrate that gunpowder could be effectively detonated underwater. Given his sympathy for the cause of American colonial rights and the potential threat posed by the Royal Navy should growing unrest lead to open war, Bushnell was quick to recognize the potential of underwater explosives for attacking ships. By 1774, in casting about for a means to deliver a gunpowder charge against the side of an enemy warship without being detected, he had formulated the design of a manned submersible, which he later called the *Turtle.*

With the outbreak of the American Revolution in April 1775, Bushnell began constructing the *Turtle* in a shed on the Connecticut River near his home town. Fabricated of oak and reinforced by iron bands, the *Turtle*'s tar-caulked hull was vaguely egg-shaped and oriented vertically, approximately seven feet high. At the top was a hinged hatch cover that, fitted with six small windows, constituted a miniature conning tower, normally just awash. The seated operator could maneuver the craft horizontally and vertically with a pair of hand-cranked propellers, aided by a small rudder aft, and a foot-operated water inlet valve and hand-operated ballast pumps controlled buoyancy to facilitate complete submergence. The *Turtle* carried a detachable, 150-pound, oak-bodied mine—fitted with a clockwork detonator—piggy-backed on the hull behind the operator. In concept, the craft was intended to approach its victim at night, with the windowed hatch just above the water, and fully submerge to work its way under the enemy ship. The operator would then attach the mine to the wooden hull using a hand-cranked auger that would be left behind with the mine on a tether. The *Turtle* would make its escape before the mine's clockwork mechanism counted down and detonated the charge.[2]

Bushnell completed his submersible by late summer 1775 and trained his brother as an operator. By the early fall, he had culminated a test series in Long Island Sound by submerging, successfully attaching a mine to an old hulk, and blowing it up. Thus encouraged, Bushnell and his fellow Connecticut patriots made plans to attack the British fleet in Boston Harbor. But winter intervened to cause a postponement of the operation, and it was further thwarted when the British fleet withdrew to Halifax in March 1776. However, new opportunities arose when the British force under Admiral Lord Richard Howe—who had relieved Shuldham—reappeared off New York Harbor in late June and seized Staten Island.

Just after the subsequent loss of Long Island by colonial forces under General George Washington, the *Turtle* was moved to lower Manhattan for an attempt on the British fleet. Bushnell had suffered a serious setback in mid-August when his brother was stricken by typhoid fever, necessitating a last-minute scramble to find and train a new operator. Several volunteers hurriedly began training, and the best of these, a 27-year-old Connecticut militia sergeant named Ezra Lee, was chosen for the *Turtle*'s first combat mission.

On the night of 6 September 1776, the *Turtle*—with Ezra Lee piloting—was towed from the Manhattan's South Ferry Landing toward the British ships swinging at anchor in Upper New York Bay. Lee's specific target was HMS *Eagle*,

Admiral Howe's 64-gun flagship, moored off Bedloe's Island (where the Statue of Liberty stands today). The patriots had hoped to time the *Turtle*'s attack to coincide with slack water, but, in the event, Lee found himself fighting an ebb tide that threatened to sweep him southward toward the Narrows. Nonetheless, with considerable exertion, he managed to reach the *Eagle*, submerge beneath her stern, and raise his auger against the ship's bottom. Despite repeated attempts, Lee, nearly exhausted from his unexpectedly long approach, was unable to penetrate the hull and affix the mine to the ship. Subsequently, it was concluded that Lee had encountered the iron fittings that fastened the *Eagle*'s rudder to the hull.[3] Lee tried maneuvering to a more favorable spot, lost control of his buoyancy, and bobbed to the surface. At this point, with daybreak approaching, he decided to give up the attempt and escape the area. By the time he passed British-occupied Governor's Island the sun was up, and he was spotted and chased by an oared barge. To lighten his load and create a diversion, Lee jettisoned the mine—which later caused an impressive explosion—and after a period of furious cranking he was met by his confederates and was towed to safety.

Despite Bushnell's considerable ingenuity and Ezra Lee's extraordinary courage, the *Turtle*'s attack on the *Eagle* had failed, as did two subsequent underwater forays by the craft against British frigates lying in the Hudson River off northern Manhattan. Nonetheless, the British were motivated by this new underwater threat—and that of fireships—to redouble their guard around ships at anchor and to move the fleet farther upriver. One might almost say that this reaction—in 1776—represents the first anti-submarine measures adopted by a navy at war. In October of that year the ship that had been used to house and transport the *Turtle* was sunk by British shellfire, and although the submersible itself is known to have been salvaged, it was apparently disposed of without being used again.

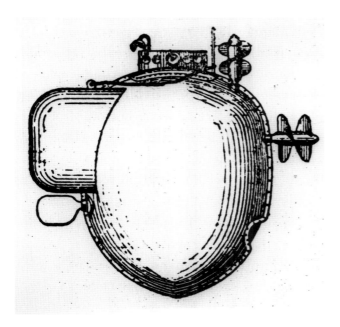

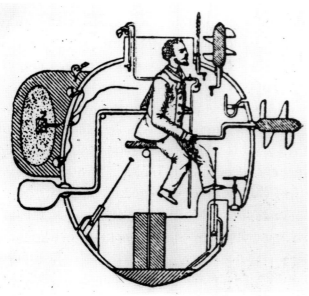

American inventor Dave Bushnell's submersible *Turtle* was the first undersea craft to attack an enemy ship. The *Turtle*'s target in 1776 was the flotilla of British warships in New York Harbor supporting the troops fighting against the American Revolution. *U.S. Navy*

Despite David Bushnell's prominence in the history of undersea warfare, he was certainly not the first to build a submersible vehicle, and it is likely that he derived many of his ideas from the accounts of earlier inventors. Diving bells had been in use for hundreds of years, and as early as 1623, a successful man-powered, oared submarine had been demonstrated in the Thames at London.[4] Subsequent to Bushnell's adventure and several attempts by American Robert Fulton (of steamboat fame) to sell a pioneering submersible to Napoleon, enterprising inventors in Russia, France, Spain, Germany, and England built and tested a wide variety of underwater craft with varying but limited success. Soon, the first proposals for moving beyond human power—initially with steam and electricity—began to be heard, but with the outbreak of the American Civil War in 1861, the focus shifted decisively across the Atlantic.

The American Civil War

Although both sides in the Civil War built and used undersea craft—some two dozen initiatives have been identified—the strategic situation facing the Confederacy prompted the South to become significantly more pro-active than the North in developing submarines and submersible vessels.[5] Many of these never left the design stage, and of those that did only a handful reached full fruition and saw action. Moreover, with a few exceptions, much of the information available about these efforts—particularly the smaller craft—remains fragmentary and contradictory.[6]

With a Union blockade of its major ports beginning to take effect within weeks of the opening of hostilities at Fort Sumter on 12 April 1861, the Confederacy turned quickly to submarine warfare as a means to offset its shortage of conventional warships and break the blockade. Within months submarine initiatives had sprouted in New Orleans, Mobile, Richmond, and other Southern ports. Probably the earliest of the South's operational submarines was built at the Tredegar Iron Works in Richmond by William Cheeney, an engineer with the Confederate Navy Department. This was a small, three-man craft with a hand-cranked propeller and a lock-out chamber to allow a diver to exit the hull to emplace underwater explosives. Air was supplied to the crew through a flexible pipe leading to a camouflaged surface float. Although a Union spy's report on the trials of the Cheeney boat had reached Washington in the early autumn of 1861, by that time the submarine had already been shipped to Hampton Roads, across from Norfolk, Virginia.

On 12 October, an enterprising newsman reported that there had been an attempted underwater attack on the USS *Minnesota*, flagship of the Union blockading squadron, by a Confederate submersible that had reached the ship undetected, but had been unable to attach its limpet mine.[7] Although this attack had failed, and the submarine had escaped, Flag Officer Louis M. Goldsborough, commander of the Union squadron, on 27 October warned all the ships under his command to be on the alert for "submarine infernal machines." Moreover, on 4 November, William Smith, captain of the frigate *Congress,* wrote to Flag Officer Goldsborough that he had devised and installed an underwater net suspended from a horizontal A-frame rigged out over the bow of his ship to prevent the near approach of enemy underwater craft. These nets, one of the first identifiable anti-submarine measures of the modern era, were soon instituted squadron-wide at Hampton Roads.[8] (Cheeney and the Tredegar Iron Works later modified their original boat and evidently built and tested a second version, but little is known of any additional tactical operations.)

The most successful submarine builders for the Confederate cause were James McClintock and Baxter Watson, owners of a New Orleans steam-gauge company, who launched their first undersea boat, the *Pioneer,* in March 1862, shortly after the epic battle between the ironclads *Monitor* and *Virginia* (née *Merrimack*). The three-man, cigar-shaped *Pioneer* was 34 feet long and four feet in diameter, and its builders hoped to operate her as a privateer against the Union blockading squadron downriver from New Orleans. However, it is unlikely that the *Pioneer* saw action before the fall of New Orleans to Union forces on 25 April. She was abandoned there as McClintock and Watson decamped to Mobile, Alabama—also blockaded—where they continued their submarine activities.

The two Louisianans were joined by a third, the wealthy New Orleans lawyer Horace L. Hunley, who apparently bankrolled the construction of a second, larger submarine in Mobile, the *Pioneer II.* After experimenting unsuccessfully with both an electric motor and a small steam engine to propel the craft, the builders reverted to human propulsion with a crew of five. Launched in late January 1863, the *Pioneer II* may have attempted unsuccessful sorties against the Union's blockading ships, but the record is unclear. In the event, she foundered in an accident in early February—without loss of life—and was never recovered.

Undaunted, McClintock, Watson, and Hunley embarked on the construction of their third and most famous submarine, the *H. L. Hunley,* named after the third of her sponsors. Fabricated from an iron boiler, the *Hunley* was 25 feet long, four feet wide, and just over five feet high, with wedge-shaped bow and stern. Two small, windowed conning towers were mounted atop the hull, and buoyancy was controlled by fore and aft ballast tanks, which—not being roofed over—could overflow into the passenger space if overfilled. The *Hunley*'s four-foot, two-blade propeller was connected directly to a longitudinal crankshaft turned by seven crewmen seated facing inboard.[9] There was also an "air box" at the top of the hull from which a tube could be raised to the surface to replenish the oxygen inside, a primitive "snorkel" device. To attack an enemy ship, the *Hunley* was to approach the target with the conning tower barely awash and then submerge underneath the enemy ship to tow a floating torpedo against the hull, where it would be exploded by pulling a lanyard from within the submarine. The submarine's captain navigated the craft by standing under the conning tower and peering through its windows, while operating the rudder and manipulating the valves and pumps that controlled buoyancy.

The *Hunley* was launched into Mobile Bay in July 1863 and successfully demonstrated her capabilities by sinking a derelict flatboat on the Mobile River with a towed torpedo. Because the shallowness and substantial length of Mobile Bay militated against attacking the Federal ships standing offshore, the Confederate authorities decided to move the submarine to Charleston, South Carolina, and operate her against the Union blockading fleet there. The *Hunley* was transported by rail across the South to Charleston, arriving on 12 August 1863, and was immediately prepared for action at a base near Fort Moultrie. By the third week of August, the submarine had made three night-time forays against the Union ships anchored outside the harbor mouth, and although she never succeeded in approaching one, the crew gained useful experience operating the boat underwater and navigating the complexities of the harbor. Confederate authorities made little attempt to conceal her presence in Charleston. Rear Admiral John A. Dahlgren, commanding the Union blockading squadron, was soon informed of this threat, but he appears to have taken no action.

In the Confederate camp, impatience with the *Hunley*'s lack of initiative in attacking the Union fleet, especially after several punishing bombardments of the city, led military authorities to seize the craft from its civilian owners on 23 August and recruit a crew of Confederate Navy volunteers. Although the new crew's initial training went well, disaster struck on 29 August, when the boat was swamped while approaching a pier and sank rapidly, drowning five of her eight-man crew.

After the boat was raised on 13 September, Horace Hunley himself took on the responsibility of recruiting and training a new crew, which likely included some of the original civilians. Once again, disaster intruded. On 15 October, in a practice attack against a cooperating target, the *Hunley* submerged to pass under its "victim" and disappeared into the deep amid a gout of escaping air. All eight men on board, including Hunley, lost their lives. Once again the boat was raised, and by mid-December, with still another crew trained up under Lieutenant George Dixon, she was ready to go to sea again.

On 5 October, ten days before the second loss of the *Hunley,* another Confederate "secret weapon"—a small, steam-powered, *semi*-submersible craft called *David,* presumably by comparison with David and Goliath—had succeeded in attacking the *New Ironsides,* one of the most powerful Union ships blockading Charleston, with a spar torpedo that caused significant damage.[10] This incident and his growing awareness of the *Hunley*'s capabilities led Admiral Dahlgren on 7 January 1864 to issue a general order that began, "I have reliable information that the Rebels have two torpedo boats ready for service, which may be expected on the first night when the weather is suitable for their movement.

The Confederate submersible *H. L. Hunley* was the first undersea craft to sink an enemy ship—the Federal screw-sloop *Housatonic* on the evening of 17 February 1864. The *Hunley* had earlier taken the lives of many of her own crew, including her namesake. This drawing of the *Hunley* was based on a photograph taken in 1863 by George S. Cook. *U.S. Navy*

One of these is the *David,* which attacked the *Ironsides* in October, the other is similar to it." He went on to describe the *Hunley* as a boat "of another kind,"

which is nearly submerged, and can be entirely so; it is intended to go under the bottoms of vessels and there operate. This is believed by my informant to be sure of well working, though from bad management it has hereto met with accidents, and was lying off Mount Pleasant two nights since. There being every reason to expect a visit from some or all of these torpedoes, the greatest vigilance will be needed to guard against them. The ironclads must have their fenders rigged out, and have their own boats in motion around them. A netting must be dropped overboard from the ends of the fenders, kept down with shot, and extended along the whole length of the sides; howitzers loaded with canister on the decks and a calcium light for each monitor. The tugs and picket boats must be incessantly on the lookout, when the water is not rough, whether the weather is clear or rainy.[11]

Admiral Dahlgren also advised his ironclads to anchor in the shallower parts of the harbor and directed his wooden ships to move farther out to sea. By that time the *Hunley,* under Lieutenant Dixon, had already begun operations to engage the Union fleet by using the steam-powered *David* to tow the submarine to the outer harbor and then turning her loose under human power to attempt attacks. On one of these forays, however, the *Hunley*'s towed, contact-detonated torpedo drifted dangerously close to the *David,* and the latter's frightened crew refused further towing assignments. Consequently, the limited stamina of the submarine's human crew forced a move to a new base of operations on Sullivan's Island at the harbor mouth, considerably nearer to the Union Navy's wooden ships standing guard. Additionally, it was decided that the existing method of attack by diving under the target while towing a floating explosive charge was too dangerous, and a spar torpedo—extending forward from the *Hunley*'s bow like the *David*'s weapon—was substituted.

In January 1864, to tighten the blockade against clandestine coastal traffic, the Union command ordered the steam sloop-of-war *Housatonic*—207 feet long with 12 heavy guns—to anchor approximately three miles off Sullivan's Island, where she was clearly visible to the crew of the waiting *Hunley*. Certainly not oblivious to the threat of an underwater attack, particularly at night, the *Housatonic* was kept at a high state of readiness: steam pressure was maintained in the boilers, extra lookouts were set, guns were loaded, and the anchor chains were rigged for quick release and getting under way. Because of the winter sea conditions, it was not until 17 February 1864, that the *Housatonic* enjoyed a calm night at her new station, but it was the opportunity Lieutenant Dixon and his *Hunley* crew had been waiting for. At 7 p.m., Dixon took the *Hunley* to sea, his crew vigorously cranking the craft toward the unsuspecting *Housatonic*. At approximately 8:45, with the submarine only 75 to 100 yards away, the *Housatonic*'s deck officer spotted what he said "looked to me like a porpoise coming to the surface to blow," raised the alarm, and ordered the ship to get under way. He was too late. Despite a hail of small-arms fire directed at her conning tower, the *Hunley* moved inexorably toward her quarry's starboard beam, stabbed her spar torpedo into the hull and, while attempting to back away, detonated the 130-pound gunpowder charge. The ensuing explosion tore an enormous breach in the *Housatonic*'s hull, and the ship settled onto the shallow bottom, her rigging still largely above the surface. Five Union crewmen were killed, and a number of others—including the captain— were seriously injured.

For the first time in history, a submarine had succeeded in sinking a warship. The loss of the *Housatonic* caused enormous consternation in the North, provoking heated editorial comment such as that of the *Army & Navy Journal*, which noted on 19 March 1864, that "the destruction of the sloop-of-war *Housatonic*, off of Charleston Harbor, demonstrates very conclusively that the Rebels have anticipated us in the practical application of engines of submarine warfare."[12]

Despite their startling achievement, Lieutenant Dixon and his crew never returned from their mission. After it was realized by the Confederates that the *Hunley* had been lost, they assumed naturally that she had perished in the same explosion that destroyed the *Housatonic*. In fact, however, when a search team under author and underwater explorer Clive Cussler found the wreck of the *Hunley* in 1995 it was a significant distance from the site of the *Housatonic*'s remains, indicating that Dixon had successfully backed away from the sinking warship and was attempting to return to land when, for some unknown reason, the *Hunley* foundered. This conclusion is consistent with the apparent sighting on shore that night of a light signal from the submarine, which had been prearranged to request a beacon fire to guide the craft home after the engagement.[13]

Although both the North and South continued to experiment with undersea craft for the remaining year of the Civil War, everything following the sinking of the *Housatonic* was anti-climactic. The Confederacy continued a number of last-ditch submarine projects, including several intended to repeat the *Hunley*'s success at Charleston against the Union blockading fleet at Mobile Bay. At least one of these boats was steam-powered, and it appears that Baxter Watson of the *Hunley* team was involved in several others. There are fragmentary accounts of one or more of these craft participating in the Battle of Mobile Bay on 5 August 1864, but no unambiguous evidence of any tactical effect. Toward the end of the conflict, the Confederacy also attempted several submarine initiatives in the trans-Mississippi theater, with small craft building at Houston, Texas, and Shreveport, Louisiana—the latter for operation on the Red River—

but the Confederate surrender at Appomattox Court House on 9 April 1865 put an end to these efforts.

There was little interest in submarines in the North. The principal exception came in 1863 when a group of Northern speculators formed the American Submarine Company. The firm built the submarine *Intelligent Whale*—28 ²/₃ feet long, propelled by crank turning, and intended to lock out a diver to attach explosives on the bottoms of enemy ships. The craft was not completed until 1866 (after the war ended) and did not undergo trials for the Navy until 1872. The *Intelligent Whale* was a failure, and the craft languished in the New York Navy Yard (Brooklyn) for decades. (It is now on display in a museum at Sea Girt, New Jersey.)

Submarines Approach Maturity—
with Torpedoes

The failure of the *Intelligent Whale* discouraged U.S. Navy interest in undersea craft for several decades after the Civil War, and Europe again became the principal center for submarine development. Even before the end of the Civil War in America, the French Navy had built and tested a large submarine at Rochefort called *Le Plongeur* (The Diver).[14] One of the earliest submersibles to exploit non-human propulsion, the 140-foot craft stored a huge quantity of compressed air to power a compound reciprocating air engine that could propel her at five knots underwater. *Le Plongeur,* manned by a crew of 12, was intended to carry a spar torpedo and was tested painstakingly for three years before inadequate longitudinal (fore-and-aft) stability—the bane of virtually all early cigar-shaped submarines—caused abandonment of the project in 1866.[15]

Simultaneously, a growing number of submarine experimenters became active in other countries, and one of the most innovative of these was George Garrett, a part-time cleric in England, whose most successful design, named the *Resurgam* (Latin for "I will rise again") was powered by a coal-burning boiler and a six-horsepower steam engine that drove the craft on the surface in the usual manner. To submerge, the fire was banked, the submarine sealed up, and the head of steam stored in the boiler was used to propel the boat at two to three knots underwater, reportedly for as much as three hours.[16]

Garrett's novel use of steam power drew the attention of Swedish arms manufacturer Thorsten Nordenfelt, who was attracted by the submarine's naval potential and entered into a partnership with the Englishman to build four prototypes between 1882 and 1888. The first of these was sold to the Greek Navy and the second two to the Turkish Navy; the final craft in the series was lost at sea on its way to a demonstration in Russia.

Nordenfelt's craft were among the earliest to be equipped with what would become their primary armament—torpedoes. Earlier craft were hampered in their offensive capability by the lack of an effective underwater weapon that could be employed against enemy warships at a significant stand-off distance. Limitations of hand-emplaced limpet mines, spar torpedoes, and towed explosive charges often put underwater attackers in as much jeopardy as their intended victims. What was needed was some kind of *self-propelled* weapon that could be launched at a target from a safe distance—what modern naval personnel would recognize as a *torpedo*. The torpedo would cause a revolution in submarine warfare as well as anti-submarine warfare.

Although during the Civil War inventors from both the North and South experimented with rocket-propelled mines, the development of the torpedo as known today began in Europe.[17] In 1864, Giovanni de Luppis, a retired Austrian naval officer, conceived the idea of placing an explosive charge in a small, clockwork-powered, underwater attack craft that could be guided by wires from the shore. After a lukewarm reception from the Austrian Navy, he approached Robert Whitehead, an expatriate British engineer, for help. Whitehead was sufficiently interested in the basic concept to begin development on his own of a mobile underwater weapon. By 1866, he had designed and built a prototype that could carry 20 pounds of dynamite for a distance of 200 yards at approximately six knots. Whitehead's first torpedo was 12 feet long and 14 inches in diameter, and it was powered by a reciprocating engine using stored compressed air. Although the Austrian Navy was quick to adopt it, the new weapon's erratic depth-keeping remained a serious problem until, after two more years of work, Whitehead devised a mechanical feedback mechanism that amplified the movement of a flexible diaphragm under hydrostatic pressure to control elevator flaps. The resulting improvement in the torpedo's performance led directly to growing interest in the invention by several other navies, and after it was successfully demonstrated to the British in 1870, Whitehead's commercial success was assured. In 1875 he established a company in Fiume (now Rijecka, Croatia) to build the weapons in quantity and rapidly became the world's foremost torpedo manufacturer, also licensing his designs to several foreign firms. These were the weapons first used on Nordenfelt's submarines.

By this time advances in electrical technology—particularly in motors and batteries—had attracted increasing numbers of submarine designers to electrical power, which was certainly more amenable to underwater operations than steam. As a successor to several man-powered boats he had built as early as 1877, a Russian engineer named Stefan Drzewieki launched a battery-powered submarine in 1884 capable of making four knots submerged.

In France Claude Goubet, Henri Dupuy de Lôme, Gustav Zede, and M. Romazotti produced a succession of battery-powered electric boats for the Ministry of Marine in the decade following 1885. These submarines culminated in a breakthrough in 1898 with French constructor Maxime Laubeuf's 111-foot, 200-ton *Narval,* which used an oil-fired steam engine for running on the surface while charging batteries for running an electric motor underwater. The *Narval* was the first submarine that could recharge her batteries at sea. Within a year the French Navy ordered four more of this design.

Despite this plethora of competing European designs and growing interest in submersibles by European navies in the last decade of the 19th Century, these early submarines suffered an array of serious limitations, of which submerged endurance was key. Moreover, even so advanced a craft as the *Narval* was still troubled underwater by controllability and stability problems, and shifting from surface to submerged operations—and vice versa—took far too long for effective use in real-world tactical situations. Just at the turn of the 20th Century, however, a novel and effective submarine concept emerged across the Atlantic that revolutionized undersea warfare.

John Holland and the Modern Submarine

Within two decades of the end of the Civil War, a handful of American inventors revived interest in building undersea craft. Among these was Professor J. H. L. Tuck of San Francisco, who designed a battery-powered electric submarine in 1884 and followed it a year later with a boat he called the *Peacemaker* that used the heat generated by the reaction of caustic soda (NaOH) and water to make steam. Somewhat more ambitious was the well-connected George Baker of Chicago, who used his political influence to drum up U.S. Navy interest in a 46-foot-long steam- and electric-powered submarine that he tested successfully on Lake Michigan in 1892. At the same time, Simon Lake of New Jersey, who had been fascinated as a boy by Jules Verne's *Twenty Thousand Leagues Under the Sea,* began the underwater experiments that would culminate in his becoming an important U.S. submarine builder in the first quarter of the 20th Century.[18]

But the most innovative and successful of the American submarine pioneers—and the man whose basic concepts would establish the fundamentals of submarine design for the next five decades—was an Irish-American schoolteacher named John Holland.[19] Holland emigrated to the United States in 1873 and, while teaching at a Roman Catholic parochial school in Paterson, New Jersey, resumed experiments on underwater vehicles

Irish immigrant John P. Holland and native-born American Simon Lake were among the world's leading pioneers in submarine development. Holland built the U.S. Navy's first "official" submarine—named *Holland* (SS 1)—shown here. Holland also designed submarines for the British, Russian, and Japanese Navies, while Lake produced undersea craft for the U.S., Russian, and Japanese Navies. *U.S. Navy*

that he had started in Ireland as an avocation. In 1876, Holland attracted the attention of the Fenian Brotherhood, an anti-British secret society devoted to freeing Ireland from English rule. Intrigued by the potential of submarines to attack British warships, the Fenian authorities made a portion of their "Skirmishing Fund" available to Holland to support his submarine work. By May 1878, Holland was able to demonstrate a crude, 14-foot submersible in the Passaic River at Paterson. Although Holland failed in his attempt to propel his first boat with a Brayton-cycle gasoline engine, he was able to drive the submarine with steam piped in from an external boiler. He successfully demonstrated the ability to submerge, transit underwater, and return to the surface. The Fenians were sufficiently encouraged to fund the construction of a larger and more advanced submarine that became known as the *Fenian Ram*.

Built in 1881 in New York City, Holland's second submarine had a 31-foot, spindle-shaped hull and was powered by a two-cylinder, 17-horsepower, Brayton-cycle gasoline engine. In two years of testing in New York Harbor the *Fenian Ram* achieved a surface speed of nine knots and showed a capability to submerge safely to a depth of 50 feet.[20] More importantly, Holland used the *Fenian Ram* to demonstrate several principles he had derived to ensure controllable underwater performance. These ideas included eliminating a primary source of longitudinal instability by completely filling the internal ballast tanks so that the water in them could not slosh back and forth to upset the trim. Additionally, he operated the *Fenian Ram* underwater with a small net positive buoyancy, using the hydrodynamic forces generated by external planes to dive the submarine and keep it down. This novel approach was facilitated by a hull relatively free of external protuberances and smooth maneuvers that maintained forward momentum at all times.

As the result of dissension within the ranks of the Fenian Brotherhood, a faction within the movement seized the *Fenian Ram* in 1883 and put an abrupt end to Holland's experiments. Although a third submarine built in partnership with Lieutenant Edmund Zalinsky of the U.S. Army was launched in 1885 and proved a technical success, the venture failed for lack of funds, and Holland suffered several years of hard times. However, in 1887 and again in 1888 the U.S. Navy showed a new interest in undersea craft by promulgating a circular of requirements and inviting potential submarine builders to submit candidate design concepts. Holland teamed with the Philadelphia shipbuilders William Cramp & Sons, and although their design won both the 1887 and 1888 competitions, budget limitations forced the Navy to defer actual construction indefinitely.

In 1893, Congress appropriated $200,000 to reopen the submarine competition, and Holland produced, under the auspices of his own John P. Holland Torpedo Boat Company, a new design that prevailed over entries by George Baker and Simon Lake. After some bureaucratic delay, the government awarded Holland a contract in 1895 to build a prototype in accordance with the original Navy requirements, which called for torpedo armament, surface and underwater speeds of 15 and eight knots, respectively, and a depth capability of 150 feet. Because of the demand for a relatively high surface speed, a large steam propulsion plant was the only viable option for the new submarine, named the *Plunger*. Accordingly, Holland's design called for an 85-foot-long, triple-screw, 168-ton behemoth, powered by two triple-expansion steam engines on the surface and a 70-horsepower electric motor underwater. (The batteries were to be charged by a separate, auxiliary steam engine.) Plagued by continuing Navy demands for changes and modifications, work on the new submarine progressed only fitfully in Baltimore during 1896 and 1897. Moreover, as Holland watched with alarm, the evolving design departed increasingly from his fundamental concepts, and he was forced to conclude that it would never meet the Navy's specifications. Indeed, when the *Plunger*'s power plant was installed and tested in dockside tests in August 1897, the unshielded boiler made the fire room uninhabitable on the surface, and its residual heat precluded submerged operation even after the boiler had been shut down.

Holland reacted by convincing his colleagues at the Holland Torpedo Boat Company to allow him to build a second submarine as a speculative venture in parallel with the *Plunger*. This "ideal" submarine—designed in strict accordance with his principles—became the *Holland VI,* laid down at Elizabethport, New Jersey, in late 1896 and constructed so rapidly that she was launched the following May.[21] Essentially a football-shaped paraboloid with a small superstructure on top, the *Holland VI* was 53 feet long with a maximum diameter of just over ten feet. She displaced 63 tons on the surface and 75 tons submerged. Holland returned to internal combustion to power the boat, using a 45-horsepower Otto-cycle gasoline engine that also drove a "dynamotor" for charging a battery of 60 wet-cells.

Thus, the *Holland VI* was likely the first submarine design that combined an internal combustion engine for surface running with an electric motor for underwater operation. This basic propulsion scheme soon was adopted worldwide and used almost universally until the advent of nuclear power 50 years later. The submarine's single screw was mounted just above the centerline, with depth planes and rudder at the stern. Even when completely ballasted, the boat was positively buoyant, and when she was submerged, dynamic forces generated by the flow of water over the stern planes held the craft down, while small trim tanks fore and aft facilitated minor adjustments. The craft could make eight knots on the surface, and underwater endurance with the battery powering the dynamotor was eight hours at five knots. Her maximum operating depth was rated at 75 feet. Initially, *Holland VI*'s armament consisted of two pneumatic "dynamite guns," bow and stern, and an 18-inch torpedo tube forward.[22] Seven projectiles could be carried for the dynamite guns, and two reload torpedoes were carried in addition to one in the tube.

During a year of testing, Holland made incremental improvements in the *Holland VI* but so depleted his company's financial resources that bankruptcy loomed. At this point, Isaac Rice, a German-American businessman, stepped in and offered to acquire Holland's firm as the key holding of a new Electric Boat Company that in the next decade would hold a virtual monopoly on U.S. submarines and the manufacture of large storage batteries for them. Thus, by February 1899 Holland at last had the financial backing— and political clout—for a forceful approach to the Navy on behalf of his new design. Following highly successful demonstrations of the new submarine to Navy authorities in both New York and Washington, and after vigorous lobbying by Rice and his colleagues, the Navy finally agreed in April 1900 to buy the *Holland VI*—its first "modern" submarine. Moreover, by October, it had resolved to abandon the *Plunger* and buy seven more submarines of the improved Holland type.

Although it took Congress until 1903 to appropriate funding for a second series of Holland submarines, the superiority of Holland's design to all of the contemporary alternatives soon was recognized by foreign navies, and Electric Boat moved quickly to license the right to build variants of Holland's basic configuration overseas. Britain built five of these, including the Royal Navy's first submarine, the *Holland I,* launched in October 1901, and the Russian, Japanese, and Dutch Navies soon followed. Thus, within five years of the U.S. Navy's initial purchase, 25 submarines of Holland's revolutionary design were operating worldwide, and the impetus given to undersea warfare by their maneuverability, endurance, and reliability soon attracted most major navies to grudging expansions of their submarine forces in the decade before World War I.[23] Of particular note, however, is the fact that not until 1906 did the German Navy commission its first submarine, the *U-1.*

By this same time, additional improvements in the propulsion and control of torpedoes had been incorporated in a new generation of submarine armament. In 1892, Whitehead adopted the Obry steering gear, which used a gyroscope to maintain the weapon's heading in azimuth with greatly increased accuracy. By the time of the Russo-Japanese War (1904–1905), torpedoes were in wide use as surface-launched weapons in most navies and could carry warheads of several hundred pounds for distances of 4,000 to 5,000 yards at about 20 knots. Other manufacturers, such as Schwarzkopf in Germany and Bliss-Leavitt in the United States, brought their own innovations, notably the burning of alcohol or fuel oil to augment the energy of the compressed-air propulsion charge. Thus, by the outbreak of World War I, state-of-the-art torpedoes—now 18 or 21 inches in diameter—could carry a 450-pound warhead to 16,000 yards at 36 knots. These were formidable

underwater weapons indeed, and with the rapidly maturing submarine, they brought a new and lethal combination to naval warfare.

Reaction to the Submarine

Although a handful of visionary naval officers sensed the full potential of undersea craft in the late 19th and early 20th Centuries, the great majority of their colleagues regarded the fledgling submarine as little more than a "plaything," useful only for local and harbor defense. Moreover, in many traditional naval circles there was a strong antipathy to the use of submarines on the grounds that a surprise underwater attack violated the rules of fair play and undermined the ethos of naval warfare as a chivalrous and open-handed endeavor. Submarine warfare was widely viewed as little more than piracy, a perception that had already been acknowledged a century earlier by Robert Fulton when he requested a "special commission" from the French government to ensure that he and the crew of his proposed submarine would be treated as prisoners of war and not pirates if captured. Similarly, in 1864, Horace Hunley requested a set of Confederate uniforms for his civilian *Hunley* crew to establish their status as combatants and not brigands. His concerns were not misplaced. Reacting to the capture of two crewmen from the Confederate *David* after its attack on the *New Ironsides,* the Union's Admiral Dahlgren suggested that they be transported to New York, tried, and hanged "for using an engine of war not recognized by civilized nations."[24] The most often-quoted expression of this point of view is attributed to Admiral Sir Arthur Wilson, the Controller of the Royal Navy, who was reported to have said in 1901 that submarines were "underhand, unfair and damned un-English. They'll never be used in any war and

I'll tell you why: I'm going to get the First Lord to announce that we intend to treat all submarines as pirate vessels in wartime and that we'll hang all the crews."[25]

Additionally, the submarine's tactical usefulness remained suspect despite performance enhancements that stemmed primarily from Holland's innovations. Unable to work closely with the battle fleet because of their limited speed, range, and sea-keeping ability, submarines were also vulnerable on the surface to ramming and gunfire and offered little of value to naval planners within the context of contemporary operational experience. Nonetheless, as early submarine forces began to make their presence felt in fleet exercises, attitudes began to change. Fleet defense against undersea craft assumed increasing significance, as the threat to capital ships of both surface- and submarine-launched torpedoes began to be realized.

By 1907, Admiral Wilson—quoted above—had recognized the danger of exposing his fleet to enemy submarine attacks and called for minimizing the presence of British heavy units in the North Sea and the approaches to the German ports.[26] This was confirmed by the outcome of the Royal Navy's 1912 maneuvers, which showed that their increasing capabilities made it very likely that German submarines would expand their coastal defense role to pose a significant threat to British fleet operations in the North Sea. On 5 June 1914—the eve of World War I—Sir Percy Scott, a technically savvy, recently retired British admiral who had almost single-handedly improved the fleet's gunnery some years before, argued in *The Times* of London that the era of the battleship was over: "Submarines and aeroplanes have entirely revolutionized naval warfare; No fleet can hide itself from the aeroplane eye, and the submarine can deliver a deadly attack even in broad daylight."[27]

Admiral Scott's opinion was too far ahead of its time to be taken very seriously, and despite growing evidence that offensive submarine warfare was increasingly feasible, most British naval officers before the war viewed the principal role of submarines as primarily that of coastal defense. Ominously, by that time the Germans had more ocean-going submarines built, building, and projected than the Royal Navy, despite the later German start.

Those British officers who did recognize a potential menace in submarine warfare had begun to search for countermeasures as early as 1885, when Captain C. A. McEvoy, at the Royal Navy's torpedo school experimented with an induction balance for detecting underwater threats by suspending electrical coils in the water. In 1893, McEvoy commenced a series of experiments with electrical listening devices underwater, but within a decade this approach had been abandoned as unreliable. The first British reference to anti-submarine tactics occurred in late 1903 when the Commander-in-Chief Home Fleet proposed an exercise to determine "the best methods of destroying submarines or frustrating their attacks."[28]

In the ensuing trials, which took place in March 1904, the Royal Navy tried several crude methods to engage underwater craft, such as attaching explosive charges to their exposed periscopes with boat hooks and attempting to snare submerged targets with grapples deployed from destroyers. None of these worked. In 1910, the Admiralty established a Submarine Committee to develop both pro- and anti-submarine tactics, and it was active until World War I broke out in August 1914. Under its auspices, the Navy experimented with a number of anti-submarine techniques, including destroying periscopes with machine-gun fire, spotting submerged submarines from the air, attacking them with destroyer torpedoes, and firing high-explosive shells into the water as a crude form of depth charge. Despite these efforts, neither the Royal Navy nor any other would enter the coming war with any means for detecting or attacking submarines underwater. Thus, in a lecture at the Royal Navy's War College in April 1914, Vice-Admiral Sir Doveton Sturdee, who in 1911 had chaired a subcommittee on defense against submarine attack, "deplored the fact that we appeared to have no means of preventing the destruction of surface vessels."[29]

At that stage of the submarine's development, few naval authorities anticipated any significant role for undersea craft in a campaign of anti-commerce warfare. To most officials, it seemed unlikely that submarines could seize or destroy merchant ships on the high seas in accordance with the customary rules of war that governed such encounters. These rules had recently been codified in the 1909 Declaration of London, which had been drafted by a conference of the leading maritime nations that had been convened because the 1907 Second Hague Peace Conference left unanswered many questions about the rights of neutral shipping in a war zone. The 1909 declaration permitted belligerents to seize or destroy suspect merchant vessels on the high seas only if they were carrying enemy contraband—essentially war material or troops. Moreover, Article 50 of the declaration required that before any merchant vessel could be destroyed at sea, all passengers and crew on board had to be "placed in safety," a phrase that demanded more than just allowing them to take to the lifeboats.[30] In practice, abiding by the letter of the declaration required that before a warship could capture or sink a merchant ship, it had to stop the vessel and send over a boarding party to determine its identity, destination, and the nature of its cargo. Only then could it proceed with sinking or seizure, *if* warranted by the contraband regulations. Thus, it was forbidden under virtually all circumstances to sink a merchant ship without warning and without making arrangements for the safety of the passengers and crew, who, in effect, were considered analogous to civilian non-combatants in land warfare.[31]

The navies of the major powers subsumed the provisions of the London Declaration into their own naval doctrines, where they became known as the Prize Regulations, binding on all naval officers engaged in anti-shipping warfare. Although the London Declaration had been drafted with surface commerce raiders in mind, it applied to *all* belligerent warships, with submarines also falling under its jurisdiction. In contrast to unrestricted submarine warfare—in which, for example, all ships in a designated war zone were liable to be sunk without warning—the Prize Regulations placed submarines engaged in anti-shipping campaigns at a serious disadvantage, exposing them to significant danger when they were most vulnerable—on the surface. These strictures would have a major effect on the course of submarine and anti-submarine warfare in the coming world conflict.

Just as submarines were becoming increasingly more effective as weapons of naval warfare, international unrest was rising rapidly. France's desire for *revanche* after her loss of Alsace-Lorraine in the Franco-Prussian War of 1870–1871, Germany's rampant militarism and her desire for "a place in the sun," instability in the Austro-Hungarian and Ottoman Empires, political turmoil in the Balkans, and the rise of Japan as a major Asiatic power all contributed to widespread national anxiety. In addition to provoking such incidents as the Russo-Japanese War (1904–1905), the Agadir Crisis

(1911), and the Balkan Wars (1912–1913), growing tensions led inexorably to a general arms race and a series of interlocking international agreements in which nations pledged military support to each other in the event of armed conflict with third parties.[32] These agreements—several with destabilizing secret protocols—in turn led to the preparation of precisely timed and carefully coordinated national mobilization plans, which, once initiated, were virtually impossible to delay or set back. Thus, by 1914, the "European system" had been transformed into a fragile house of cards that required only a small disturbance to cause a general collapse.

Then, on 28 June of that year in Sarajevo, a Serbian student *cum* terrorist named Gavrilo Princip assassinated Archduke Franz Ferdinand, the heir to the Austrian throne, and his wife. Within a month, the major European powers had chosen sides and gone to war.

2

The First ASW Challenge

On 20 October 1914, two and one-half months after the start of World War I, the German submarine *U-17*, commanded by *Kapitänleutnant-zur-See* Johannes Feldkirchner, came upon the small British freighter *Glitra* of 866 tons some 14 miles off the coast of neutral Norway, carrying a mixed cargo of coal, coke, and iron into Stavanger. Feldkirchner had no specific orders to attack enemy merchant vessels, but he signaled the *Glitra*'s crew to heave to and abandon ship, and although the *U-17* lacked a deck gun to enforce this demand, the *Glitra*'s master and crew took to their boats. Feldkirchner then sent over a boarding party that removed charts and other documents of intelligence value and opened the sea cocks to sink the freighter. The *U-17* stood by for the two hours that it took the ship to sink. With the *Glitra* gone, Feldkirchner towed her life-boats and crew toward the coast until he met a pair of Norwegian patrol craft, which assumed responsibility for the hapless victims. Feldkirchner and the *U-17* then departed the area to resume their patrol. This was the first-ever sinking of a merchant ship by a submarine in time of war.

Although the provisions of the 1909 Declaration of London clearly permitted belligerent warships, including submarines, to destroy enemy merchantmen, almost three months had elapsed since the outbreak of the war in early August 1914 before the *Glitra* become the first merchant victim of a submarine attack. By warning the *Glitra*'s crew and removing it to "a place of safety" before sinking the ship, Feldkirchner had acted in strict accordance with the Prize Regulations of the declaration. Both sides viewed the *Glitra*'s sinking as

The *U-16* was typical of Germany's World War I submarines. Completed in 1911, she served throughout the conflict and was credited with sinking 11 ships of 11,730 tons. This photo shows her in 1917; she was lost in an accident two years later, in February 1919, while en route to England to surrender. *Leo van Ginderen collection*

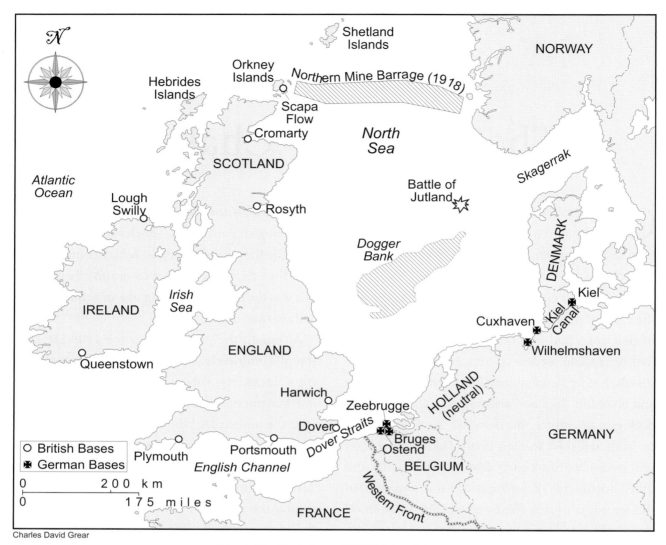

Map 1. The North Sea and British Home Waters

an isolated and unusual incident and unlikely to be a harbinger of the future war at sea. Even when, six days later, the French liner *Amiral Ganteaume* with 2,500 Belgian refugees on board was mistaken for a troopship by the *U-24* and torpedoed without warning in the English Channel—but not sunk—and two additional British merchant ships were destroyed by the *U-21* off the coast of Normandy in November, the danger of a concerted German submarine campaign against Allied merchant shipping seemed minimal. That casual interpretation of events would change quickly as

the realities of the strategic situation became clear to the belligerents.

Making use of their vastly larger fleet and global presence, the British had declared a naval blockade of German ports at the beginning of the conflict and had taken prompt measures to seize German merchant ships, intercept neutral shipping carrying contraband to German ports, and hunt down the German naval squadrons and commerce raiders that had been at sea when war was declared. Because Germany's limited coastline gave access to the high seas only through the North Sea and the Baltic, over routes easily interdicted by the Royal Navy, Britain could effectively choke off all of Germany's trade with the world beyond Europe. Furthermore, by controlling the Mediterranean, she could enforce these same measures against Germany's allies, Austria and Turkey. Although Britain generally acceded to the Declaration of London, it had never actually signed that document and was able to pick and choose among its provisions for greatest advantage. Thus, instead of implementing a "close" blockade with ships stationed immediately off the enemy coast—as required in accordance with international law—the Royal Navy elected a "distant" blockade of Germany, mostly from its bases in England and Scotland, where its ships would be less vulnerable to enemy mines and warship sallies. Additionally, in defiance of the declaration, Britain soon extended the definition of contraband to include food bound for Germany, and what began as a blockade rapidly became a de facto "starvation campaign," bitterly criticized in German propaganda of the time.

Thus, as the ground war on the Western Front degenerated into stalemate, and the prospect loomed of a much longer conflict than the Central Powers had anticipated, the potential effects of the British economic blockade on Germany's war effort became increasingly worrisome. Furthermore, with the German High Seas Fleet essentially bottled up in bases in the Helgoland Bight by the larger British "fleet in being" across the North Sea, only German submarines remained capable of carrying the fight to the enemy.

But Britain—an island nation—had a glaring strategic vulnerability of her own: a crucial dependence on overseas trade, not only for war materials but also for the very necessities of life. According to some analyses, Britain in 1913 imported 80 percent of its wheat, 50 percent of its meat, one-half of the ore needed for the production of pig iron, and *all*

of the oil that fueled an increasing number of the Royal Navy's ships. Consequently, it was practically inevitable that the German Navy would gravitate toward a submarine anti-shipping campaign as the military deadlock on land continued.

When the war began in August 1914, only 14 years had elapsed since John Holland had sold what is often described as "the first modern submarine" to the U.S. Navy. Indeed, Holland's basic design was so successful that by 1905 nearly 50 submarines of that general configuration were in service with the major navies of the world, and nearly as many more were under construction.[1] Initially, these early boats were so limited in range and endurance that they were acquired solely for harbor and coastal defense. Both Russia and Japan employed their first rudimentary submarines in this fashion—without effect—during the Russo-Japanese War of 1904–1905. During this early era, very few senior naval officers recognized any greater potential for the submarine in naval operations. One of the few who did, however, was the Royal Navy's visionary Admiral Sir John (Jackie) Fisher, who became the First Sea Lord in 1904 and wrote that same year, "I don't think it is even *faintly* realized—*the immense pending revolution which the submarines will effect as offensive weapons of war.*"[2] Indeed, as the submarine's capabilities improved rapidly during the first dozen years of its adoption by the major powers, the potential for longer-range scouting, patrolling, and offensive operations became apparent, and the first long-endurance, ocean-going boats had already appeared by the opening of the World War I.[3] As shown in table 2-1, the future belligerent powers could then put to sea more than 250 submarines. Of these, however, only one-fifth—28 German and 18 British boats—could be considered truly ocean-going craft.

Table 2-1.
Operational Submarines in August 1914

Great Britain	75
France	50
United States	32
Germany	30
Russia	25
Italy	18
Japan	13
Austria-Hungary	11

Source: Compiled from Fred T. Jane, *Jane's Fighting Ships 1914* (London: Sampson Lowe Marston, 1914).

At the outset of the conflict, the British and Germans believed that the primary role of their first-line submarines would be to fight enemy warships. This entailed patrolling off hostile coasts, awaiting opportunities to attack surface warships, and supporting fleet operations as "mobile minefields" over which the enemy could be drawn by feints and probing maneuvers. Initially, the Germans had no plans for mounting the anti-shipping campaign against Britain that subsequently developed; Britain, in turn, did not anticipate a major need to defend merchant shipping against submarine attack. These assumptions were strongly influenced by the terms of the Declaration of London, which placed belligerent submarines engaged in anti-shipping campaigns at a serious disadvantage. Therefore, an Admiralty memorandum of December 1912 declared flatly that the submarine had "the smallest value of any vessel for the direct attack upon trade. She does not carry a crew which is capable of taking charge of a prize, she cannot remove passengers and other persons if she wishes to sink one. Therefore she will not affect the direct action in attack, which must be made by cruisers and other surface traveling vessels."[4]

Even with the expectation that submarines would be used primarily against enemy warships, their operating limitations and the earlier restriction to coastal and harbor-defense roles caused both sides to underestimate the offensive power of submarines operating pro-actively against surface combatants. For this reason, little effort was expended on developing anti-submarine defenses. Within weeks, successes by both German and British submarines forced a reassessment.

On 5 September 1914, only a month after the war began, the German submarine *U-21* torpedoed and sank the British light cruiser *Pathfinder* in the North Sea. Less than three weeks later, on 22 September—*within a single hour*—the *U-9* sank three obsolescent British armored cruisers—the *Aboukir, Cressy,* and *Hogue*—some 20 miles off the coast of Holland. A single submarine of some 500 tons with a crew of less than 30 had sent to the bottom three warships totaling 36,000 tons with the loss of nearly 1,500 men. (Eight days earlier, the light cruiser *Hela*, the first German warship to fall victim to submarine attack, had been torpedoed and sunk off Helgoland by the Royal Navy submarine *E-9*.)[5]

Then, on New Year's Day 1915, in the English Channel near Portland, the *U-24* torpedoed and sank the British pre-dreadnought battleship *Formidable* with the loss of more than 550 men. By the beginning of the first full year of the war, submarines on both sides had clearly demonstrated their offensive capabilities against surface warships.

The Royal Navy's early losses caused Admiral Sir John Jellicoe, Commander-in-Chief of the Grand Fleet, such serious concern about the lack of submarine defenses at his main fleet anchorage of

Scapa Flow in the Orkney Islands north of Scotland that his fleet spent as little time there as possible for the first six months of the war. After covering the crossing of the British Army to France and Belgium in the opening phase, Jellicoe withdrew the bulk of his heavy ships to the west, where they could cover the northern exit of the North Sea while remaining within striking distance of German bases. But as he wrote in a letter to Winston Churchill, "I *long* for a submarine defense at Scapa; it would give such a feeling of confidence. I can't sleep half so well inside as when outside, mainly because I feel we are risking such a mass of valuable ships in a place where, if a submarine where to get in, she practically has the British dreadnought Fleet at her mercy up to the number of her torpedoes."[6]

Therefore, while defensive nets, booms, and minefields were being installed at Scapa Flow, the Grand Fleet sought temporary refuge in Loch Ewe in northwestern Scotland and later in Loch na Keal (near the Isle of Mull) and Lough Swilly in Northern Ireland. Only after anti-submarine defenses were completed in mid-February 1915 did the Grand Fleet return to Scapa Flow, its principal anchorage for the rest of the war. This caution was not misplaced. After several disruptive false alarms in September and October 1914, the German submarine *U-18 did* succeed in reaching Hoxa Sound, one of the entrances to the Scapa Flow anchorage, where on 23 November she was rammed by a trawler and forced to scuttle.

Initial Anti-Submarine Measures

Because the submarine offensive against merchant shipping was so largely unexpected and the effectiveness of submarines against surface warships widely doubted before the loss of the *Aboukir, Cressy,* and *Hogue,* neither the Allies nor the Central Powers began the war with either an ASW strategy or the specialized tools—weapons, sensors, and tactics—needed to implement one. Faced with the urgent need to take some action, both sides quickly improvised a number of rudimentary—and largely ineffective—countermeasures using whatever resources came to hand. Only as the experience of war revealed the true magnitude of the threat were sufficient time, money, and fleet assets devoted to waging what amounted to an entirely new kind of warfare that demanded novel tactics, techniques, and material.

In this context, it was Britain—with the most to lose—that eventually mounted the most intensive anti-submarine campaign and made the greatest contributions to developing the first generation of ASW platforms, tactics, sensors, and weapons. The French, preoccupied with the land struggle on the Western Front—largely on their territory—were mostly content to follow the lead of their ally across the Channel, and although the United States also would prove highly inventive when it entered the war in April 1917, the British had already had almost three years of innovation and operational experience by that time. The Germans, lacking the overriding strategic necessity to protect merchant shipping—and with their Navy largely restricted to home waters—lagged well behind the Allies in every aspect of ASW except mining, although they were frequently opportunistic in adapting enemy techniques for their own use.

The British simply did more ASW than anyone else. At the beginning of the war the Royal Navy had approximately 220 destroyers in commission, although most of these ships were outdated—if not obsolete—with some dating back to the late 1890s. In addition, there were more than 100 smaller torpedo boats, the most recent of which had been launched in 1908. Just coming into the fleet in 1914 were the more modern destroyers of the M class, displacing about 1,000 tons, armed with three 4-inch guns and four 21-inch torpedo tubes, and capable of steaming at 35 knots. However, no destroyers had been built for the ASW role because the submarine threat was too new and too uncertain to have figured significantly in their designs. Rather, on both sides of the North Sea the destroyer had evolved from its beginnings as a "torpedo boat destroyer" into a general-purpose ship supporting the battle fleet: to be deployed in large numbers to screen the battle line and to deliver slashing, high-speed torpedo attacks on the enemy's major warships. Two of the most modern destroyer flotillas—just over 40 ships—were attached to the Grand Fleet; 36 other destroyers were serving with the Harwich Force, on the North Sea coast of England; and other flotillas—and penny packets of torpedo boats—were assigned to the Dover, Humber, Tyne, and Firth of Forth patrols, the Channel Fleet, the Mediterranean, and several foreign stations. In particular, most of the destroyers in the east of England were maintained as a quick-reaction force for defending the coast against possible German warship attacks, protecting cross-Channel shipping, and screening larger combatants. The oldest destroyers and torpedo boats, unfit for any other service, provided local defense for the Thames Estuary and such ports as Portsmouth, Devonport, Newhaven, Portland, and Pembroke against possible—if highly unlikely—German naval bombardments.

Unwilling to redirect significant numbers of destroyers and torpedo boats from their existing missions to the ASW role, the Royal Navy initially attempted to address the emerging U-boat problem by pressing into service a wide variety of impromptu, armed patrol craft, partially manned by naval reservists. However, as Lieutenant-Commander Kenneth Edwards reported, their ASW weaponry was rudimentary at best:

> The first anti-submarine patrol off Portland harbor, for instance, was carried out by picket boats (small steam-boats). Their anti-submarine armament consisted of a blacksmith's hammer and a canvas bag. The idea was that the hammer should be used to smash the periscope of a submarine, and the canvas bag to "blind" a submarine by being tied over the top of its periscope, but whether the periscope was to be tied up in the bag before being battered by the hammer or, for the sake of decency, afterwards, was never quite clear.[7]

Within a week of the opening of hostilities the British had deployed some 80 civilian trawlers to sweep mines and patrol for German U-boats, largely in the English Channel and the Strait of Dover. Within a month that number had grown to 250 craft, the first echelon of what would become the Royal Navy's Auxiliary Patrol, which by the time of the Armistice in late 1918 controlled nearly 3,200 vessels of all kinds, most of them armed yachts, trawlers, and drifters.

As the Royal Navy had no reliable means of detecting and attacking submarines underwater, the ASW strategy inherent in its initial use of small warships and armed civilian vessels was to hold German U-boats underwater until their batteries became exhausted, forcing them to the surface and leaving them vulnerable to gunfire and ramming. In the event, this simplistic approach was relatively ineffective, because the submarines generally had sufficient underwater endurance to slip away undetected from potential encounters. Although the *U-15,* the first German submarine lost to hostile action, was rammed by the cruiser *Birmingham* in the first week of the war, it was only because she had been surprised on the surface while attempting to make repairs. In neither that incident nor the loss of the *U-18* at Scapa Flow had the victim been forced to surface by exhausted batteries. Although by the end of the conflict 23 U-boats had been sunk by ramming, it was in general relatively easy for a submarine to submerge and evade its pursuers unless it was caught unawares.[8] Surface gunnery was even less effective. Most German submarines lacked deck guns until well into 1915, and early surface encounters between U-boats and armed patrol craft were relatively one-sided. Even so, only nine German U-boats were destroyed by surface gunfire throughout World War I.

Despite the limited effectiveness of British and French ASW during the first months of the war—largely because there was as yet no way to identify and attack submarines underwater—many German U-boat commanders were intimidated at first by the density of the surface patrols they encountered in the English Channel and the Strait of Dover. Moreover, the strictures of the Prize Regulations made it necessary for them to discriminate troopships and those carrying military cargo from ordinary merchantmen before attacking. Consequently, in a strategic blunder, the Germans made little attempt to interdict the cross-Channel movement of the British Expeditionary Force and its logistics train from British ports to France and Belgium between mid-August and early September 1914. During that period, 100,000 men, their weapons, vehicles, horses, and supplies were transported *without any loss* across the Channel to play a crucial role in frustrating the German Army's drive on Paris, which, if successful, could have ended the war by the close of 1914.

Although the German plan to envelop Paris was narrowly thwarted at the Battle of the Marne in early

and mid-September, the ensuing "Race to the Sea" between the German and British armies that extended into October 1914 was to have a major impact on submarine and anti-submarine operations in the area. By the time the conflict's opening offensives became stalemated in late October, the northern end of the Western Front had reached the North Sea just to the east of the town of Nieuport in Belgium, leaving the Germans in possession of a 30-mile stretch of coastline that extended to the border with neutral Holland to the northeast. Despite the narrowness of this access to the North Sea, the German Navy fully exploited its opportunity by establishing key basing and repair facilities for submarines and destroyers at Bruges, some eight miles inland and connected to the ports of Zeebrugge and Ostend by canals. Of these, the modern eight-mile canal to Zeebrugge was the more important because it could handle warships up to the size of a light cruiser. By the end of 1914, four U-boats were stationed there, and by October 1915, the Germans had 16 U-boats in a Flanders Flotilla operating from Zeebrugge and Ostend, within easy striking distance of the southern North Sea, the Strait of Dover, and the English Channel.

In response to the threat to British communications with France posed by the German lodgment in Flanders, the Admiralty established in October 1914 a separate command—the Dover Patrol—and placed a motley collection of 4 light cruisers, 24 destroyers, 13 old submarines, and a number of Auxiliary Patrol craft under Rear-Admiral Horace Hunt to shoulder that responsibility. Subsequently, under the command of Admiral Sir Reginald Bacon (after April 1915), the Dover Patrol would become the principal focus for ASW operations off England's east coast, playing a central role in establishing patrol areas, organizing submarine counter-offensives, and implementing the elaborate system of minefields and barrier nets that became a principal defensive measure. Later—in mid-war—as German submarine attacks on shipping ranged wider afield, a similar ASW command for the Western Approaches to the English Channel was established at Queenstown (now Cobh), Ireland, under Vice-Admiral Sir Lewis Bayly.

Mines versus Submarines

At this early stage of the war the only weapon that offered the potential for destroying submarines underwater was the sea mine. Mining had come into its own as a naval weapon as early as the American Civil War and had been used effectively by both sides in the Russo-Japanese War of 1904–1905, in which 16 warships on both sides were sunk by mines.[9] On 2 October 1914, in the first use of mining specifically as an ASW measure, the British laid a large minefield across the northern entrance to the Strait of Dover, approximately 20 miles northeast of the Dover–Calais line and extending almost to the coast of Belgium. The primary purpose of this minefield was to prevent German submarines from attacking the increasingly important cross-Channel supply line. Because the southern North Sea is relatively shallow—mostly on the order of 100 feet deep—the field consisted entirely of moored spherical mines, tethered to anchors by steel cables whose length was measured out automatically to keep the warheads themselves at a predetermined distance above the sea floor. As the minefield also posed a threat to surface ships, the Royal Navy was forced to intercept friendly ships and either warn them away from the danger area or escort them through safe-passage lanes in the field.

German submariners quickly learned of the minefield's existence and treated it with significant respect, but it soon was apparent that the field's overall effectiveness was minimal. Because the mooring system of the British mines was under-designed, the warheads frequently broke their cables during rough weather and, as "floaters," became serious dangers to Allied shipping. Moreover, the mine's mechanical triggering device proved unreliable. The large tidal range of the North Sea and the English Channel—up to 20 feet in some places—posed another problem. Because the mines were moored to be about 10 to15 feet below the surface at high tide to make them effective not only against submarines, but surface ships also, the arrival of low tide frequently left the warheads floating on the surface in clear view. Thus, it was relatively simple for the Germans to determine the extent and location of the minefield and either avoid it or—more commonly—submerge deeply enough to run underneath the mines, accepting as a matter of course the nerve-wracking screech of the mooring cables scraping along the hull.

Although their several deficiencies reduced these early minefields to more of an annoyance or a deterrent than an actual threat, there was still the danger of snagging a cable and dragging the mine down to the submarine, with fatal results. In fact, the fourth and fifth U-boats lost in the war—the *U-11* and *U-5*—were destroyed by mines near the northeast corner of the field on 9 and 18 December, respectively. A month later, in January 1915, the *U-31* disappeared without trace off the eastern coast of England and also may well have been mined.

The German Navy laid several large, defensive minefields in the Helgoland Bight. Although intended primarily to deny freedom of maneuver to British surface warships, they also were a serious threat to submarines attempting to penetrate German home waters early in the war. The first successful British submarine patrol into the Helgoland Bight commenced on the first day of the conflict, and as early as 25 September 1914, the *E-6* fouled two mines there but managed to escape. The *E-10* was not so lucky; she was lost in the Bight with all hands on 18 January 1915, probably the victim of a German mine.

Meanwhile, in the Baltic, the Russian Navy laid 2,200 moored mines at the entrance to the Gulf of Finland to protect Petrograd (St. Petersburg) from attack by sea, but not until August 1915 did these mines claim a submarine, the *U-26*. Despite relatively few early successes against submarines of either side, mines would become an increasingly potent undersea weapon as the war drew on and

Mines were an important submarine *and* ASW weapon in both world wars as well as in the Cold War. These German sailors are loading a mine into a UC-class coastal minelaying submarine in Zeebrugge harbor in 1917. *Imperial War Museum*

both their effectiveness and the tactics for employing them improved.

"Fishing" for Submarines

Recognizing the need to take the offensive and to develop more pro-active techniques for attacking submerged submarines, the British Admiralty on 8 December 1914 organized a Submarine Attack Committee of naval and civilian experts to oversee the progress of existing ASW programs and to investigate new weapon and detection approaches to use against U-boats. Perhaps indicative of the few real alternatives available to the committee is the fact that most of its early projects seem to have been directly inspired by time-honored commercial fishing methods—trolling, seining, and harpooning.[10]

As early as 1910, the British began developing what was called an "explosive sweep" that consisted of a towed, 80-pound explosive charge streamed at a depth of 40 feet by the combination of a hydroplane at the surface and an underwater kite. The tow cable was supposed to foul the hull of any submarine it encountered, and the charge would be exploded electrically to destroy the target. This single sweep was in use at the beginning of the war, but it was soon supplanted by a more elaborate version that deployed two parallel cables, one above the other. The uppermost of these was fitted with a series of buoyant floats, from which the lower cable—with nine charges spaced 100 feet apart—was suspended. In this later version, of which more than 1,000 were issued to the fleet, the charges could be detonated either electrically or by contact with the target. By 1916 the modified sweep had been replaced by a more advanced system that carried 400-pound explosive charges in a pair of paravanes streamed to either side of the towing ship at selectable depths down to 200 feet. This paravane sweep was introduced in a high-speed version for destroyers and a low-speed variant for trawlers and drifters. By mid-1917, the former had begun to be phased out in favor of the increasing use of depth charges.

Both the French and Italian Navies developed similar weapons during the conflict, but only the British were large users of explosive sweeps in World War I. Ironically, it appears that only one German submarine—the *U-8*, on 4 March 1915—was destroyed by an explosive sweep, and then only because she had fouled an anti-submarine net shortly before. Later in the war, paravane sweeps were detonated more than 50 times in individual attempts to destroy suspected U-boats, but no confirmed kills resulted.

Many types of underwater nets, both fixed and mobile, also were used in ASW by all of the belligerents. In addition to the defensive anti-submarine nets installed almost universally at harbor entrances and in restricted passages leading to fleet anchorages, the British also developed several net systems for pro-active anti-submarine operations. The Admiralty's first attempt to deploy a large, at-sea net complex was supposed to create a fixed, anti-submarine barrier across the Dover Strait from Folkestone to Cape Gris-Nez on the French coast, with a tightly controlled gate at each end to allow passage of friendly ships. Begun in February 1915, the net consisted of a connected series of large vertical mesh panels, each 100 feet deep and 200 feet long, suspended from wooden surface floats that were anchored to the bottom with mooring cables. The sheer magnitude of the task (over a length of some 25 miles), the huge size of the components, and adverse tidal and sea conditions in the strait forced cancellation of the project in May 1915, with the barrier only half-complete.[11]

Thereafter, the British reverted to using smaller and more tactically oriented "indicator nets," which combined a surface-suspended cable mesh with an alarm device that made a visual signal when the net was fouled by a transiting U-boat. These nets—with a mesh size on the order of 12 feet—were manufactured as 100-yard-long panels in a variety of depths from 30 to 120 feet. Each panel was suspended from a line of surface floats and fitted with a chemical smoke generator that would activate if the "quick-disconnect" clip that joined it to its neighbor was pulled free when a submarine became entangled in a panel. The smoking indicator on the surface would then mark the U-boat's moving position.

The indicator nets could be moored to the bottom as fixed barriers or towed by herring drifters pressed into the Auxiliary Patrol. Up to ten of the modules could be fastened together to form a barrier as much as 3,000 feet long, and several of these were often deployed in echelon. Normally, a single drifter would tow the indicator net in a line behind it, so that its "aperture" was parallel to the ship's course. Armed trawlers stood by to attack U-boats caught in the nets with gunfire, ramming, or explosive sweeps. Another, more challenging technique was to use two drifters steaming on parallel courses with the net streamed between them to "sweep out" an underwater area in the direction of travel. In the event, towing the nets was often complicated by tangles, bottom obstructions, leaking surface floats, and unreliable connectors, which often parted from tidal or wave action alone.

The Royal Navy used moored indicator nets in areas around the British Isles, such as the mouth of the Thames Estuary, suspected of heavy enemy submarine activity. Attempts to use the nets farther from shore in more ambitious installations were thwarted by tides and currents that destroyed the integrity of the barriers. Moreover, the associated surface buoys quickly revealed the locations of the nets to the U-boats, making the barriers easy to avoid by going around or running under them. The most elaborate towed net defense was in the North Channel of the Irish Sea, between Scotland and Northern Ireland, where the great depth of water precluded a moored installation. Even though German submarines could dive beneath the deepest British nets, the Royal Navy hoped to keep U-boats transiting the barrier submerged for at least 30 miles by maintaining a series of parallel net lines. Then, when they were forced to surface to recharge their batteries, destroyers and patrol craft could attack.

By the beginning of 1915 it was realized that the marriage of indicator nets and underwater mines might offer significant ASW potential. In February, the Admiralty ordered the Submarine Attack Committee to develop a small Electro-Contact (EC) mine for mounting on an indicator net panel, so that if the panel tore away, the 45-pound explosive charge would be drawn to the submarine's hull and detonate. At first it was thought that this innovation could be used with both moored and towed nets, but by April 1915, it had become apparent that it posed too great a danger to the drifters and their crews. All of the EC mine nets eventually deployed were moored versions, which required special provisions for housing the associated batteries as well as troublesome maintenance procedures.

The first mine-net barrage was planted off the Belgian coast from Ostend to the River Scheldt in late April 1915, to impede operations of the German Flanders Flotilla, but the most ambitious mine-net project was a 28-mile line from the Goodwin Sands off eastern Kent to Dunkirk, installed in September and October 1916. In both cases, the British intention was to impede submarine access to the English Channel from

bases in Germany or on the occupied Belgian coast. And the same difficulties in maintaining the integrity of the barrier in the face of wind and sea conditions that had bedeviled the earlier indicator nets—plus the ease with which the Germans could dive beneath the deep-water portions—minimized the effectiveness of the mine nets also.

Despite many additional claims, it appears that indicator nets contributed significantly to the loss of only two German submarines—the *U-8* (mentioned above) and the *UB-26,* depth-charged on 5 April 1916, after fouling an indicator net near Le Havre. Additionally, an Austrian submarine was lost in a similar way a month later in the Strait of Otranto in the Mediterranean. The EC mine nets were even less successful. Other than the strong probability that the *UC-7* was sunk by one of the net lines off the Belgian coast in July 1916, there were no likely kills by either that barrage or any other mine-net deployment. Despite so little effectiveness in sinking submarines, the several net variants fielded by the Allies in World War I often inhibited the free maneuver of the German boats and created a significant deterrent to unfettered submarine operations in the areas where they were used.

In the area of shipboard ASW weapons, the hand-thrown "lance bomb" was something of a cross between a harpoon and a hand grenade, and it was one of the more bizarre British attempts to field a weapon for small craft. First put into service in April 1915, it consisted of a wooden lance approximately five feet long tipped with a seven-pound, contact-fuzed explosive charge. Issued to the trawlers and drifters of the Auxiliary Patrol, it was supposed to be aimed at a close-aboard U-boat either on or just below the surface. Reportedly, the lance bomb could be thrown as far as 75 feet, but only by using a dangerous approximation of the

Before depth charges became the "weapon of choice" against submerged submarines, the Royal Navy experimented with a variety of weapons—from sea lions carrying explosives to this hand-thrown "submarine dart" or "lance bomb" device. *U.S. Navy*

technique used by Olympic hammer-throwers—gaining momentum by swinging it in a circle and then releasing it in the direction of the target. Although 20,000 of the weapons were produced, they were withdrawn from service in 1917 without having scored a single success.[12]

Q-Ships—*Ruses de Guerre*

Significantly more effective was another early British ASW measure devised to take advantage of the stop-and-search requirements of the Prize Regulations. These were the decoy ships of the Special Vessel Service, better known as "Q" or "mystery" ships, and once described as "a live trap baited with human flesh to catch unsuspecting prey."[13] Nor-

mally, the mystery ships were small, nondescript merchant or fishing vessels that were heavily armed with concealed naval guns and, later, depth charges and torpedo tubes. If a Q-ship was stopped by an enemy submarine to be inspected for contraband, it was supposed to heave to while a "panic party" of seaman—some disguised as women—took to the lifeboats, hurriedly abandoning ship. Then, when the unsuspecting U-boat had been enticed to draw nearer, the Q-ship's guns were unmasked to deliver a hail of close-range fire on the enemy.

The Special Vessel program began modestly in November 1914, when Winston Churchill, as First Lord of the Admiralty, ordered the Royal Navy to fit out a small steamer with concealed armament to trap German submarines operating off Le Havre. By the end of the war the British had deployed 180 decoy ships, with the number at sea peaking in 1916–1917. The first of these to sink U-boats were the *Prince Charles*, which took the *U-36* unawares near the Hebrides on 23 July 1915, and the armed smack *Inverlyon*, which destroyed the *UB-4* near Yarmouth three weeks later.

First tried in May 1915, an early variant of the Q-ship approach used trawlers as decoys, each towing a submerged submarine with a cable incorporating a telephone line. If an enemy submarine was spotted on the surface, the sighting report was passed to the friendly submarine, which cast off the tow and—still under water—went over to the attack. Although this approach was discontinued in October 1915 after German submariners caught on to the ruse, the trawler-submarine combination trapped two U-boats, the first of which, the *U-40,* was destroyed by the trawler *Taranaki* and the British submarine *C-24* on 23 June 1915, even before the first conventional Q-ship kill by *Prince Charles.* Interestingly, the Germans experimented briefly with this same tactic in the Baltic later that year, while in late 1917, the Royal Navy designed a new class of submarines specifically for the ASW role, the R class (see Chapter 3).

All told, Q-ships and the trawler-submarine combination accounted for the destruction of an impressive 14 German submarines during the war. The most successful of the Royal Navy's Q-ship captains was Lieutenant-Commander Gordon Campbell, who sank two U-boats while in command of the ex-tramp steamer *Farnborough*—suffering mortal damage to his own ship in the second encounter—and a third as captain of the ex-collier *Pargust*.[14]

Nine of the total number of Q-ship kills were scored before February 1917, when German submarines operated largely under the Declaration of London restrictions. Subsequently, unrestricted submarine warfare and the introduction of convoying eliminated the raison d'etre of decoy ships as German submariners treated vessels traveling alone with heightened suspicion. As a result, the number of Q-ship encounters dropped off rapidly, and the last sinking of a submarine by a Q-ship took place in August 1917 in the Bay of Biscay. When the convoying of merchant ships became virtually universal, Q-ships were often used as ocean escorts, occasionally playing the part of a straggler lagging behind the convoy.

It can be argued that Britain's earlier use of the Q-ships served largely to undermine the strictures of the Prize Regulations, since it motivated U-boat captains to "shoot first and ask questions later." Because of the highly secret nature of the Special Vessel Service, most sources differ on the number of British Q-ships lost to the Germans. In the very last encounter between a decoy ship and a submarine on 30 July 1918, it was the Q-ship, the ex-coastal steamer *Stock Force*, that was lost:

Not worth a torpedo to a U-boat: the nondescript barquentine *Rentoul* was employed as a heavily armed Q-ship but also was used to carry coal from Britain to France. Taken into British service in 1918, she was armed with one 4-inch gun, two 12-pounders, and a 7.5-inch howitzer. *Imperial War Museum*

Vice-Admiral Gordon Campbell, Royal Navy
(B. 1886 D. 1953)

The most famous of the Royal Navy's Q-ship commanders in World War I, Campbell was born in Upper Norwood, near London, the son of a former officer in the Royal Artillery. He entered the Navy as a cadet at the age of 14 and spent his first assignments at sea in the battleship *Prince George* in the Mediterranean and in the cruiser *Flora* in Canadian and South American waters. Later, after attending naval college at Greenwich, he served in the destroyer *Arun* and then spent two and one-half years on the China Station in the armored cruiser *King Alfred*. After his return to England in mid-1910, Campbell was assigned to the staff of the boys' training ship *Impregnable* for two years, followed by command of the destroyers *Ranger* and then *Bittern*, holding the latter position for the first year of World War I.

He was selected for the Q-ship service in September 1915, implemented the conversion of the collier *Loderer* to the Q-ship *Farnborough* and, as a lieutenant-commander, took her to sea for the first time in November 1915, operating out of Queenstown, Ireland. On 22 March 1916, the *Farnborough* encountered the German submarine *U-35* some 20 miles off the southwest coast of Ireland and, after ignoring a torpedo near-miss, decoyed the submarine within gunnery range and destroyed it with a combination of gunfire and depth charges. Campbell was promoted to commander as a result of this success. Eleven months later, on 17 February 1917, the *Farnborough* was torpedoed without warning by the *U-83* but nonetheless executed her Q-ship ruse flawlessly to draw the submarine close alongside, at which point she revealed her identity and sank her with gunfire. The sinking *Farnborough* was towed to Berehaven and beached at the harbor entrance, later to be salvaged for another career as a tramp steamer.

Campbell was awarded the Victoria Cross for this second success, and he was immediately assigned another Q-ship, HMS *Pargust*. He destroyed his third U-boat, the *UC-29*, west of Ireland on 7 June 1917, in an action in which his own ship was torpedoed, but was able to return to port. He then fitted out his third Q-ship, HMS *Dunraven*, at Devonport, and sailed on 4 August 1917. She was sighted by the submarine *UC-71* four days later, 100 miles southwest of Land's End, England. After a lengthy "chase," with the *Dunraven* feigning an attempt to escape from the U-boat, the two ships engaged in a vicious gun battle in which the Q-ship was mortally wounded when one of her magazines blew up. The *UC-71* escaped unscathed; the *Dunraven* sank under tow that night. Soon thereafter, Campbell was reassigned as Admiral Lewis Bayly's flag captain at Queenstown and then, as captain of the light cruiser *Patrol*, served the rest of the war in charge of escort operations in the Irish Sea.

Campbell returned to training duties immediately after the Armistice, first taking HMS *Cumberland* to the West Indies on a training cruise and then serving as commanding officer of the shore training facility HMS Impregnable. Subsequently, he served as the captain-in-charge of the naval base at Simonstown, South Africa, and commanded the battle cruiser *Tiger* before his retirement from the Navy as a rear-admiral in May 1928. He represented the town of Burney as a member of Parliament from 1931 to 1935 and in retirement was promoted to the rank of vice-admiral in 1932.

torpedoed without warning by a U-boat but still managing to score several 4-inch gun hits on her adversary before going down. In the event, approximately two dozen of the mystery ships appear to have been sunk, half of which were torpedoed without warning. Thus, the exchange ratio between the decoy ships and their supposed quarry was roughly two to one, which raises serious questions about their overall ASW effectiveness.

The U.S. Navy attempted only one true Q-ship initiative during World War I: in late 1917 the Royal Navy transferred a Q-ship to U.S. control, and on 27 November of that year she was commissioned as the USS *Santee* for operations out of Queenstown, Ireland. Unfortunately, just over a month later, while at sea on a training cruise, the *Santee* was torpedoed without warning by a German U-boat, and although she survived the encounter to be towed back to port, she was returned to the British and never employed by the U.S. Navy again.[15]

Germany Raises the Stakes

In 1915, as the struggle on the Western Front devolved into a static war of attrition, and the economic effects of the British naval blockade became more telling, influential officials in Germany began calling for a new naval strategy to break the stalemate. There had been advocates of unrestricted submarine warfare in Germany as soon as the disadvantages of the Prize Regulations became apparent at the beginning of the war. Notably, in mid-October 1914, the head of the German U-boat arm, *Korvettenkapitän* Hermann Bauer, responding to the planting of the first large British minefield in the North Sea earlier that month, had advocated an unrestricted campaign against all shipping in British waters. He was promptly supported in this view by the father of the modern German Navy, *Grossadmiral* Alfred von Tirpitz, state secretary of the Imperial

Naval Office since 1897, and by several high-ranking flag officers, including *Vizeadmiral* Reinhard Scheer, future commander of the High Seas Fleet. The principal opposition to such a move was centered in the German Foreign Office and the chancellor, Theobald von Bethmann-Hollweg, who feared its effect on neutral countries and, in particular, the likelihood of drawing the United States into the war on the Allied side.

With both camps clamoring for the ear of Kaiser Wilhelm II, there ensued two years of indecision over the self-imposed limits on German submarine warfare, with first one side prevailing and then the other. First, in February 1915—ostensibly because the British had begun to sail their ships under false neutral flags—the waters around the British Isles were declared a war zone in which every merchant ship encountered would be destroyed, possibly without guaranteeing the safety of the passengers and crew. At the opening of this first unrestricted campaign, the Germans could put to sea 37 submarines of all types, of which only 25 were suitable for blockade duty.[16] Even so, the declaration met a storm of protest from the neutral powers, notably the United States, which demanded reinstatement of the Prize Regulations. In response, the Kaiser ordered that if their identity could be ascertained, no neutral ships should be attacked without warning, thus de-escalating the diplomatic crisis, but severely hampering German freedom of action.

Then, on 5 May 1915, the Cunard liner RMS *Lusitania* was torpedoed off the coast of Ireland by the *U-20* with the loss of 1,201 lives, including 128 Americans. This event reignited the controversy and moved the Kaiser in June to place large passenger ships off-limits, regardless of nationality; in August, this edict was extended to all passenger ships. Finally, in mid-September, out of frustration with these increasingly unworkable restrictions, the

German naval staff (the Admiralstab) announced a return to the Prize Regulations, essentially ending unrestricted submarine warfare until further notice.

Despite this policy reversal, the number of British merchant ships lost to submarine attack in 1915 totaled 227, of nearly 860,000 gross tons, peaking in August but tailing off somewhat when the Prize Regulations were reinstated. However, by late in the year Germany's initial submarine force had been augmented by nearly 20 boats that had been under construction at the beginning of the war and by a total of 32 newly designed, smaller coastal and minelaying submarines of the UB and UC classes, many of them assigned to the Flanders Flotilla. As new construction ramped up in 1916, the growing numbers of German submarines at sea began to make their presence felt even in the face of stricter observance of maritime law by the Admiralstab. In the first half of 1916, the U-boats sank 610,000 gross tons of shipping of all flags, and by the end of the year, sinkings had reached approximately 330,000 tons per month.

In December 1916, with the effects of the British blockade causing growing dislocation of the German economy, the head of the Admiralstab, Admiral Henning von Holtzendorf, reopened the question of unrestricted submarine warfare. In a memorandum on the 22nd of that month, he wrote,

> A decision must be reached in the war before the autumn of 1917, if it is not to end in the exhaustion of all parties and consequently disastrously for us. Of our enemies, Italy and France are economically so hard hit that they are only upheld by England's energy and activity. If we can break England's back the war will at once be decided in our favor. Now England's mainstay is her shipping, which brings to the British Isles the necessary supplies of food and materials for war industries and ensures their solvency abroad.[17]

With an associated statistical analysis, Holtzendorf demonstrated that if German submarines could achieve the destruction of 600,000 tons of British and Allied shipping each month, Britain—which imported two-thirds of its food—would be brought to the brink of starvation in five months. These losses, which could only be attained by returning to unrestricted submarine warfare, would also cause severe disruption of the French and Italian war economies by depriving them of their necessary supplies of British coal. Moreover, even if the United States were provoked to join the Allies, Britain would be defeated before America's power could be brought to bear from across the Atlantic.

Admiral Holtzendorf's plan for an unrestricted submarine campaign to force a quick end to the war soon gained momentum with the German General Staff and the Kaiser, leaving Chancellor Bethman-Hollweg little choice but to withdraw his earlier objections. Accordingly, on 31 January 1917, Germany announced its fateful decision to begin unrestricted submarine warfare in the approaches to the British Isles and over most of the Mediterranean, effective the next day, 1 February. By that time the German Navy had 105 submarines available for its desperate campaign.

The effects were almost immediate. Within two days the United States severed diplomatic relations with Germany, and two months later, on 6 April, it declared war.[18] At the same time, Allied shipping losses mounted precipitously until they reached a peak of over 860,000 tons in April, when 167 merchant ships were lost for every submarine destroyed. Moreover, neutral shipping was increasingly reluctant to accept war cargoes and sail into the war zone, even though the Admiralty attempted to mitigate the increasing threat by funneling ocean traffic through carefully patrolled routes close to shore and traversing submarine danger areas at night. Still the number of ships and cargoes lost continued to rise. In the British official history of the war, Sir Henry Newbolt later wrote,

> Everything [in April 1917], indeed, combined to show that the Allies were really within sight of disaster. The lists of sinkings, the numbers of successful attacks, the increasing use of the torpedo, the moderate rate of German submarine losses all told the same story. Admiral von Holtzendorf's prophecy of victory was apparently verging toward fulfilment, and only a change in our system of defense could turn the tide.[19]

As the depredations continued into the summer of 1917, stocks of food staples in the British Isles were reduced to a six-week supply, and the Grand Fleet was forced to curtail its at-sea exercises for lack of oil. Thus, with the German High Seas Fleet largely restricted to the Helgoland Bight since the Battle of Jutland in June of the preceding year, countering the enemy submarine campaign become the most pressing issue of the naval war in 1917, and the Admiralty focused increasingly on devising new ASW weapons and techniques.

The Allied ASW Crisis

In January 1917, Admiral Jellicoe, by then First Sea Lord, succinctly summarized the ASW problem: "There were only three ways of dealing with the submarine menace. The first, naturally, was to prevent the vessels from putting to sea; the second was to sink them after they were at sea; and the third was to protect the merchant ships from attack."[20] He concluded that the second of these

was the most promising approach and opted for stepped-up development of new platforms, sensors, and weapons. A month earlier, in December 1916, he had founded an Anti-Submarine Division at the Admiralty, at first headed by Rear Admiral Sir Alexander Duff, and that organization soon took total responsibility for coordinating the British ASW effort. Fortunately, the experience of more than two years of war and several key research and engineering efforts initiated earlier had produced significant advances in both tactics and weaponry. The first of these was the development and introduction of the depth charge.[21]

By early 1915, the Admiralty had provided limited numbers of rudimentary depth charges to the Auxiliary Patrol. These devices, initially manufactured in four sizes and loaded with up to 100 pounds of guncotton, were made up of a detachable surface float tethered by a lanyard to the warhead. After the weapon was thrown overboard, the sinking charge would pay out the lanyard until it reached the end of its pre-set length, when it would jerk tight and pull the firing pin. There were also two air-dropped versions, and France and the United States eventually developed similar weapons for their own anti-submarine aircraft. In practice, no kills were recorded for these early depth charges, both because they were produced only in limited quantities and because the explosive charge was too small to cause significant damage except from a near-direct hit. But it was a beginning.

After a rapid development and procurement program during most of 1915, the Royal Navy issued the first of an order for 1,000 improved Type D depth charges in January 1916. The Type D used a hydrostatic pistol to fire the weapon at selectable depths, and it came in two versions—one charged with 300 pounds of amatol for destroyers and torpedo boats and a second with

120 pounds of explosive for use by the slower-moving trawlers and drifters. Supposedly, the explosive effects of the larger weapon were sufficient to destroy a submarine within 70 feet and to cause heavy damage within 140 feet.

Initially, depth-charge quantities were so limited that only two of the new weapons could be issued to each vessel, increasing to four each in early 1917. Not until the middle of that year did the Royal Navy have sufficient depth charges on hand to meet operational needs. Despite some uncertainty, it appears that the first German U-boat to fall victim to a depth charge attack was the *U-68*, sunk by Commander Campbell's Q-ship *Farnborough* on 22 March 1916. Only one additional submarine was killed by depth charges that year, but there would be six in 1917 and 22 during the last ten months of the war.

Although the French Navy attempted to develop its own depth charges—the Guiraud model, with explosive weights of 90 and 156 pounds—insufficient numbers and poor reliability essentially nullified their operational effectiveness. In contrast, the U.S. Navy became a key developer and major supplier of these weapons by the end of the conflict. The American Mark I depth charge, a float-and-lanyard design with only 50 pounds of explosive, was adopted in early 1917 and manufactured in quantity, but it was soon supplanted for the same reasons that doomed the similar British weapon. It was replaced by the more powerful Mark II, which contained 300 pounds of TNT that could be detonated hydrostatically at depths from 50 to 200 feet. The U.S. Navy ordered 30,000 Mark II depth charges, followed by 10,000 Mark IIIs, which could reach 300 feet, and also by, finally, 1,000 Mark IVs, with a 600-pound warhead. The only confirmed kill of an enemy submarine by a U.S. Navy ship or aircraft during World War I was the *U-58*, mortally wounded by depth charges from the destroyer *Fanning* (DD 37) south of Ireland on 17 November 1917.

Crewmen crowd the deck of the *U-58* as she sinks south of Ireland after being depth-charged by the U.S. destroyer *Fanning* (DD 37) on 17 November 1917. Two of the *U-58*'s crew were killed; there were 38 survivors. The *U-58* was the only confirmed U-boat kill by U.S. warships in World War I. *U.S. Navy*

The overall effectiveness of the larger, fast-sinking depth charges introduced in 1916 and 1917 was further enhanced by a better-engineered depth-charge rack that could release timed patterns of charges off the stern by remote control. The earliest racks held eight and later 13 weapons, and they were installed in pairs on U.S. destroyers starting in June 1918. However, attacking a submarine with depth charges rolled over the stern required the attacker to maneuver smartly to intersect the presumed course of the quarry at just the right moment, and the resulting linear pattern provided only limited area coverage.

In an attempt to extend the reach of their earlier depth bombs, the British developed several types of shipboard artillery, both rifled howitzers and smooth-bore bomb throwers, to loft the explosive charges to the predicted position of the target, particularly one caught in the act of submerging. The most common of the howitzers was a 7.5-inch piece that could throw 100- or 500-pound projectiles 2,100 yards and 300 yards, respectively, the charges fitted with both contact exploders and hydrostatic pistols. The bomb throwers fired stick bombs—looking much like lollipops—that married the warhead to a cylindrical shaft that slid into a 3.5-inch gun barrel containing the propelling charge. Typical bomb throwers could achieve a range of 1,200 yards with a 200-pound projectile and 650 yards with a 350-pound version, both with variable depth settings.

The Royal Navy began issuing both howitzers and bomb throwers to Q-ships and vessels of the Auxiliary Patrol in June 1917. Also developed for the Auxiliary Patrol was a similar design that adapted already-installed 12-pounder guns to fire what amounted to a 200-pound ASW rifle grenade.[22] Although 3,100 of these were produced, they shared the disadvantage of the earlier projectile systems: they were essentially single-shot, ahead-firing weapons with only limited azimuthal coverage, and although widely used, they scored no known submarine kills. What was really needed was the ability to saturate a suspected target area with multiple explosive charges, and that required something more.

For the Royal Navy, the solution was the Thornycroft depth-charge thrower, which entered service in August 1917. Somewhat similar to the earlier stick-bomb thrower, the new launcher used an explosive charge inside a canted barrel to loft a Type D depth charge a distance of 40 yards. The British mounted the weapons aft on destroyers, patrol boats, and sloops, so that while depth charges were being rolled off the stern, others could be thrown to the side at right angles to the heading of the ship.

The depth charge Y-gun developed by the United States went the Thornycroft model one better by incorporating two barrels canted at 45 degrees in opposite directions—hence the name—with a single 3-inch blank cartridge at the base to throw a depth bomb to each side simultaneously. These launchers could loft a pair of Mark II depth charges 50, 60, or 80 yards, depending on the size of the firing cartridge. From December 1917 to the end of the war, nearly 1,000 Y-guns were installed on U.S. destroyers and submarine chasers. At the same time, both navies developed innovative attack maneuvers, such as steaming in a "figure-eight" pattern over the suspected target position to exploit the new advantage conveyed by dense patterns of depth charges.

With the start of unrestricted submarine warfare, mines—already important early in the conflict—attracted new attention from the British. Acknowledging the serious reliability problems in its first mining campaigns, the Admiralty worked feverishly to

Chief petty officers and a sailor load depth charges on the Y-gun of a U.S. destroyer. Firing depth charges off both sides of the ship with a Y-gun simultaneously with rolling depth charges from stern racks provided a "pattern" more likely to damage a U-boat than either method alone. *U.S. Navy*

improve mine designs during 1915 and 1916. Unlike the Royal Navy, the Germans had already deployed two excellent undersea mines, the 330-pound E-mine and the smaller, 44-pound U-mine, intended for ASW service. Both enjoyed a superior anchoring system and reliable contact detonators in which the crushing of malleable metallic "horns" generated an electrical firing current by releasing a stored electrolyte into a small battery. To save time, the Royal Navy exploited several captured German E-mines to develop its own versions—the H2, with a 300-pound warhead, and the H4, with a 150-pound charge.[23] When these and American counterparts became available in quantity late in 1917, the Allies embarked on two ambitious anti-submarine mine barrages.

German U-boats sailing from their main bases in the Helgoland Bight could reach the English Channel and the Atlantic trade routes most directly by sailing southwesterly through the North Sea and threading the Strait of Dover. An alternate route—

1,500 miles longer—led around the north of Scotland and then southward on either side of Ireland. This lengthy detour significantly shortened the time that submarines could stay on patrol. Moreover, German submarines based on the occupied coast of Flanders were well positioned to make use of the Dover Strait, just to the south, to achieve access to British shipping. Thus, as the toll of ships and cargoes lost mounted sharply in the summer of 1917, the British renewed their determination to close the Dover Strait to U-boats and revived their earlier, unsuccessful attempt to create a layered barrier minefield between Folkestone and Cape Gris-Nez.

Beginning in November 1917, the Royal Navy laid the first of a new series of densely populated minefields across the strait, using H2 mines in multiple parallel rows at depths from 40 to 100 feet. Guarded "gate" passages at each end protected by underwater sensors and sown with remotely detonated mines were established to allow the transit of friendly shipping, and the entire field was illuminated at night by searchlights from the shore and chemical flares deployed by patrolling guard vessels. This lighting was intended to prevent submarines from traversing the field on the surface under cover of darkness, thus forcing them to hazard the passage submerged. As more mines became available, the British kept adding to the Folkestone–Cape Gris-Nez barrage, and at its completion in August 1918, it contained more than 10,000 mines. The field claimed its first victim, the Flanders-based *UB-56*, less than a month after the first lines were laid. All told, ten German U-boats perished in its toils. Although the Strait of Dover still remained passable to determined—and lucky—submarines, the increasing danger posed by the new barrage forced most U-boats to take the northern route, both outbound and returning for the remainder of the war.

Initially, the U.S. Navy had planned to build up its own mine reserves by manufacturing the British service mine, but when the poor performance of the earlier British models became apparent, the Navy opted for an original design with a clever galvanic firing mechanism that significantly enhanced its volume coverage. This was the U.S. Mark 6, a conventional, self-mooring spherical mine with contact horns, a 300-pound charge, and a bottom anchor. In addition to the usual detonators, however, it also deployed a 100-foot copper-wire "antenna" held aloft by a float above the main case, which itself was fitted with an insulated copper electrode. If a steel hull brushed against the antenna, galvanic action—which takes place between two dissimilar metal electrodes in an electrolyte—generated sufficient electric current to fire the mine.[24] But the Mark 6 was not without its problems. It tended to detonate prematurely and could cause mines nearby to explode sympatheti-

cally. Nonetheless, continuous refinement and its superior volume coverage—a tall vertical cylinder, vice a relatively small sphere around the warhead itself—made it useful in World War II, and it was still in the stockpile for a decade after that.

After the United States actively joined the Allies in April 1917, the U.S. Navy proposed exploiting the large volume-coverage properties of the Mark 6 mine to implement a mine barrier of unprecedented size to close off the northern route used by German submarines to reach the Atlantic. Overcoming British misgivings, the United States gained agreement for a collaborative effort to plant a multi-layered, deep minefield stretching across the top of the North Sea from the Orkney Islands to the coast of Norway near Bergen. The area to be covered by the field was approximately 235 miles long by 50 miles wide. It was divided into three sectors, of which the British took responsibility for the two nearest shore on either end, using H2 weapons. To cover the 134-mile-long deep-water section in the middle the U.S. Navy ordered 100,000 Mark 6 mines in October 1917 and began assembling them at depots in Scotland in February 1918, when the first mines were laid. The "Great Northern Barrage" was only about 85 percent complete when the last mines were planted two weeks before the end of the war in November 1918. Even so, nearly 73,000 mines were laid, over three-quarters by the U.S. Navy. And although it was possible for U-boats to sneak around the eastern end of the minefield through Norwegian territorial waters, probably six submarines were destroyed in attempting passage. Whether this number and the deterrent effect of the Northern Barrage justified its enormous cost and the diversion of resources needed to create it still are debated today. If the war had lasted another year perhaps its longer-term effect would have been more telling.

Radio Intelligence

Another new technology that grew rapidly in importance as the ASW crisis unfolded in mid-1917 was radio intelligence. Although less than 15 years had elapsed since Marconi's first successful transatlantic radio transmission in 1901, by the beginning of the war, all of the world's major navies had adopted wireless telegraphy for long-distance communications. The first U.S. patent for Radio Direction-Finding (RDF) was granted in 1911, and the belligerents were quick to realize that RDF offered a useful technique for esti-mating the positions of enemy warships by tracking their long-range radio transmissions. From the beginning, virtually all submarines on both sides of the conflict maintained radio contact with their headquarters, and the German U-boats in particular communicated regularly while on patrol. Even before the declaration of war—and at first largely by chance—Royal Navy radio facilities and their commercial counterparts began detecting German naval communications. Faced at first with the choice of jamming or intercepting these signals, the government opted for the

Sir James Alfred Ewing
(B. 1855 D. 1935)

Scottish physicist and engineer James Ewing is famous primarily for his research into the magnetic properties of metals, investigations that led to his discovery of the phenomenon of *hysteresis*. During most of World War I he managed the British Admiralty's codebreaking section, the highly successful Room 40, which contributed significantly to the Royal Navy's ASW effort.

Ewing was born in Dundee, the son of a Church of Scotland minister. He studied engineering at the University of Edinburgh under the prominent scientists William Thomson and Lord Kelvin and then spent the years 1878–1883 teaching physics in Japan during that nation's "opening to the West." After returning to Scotland he became an engineering professor at University College, Dundee. In 1890, Ewing was appointed the Professor of Mechanism and Applied Mechanics at Cambridge, where he initiated the research into magnetic induction and the crystalline structure of metals for which he was awarded the Gold Medal of the Royal Society in 1895.

Having earlier proposed several reforms in Royal Navy technical training, Ewing was selected by the Admiralty in April 1903 for the newly created post of Director of Naval Education (DNE) at Greenwich, where he became responsible for all education and training programs in the Royal Navy. He was knighted in 1906 for his services in that position. It was in his capacity as DNE that Ewing was approached by Rear-Admiral Henry F. Oliver, then the Director of Naval Intelligence, early in World War I for assistance in decoding the growing number of German naval messages intercepted by British radio stations. Ewing recruited a cadre of amateur codebreakers to form the Room 40 organization. His team proved highly successful, not only in breaking the German naval codes but also in deciphering the infamous Zimmermann telegram, the revelation of which had a large part in bringing the United States into the war.

Ewing managed the Room 40 operation until May 1917, when he became the vice-chancellor of the University of Edinburgh, a position he held until his retirement in 1929.

intelligence value of the latter and established a string of RDF stations along the eastern coast of England and Scotland. Eventually, there were 14 such stations, capable of triangulating on enemy radio signals from both the North Sea and the eastern Atlantic to provide submarine position estimates with error circles ranging from 20 to 50 miles in radius.[25] Although the poor accuracy of this locating information reduced its usefulness for tactical prosecution, it provided valuable clues about the number of U-boats at sea and areas to be avoided by merchant ships and—later—by convoys. Soon, information of even greater value emerged when the content of these intercepted transmissions yielded to British cryptography.

The application of codebreaking techniques to the text of the German signals picked up by the RDF stations began in a somewhat ad hoc manner: On the first day of the war, Rear Admiral Henry F. Oliver, Director of Naval Intelligence, asked the Director of Naval Education, Sir Alfred Ewing, if he would be interested in examining the accumulating number of German coded messages that were being intercepted. Ewing assembled a small staff to begin an attempt to solve the naval codes, eventually using Room 40 of the Old Admiralty Building in London, which became the focal point of British cryptographic activities.[26] At first, Ewing's band of amateurs made little headway in deciphering the German messages, but in mid-October they benefited from an extraordinary windfall.

In late August, the German light cruiser *Magdeburg* had run aground in the Baltic and was seized by the Russians. Despite attempts at destruction, several copies of the current German signal books, including codes, keys, and gridded maps, were retrieved from the wreck, and this material was duly forwarded to London by the Russians. It then emerged

that the intercepted radio code groups had themselves been superenciphered so that an additional codebreaking step was required to make use of the *Magdeburg* code material. Ewing's team had surmounted that last barrier by mid-November and for the rest of the war was able to read a large portion of German naval communications.[27] The British codebreakers were aided in this by two other lucky "finds," a copy of the German merchant-ship code seized from a freighter interned in Australia at the onset of hostilities and a complete set of jettisoned code books from a German destroyer lost in the Battle of the Helgoland Bight in October 1916 and fished out of the sea, purely by accident, by a British trawler. Additionally, in late 1917, the British began using divers systematically to explore German U-boats sunk in shallow water for code books and other tactical intelligence. Some significant material resulted from that effort.[28]

By the end of 1914, Room 40 was playing an important part in plans for the Royal Navy's day-to-day response to both major moves by the German fleet and anti-shipping patrols by U-boats. Advance warning gleaned from intercepted German communications resulted directly in the British victory in the Battle of the Dogger Bank in January 1915 and the cataclysmic, but inconclusive, fleet encounter at the Battle of Jutland in May–June 1916. Perhaps more important, it provided the anti-submarine section of the Admiralty with daily reports on U-boats at sea, their approximate locations, and intended patrol or minelaying areas. Thus, the two principal ASW commands, at Dover and Queenstown, became key beneficiaries of the elaborate and successful ASW intelligence effort that evolved during the war.

After October 1917, when Room 40 came under the direct control of the legendary Captain William Hall, the Director of Naval Intelligence and likely the most brilliant intelligence official on either side, its increasing skill in puzzling out call signs, coping with abrupt code and key list changes, and warning of German initiatives made possible several operations in which U-boats were "ambushed" by British submarines stationed at predicted locations. In May 1918, for example, a communications intercept revealed that two large German "cruiser" submarines, the *U-153* and *U-154,* had been directed to meet at sea on the 11th of that month 150 miles

Admiral Sir William Reginald Hall, Royal Navy
(B. 1870 D. 1943)

William "Blinker" Hall became the Director of Naval Intelligence (DNI) in October 1914 and held that position for the rest of World War I. Under his leadership, the Admiralty's Naval Intelligence Division soon became acknowledged as the most effective intelligence operation in Britain, if not the world.

Hall was born in Wiltshire, coincidentally as the son of the Royal Navy's *first* head of naval intelligence. The junior Hall entered the Navy in 1884, joining the naval training ship *Britannia.* He served in a series of surface ships while moving up the ranks and qualifying as a gunnery officer, eventually taking command of the battleship *Cornwallis* in 1904. In late 1905 he was promoted to captain and appointed the head of Mechanical Training Establishments, which provided technical training to sailors. Subsequently, as captain of the cadet training ship *Cornwall,* he first got involved with naval intelligence work as that ship toured various foreign ports. Following command of the armored cruiser *Natal* and shore duty as assistant to the Controller of the Navy, Hall became captain of the new battle cruiser *Queen Mary* in 1913. Early in the war the ship took part in the Battle of the Helgoland Bight (August 1914). Because of deteriorating health, he asked to be relieved of command at sea and was appointed Director of the Naval Intelligence (DNI) in October, relieving Captain Henry Oliver.

In addition to encouraging and expanding the division's codebreaking activities under Sir James Ewing, Hall pioneered the effective use of what would today be called "all-source intelligence," particularly using radio intercept and direction-finding and by maintaining strong relationships with other British intelligence agencies. In addition to creating that era's most effective ASW intelligence capability, Hall's DNI organization played a crucial wartime role in confronting Ireland's Easter Rebellion of April 1916, the interception and decoding of the Zimmermann telegram in January 1917, and thwarting German espionage activities in Britain.

In 1917, Hall was promoted to rear-admiral, was knighted in 1918, and in the 1920s was advanced to vice-admiral and then to admiral while on the retired list. After his retirement in January 1919, Hall served as a Conservative member of Parliament until 1923 and then again from 1925 to 1929. In the 1920s and 1930s, he traveled widely, lecturing on intelligence matters. Although he was too old to serve on active duty in World War II, Hall was a member of the Home Guard until he died in 1943.

Hall's nickname, "Blinker," arose from a chronic facial twitch, which caused one of his eyes—somewhat unexpectedly—to blink repeatedly.

west of Cape St. Vincent, Portugal. Accordingly, the Admiralty dispatched the submarines *J-1* and *E-35* to lie in wait at two possible rendezvous points. When the *U-154* arrived on schedule she was sent to the bottom with all hands by two torpedoes from the *E-35*. The *U-153* observed the sinking from a distance of several miles, but was unable to mount a counterattack.

The fact that the British were able to anticipate their moves with increasing regularity never convinced the Germans that their codes had been compromised, and except for more frequent changes in key lists and superencipherment, they used the same basic systems throughout the war. For their part, the Germans succeeded in breaking the lower-level British codes, such as the one used to report successful mine-clearance operations, but their more limited successes had much less effect than British cryptography had on the U-boat campaign or on fleet operations in general.

The Introduction of Convoying

Despite rapid progress in fielding new and improved weapons, sensors, and ASW techniques in early 1917, Allied merchant shipping losses continued at a ruinous level. The first three months of unrestricted submarine warfare reduced the world's merchant tonnage by two million tons—out of approximately 30 million tons—and the chance of a ship safely completing a round-trip from Britain to a port beyond Gibraltar fell to one in four.[29] The Admiralty's initial response to the growing crisis was to attempt to take the offensive by mounting more aggressive anti-submarine patrols in key danger areas. Concerted sweeps by destroyers, sloops, and aircraft scoured the areas where intelligence and cryptographic information predicted that U-boats were likely to congregate. Surface hunter-killer groups, equipped with newly developed underwater

listening devices and armed with depth charges as they became available, used cooperative sweep tactics intended to detect and harry enemy submarines in known operating areas.

The results were disappointing. From the onset of unrestricted submarine warfare at the beginning of February to the end of June 1917, only three of the 18 German U-boats lost near the British Isles were destroyed by surface action. Hunting submarines in this way was, as Vice-Admiral David Beatty noted, "a prodigious job, as it is like looking for a needle in a bundle of hay, and, when you have found it, trying to strike it with another needle."[30]

Eventually, under mounting pressure from Britain's civilian War Cabinet, the Admiralty was driven in desperation to an expedient that had been lurking in the wings all along—convoys. Escorting merchant ships in convoy had been a regular feature of naval warfare in the age of sail, when enemy raiders or privateers had been the principal threat. Moreover, the movement of troops from Canada, India, Australia, and New Zealand to Europe and the Middle East in 1914 and 1915 had been under convoy protection; their home governments had insisted upon it. Even more relevant was the successful experience of several short convoy routes that had been organized under the pressure of events only months before. To protect trade between the neutral Netherlands and Great Britain from enemy warships based in the Helgoland Bight or Flanders, British destroyers had been escorting small convoys of merchant ships across the southern North Sea from the Hook of Holland since late July 1916. By the end of the war there had been only six sinkings in nearly 1,900 sailings.

Heavy merchant losses in the last quarter of 1916 had moved the Admiralty to bow to pressure from both the French and Norwegian governments for similar arrangements. The most elaborate of these was a carefully organized convoy system for protecting colliers transporting British coal across the English Channel from southern England to ports in northwestern France, and later, the Bay of Biscay. Since English coal was vital to the French war effort, the French proposal to safeguard the coal supply was quickly agreed to, and the first convoy sailed in late January. Protected on the British end largely by armed trawlers from the Auxiliary Patrol, more than 4,000 crossings had taken place by May 1917 with only nine ships lost. After neutral Norway had 27 ships torpedoed in March, the Royal Navy organized another series of convoy routes across the North Sea from Bergen, Norway, to Lerwick in the Shetland Islands and down the eastern coast of Scotland. These measures were initiated in April 1917, but were subsumed into the larger convoy arrangements that followed too soon to gauge their efficacy.

Despite these successes, both the Admiralty and the merchant marine community were strongly opposed to adopting a comprehensive convoy system for protecting merchant shipping against submarine attack. Fundamentally, the Royal Navy—with a venerable tradition of seizing the offensive at sea—found itself inherently resistant to adopting the "defensive" posture that convoys represented. The Admiralty quickly seized on a number of reasons to dismiss the convoy idea. First, it argued, sailing significant numbers of ships together only made them a larger and more detectable target and thus more vulnerable to attack. An Admiralty staff paper in January 1917 stated flatly,

> Wherever possible, vessels should sail singly, escorted as considered necessary. The system of several ships sailing in company, as a convoy, is not recommended in any area where submarine attack is a possibility. It is evident that the larger the number of ships forming the convoy, the greater the chance of a submarine being enabled to attack successfully,

and the greater the difficulty of the escort in preventing such an attack.[31]

Second, the authorities claimed that finding the large number of escorts required for convoy duty would conflict with the Grand Fleet's continuing need for destroyers and with existing commitments to area patrols and "offensive" ASW. Third, administrative and practical objections were raised—and echoed by the shipping companies: time delays, port congestion, the inability of merchant ships with different speed and sea-keeping capabilities to maintain station and zig-zag defensively. Even with the likelihood of ships being torpedoed without warning, both the Navy and the civilian maritime community remained convinced that arming merchant vessels with deck guns and sailing them independently was a more effective defense.

Nonetheless, with the British government clamoring for a solution, the organizer of the French coal convoys, Britain's Captain R. G. H. Henderson, was able to demonstrate that by including short coastal voyages, the Admiralty had overestimated the number of merchant ships needing convoy protection by a factor of 20. This realization and the pressure of events finally forced Admiral Jellicoe, then First Sea Lord, to agree in late April to the convoying of all vessels bound from the North and South Atlantic to Great Britain.[32] In the first trial of the concept, 16 merchant vessels left Gibraltar for England on 10 May, escorted en route by two Q-ships and then joined by three destroyers for the final leg. The convoy reached its dispersal point off the south coast of England on 20 May with no losses.

Even before its safe arrival, the Admiralty had appointed an Atlantic Trade Convoy Committee to devise a formal system for broader implementation, and a Convoy Section in the Admiralty itself soon followed. The first trans-Atlantic convoy from the United States left Hampton Roads on 24 May with 12 merchantmen escorted by a British armored cruiser. At 16 degrees west longitude—about 500 miles west of England—escort duties were assumed by destroyers from Devonport. Unable to maintain the required speed, two merchant ships were forced to drop out, and significantly, one of these was the

Admiral Reginald Guy Henderson, Royal Navy
(B. 1881 D. 1939)

As a commander, Henderson was largely responsible for the Royal Navy's reluctant acceptance of trans-Atlantic merchant convoys in 1917, and he subsequently played a key role in organizing and running the convoy system. In his memoirs, British prime minister David Lloyd-George largely credited Henderson with breaking down Admiralty resistance to convoying and ensuring its ultimate success. Many of Henderson's innovations formed the basis for similar convoy arrangements in World War II.

Henderson, who entered the Navy in 1894, came from an old Royal Navy family—both his father and an uncle were flag officers. He moved up rapidly through the ranks as a gunnery specialist and by 1914 had become executive officer of the battleship *Erin* and was on board the *Erin* when she took part in the Battle of Jutland. Shortly thereafter he was assigned as the naval assistant to Admiral Sir Alexander Duff, the head of the Anti-Submarine Division in the Admiralty. There Henderson organized the limited cross-Channel convoy system that protected exports of British coal to France, and with its success he became convinced that convoying in general was the key to reversing the rising toll of merchant shipping losses. In the face of determined Admiralty opposition—based largely on the erroneous claim that more than 5,000 ships weekly (the total of *all* arrivals and departures) had to be protected—he was able to show by a more realistic statistical analysis, one that counted only actual ocean-going traffic, that the number of ships requiring convoying was only about 130 per week, a much more manageable problem. When the Admiralty continued to drag its feet, Henderson went outside of official channels to approach Lloyd-George directly, and after pressure from the latter, the Royal Navy acquiesced to a trial period in May 1917. Subsequently, in conjunction with the Ministry of Shipping, Henderson was instrumental in implementing and directing the worldwide system of convoys that broke the back of the German submarine offensive. He was rewarded for that role by promotion to captain in October of the same year. In 1919, he was knighted in recognition of his contribution to the war effort.

After the war Henderson served on the China Station and on the staff of the Royal Naval College at Greenwich, during which time he became an early proponent of the Fleet Air Arm. Following his command of the aircraft carrier *Furious* in the late 1920s, he was promoted to flag rank and served as the first Rear-Admiral, Aircraft Carriers in the early 1930s, in which billet he wielded a key influence on the evolution of British naval aviation. Promoted to vice-admiral in 1934, he was appointed Third Sea Lord and Controller of the Navy, with major responsibilities for expanding the fleet just prior to World War II. Soon after he was raised to full admiral in 1939, he became seriously ill—reportedly from overwork—and died that year at the age of 58.

only ship lost to a U-boat. Moreover, of 71 merchant ships in the five Hampton Roads convoys that sailed in June, none was sunk, although one was damaged by a torpedo hit after dispersal. Despite the preponderance of earlier "expert" opinion, it was clear that convoying worked.

Eventually, the British, Canadian, and U.S. Navies organized a regular schedule of convoys for ships from Hampton Roads, New York, and Sydney in Nova Scotia, with Halifax as an alternate. By late July, there was also a regular Gibraltar run, followed quickly by convoy service through the Mediterranean and to and from Dakar and Sierra Leone on the western coast of Africa. Finally, the rapid build-up of American troops in France in 1918 required adding, in April of that year, additional convoy routes from New York to French ports on the Bay of Biscay. Because the German unrestricted submarine warfare strategy focused as much on destroying carrying capacity as on interdicting food and supplies, it was important on each of these routes to plan for and organize the convoying of ships on return voyages, most of them in ballast. Thus, within a few months, the convoy system had grown into a huge maritime enterprise, protecting virtually all ships in the war zone.

At the onset of unrestricted submarine warfare in February 1917, the Germans had declared a "prohibited area" in the Atlantic that extended out to 20 degrees west longitude and southward as far as the northwest corner of Spain. Within this region any ship, even neutral, was liable to be sunk without warning. For this reason, and also because of the range limitations of the earlier German submarines, the zone of greatest danger for merchant convoys lay within 300 to 500 miles of the British Isles. Thus, convoy protection during the greater part of the crossing could be less rigorous than that required closer to the destination and was normally entrusted to "ocean escorts." For the most part, these were older, second-line warships, such as light and armored cruisers, pre-dreadnought battleships, and armed merchant cruisers, intended to protect as much against surface threats as against U-boats.[33] At a rendezvous at the outer edge of the danger zone, the ocean escorts were relieved by destroyers from Devonport, Queenstown (in southern Ireland), or Buncrana (in northern Ireland), which shepherded the merchant ships through the final leg of the crossing, where U-boats were most likely to be encountered. Normally the operations were timed so that

In World War I, Allied ships—mostly fast liners and destroyers—were camouflaged to make it more difficult for a U-boat commander eyeing a target through a periscope to estimate a ship's size and speed. This painting of the *Mauretania* in "dazzle" camouflage was executed by Burnell Poole. *U.S. Navy*

destroyers relinquishing an out-going convoy to its ocean escort could turn around and assume responsibility for an incoming counterpart. Destroyers remained in particular demand for this "end-game" mission, because of their speed, agility, and sea-keeping abilities. As a result there were never enough of them to meet the need, and by the end of the conflict, more than 40 U.S. destroyers were operating in European waters, largely as convoy escorts.

The first division of six U.S. destroyers, under the command of Commander Joseph K. Taussig, arrived at Queenstown on 4 May 1917, less than a month after the U.S. declaration of war. When asked on reporting to Vice-Admiral Bayly when his ships would be ready for sea, Commander Taussig responded famously, "We are ready now, sir, that is as soon as we finish refueling. Of course you know how destroyers are—always wanting something done to them. But this is war, and we are ready to make the best of things and go to sea immediately."[34]

In practice, the Admiralty's Convoy Section directed day-to-day operations of the convoy system from a centralized "war room," of which the principal feature was a wall-sized, comprehensive track chart showing the current positions of all convoys at sea and the presumed locations of enemy submarines, gleaned from radio direction-finding, cryptography, or other intelligence. High-frequency radio contact with each convoy commander made possible the diversion of convoys around potential threats, and seemingly random course changes at irregular intervals further complicated the task of a U-boat commander attempting an intercept. The sailings themselves were organized in accordance with the types of cargo, destinations, and the speed of individual merchantmen. "Slow" convoys moved at less than ten knots, in contrast to higher-speed counterparts, which could sustain 13.5 knots. Thus, including the effects of zig-zagging, a trans-Atlantic convoy

could take between ten days and two weeks to cross the ocean. The number of ships traveling together rose steadily as confidence in the system increased, and by the end of the war, 40-ship convoys were not unusual.

Merchant ship losses decreased sharply after the introduction of convoying in May 1917. From the high of over 860,000 tons in April, the tonnage sunk by U-boats dropped steadily until September, when just under 354,000 tons were lost. There was an upsurge to over 466,000 tons in October, but this was the worst month for the rest of the war, and in October 1918—the last full month—only 112,000 tons were destroyed.[35] Although these numbers still represented significant losses of ships and cargo, and imports to Britain were down 20 percent in 1917 from the previous year, they were well below the ruinous toll that had immediately followed the beginning of unrestricted submarine warfare in February.

As early as 1 November 1917, Sir Eric Geddes, since July the First Lord of the Admiralty, was able to report in his maiden speech to the House of Commons, "In September 90 percent of the total ships sailing in all Atlantic trade were convoyed, and since the convoy system was started—and it has been criticized in some quarters—the total percentage of loss per convoyed vessel passed through the danger zone is 0.5 percent or 1 in 200."[36]

The fundamental reason why the convoy system was so effective in reducing shipping losses is that for a given total of ship crossings it minimized opportunities for U-boat attacks. When merchantmen sailed independently and spread themselves around the ocean along known shipping routes, German submarines would be likely to encounter one or two in their patrol areas each day. On an oceanic scale, however, the tightly concentrated group of ships constituting a convoy was little more likely to be encountered and attacked than a single ship. Moreover, it could easily sweep through a submarine's patrol area before the latter could position itself for firing torpedoes effectively. A secondary factor was the power of the convoy to decoy enemy submarines within range of its escorts and provide the latter with attack opportunities that otherwise would not have appeared. Although only five of 43 German U-boats sunk between July 1917 and the end of the year were lost to convoy escorts—most of the rest succumbed to mines—the exchange ratio between merchant ships lost and submarines destroyed decreased from 167 in April to an average of only 16 for the six-month period from August 1917 to January 1918.[37]

It was clear that a corner had been turned, and shipping losses to German U-boats no longer threatened to cripple the Allied war effort before the power of the United States could be brought to bear. Prime Minister David Lloyd George would later remark in his war memoirs, "The greatest triumph of 1917 was the gradual beating off of the submarine attack. This was the real decision of the War, for the sea front turned out to be the decisive flank in the gigantic battlefield."[38]

3

ASW in Other Areas

While the principal focus of Allied ASW efforts remained on the waters around the British Isles throughout the war, significant U-boat activity in the Mediterranean Sea required a major anti-submarine campaign there, too. Indeed, for much of the conflict, approximately one-third of the shipping losses suffered by the Allies occurred in the Mediterranean, where a handful of German and Austro-Hungarian submarines enjoyed relative impunity from the limited British and French ASW capabilities. Additionally, while British and Russian submarines were attacking German shipping in the Baltic, their German counterparts operated freely against Russian supply lines in the Black Sea in support of their Turkish confederates. These smaller submarine campaigns also necessitated a series of anti-submarine measures.[1]

The Dardanelles Campaign

In a contentious public debate in 1912 on naval force levels around the world, a major British newspaper described the Mediterranean as "the carotid artery of the Empire."[2] Indeed, the security of the sea routes to the Suez Canal and beyond loomed large in British strategic thinking. For the French, free access to their North African colonies across the narrow sea was of similar importance.

Thus, with the entry of Turkey into the war on the side of Germany and Austria-Hungary in November 1914, and with Italy leaning toward the Allied camp but still neutral, the British and French were compelled to maintain significant naval forces in the Mediterranean despite high-priority needs elsewhere. Moreover, in an attempt to drive Turkey out of the war and establish sea lines of communication to Russia through the Black Sea, a powerful Anglo-French naval armada tried to "force" the Dardanelles—connecting the Mediterranean and the Black Sea—and reach Constantinople in mid-March of 1915. When that effort failed in the face of dense Turkish minefields and coastal artillery, a subsequent amphibious landing in late April 1915 succeeded in establishing a tenuous Allied beachhead on the adjacent Gallipoli Peninsula, into which the British eventually poured more than 400,000 troops, largely from Australia and New Zealand. Although the Gallipoli campaign would end with ignominious Allied withdrawals in the winter of 1915–1916, the threat of a British and French blockade force at the Dardanelles had led the Turks to appeal to their German partners for relief even before the Gallipoli loadings.

The Germans responded by shipping four UB-class coastal submarines by rail for final assembly at Pola, an Austrian port in southern Istria, where they could augment the small Austro-Hungarian submarine force of seven second-line boats operating out of bases in the Adriatic Sea. These first four German submarines arrived between March and July 1915, and two more followed soon after. Also, on 5 April, the same day as the first landing at Gallipoli, the German submarine *U-21* left the Helgoland Bight bound for the Dardanelles via the Strait of Gibraltar, with a stop at the Austrian base at Cattaro, on the Dalmation coast of the Adriatic. Within two days of reaching the Dardanelles on 25 May, the *U-21,* without warning, torpedoed and sank two British pre-dreadnought battleships, the *Majestic* and *Triumph.* The U-boat then passed through the strait and the Sea of Marmara to reach Constantinople. And, on 13 August, the *UB-14* torpedoed the British transport *Royal Edward* in the Aegean Sea, with the loss of more than 900 lives. Thus, the earliest German U-boat operations in the Mediterranean had an immediate and devastating impact.

The Gallipoli campaign also brought a significant number of British and French submarines to the eastern Mediterranean in the expectation that they, too, could penetrate the Dardanelles into the Sea of Marmara and attack Turkish supply lines to the peninsula. But in addition to deploying both coastal artillery and mines to defend the strait against a potential Allied assault, the Turks had emplaced a series of well-patrolled submarine nets across the passage, particularly where it narrowed to less than a mile wide at Canakkale, with water only 200 feet deep. Nonetheless, in December 1914, well before the Allied naval attack of March 1915 and the invasion of the Gallipoli Peninsula in April, the British submarine *B-11* managed to penetrate the Dardanelles far enough to torpedo the old Turkish battleship *Messoudieh* just south of the narrows at Canakkale.

The submarine and the torpedo became a deadly "weapons system" during World War I. These German submariners are preparing torpedoes as their U-boat goes to sea. *Imperial War Museum*

Later, in support of the land campaign itself, additional Allied submarines, mostly British, succeeded in breaking all the way through the Turkish defenses in the Dardanelles to reach the Sea of Marmara, where they preyed easily on enemy shipping.[3] The first Allied submarine to reach the Marmara was the Australian *AE-2* on 25 April, although she was sunk by a Turkish torpedo boat only four days later. One of the more unusual ASW actions of World War I occurred on 27 April during the British *E-14*'s first successful attempt to negotiate the passage. After an initial sighting, Turkish sailors on small patrol craft sought desperately to lasso the boat's periscope whenever it appeared above the surface to get a fleeting navigational fix.

The most extraordinary Allied submarine success during the Gallipoli campaign was achieved by the British *E-11*, which, under Lieutenant-Commander (later Admiral) Martin Dunbar-Nasmith, entered the Sea of Marmara on 19 May and remained for two and a half weeks. After sinking four large steamers, two ammunition ships, and a gunboat, Dunbar-Nasmith sailed as far as Constantinople, where he torpedoed a transport just outside the Golden Horn; he sank yet another transport when he left the Dardanelles on 6 June.

Allied submarine casualties were considerable. Before the Dardanelles campaign wound down in early 1916, 13 Allied submarines had taken part in the operation, making 27 successful passages through the Turkish straits. Eight submarines—four British and four French—were lost in the straits and in the Sea of Marmara. Turkish ASW, which relied primarily on surface craft, was relatively ineffective, but the shallow, twisting passage at the narrows, with unpredictable cross currents and overlying layers of salt and fresh water, frequently forced submarines to broach or become fouled in the nets, leaving them easy prey to shore guns.

After the Allies withdrew from Gallipoli, several German U-boats—presumably with Turkish assistance—followed the *U-21*'s earlier example in running the Dardanelles to reach Constantinople despite British and French guardships at the entrance to the strait. As a result, by May 1916 seven German submarines were operating in the Black Sea against Russian shipping. Russian ASW measures there were limited largely to defensive mining, and the German boats exacted a heavy toll before the Bolshevik revolution forced Russia out of the war in late 1917.

Operations in the Adriatic

Even before the arrival of German U-boat reinforcements in the Mediterranean, the small Austro-Hungarian submarine force had given a good account of itself in its limited area of operations. As early as 21 December 1914, the Austrian submarine *U-12* damaged the French dreadnought battleship *Jean Bart* with a torpedo hit while the latter was leading a surface sweep into the lower Adriatic. The French were struck again on 27 April 1915, when the Austrian *U-5* sank the French armored cruiser *Léon Gambetta* patrolling at the Strait of Otranto.[4] Moreover, the first submarine lost in the Mediterranean theater during the war was the French *Curie*, sunk by gunfire from an Austrian destroyer on 20 December 1914, when she was forced to surface after fouling a submarine net protecting the approaches to Pola.

The conflict in the Adriatic flared up in earnest on 23 May 1915, when Italy declared war on Austria-Hungary but not on Germany. Under these new conditions—with Italy and Germany not formally antagonists—German submarines operating in the Mediterranean and Adriatic had to resort to subterfuge to support their Austrian allies. When the German *UB-15* sank the Italian submarine *Medusa* on 1 June, and the *UB-14* torpedoed the Italian armored cruiser *Amalfi* in the upper Adriatic on 7 July—Italy's first major naval loss—both of the German UB boats were flying the Austrian flag. Two days later, the Austrian *U-4* torpedoed the British light cruiser *Dublin* in the lower

Adriatic, causing extensive damage. Subsequently, German and Austrian submarines based in Pola and Cattaro, and Italian and British counterparts operating out of Venice and Brindisi, plus lighter craft such as torpedo boats, imposed in the Adriatic a stalemate that lasted for most of the war. The Austro-Hungarian battle fleet, already bottled up by superior French and Italian forces at the Strait of Otranto, was kept close to home also by the threat of submarines and torpedo boats from bases on the Italian coast, and French and Italian capital ships in the Mediterranean were discouraged from entering the Adriatic by the similar threat of enemy submarines based in Dalmatia.

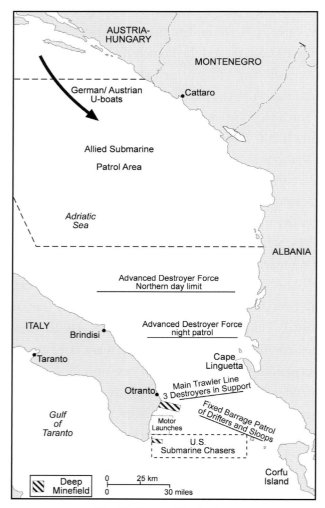

Map 2. Otranto Straits Barrage
Source: Arthur Marder, *From the Dreadnought to Scapa Flow* volume 5 (Barnsley, U.K.: Seaforth Publishing, 2014).

This stalemate, however, had little effect on the ability of German and Austrian submarines based at Pola, Cattaro, and several smaller ports to achieve access to the wider Mediterranean and its lucrative shipping targets by threading their way through the Strait of Otranto. Within a year of the *U-21*'s arrival from Germany, more than a dozen U-boats were operating in the Mediterranean, together with the six (noted above) supporting the Turks against the Russians in the Black Sea. In this same period, the Germans and Austrians lost three submarines each in the theater, but more than half of the loss of Allied shipping during late 1915 and the first half of 1916 was suffered in the Mediterranean.

In addition to the vulnerable supply routes through the Mediterranean necessitated by the Gallipoli campaign, the Anglo-French expeditionary force sent to Salonika in neutral Greece in October 1915 to support the beleaguered Serbians provided even more opportunities for the U-boats, particularly in the Aegean. Recognizing this growing danger, the British, French, and Italians created an anti-submarine barrier across the 50-mile-wide Strait of Otranto, beginning with a mobile net barrage deployed by British drifters in September 1915. The drifters, more than 90 of which were operating out of Brindisi by December, represented the principal element of a layered defense, with a line of Italian auxiliary craft posted across the strait to their north and French submarines and patrol boats to the south. Much like similar British measures in the Irish Sea, the Otranto defenses were intended to force enemy submarines to transit the strait submerged, both to drive them into the nets and to deplete their batteries by requiring them to remain underwater for extended periods. Initially, however, the British nets reached only down to 40 feet, and not until April 1916 was this depth capability extended to 150 feet. Even so, there were never enough drifters available to cover the entire strait—at least 50 needed to be at sea at all times—and a strong tidal flow and unpredictable currents made it impossible to maintain a reliable barrier. Additionally, coordination among the Allies left much to be desired, and the French and Italian patrol stations were often unoccupied.

Thus, although there were four confirmed instances during 1916 when German or Austrian U-boats became entangled in the Otranto net barrier, only one—the Austrian *U-6*—was actually sunk, in mid-May. It was not particularly challenging for transiting submarines to dive under the nets, but the sporadic nature of surface patrols made it even easier to run through the barrier on the surface under cover of darkness, and most of the submarines did. In addition, the light patrol craft and drifters guarding the nets were easy prey for raids by Austrian destroyers, which precipitated several sharp surface actions in mid-year. All told, the anti-submarine defenses in the Strait of Otranto did little to inhibit access to the Mediterranean by German and Austrian submarines.

Even though the U-boats generally adhered strictly to the London Declaration's prize rules, Allied merchant sinkings continued to rise throughout 1916. A particularly damaging loss occurred in late February 1916, when the *U-35* sank the French transport *Provence* south of Cape Matapan, with the loss of more than 1,000 troops. At the end of the year, Admiral Sir Henry Oliver, Chief of the Admiralty War Staff, was forced to note that "the inefficiency of this barrage [at the Strait of Otranto] is the root of all the submarine trouble in the Mediterranean."[5]

The Wider Mediterranean

In response to the apparent submarine threat in the Mediterranean theater, an earlier agreement reached among the Allied powers in Paris in early December 1915 divided the area into 18 ASW zones, variously assigned to the British, French, and Italian Navies. This partitioning was further refined three months later at a meeting in Malta, which established a system of patrolled shipping routes, with close escorts provided only for special cases, such as troopships. Not surprisingly, these first organized anti-submarine measures in the Mediterranean merely duplicated the "zone-defense" approach of patrolling dangerous areas that had been adopted in the North Atlantic earlier in the war—with the same lack of success. Moreover, when Italy finally declared war on Germany in late August 1916, German U-boats enjoyed even greater freedom of action in that they no longer had to be circumspect in attacking Italian ships. Naval historian Arthur Marder noted, "The U-boats got good results in the Mediterranean because, *inter alia,* they sent the best boats there, and under the command of the most experienced officers; operating conditions were unusually favourable; steamer routes were easy to find, and weather and visibility conditions were vastly better than in the North Sea; and counter-offensive measures were extremely inadequate."[6]

As Mediterranean losses in the last quarter of 1916 approached an annual total of 430,000 tons, the Allies adopted more desperate measures. Troops bound for the eastern Mediterranean were transported overland to Marseilles and only then took ship for points farther east. The use of the Suez Canal was restricted to ships bound for Indian ports west of Ceylon, forcing those headed for the Bay of Bengal to avoid the Mediterranean altogether and take the long detour around Africa. When pressure mounted inevitably to adopt a convoy system, the British and French instead responded ineffectually by instituting a series of well-protected "ports of refuge" west of Sicily. In these harbors, merchant shipping could find safe haven during daylight hours, venturing forth only at night and close to shore to reach the next port in the chain. In the eastern Mediterranean, shipping was dispersed widely over diverse routes to Malta, Egypt, and the Aegean.

This system of patrolled routes, ports of refuge, and subsequent dispersal proved completely inadequate to counter the unrestricted submarine warfare campaign unleashed by the Germans in February 1917. With the entire Mediterranean now a war zone—and with 16 German and Austrian submarines at sea there by April—shipping losses in the theater that month exceeded 275,000 tons, and for the second quarter of 1917 they reached nearly 630,000 tons, more than twice the total of the preceding three months. At a conference at Corfu at the beginning of May, the Allies adopted a new set of half-measures in which ships entering the Mediterranean were required to call at Gibraltar to be organized into a hybrid succession of small convoys and protected routes for moving eastward. Additionally, the Corfu conference gave the British effective control over the entire ASW effort in the theater, but coordination among the three major allies remained uneven, and the "handing over" of responsibility for groups of ships moving from area to area frequently failed.

By this time there were a total of more than 850 British, French, Italian, *and Japanese* patrol craft of various sizes and types operating in the Mediterranean.[7] Japan had joined the Allies in the first month of the war but at first had restricted its actions to seizing German island possessions in the Pacific and attacking German port concessions in China. Then, in mid-April 1917, acceding to the request of the other Allies, the Japanese Navy sent six destroyers and the armored cruiser *Akashi* to the Mediterranean to assist in the ASW effort. In August, eight more Japanese destroyers and the armored cruiser *Idzumo* arrived, the latter to relieve the *Akashi*. The cruiser and these 14 destroyers, under loose British control, were valuable additions to the Allied force at a time when destroyers were in short supply. On nearly three dozen occasions, Japanese destroyers engaged German and Austrian U-boats in the Mediterranean, but not without loss: in June 1917, the destroyer *Sakaki* was torpedoed northwest of Crete by the Austrian submarine *U-27* and, although kept afloat, lost her bow and 65 of her crew.

With mounting impatience over shipping losses in the Mediterranean that amounted still to a disproportionate one-third of the worldwide total, another Allied naval conference, in London in early September 1917, agreed to a formal convoy system in that theater. Immediately, convoys were organized and escorted from Gibraltar to Genoa (to bring coal to Italy); from Gibraltar to Egypt and the Suez Canal (via Bizerte); and across the Mediterranean between France and its North African colonies. By mid-October the Royal Navy had instituted regularly scheduled convoys all the way from Britain to Port Said and back, timed to pass Cape Bon during darkness. These long-distance convoys normally consisted of from 16 to 20 ships, all capable of making more than ten knots, and escort duties were shared among the Allied navies along their path. Although the loss to U-boats of two ships from the first outbound convoy and three from its returning counterpart revived the old arguments against convoying in favor of more offensive ASW tactics, the next four outbound convoys suffered no losses, and the Mediterranean convoy system was expanded continually until the end of the war.

Although the Germans had as many as 18 submarines in the Mediterranean in mid-1917, several were ordered to the Levant to support the Turks in resisting the British campaign in Palestine, which captured Jerusalem on 12 December and pressed northward into Syria. This diversion and the introduction of the convoy system caused the number of sinkings to drop significantly in the last half of 1917, and although there were occasional flare-ups, the trend continued downward for the rest of the war. Despite the presence of 28 German U-boats in the Mediterranean theater in August 1918, only 65,000 tons of shipping were lost that month. As in the North Atlantic, U-boat commanders found merchant ships in convoy harder to locate and better defended, and the extension of Allied radio direction-finding and dedicated cryptography to the Mediterranean in mid-1917 made possible the avoidance of many submarine patrol areas. Nonetheless, the Allied convoy authorities faced a more difficult challenge in the Mediterranean than in the North Atlantic, where the submarine danger was restricted largely to ocean areas within 500 miles of the British Isles. The Mediterranean was relatively narrow, with several critical passages that simplified submarines locating Allied targets. Also, the entirety of the Mediterranean was within easy striking range of Austrian bases, and Allied ships had to be convoyed from end to end.

As an adjunct to the introduction of the convoy system in the fall of 1917, the French and Italian Navies mounted a major effort to increase the effectiveness of the Otranto net barrage. In April 1918, they began deploying a fixed anti-submarine net 200 feet deep between Cape Santa Maria di Leuca on the heel of Italy and Fano Island near Corfu. Although this net line—south of the existing defenses—was completed only six weeks before the end of the war, it snagged one luckless German submarine, the *UB-53*, which was forced to the surface and scuttled.

Further, in June 1918, somewhat more than a year after the United States entered the war, a force of 36 wood-hull U.S. Navy subchasers arrived at Corfu to reinforce local anti-submarine measures. In the remaining months of the war this American "splinter fleet" mounted numerous patrols in support of the Otranto barrage and claimed 19 submarine "kills" at the time, although no submarine losses could be confirmed after the fact.[8] Ironically, except for destroying the *U-6* and *UB-53*, and possibly two other U-boats lost to unknown causes, the enormous ASW effort mounted in the Strait of Otranto was almost entirely fruitless.

In total, the German Navy lost 19 submarines in the Mediterranean and Black Seas, and the Austrians nine—approximately 14 percent of the total number of U-boats lost to the Central Powers. Among their enemies, the French lost 11 submarines, the Italians ten, and the British six. All but one of the Italian losses were in the Adriatic, as were six of the French submarines sunk. The area around the Dardanelles and the Sea of Marmara claimed all but one of the British losses, and the French lost five submarines there, including one sunk in a collision with a British armed steamer.[9] In mid-October 1918, when the Austro-Hungarian government began peace negotiations, the German submarines at Pola and Cattaro made preparations for evacuation, and by the end of the month 12 U-boats had departed for Germany. Ten more—unable to make the long voyage—were scuttled in the Adriatic. The Armistice ending World War I followed within two weeks.

The Baltic Campaign

Like the Black Sea, the Baltic was of secondary importance in the war at sea, but it was the only theater in which German shipping was targeted in an anti-commerce campaign and where there were extensive German ASW efforts. The Russian Navy was interested primarily in defending the

Gulf of Finland and the approaches to the capital at Petrograd (St. Petersburg), whereas the Germans had a major strategic interest in protecting iron ore shipments from neutral—but German-leaning—Sweden to their northern ports. In 1915 and 1916, as the German Army pushed northeasterly along the southern shore of the Baltic toward the Gulf of Riga, naval forces on both sides supported the seaward flanks of their respective armies, leading to a series of small-scale but violent clashes at sea. Interestingly, because of inclement weather and ice cover, the "campaigning season" in these more northerly waters was generally limited to the period from April to early November.

During 1915 and 1916, nine Royal Navy submarines reached the Baltic to operate from Russian bases. The first five—all E class—arrived via the Kattegat and the Belts between Sweden and Denmark despite intense German patrolling, whereas the final four—smaller C-class boats—were barged down from the northern port of Archangel on the White Sea via inland waterways. Although the early arriving E-class boats initially concentrated on attacking German warships, they joined a similar number of less-capable Russian submarines in September 1915 to mount a concerted campaign against the Swedish iron ore traffic. Allied submarines sank 14 small freighters—a total of 28,000 tons—during this first effort, but the effect on the enemy war economy was minimal, particularly after the Germans began convoying the ore carriers in April 1916, while also adopting many of the ASW innovations pioneered by the British, such as depth charges, explosive sweeps, and Q-ships.

In 1914, the German Navy had established a Technische Versuchskommission to develop ASW weapons and devices, but only a single depth-charge design appeared during the war. This was the C-15, a 200-pound float-and-lanyard type, and it proved as unreliable as its earlier British equivalent.[10] Moreover, it was never available in the quantities needed for effectiveness, and the Germans failed to develop the proficiency in ASW that necessity had forced on the British. Like their Royal Navy counterparts in the waters around the British Isles, the Germans organized a series of ASW hunter groups in the Baltic Sea, but these groups were even less effective than the Allied equivalents. Nonetheless, four Russian and two Royal Navy submarines were lost in the Baltic, plus another British boat that was interned in Denmark after grounding in territorial waters on the way into the area. After Russia formally left the war in February 1918 under the punitive terms of the Treaty of Brest-Litovsk, the seven surviving British submarines in the Baltic were scuttled in the Gulf of Finland to prevent their capture by the Germans, and over a dozen Russian boats were scuttled in the throes of the Russian Revolution.

Allied ASW in the End Game

The introduction of convoying in May 1917 and its subsequent expansion to cover virtually all of the major Allied shipping routes had broken the back of the German anti-shipping campaign by the end of that year. Although Allied merchant ship losses remained at considerable levels into 1918, with a maximum of nearly 369,000 tons in March, the exchange ratio—merchant ships sunk for each submarine lost—had shifted dramatically in the Allied direction. From the peak of 167, achieved in April 1917, the exchange ratio averaged only 16 between August and January 1918 and reached a minimum of ten in May 1918, a month in which the Germans lost 15 U-boats.

Although massive new construction enabled the Germans to keep more boats at sea, the sheer weight of ASW numbers that the entry of the United States into the war brought to bear and several years of cumulative improvement in ASW weapons, sensors, and tactics had forced the U-boats onto the defensive. In the face of a relentless Allied ASW campaign, their losses mounted sharply.

Nonetheless, several vexing ASW problems remained. Among these, the well-positioned Flanders U-boat flotilla remained a thorn in the Allied side, giving German submarines easy access to the southern North Sea and Britain's eastern coast. Despite their strategic location, however, the ports of Zeebrugge and Ostend—connected by canals to the larger inland base at Bruges—suffered a significant disadvantage. To accommodate the 15-foot tidal range in the area, both canals required locks at the coastline, and the lock gates and the canals themselves created a significant vulnerability that the British first attempted to exploit in 1915. Recognizing the need to defend Zeebrugge and Ostend from the sea, the Germans had emplaced substantial batteries of coast artillery near both ports with guns as large as 15 inches in caliber.

The Royal Navy's first concerted attempt to prevent the egress of German submarines and destroyers from their Flanders bases took place on 23 August 1915. A strongly supported British force of three monitors attempted to destroy the lock gates at Zeebrugge, a half-mile inland, by shellfire from the sea.[11] Despite elaborate preparations, which included mounting huge tripods on the seabed to establish aiming points, the attempt was a total fiasco because of material failures on two of the three monitors, the small target area of the gates themselves, and the German shore batteries, which easily outranged the British guns. A similar attempt to bombard the lock gates at Ostend on 7 September also was unsuccessful.

Subsequently, in conjunction with offensives by the British Expeditionary Force in Belgium, the Royal Navy conducted additional bombardments of the Zeebrugge–Ostend area in January, September, and December 1916, without affecting the viability of the ports for submarine and destroyer operations. These forays had expanded by then to include raids on both cross-Channel traffic and the Dover mine barrage. Thus, at least partly in response to pressure from the Navy, the British Army mounted a major land offensive in July 1917 intended to seize the coastline and eliminate the German naval bases there. The result was the third battle of Ypres—also known as Passchendaele—which killed 70,000 British soldiers for virtually no gain and severely strained relations between the Army and the Royal Navy.

The final—and most daring—attempt to prevent German warships and submarines from using Zeebrugge and Ostend took place on 23 April 1918, when Commodore Roger Keyes, the new commander of the Dover Patrol, launched a large-scale commando raid to block both canals. The primary objective of this intricate operation, which involved 165 ships and nearly 1,800 officers and men, was to sink three blockships in the canal entrance at Zeebrugge and two more in the harbor at Ostend. At Zeebrugge this required landing a force of Royal Marines to overcome German defenses on the mole that protected the harbor and detonating an explosives-laden submarine under the viaduct that connected it with the land. Despite fierce German resistance, the raiders accomplished these actions, and two of the three blockships reached the canal and were successfully scuttled, seemingly blocking the entrance. Meanwhile, the operation at Ostend went badly awry, largely because the Germans had moved the light buoy marking the channel, and the blockships were sunk a mile out of position.

Because subsequent aerial photographs appeared to show that the Zeebrugge canal had indeed been severed, the Zeebrugge-Ostend raid was declared a major victory despite more than 600 men killed, wounded, or missing. Eleven Victoria Crosses were awarded, and Keyes was knighted, eventually becoming Lord Keyes of Zeebrugge and Dover. The reality was less encouraging. Within two days, the Germans had cleared the channel sufficiently to allow the passage of both submarines and torpedo boats, and in three weeks destroyers were again operating from the port. Only in October 1918, when the final retreat of the German Army forced the abandonment of the Flanders coast, did the last submarines and destroyers depart for Germany.

In response to the proven effectiveness of the convoy system in cutting Allied shipping losses in the eastern Atlantic, the German authorities decided in the spring of 1918 to extend their anti-shipping campaign to the east coast of the United States. This was not without precedent. Earlier, in October 1916—well before the Americans had entered the fray—the German submarine U-53 had paid a port call on Newport, Rhode Island, and, departing within 24 hours as required by the neutrality laws, sank five Allied merchantmen just outside the three-mile limit. Moreover, the Germans had built several large, unarmed merchant submarines—with 1,875 tons submerged displacement on a length of 213 feet—specifically for importing desperately needed strategic materials through the British blockade. The most famous of these, the *Deutschland,* made two successful round trips to the United States in the summer and fall of that same year.[12]

Subsequently, the German Navy armed these cargo-carrying submarines for naval service and built sufficient additional boats in mid-1917 to create a homogeneous class of long-range "cruiser" submarines designated *U-151* through *U-157,* with the *Deutschland* emerging as the *U-155.* Despite the large distances and transit times involved, these large, capable boats proved quite effective in the brief, but disruptive, submarine campaign that ensued. Surprisingly for this later period of the war, it was conducted in strict accordance with the rules of cruiser warfare, to avoid antagonizing even more neutrals and prejudicing an eventual peace settlement on the basis of U.S. president Woodrow Wilson's "14 Points."

The first cruiser submarine to appear in the western Atlantic was the *U-151,* which arrived in May 1918 on a 94-day patrol that ultimately emerged as the most successful of the campaign. Operating between New York and Cape Hatteras, the *U-151* laid mines, cut undersea communication cables, and sank 23 ships totaling over 51,000 tons before returning to Germany in July. This foray was followed by five more patrols by three "cruisers" and two large submarine minelayers, and when the campaign ended in October, 93 Allied vessels of 166,907 tons had been lost to U-boats. Additionally, the *U-156* laid off Fire Island, New York, a minefield that sank the armored cruiser *San Diego* (ACR 6) on 19 July, and the pre-dreadnought battleship *Minnesota* (BB 22) was severely damaged—but without casualties—on 29 September by a mine planted by the minelayer *U-117* near the mouth of Delaware Bay.

Although the *U-156* appears to have been lost in the Northern Mine Barrage on her return trip to Germany, U.S. anti-submarine efforts in response to the German campaign were largely ineffective. Soon after the United States entered the war the Navy had employed its available patrol boats, subchasers, and aircraft for ASW sweeps off the Atlantic seaboard, but lack of resources forced the stopgap measure of using U.S. submarines themselves in ASW operations there and on the Gulf Coast. Ultimately, two submarine divisions were shifted from Hawaii and Puget Sound for that purpose, and by the beginning of 1918, small detachments of older U.S. undersea craft were operating from Provincetown (Massachusetts), New London (Connecticut), Cape May, the Delaware Breakwater, Philadelphia, Hampton Roads, Charleston, Key West (Florida), Galveston (Texas), the Virgin Islands, Bermuda, and Coco Solo in the Panama Canal Zone.

As an additional measure, reminiscent of the trawler/towed-submarine tactic tried earlier by the British, the U.S. Navy in mid-1918 commissioned two four-masted schooners, the *Robert H. McCurdy* and the *James Whittemore,* as well as the smaller New England fishing schooner *Arabia,* to serve as decoy ships intended to lure German U-boats within range of U.S. submarines lurking nearby. But as in Europe, this random patrolling produced little, except for a single encounter off Cape May in August 1918, when aircraft and several subchasers forced the *U-117* to submerge and abort an attack. The only other notable ASW achievement in U.S. waters occurred a month later, when the destroyer *Stringham* (DD 83) damaged the *U-140* in a depth charge attack off the coast of North Carolina, four days after the submarine had sunk the Diamond Shoals lightship.

A lieutenant moves forward on a U.S. four-stack destroyer as sailors stand by the stern depth-charge racks. These were the first effective weapons against a submerged U-boat. The destroyer's after 4-inch/50-caliber gun is in the foreground. *U.S. Navy*

Despite the appearance of German success and the ineffectiveness of the rudimentary ASW measures then available to the United States, the brief U-boat campaign off the East Coast came too late to affect the outcome of the war. The total loss of Allied shipping was only one-third or so of that sunk in a single month during the height of the conflict in European waters, and the growing industrial capacity of the United States was fully capable of offsetting an even more dramatic toll. Nonetheless, the Germans had demonstrated convincingly that modern submarines could operate effectively over transoceanic distances and that a mere handful could divert a disproportionate share of naval resources to coastal defense.

Submarine versus Submarine

As the war entered its third and fourth years, there was a significant increase in the role of the submarine itself as an ASW platform. Allied submarines sank 19 German U-boats and an Austro-Hungarian submarine during the conflict, with more than half of these kills scored in the last 15 months of the war.[13] German and Austrian boats sank nine Allied submarines: five British, two Italian, and two French. Additionally, the German *U-7* was destroyed off the Dutch coast in January 1915 by the *U-22* in a "blue-on-blue" encounter, and the Italian *H-5* was similarly destroyed by the British submarine *H-1* in the Adriatic in April 1918. Since all the submarine victims were caught on the surface, most of these incidents differed little from conventional submerged attacks on surface ships.

The British in particular began to use submarines as regular members of hunter-killer groups in mid-war, as well as using their own boats to "stake out" known U-boat transit routes and operating areas.

Rear Admiral William S. Sims, the commander of U.S. naval forces in Europe, later was to claim that the relative success of Allied submarines in hunting their German counterparts had been due to the close proximity of the Allied bases, which enabled Allied boats to operate submerged for a much greater percentage of the time. Moreover, the German anti-shipping campaign required the German U-boats to operate largely on the surface to maximize their area coverage.[14]

In addition to the several destroyer flotillas sent to Europe after its entry into the war, the United States dispatched 12 submarines to the Azores and southern Ireland, specifically to bolster the Royal Navy's anti-submarine campaign in the eastern Atlantic. Because their limited range prevented them from making the ocean transit under their own power, the U.S. boats were first towed to the Azores—where five K-class boats remained—and thence to Bantry Bay, Ireland, where seven L-class submarines operated with the British between January 1918 and the end of the war. The American boats were assigned patrol areas south of Ireland and up into St. George's Channel, and during most of 1918 three of the seven boats would be at sea on eight-day patrols, largely submerged during the day, lying in wait for the enemy. Although this intensive effort led to 21 claimed U-boat sightings and four torpedo attacks, the U.S. boats scored no kills. In the autumn of 1918, two more U.S. submarine divisions departed for Europe, to arrive just as the Armistice was declared. They were quickly recalled. (By early 1919, the last U.S. boats in European waters had returned home.)

Recognizing the growing potential for using submarines to attack their enemy counterparts, the Royal Navy in late 1917 laid down 12 boats of the R class, the world's first submarines designed

The ten British R-class submarines completed in 1918–1919 were the world's first undersea craft designed specifically for the hunter-killer (SSK) role. Relatively small with a surface displacement of 410 tons and a length of 163 feet, they were fast and highly maneuverable underwater. All had been discarded by 1925.
Imperial War Museum

specifically as a U-boat hunter-killer. Relatively small for their time—only 500 tons submerged on a length of 163 feet—the R-boats were powerful enough to make 15 knots underwater (greater than their surface speed of nine and one-half knots) and were well armed, with six 18-inch torpedo tubes and an advanced hydrophone installation. Although ten were completed in 1918 and undertook patrols, only the *R-8* was able to engage a U-boat—and her torpedo failed. The R class, although an interesting harbinger of the future, was significantly ahead of its time; all but two had been disposed of by 1923.

The Final Curtain

By late summer 1918, it was apparent that the German gamble on unrestricted submarine warfare to force a British capitulation before the arrival of superior U.S. forces had failed. Faced by a growing American troop and aviation presence in France, the German Army commenced withdrawing in September to defensive positions along the Hindenburg Line, but under the pressure of a concerted Allied offensive along the entire Western Front late that month, it began retreating inexorably from its early gains in Flanders and France. Meanwhile, behind the lines, both political and military resistance was crumbling, and on 4 Octo-

ber, Germany's newly appointed chancellor, the moderate Prince Max of Baden, joined Austria in appealing to President Wilson for a general armistice on the basis of Wilson's 14 Points.

By then, in response to the steady British advance in the north, the German Navy had already evacuated its Flanders Force from Ostend, Zeebrugge, and Bruges, and had been forced to destroy three submarines unable to get away. On 21 October, as a consequence of the initial peace negotiations, the German naval command ordered all U-boats at sea to return to their home bases in the Helgoland Bight. Despite the imminent end of the war, the command of the High Seas Fleet—notably the commander-in-chief, Admiral Scheer—still hoped to mount one last "death-or-glory" sortie to draw the Royal Navy's Grand Fleet into battle by attacking the Flanders coast and the Thames Estuary. Detailed plans were drawn up for this final operation, to commence on 30 October; two days earlier approximately 25 submarines left port to assume their assigned positions athwart the path of an expected British riposte. When the disgruntled crews of the German battle fleet learned of these intentions, however, their simmering unrest erupted into full-scale mutiny, and the operation was quickly aborted. The High Seas Fleet had essentially ceased to exist as a coherent entity.

After brief final negotiations, the Armistice went into effect at 11 a.m. on 11 November 1918. A key provision of the naval agreement was the requirement that the German Navy surrender its entire submarine force to the Allies at Harwich on the eastern coast of England. Accordingly, the first 20 submarines arrived on 20 November, and by the end of December, a total of 114 had been turned over to the British. In Germany, an additional 62 boats were found to be seaworthy, plus nearly 150 under construction. The latter were broken up, but Germany ultimately transferred 176 submarines to Allied control, plus another eight boats that had been interned in neutral ports. Thus ended the first war in which submarine and anti-submarine operations played a major role.

Lessons Learned, New Platforms, and New Technologies

The early decades of the 20th Century were years of accelerating technical and industrial progress that built on the unprecedented scientific and engineering advances of the preceding 50 years. It was an era that saw the beginnings of military aviation and radio communications, broad advances in electro-mechanical technology, and innovations at sea like the steam turbine and director-controlled gunnery. The unexpected war emergency created by the submarine threat stimulated vigorous efforts on both sides to exploit these new technologies for the development of anti-submarine weapons, platforms, and sensors. As Winston Churchill later noted,

> It was a warfare hitherto undreamed-of among men, a warfare at once more merciless and complicated than had ever been conceived. All the known sciences, every adaptation of mechanics, optics, and acoustics that could play a part were pressed into its service. It was a war of charts and calculations, of dials and switches, of experts who were also heroes, of tense, patient thought interrupted by explosions and death.[1]

The Role of Aviation

Progress in aviation since the Wright Brother's first flight in 1903 had been even more rapid than developments in the submarine world and, like submarines, military aircraft first came into their own in World War I. By 1914, both the Allies and the Central Powers had significant numbers of relatively capable aircraft, used at first for scouting and reconnaissance but soon also for bombing and air-to-air combat. In August 1917, a report by the British prime minister's Committee on Air Organisation and Home Defence Against Air Raids had opined, "Air supremacy may in the long run become as important a factor in the defence of the Empire as sea supremacy."[2] Not surprisingly, both sides introduced aircraft for anti-submarine operations early in the war, and their use for ASW had become widespread by the end of the conflict in November 1918.

Because of their long endurance and relative safety over water, lighter-than-air craft—airships— were at first the most widely used ASW aircraft. Airships in various forms had become relatively common by the mid-19th Century. The pioneering efforts of the Brazilian Alberto Santos Dumont, who built the first completely practical airship in France in 1898, and the German Count Ferdinand von Zeppelin, the first of whose giant rigid-frame dirigibles flew in 1900, had attracted significant commercial and military attention.[3] The German Army bought its first Zeppelin in 1909, followed three years later by the Navy, and in August 1914, there were seven Army airships in service and one Navy. These numbers increased rapidly, and by the end of the war, the Germans had built more than 100 military airships and employed them widely for reconnaissance, strategic bombing, and long-range scouting in support of the High Seas Fleet. German airships patrolled regularly over the Helgoland Bight and the western Baltic, searching for both enemy surface forces and submarines. On Christmas Day 1914, the naval Zeppelin *L-5* bombed the British submarine *E-11* in the North Sea, albeit without inflicting damage. Five months later, in May 1915, the *L-9* attacked three British submarines in three hours but succeeded only in scoring a near miss on the *D-4*. Although no other Zeppelin came as close to scoring a kill during the war, their presence constituted a powerful threat to submarines.

Neither the British nor the other Allied powers ever overcame the German lead in rigid airships, but they were quick to improvise lighter-than-air platforms of their own.[4] In March 1915, the Royal Navy introduced its first purpose-built ASW aircraft by suspending the fuselage of an obsolescent BE-2 bomber beneath an elongated, hydrogen-filled "gas bag" to create the Submarine Scout series of non-rigid airships. These aircraft—for which the term "blimp" was soon coined—simply used the BE-2's 70-horsepower Renault engine for motive power and could carry two 112-pound bombs.[5] As the war progressed, the Submarine Scouts were supplanted by larger, more-capable blimps of the Coastal, Coastal Star, and Zero classes. By late 1918 the British had more than 100 non-rigid airships—blimps—engaged in coastal and ASW surveillance. Their long endurance, beginning with four- to eight-hour patrols in 1915 and extending to 12 hours by the war's end, was ideal for escorting convoys in home waters. Although generally too slow to prosecute direct attacks when surfaced submarines were spotted, the blimps collaborated well with surface escorts, which could be quickly vectored to targets sighted from the air by means of either visual or radio signaling. Additionally, the mere presence of an airship over a convoy often sufficed to keep shadowing

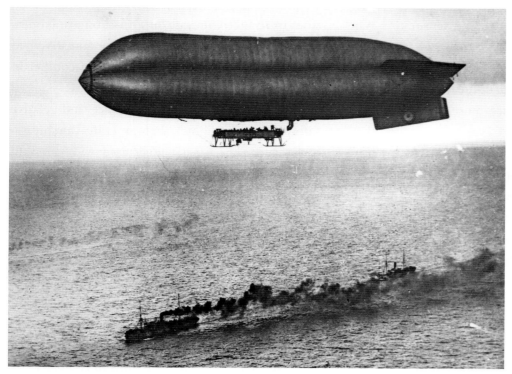

A British Coastal-class airship over a convoy in December 1917. The gondola suspended under the airship was a modified aircraft fuselage; the craft had aircraft-type engines forward and aft to propel it and was flown by a crew of five or six. These airships could carry four 112-pound bombs or two 230-pound bombs or depth charges. *Imperial War Museum*

U-boats submerged, thus restricting their speed and depleting their batteries. From mid-1915 until the end of the war only two ships were sunk while under convoy by British blimps.

Another lighter-than-air surveillance platform was the kite balloon, first deployed in 1915 at about the same time as the Submarine Scout. The kite balloon was a manned, tethered "aerostat," most of them towed by a surface patrol craft to achieve significantly greater "height of eye" than possible for the ship's own lookouts. After convoying was initiated, kite balloons were often flown by the accompanying escorts for detecting not only surfaced U-boats or periscope "feathers" at a distance but also incoming torpedo tracks. However, many authorities worried that kite balloons provided patrolling submarines easily identifiable markers for detecting hull-down convoys from miles away, and for this reason their use in convoy protection was discontinued during the final months of the war. Nonetheless, kite balloons continued to be used for ASW area patrols, and they are credited with the initial detection of at least two U-boats—the *U-69* in July 1917 and the *UB-83* in September 1918—that subsequently were destroyed by depth charges from the destroyers flying them.[6]

Until late 1916 the Royal Navy made comparatively little use of heavier-than-air aircraft for ASW operations. Previously there were sporadic patrols by land-based aircraft and seaplanes over inshore areas where merchant shipping was most densely concentrated, such as the approach routes to British ports. Although conventional land-based aircraft could carry heavier payloads, seaplanes had the advantage of being able to take off and alight on water in the all-too-frequent event of engine failure. At the beginning of the war, land-based aircraft were too unreliable to be flown more than a few tens of miles from the coast; as for seaplanes, although the 50 available to the Royal Navy could safely range farther out, their limited armament, low speed, and vulnerability to rough seas restricted ASW operations. From mid-1915 the large Short Brothers Type 184 single-engine floatplane—originally designed as a torpedo bomber—was pressed into service for reconnaissance and coastal patrol, but its small payload and erratic performance on all but the calmest water spurred the search for a better alternative.[7]

Within a year the Type 184s were supplanted by a series of twin-engine flying boats that derived from the *America,* an innovative design of Curtiss Aircraft in the United States and proposed for a North Atlantic crossing in 1914. When the coming of war prevented the *America*'s trans-Atlantic flight, Commander John C. Porte of the Royal Naval Air Service (RNAS) convinced naval authorities to buy the two Curtiss aircraft already completed, and, eventually, the Admiralty ordered 62 more, assembling most of them in Britain. These first *America* aircraft proved too small and under-powered for the ASW role; thus Curtiss produced a larger version that appeared in July 1916, the *Large America* flying boat. By the end of 1918, 270 *Large America*s in several improved models had been delivered to both the RNAS and the U.S. Naval Air Service, roughly half to each service.

In a final evolution, Porte, by then the Royal Navy's foremost expert on flying boats, introduced a series of modifications to the *Large America*s—principally a more seaworthy hull and more powerful engines—to yield the excellent Felixstowe F-2A flying boats, first delivered in November 1917. Of the 110 F-2As built for the RNAS, 53 were in service at war's end as the primary British ASW aircraft. Carrying a bomb load of 460 pounds and as many as seven Lewis machine guns for defense, the F-2A had a nominal endurance of six hours but in an overload condition could stow enough fuel to stay aloft for nine. In the spring of 1918, the Royal Navy tried towing Felixstowe flying boats on lighters behind destroyers to give them even longer legs, but little came of the concept.

With the advantage of increasingly capable aircraft, airborne ASW tactics grew in sophistication and effectiveness as the war progressed. Coordinated operations by multiple aircraft made possible the sweeping of broad ocean areas farther from land, and sequential sorties provided the continuous presence needed to keep patrolling U-boats underwater, where their speed, endurance, and visibility were severely limited. In mid-April 1917, the Royal Navy initiated intensive ASW area coverage with "Spider Web" patrols in the southern North Sea, in which an octagonal grid 60 miles in diameter was patrolled continuously by flying boats based in England. The search grid was centered on the North Hinder lightship, midway between Harwich and the Hook of Holland, and athwart the main U-boat transit route into the English Channel. In the first two weeks of Spider Web patrols, eight U-boats were detected from the air and three were attacked. On 22 September 1917, one of the few "kills" scored by aircraft in the war occurred when an RNAS *Large America* spotted a U-boat on the surface in the Spider Web area and dropped two 230-pound bombs close aboard as she attempted to submerge. The submarine was seen to heel over and sink, and its loss corresponded with the disappearance that day of the *UB-32*, inbound for Zeebrugge on the Belgian coast. While official records show only the *UB-32* sunk in the Spider Web, early eyewitness sources—and some later reports—credit a Curtiss H.12 flying boat with having sunk the *UC-6* in the Spider Web at 8:30 a.m. on 28 September while she was leading a column of four U-boats and three destroyers. The authors of this volume adhere to the official records.[8]

Although early air-dropped depth charges were small and ineffective, and hitting a recently submerged or rapidly diving submarine with an air-dropped weapon required as much luck as skill, submariners were genuinely intimidated by the presence of enemy aircraft. Submarine commanders on both sides complained bitterly in their after-action reports of the difficulty of finding and attacking targets when aircraft kept them unable to maneuver on the surface, sight targets, or charge batteries. By 1918, most U-boats had been fitted with special periscopes called "altiscopes," enabling them to scan the horizon for threatening aircraft while submerged.

When the success of the convoy system in late 1917 forced German submarines to focus on the coastal routes leading to the convoy assembly points, the British responded in May 1918 with what they called "Scarecrow" tactics, intended to exploit the deterrent effect of air cover. These involved assembling a large number of aircraft of every description—most of them obsolete and often unarmed—simply to fly continuous patrols over coastal areas so that every point along the shipping routes was visited at least once every 20 minutes. With each appearance of a Scarecrow aircraft, enemy submarines—unsure whether it was an actual threat or not—were forced to dive, thus rendering their time on station largely ineffective.

The first large land aircraft adapted successfully by the British for ASW operations was the twin-engine Blackburn Kangaroo, which boasted a 920-pound bomb load and eight-hour endurance. The earliest deliveries of this bomber commenced late in the war—in April 1918—and only one squadron had been equipped by the war's end. Nonetheless, the Kangaroo's reliability, maneuverability, excellent visibility, and superior payload proved well suited to ASW missions over the North Sea, and in its relatively brief combat history, the Kangaroo squadron attacked 11 U-boats, including the *UC-70*, which was damaged by one of its aircraft in August 1918 and then sunk by a destroyer.

By the last month of the war the British had more than 650 aircraft assigned to ASW operations in home waters: 285 seaplanes, 272 land planes, and 100 airships.[9] At the same time, the strength of the U.S. Naval Air Service in the European area had grown to 2,500 officers, 12,000 men, and more than 400 aircraft of all types—including 12 dirigibles—with most of the aircraft supplied by the British and French. U.S. aircraft were devoted principally to ASW missions flown from French bases over the western English Channel and the Bay of Biscay. A large U.S. airbase near the mouth of the Humber River in eastern England was home to 1,900 men and nearly 50 aircraft devoted to North Sea patrols, and a Northern Bombing Group in France's Dunkirk/Calais area—with Navy and Marine Corps squadrons—regularly targeted German submarine and destroyer facilities on the coast of Flanders.[10] Meanwhile, the French themselves had been mounting an airborne ASW effort of similar magnitude.

Germany and its allies also employed conventional aircraft in hunting hostile submarines, although on a more limited scale and largely in the Baltic and Adriatic Seas. The Austro-Hungarian Naval Air Service is credited with the two first-ever "kills" of submarines by aircraft, both in 1916. In early August the British submarine *B-10,* sent to the Adriatic with five sister boats in 1915 to bolster the Italian naval effort, was destroyed in a raid by Austrian bombers while moored at the Arsenal of Venice. A month later, on 15 September, two Lohner Type-L flying boats—single-engine pusher biplanes capable of carrying bomb loads of 440 pounds—attacked the French submarine *Foucault* while she was at periscope depth off the Austrian naval base at Cattaro. Mortally wounded in the attack, the *Foucault* first plunged to the bottom, but then clawed her way back to the surface, where

her crew abandoned ship. The two Lohners then landed among the desperate survivors to rescue the entire French crew.

Particularly effective for German airborne ASW were the Hansa-Brandenburg seaplanes, designed by Ernst Heinkel. Built in five successive models, the last two of which—the W.29 and W.33—were low-wing monoplanes, the small, fast Brandenburgs were probably the most capable floatplanes produced during the war. In one celebrated incident on 6 July 1918, a flight of five Flanders-based Brandenburg W.29s came upon the British coastal submarine *C-25* on the surface east of Harwich. They attacked the submarine with bombs and machine-gun fire that killed the entire bridge watch and left her unable to dive. Although lack of fuel forced the Germans to break off the attack before sinking the boat, the *C-25* had to be towed back into port and was so badly damaged that she was never repaired.

Despite the enormous resources expended—and enthusiastic claims for countless sinkings at the time—subsequent analysis has shown that the number of submarines on both sides actually destroyed during the war by unaided aircraft was likely *only five*—two German boats, two British, and one French. Moreover, the two British losses are less than clearcut: one, the *B-10,* was bombed at her dock, and the other, the *D-3,* was sunk in a case of mistaken identity by a French airship in March 1918.

Thus, if one judges the effectiveness of airborne ASW in World War I solely by the number of submarines killed by aircraft, the result is highly disappointing. On the other hand, there were numerous incidents in which significant, non-lethal, damage was done to submarines by aircraft bombs and several encounters where damage inflicted initially by aircraft led directly to subsequent kills by surface forces or in one case to internment in a neutral port.[11] Even more important to the steady improvement in ASW toward the end of the war was the value of aircraft for providing an "eye in the sky" for spotting submarines over large areas and at long distances from their prey, as well as for cueing escorts and patrol craft for follow-on attacks. Additionally, the effectiveness of air cover in forcing submarines to remain underwater for an increasing percentage of their time on station placed serious restrictions on their freedom of action in approaching and attacking targets.

ASW Surface Craft

As noted above, the Royal Navy initially attempted to address its emerging submarine threat by pressing into service a wide variety of impromptu patrol craft—the armed yachts, trawlers, drifters, and motor boats of the Auxiliary Patrol. The Navy also embarked on a crash construction program to provide whole new classes of small ships intended specifically for ASW. In late 1915 and early 1916, the Royal Navy took delivery of 550 75-foot motor launches for inshore and coastal patrols. They had been designed and built in the United States, with final assembly in Canada to avoid U.S. neutrality restrictions. A total of 720 such craft of were built, with the remainder going to the Italian and French Navies. These motor launches were powered by twin six-cylinder gasoline engines of U.S. manufacture, could reach 19 knots, and were armed with a 3-inch gun and from two to ten depth charges.

More substantial ASW platforms were the several series of Flower-class sloops—small steamships built along merchant lines, named after native flowers, and initially planned as minesweepers. Their uncomplicated design was chosen to facilitate rapid construction by smaller shipyards under the War Emergency Program. Beginning in 1915, 72 sloops were laid down. Displacing 1,250 tons on a length of 267 feet and powered by triple-expansion steam engines, these single-screw ships could reach 15 to 17 knots. Although their armament varied widely, they generally carried two 4-inch or 12-pounder guns and later 3-pounder anti-aircraft guns, as well as depth charges. Because of their similarity to small merchant vessels, another 39 were built as Q-ships and also carried Thornycroft depth-charge throwers. Late in the war, the Flowers were upgraded with underwater listening devices and radios to facilitate team tactics in hunting submarines. The Flower-class sloops were in the thick of the fight and are credited with sinking five U-boats, four of them in the Mediterranean. Seventeen Flowers were lost to enemy action.[12]

Also, 44 of the smaller but potent P-class escorts, essentially mini-destroyers, were delivered between 1915 and 1917. Fitted with a collapsible ram bows, they displaced only 613 tons on a length of 245 feet but managed to carry a 4-inch gun, a 2-pounder anti-aircraft gun, two 14-inch torpedo tubes, and both depth-charge racks and throwers. Powered by steam turbines, the twin-screw "P-boats" could make 20 knots, faster than any other of the war's purpose-built ASW ships. Twenty more—disguised with deceptive silhouettes and with 12-pounder guns supplanting the torpedo tubes—were built as Q-ships in 1917 and 1918 (these designated the PC class). In the closing phase of the conflict, they were used regularly as convoy escorts and components of hunter-killer groups.[13]

As the war ground on, other belligerents in both camps sent their own versions of small patrol or ASW craft to sea, but two designs of particular distinction were produced by the U.S.

Navy: the wood-hull submarine chasers and their steel counterparts, the Eagle boats. Between 1917 and 1919, more than 400 subchasers, or SCs—including 100 that went to the French Navy—were built in 38 boatyards scattered around the United States. The SCs were small, yacht-like vessels that displaced 85 tons full load on a length of 110 feet. Powered by three 220-horsepower gasoline engines, they had a top speed of 18 knots and endurance of about 1,000 miles at 10 to 12 knots. They carried a 3-inch gun and two machine guns, plus 18 depth charges, which could be launched from stern racks or a Y-gun. They also were fitted with rudimentary underwater sound detection gear and radio sets for inter-ship communications. By war's end, 135 U.S. subchasers had been sent to Europe, steaming under their own power via the Azores and refueling as necessary from tenders that accompanied them.

In mid-1918, American SC squadrons began operating out of Plymouth, England; out of Queenstown, Ireland; from Corfu in the Adriatic; and in support of the Allied intervention in the Russian civil war, from Murmansk in northern Russia. After the Armistice, significant numbers were sent to Scotland to aid in clearing the Northern Mine Barrage. Six U.S. subchasers were lost in the war, none to enemy action: Five were sunk in accidents and one was destroyed when she was mistaken for an enemy submarine by an armed auxiliary in American waters in August 1918. None sank any submarines.

The Eagle boats were manufactured by the Ford Motor Company at its River Rouge plant in Michigan in an attempt to apply Henry Ford's mass-production techniques to building small warships. These were essentially U.S. counterparts of the Royal Navy's P-class escorts. Henry Ford agreed to the venture in January 1918, and as many as 500

of the craft—designated PE, for Patrol Eagle, by the Navy—were planned originally. Ultimately, 112 were ordered, but the end of the war just 11 months later caused the cancellation of 52, and only 60 were completed.

The Eagle boats displaced 430 tons on a length of 200 feet. Powered by a geared steam turbine driving a single propeller shaft, they could make 18 knots and were intended to be armed with two 4-inch guns, two 3-inch anti-aircraft guns, and a Y-gun for depth charges. Like the subchasers, they were also designed to carry both underwater listening devices and a radio. Although 12 Eagle boats had been launched by the time of the Armistice, only two of them had been accepted by the Navy, and except for a handful that were sent to northern Russia in 1919, none saw any action in the war or its aftermath. Later, a number were transferred to the U.S. Coast Guard, and eight of their sister ships saw U.S. Navy service in World War II. None of the latter was used in ASW service, but ironically, one of them, the *PE 56*, was sunk by a German submarine off the coast of Maine in April 1945.

Despite the initial Allied emphasis on building large numbers of small ASW escorts as quickly as possible, the experience of war gradually demonstrated to both sides the superiority of relatively large destroyers as ASW platforms. Large numbers were begun by most of the key belligerents during the conflict and although still configured largely for their battle-fleet roles, increasing numbers were assigned to anti-submarine duties. Table 4-1 compares the numbers of modern destroyers both operational and under construction in the major navies at the beginning and end of the conflict.

The extraordinary increase in the number of British and American destroyers reflects both the rapid wartime expansion of both fleets and growing appreciation of the value of the destroyer's

Table 4-1. Destroyer Force Levels in World War I

Nation	Number of ships* (active + building)	
	mid-1914	late-1918
Great Britain	114 +15	370 +19
France	39 + 3	39 +1
Italy	21 +16	54 + 4
Japan	39 + 2	64 + 15
Russia (Baltic and Black Seas)†	35 + 36	55 + 25
United States	34 + 12	258 + 166
Germany	101 + 12	100 + 45
Austria-Hungary	18 + 0	20 + 1

* Includes only *destroyers* laid down in 1905 and later.

† Russian figures are approximate.

Source: Compiled from *Jane's Fighting Ships 1914* and Surgeon-Lt. Oscar Parkes and Maurice Prendergast, *Jane's Fighting Ships 1919* (London: Sampson Lowe Marston, 1919).

speed, agility, and payload capacity for the growing ASW role forced on the U.S. and Royal Navies in 1917. In contrast, faced with a relatively minor submarine threat and with the High Seas Fleet blockaded in the Helgoland Bight for most of the war, Germany shifted her priorities away from building destroyers to producing more U-boats.

The last destroyers laid down by the Royal Navy before the Armistice were the 21 ships of the so-called Admiralty V class, but none was completed until 1919, and the class only saw combat in World War II. In comparison to their smaller 1914 M-class predecessors, the ships of this final class of World War I destroyers displaced 1,300 tons on a length of 312 feet and carried four 4.7-inch guns, 2-pounder anti-aircraft guns, six torpedo tubes, and depth charges. With geared turbines driving twin screws the V-class ships could reach 34 knots.

Their distinctive U.S. Navy counterparts were the famous "flush-deck four-pipers" of the similar *Caldwell, Wickes,* and *Clemson* classes, the first of which were begun in 1916. By the time this unprecedented construction program wound down in 1921, 273 destroyers had been launched, although only 44 were completed before the end of the war. Displacing between 1,125 and 1,215 tons with a length of 314 feet, the flush-deckers could reach 35 knots on twin screws powered by geared turbines. Designed before the seriousness of the ASW threat was fully revealed, they were still armed in accordance with the type's earlier mission of torpedo boat defense and battle force support with four 4-inch guns, one or two 3-inch anti-aircraft guns, and 12 21-inch torpedo tubes.[14] Depth charge racks and throwers were added as an afterthought as the weapons became available, and the escort and ASW roles assumed increasing importance. Although many of these ships were scrapped in the early 1930s, the remainder formed the core of the U.S. destroyer force for the inter-war years, and many survived to serve in U.S. and Allied Navies in World War II.[15]

The USS *Graham* (DD 192) was typical of the U.S. four-stack destroyers of World War I building programs. Completed in 1920, like most of her type, the *Graham* was too late for wartime service. Many of these ships served in World War II, with 50 four-stack destroyers going to the Royal Navy (some manned by Canadians), nine of those being retransferred to the Soviet Navy. *U.S. Navy*

Underwater Detection Systems

Submarines encountered above water could, of course, be attacked with gunfire and ramming, and most early ASW strategies were designed to force submarines to the surface, where they were most vulnerable. Nonetheless, two crucial ASW shortfalls remained: some reliable means to detect and track the enemy craft while submerged, and appropriate weapons to attack them underwater once located. While the introduction of depth charges and depth-charge throwers in the last half of the war went a long way toward satisfying the second of these needs, none of the underwater detection techniques deployed before the Armistice achieved any significant tactical success despite large research and development efforts in Britain, France, and the United States.

The desperation of the Royal Navy in seeking viable underwater detection systems left no stone unturned. After an unsuccessful attempt to induce seagulls to locate and follow enemy submarines by training the birds with a dummy periscope that ejected food, the Admiralty approved a series of ASW experiments involving sea lions between December 1916 and May 1917.[16] After training several animals from a circus to swim toward the sound of a bell in a Glasgow swimming pool, the experimenters next obtained additional animals from a zoo and trained them to follow small boats on a lake in Wales. Unfortunately, the first serious sea trial of the concept in the Solent near Portsmouth emerged a total failure, when the sea lions showed themselves perfectly willing to follow any nearby vessel that attracted their attention. Moreover, the abundance of local fish gravely undermined the trainers' reward protocols. Another scheme was to feed the sea lions only from a submarine, hoping that—with a small explosive charge attached—they would seek out U-boats when hungry. But instead they remained near the craft that had "launched" them. These ideas were quickly dropped.

Among the earliest—and simplest—underwater detectors employed successfully by the Allies were large electromagnetic "indicator loops" installed as sea-floor barriers to protect harbors, anchorages, and estuaries from incursions by enemy submarines. Also called "Bragg loops," after their inventor, British professor W. H. Bragg, these consisted of large rectangular loops of armored copper cable on the sea bed, approximately 5,000 yards long by 200 yards wide and connected to observation stations ashore. When the steel hull of a submerged submarine moved over one of these installations, the magnetic induction caused by the boat's permanent magnetization and the local disturbance of the earth's magnetic field generated a perceptible deflection of the needle of a ballistic galvanometer in the guardhouse. This indication could be used to cue patrol craft to the area or to activate remotely controlled mine lines planted in close proximity to the sensors. Between 1915 and 1918, systems of indicator loops and associated minefields were installed in the approaches to Scapa Flow, in the Thames Estuary, at both ends of the cross-Channel mine barrage, and in several major port areas around the British Isles. Shortly before the end of the conflict the U.S. Navy installed a similar indicator-loop barrier across the mouth of the Chesapeake Bay, and improved versions of the same basic system were still in use at many American sites during World War II. The very last U-boat lost in the war—the *UB-116*—was destroyed on 28 October 1918, in a controlled minefield in the approaches to Scapa Flow after detection by both magnetic and acoustic sensors.[17] There also were a handful of other incidents in which a combination of indicator loops and acoustic sensors may have contributed to the damage to or loss of German submarines.

Underwater sound offered a much more promising alternative for detecting submerged submarines, particularly from mobile platforms. (Because it is a denser medium, water transmits sound much more readily than air. The sound speed in water is approximately 4,750 feet per second, over four times greater than it is in the atmosphere. In addition, although the detailed phenomenology is complex, sound can travel much farther in water than in air, particularly at low frequencies.) By 1890, scientists in several nations were experimenting with underwater microphones—soon dubbed "hydrophones"—derived from early telephone technology.[18] Both carbon button microphones and electro-dynamic "magnetophone" receivers were used to fashion underwater listening devices by sealing them in cans fitted with metal diaphragms in contact with the surrounding water.[19] Shortly after 1900, the Submarine Signal Company was founded in the United States to develop a navigational aid that used large underwater bells located near lighthouses or danger areas and rung in a time-coded sequence as a warning to nearby ships. On the latter, pairs of hull-mounted hydrophones near the bow were used to get a rough bearing on the beacons by turning the ship until the bell sounds from the port and starboard sensors were equally loud in a set of headphones. By the time of the *Titanic* disaster in 1912 the system was well established, with warning bells installed in key hazard areas and receivers on many trans-Atlantic liners as well as several warships of the Royal Navy. Proponents on both sides of the Atlantic proposed several variants of this basic approach for underwater signaling, or "sound telegraphy," but with only limited success. With the coming of war in 1914, these systems were virtually the only underwater listening devices available to the Allies, or, for that matter, to their enemies.

It soon was apparent that the hull-mounted hydrophones used in the Submarine Signal Company's systems and their British counterparts were useless for the acoustic detection of submarines. Even when the receiving microphones were isolated in water-filled tanks separate from the hull structure, the background vibrations of the ship's engines and auxiliary machinery overwhelmed the relatively quiet, water-borne sound signature of even a nearby submarine.

Thus, early in the war the Royal Navy was compelled to embark on an accelerated program to

The Royal Navy experimented with and sent to sea a variety of acoustic devices to detect German submarines—some worked, some did not. These photos show hydrophone installations on two ASW trawlers. By war's end hundreds of trawlers and other small craft as well as destroyers had been fitted with underwater listening devices. *Imperial War Museum*

develop hydrophones specifically for anti-submarine applications. A key figure in this effort was Commander C. P. Ryan at the Hawkcraig Admiralty Experimental Station, near Aberdour, Scotland. Earlier in his career Ryan had been active in the development of wireless telegraphy, and at Inchkeith, Scotland, in the autumn of 1914 he began experimenting with several types of hydrophones for detecting submarines. His early models, derived from the Submarine Signal Company's carbon microphones, had evolved

Captain Cyril Percy Ryan, Royal Navy
(B. 1875 D. 1940)

The Royal Navy's most important developer of underwater listening devices in World War I, Ryan was born in Kilkenny and entered the Navy just before his 15th birthday. He served in the Mediterranean as a midshipman on HMS *Collingwood* until 1894, when he returned to England to enter the Royal Naval College at Greenwich. There he excelled in the torpedo course but passed the examination for a third-class officer's certificate only on his second attempt. Promoted to lieutenant in 1898, Ryan served with the Home Fleet, on the China Station, and then in the Mediterranean, where he commanded the destroyer *Zealous* and soon established a reputation as an expert on wireless telegraphy.

Ryan proposed several wireless improvements later adopted by the Admiralty, and when he was promoted to commander in 1908, he was given command of a destroyer flotilla in the Home Fleet. His performance as a flotilla leader apparently was so unsatisfactory that he nearly lost his command. Recognizing that prospects for further promotion were poor, he left the Navy in 1911, while in command of the armored cruiser *Euryalus.* Hoping to capitalize on his skills in wireless telegraphy, Ryan joined the Marconi Company.

With the coming of World War I, Ryan returned to the Navy's active list and in autumn 1914 began work on the underwater sound detection of submarines at Inchkeith in Scotland. At first largely indifferent to Ryan's experiments, the Admiralty nonetheless decided to support them in early 1915, and in December the Inchkeith work was transferred to a larger facility at Hawkcraig Point, near Aberdour, which eventually grew into the Hawkcraig Admiralty Experimental Station and hydrophone training establishment. Under the pressure of the rising submarine threat, Ryan's Hawkcraig facility developed the majority of listening devices pressed into service by the Royal Navy, including the PGS, PDS I, and PDS II hydrophones, the "Rubber Eel," and the arrays of fixed hydrophones that protected important approaches, anchorages, and staging areas against U-boat incursions. As a wireless expert, Ryan was relatively unfamiliar with the physics of underwater sound, and his empirical, cut-and-try approach to hydrophone development—plus his strong personality—soon put him at odds with the more theoretical, academic scientists of the Board of Invention and Research (BIR), with whom he was supposed to collaborate. Ultimately the BIR was shunted aside and disestablished, the Navy promoted Ryan to acting captain in late 1916, and he remained in charge of the Hawkcraig facility until it shut down in 1919. Subsequently, he became the head of the Submarine Detection Section of the Navy's Mining School until his final retirement from the Royal Navy in June 1921.

by mid-1915 into two standard versions amenable to mass production: the Portable General Service (PGS) hydrophone, intended for over-the-side use on drifters, and a fixed, tripod-mounted model for stationary, sea-bottom installations near shore. With both instruments the operator simply listened to the microphone output on headphones. Subsequently, Ryan also developed a series of hydrophones based on magnetophone technology. Although less sensitive than their carbon-microphone counterparts, these offered the advantage of not requiring battery power. Over the frequency range of interest for submarine-produced sounds—thought to be from 400 to 1,000 Hz—the 8-inch-diameter, lozenge-shaped PGS instrument was essentially omnidirectional, but its performance varied widely depending on ocean conditions and the noisiness of individual submarines. Although detection range seldom exceeded a mile or two, more than 4,500 sets were manufactured during the war, largely for use on British small craft.

Meanwhile, after four experimental installations, the Royal Navy in late 1916 began to deploy permanent fields of stationary, bottom-mounted hydrophones in strategic coastal areas, and at war's end 18 were in operation. Intended to give early warning of the approach of German U-boats, these sensor fields had up to 16 hydrophones cabled to listening stations ashore and could detect enemy submarines up to three miles away in calm weather. When the seas were rough, however, the detection range fell to only a half-mile. The use of listening devices in conjunction with shore-controlled minefields—much like indicator loops—followed directly in several areas, and ultimately two certain submarine kills, two "possibles," and two instances of serious damage were credited to them. In addition to the destruction of the *UB-116* at Scapa Flow (described above), the *UB-109* was detected by a hydrophone field at the Folkestone end of the cross-Channel mine barrage on 29 August 1918

and destroyed when nearby mines were detonated in response.

Shipboard Systems

For hunting submarines from ships at sea, early hydrophones such as the PGS had two basic drawbacks: First, because the earliest instruments were omnidirectional—equally sensitive to sound coming from all sides—it was impossible to determine the bearing of targets heard on the headphones. Second, listening for submarines often required the searching ship to come to a full stop in the water to lower hydrophones over the side; otherwise, both the sound of the searching ship's propulsion machinery and flow noise from the passage of the sensor through the water completely masked the sounds of an underwater target's motors. This latter consideration was a key factor in the decision to deploy the PGS hydrophones initially on drifters.

In parallel with a group of civilian scientists organized under the auspices of the Admiralty's Board of Invention and Research (BIR), C. P. Ryan, by then promoted to captain, attacked both problems. Lacking any theoretical background in the physics of underwater sound and attempting to field useful equipment as quickly as possible, he adopted a pragmatic, experimental approach at his Hawkcraig facility. In contrast, the BIR—staffed largely by academic researchers—opted for a more methodical, analytic strategy that often frustrated its Royal Navy sponsors.[20] Nonetheless, there was useful cross-fertilization between the groups. Ryan's successful development of directional hydrophones in 1916 and 1917 drew heavily on preliminary designs by Professor J. T. McGregor Morris and A. J. Sykes of East London College. The Portable Directional Hydrophone (PDH) Mark I added a baffle plate to the back side of a PGS hydrophone variant so that, at least at higher frequencies, the instrument would be less sensitive rearward and so would approximate a unidirectional receiver. The PDH Mark II used two diaphragms, which, facing outward in opposite directions and coupled by an internal strut, drove a carbon microphone; the result was a hydrophone that was equally sensitive to the front and rear but relatively *in*sensitive to sounds from the edge directions—in other words, a figure-eight pattern. The directional capabilities of the PDH Mark II came at the expense of overall sensitivity, but the sensor could be rotated to determine the direction of an incoming sound to within a few degrees. However, because there still remained a 180-degree ambiguity in the bearing of potential targets, it was often yoked together on a single vertical shaft with a PDH Mark I—which was unidirectional—to eliminate the forward or aft uncertainty in target direction.

For the growing numbers of British surface ships and submarines that carried them, the two portable directional hydrophones—or their use in combination—could generate reasonable bearings on targets up to three miles away. But their tactical effectiveness was still limited by the need to go dead in the water, and often to shut down auxiliary equipment, to gain even marginal performance. Not only did this inhibit timely pursuit and attack, but the stationary patrol craft themselves became highly vulnerable to a submarine torpedo. Several further attempts were made to solve this problem with flush hull-mounted hydrophones, particularly on submarines, but even with increasingly sophisticated isolation schemes, the self-noise drawback remained. In January 1916 Ryan noted that towing a hydrophone behind a ship in a streamlined body materially reduced the effects of own-ship machinery noise, and this discovery led to the adoption of several towed listening systems.

The first of Ryan's models—known as the Rubber Eel—used a streamlined rubber body 18 inches long that encased a single carbon button microphone in the aft end of a tapered, sea-water-filled brass tube to attenuate sounds coming from the towing ship. Streamed several hundred yards astern, it yielded a maximum detection range of about four miles at a speed of eight knots, but this distance diminished rapidly to only a mile and a half at ten knots, when the ship's propulsion noise began to dominate the sound field. Although the Rubber Eel was essentially omnidirectional, Ryan completed a more elaborate, directional version called the Porpoise just before the end of the war. It incorporated a baffled PDH Mark II hydrophone that could be rotated horizontally by remote control to determine the maximum sound bearing.

A competing towed hydrophone system was the Nash Fish, developed by G. H. Nash of the British Western Electric Company, which used a torpedo-like tow body roughly six feet long by one foot in diameter with thin, metallic acoustic "windows" in the sides. The Nash Fish contained both unidirectional and bidirectional hydrophones, with the latter rotated remotely, as in the Porpoise, to determine target bearing, while the unidirectional microphone resolved the left or right ambiguity. After acceptance by the Admiralty in October 1917, nearly 200 Nash Fish were procured. Although superior in bearing accuracy to Ryan's designs, they needed to be towed more slowly to achieve the same range. Both approaches were minimally useful for detecting submarines while under way at speed. Still, they were one of the earliest progenitors of the massive acoustic towed arrays of the Cold War era.

In yet another attempt to devise a hull-mounted device that could be operated while under way, the French came up with a system known as the "Walser gear," after its inventor, *Lieutenant de Vaisseau* Georges Walser. This consisted of a pair of three-to-four-foot-diameter steel blisters mounted forward on each side of the ship, each with a number of thin diaphragms communicating with an interior cavity to form something of a "sound lens," with a receiving horn at the focus. The resulting auditory signals from each side were introduced to a binaural stethoscope through variable-length tubes—much like a trombone—that could introduce small time delays and "center" the sound in the operator's head to determine the bearing. By November 1917, the French Navy had equipped 15 ASW ships with the Walser gear, and in considering its adoption for its own ships the Royal Navy made several experimental installations. British trials in 1918 showed that a submarine traveling at three knots could be heard up to a mile and a quarter away at a search speed of five knots. Ultimately, the Royal Navy declined to adopt the Walser gear, because of the large hull penetrations and internal volume required.

After 1917, Allied seaplanes and blimps were also fitted with underwater listening devices. First attempted in the Mediterranean with small seaplanes and omnidirectional hydrophones, the technique required the pilot to alight on the water, stop the engines, and dangle a sensor over the side. If contact was made with a potential target, surface ships would then be cued to the presumed location. Later, several Felixstowe and the *Large America* flying boats were fitted with directional hydrophones on swiveling booms that could be deployed vertically after the aircraft came down on the water. Not surprisingly, this cumbersome approach was entirely unsuccessful, and few operational searches were even attempted. Not only was the detection range too short to be useful, but the necessity for repeated landings and take-offs stressed the airframes and increased the likelihood of engine failure that would strand the aircraft on the water.

Blimps offered more promise for acoustic searches. With no need to alight on the water to deploy their listening devices, they offered somewhat more tactical flexibility, but their low speed hampered timely localization and attack—particularly since their engines too needed to be shut down to be able to hear a contact. With an airship drifting with the wind at speeds up to eight knots, a towed hydrophone could provide some rudimentary detection capability, but the blimp's other drawbacks militated against its successful use of listening devices. Nonetheless, just before the end of the war, hydrophones were ordered for all British blimps.

Acoustics in America

Although the U.S. Navy had done little work on submarine detection before the war, the United States embarked on an underwater sound program of its own within only a few months of entering the conflict.[21] Even before war was declared, but under government sponsorship, the Submarine Signal, General Electric, and Western Electric Companies had combined their resources to establish an acoustics research facility at Nahant, Massachusetts. Then, several months after consultations with the British and French in May and June 1917, the Navy created the Naval Experimental Station at New London, Connecticut, which—as the Naval Underwater Sound Laboratory—would later serve as the nation's premier sonar research and development center for more than a half-century. These two primary facilities and a half-dozen of somewhat lesser importance immediately commenced a "crash" program to develop hydrophones and other underwater listening apparatus. Within a few months, the first fruits of their efforts began to appear.

The first—and certainly the simplest—U.S. listening devices were the C and SC tubes. The C tube was nothing more than an inverted T made of brass tubing with two air-filled rubber bulbs mounted at the ends of the five-foot-long underwater crossbar. The bulbs were connected by rubber tubes to a binaural stethoscope worn by an observer above water, and the device could be rotated manually to "center" the sound in the operator's ears and provide a bearing to the target. Whereas the C tube was a portable device operated from a moveable framework on the ship's deck, the SC version was permanently installed below deck and penetrated the hull. Supposedly, the C and SC tubes could detect a submarine at about two miles under average conditions, but as bidirectional "ears" they suffered from the same 180-degree bearing ambiguity as the British PDH Mark II hydrophone. Nonetheless, being completely acoustic—that is, non-electrical—devices, they were so cheap and easy to produce that large numbers were used during the war, even by the British. A more elaborate version called the MB tube appeared later. It used eight rubber bulbs at each end of the crossbar in an attempt to provide more "sound-gathering" power and sharper directionality fore and aft, but like the earlier "tubes," it

still required the searching ship to come to a full stop to hear a target.

The Americans also developed and fielded several electro-acoustic designs that broke interesting new ground. The K tube was a fixed acoustic array with three rubber-encased carbon microphones installed at the vertices of an equilateral triangle, roughly four feet on a side.[22] This was suspended from a buoy some distance from the ship and connected by a buoy-supported towline and electrical cabling to the operator's station on board. To get a directional bearing on a suspected submarine, the microphones were paired two at a time and processed through a device called a "binaural compensator" that converted the electrical outputs back to sound signals in two telephone earpieces. These, in turn, drove a binaural stethoscope through a pair of acoustic tubes whose lengths could be varied with a bearing-indicating handwheel to center the sound in the listener's ears. The third hydrophone was then processed similarly to eliminate the bearing ambiguity inherent in using only two sensors.

This SC-tube listening device was mounted through the hull of the submarine *H-5* (SS 148) shortly after World War I. The SC tube was a variant of the C-tube device and consisted of two rubber bulbs connected by flexible tubing to a binaural stethoscope. By rotating the crossbar to equalize the sound level in both ears, the operator could estimate the target's bearing. *U.S. Navy*

Although separating the array from the ship eliminated much of the background noise, and notwithstanding that the K tube was credited with a detection range under ideal conditions of more than a dozen miles, it could still only be used with the mother ship virtually stopped. Subsequently, several streamlined versions were designed to allow listening and searching at moderate speeds, but a better solution was found with a towed device similar to the British Rubber Eel. Known as the "Electric Eel," or the "snake," to avoid confusion with its Royal Navy counterpart, it housed a linear array of 12 microphones in a streamlined rubber tube that was towed several hundred yards behind the ship and 100 feet deep. Half of the microphones were connected to each ear of the listener via a compensator that used electrical—instead of acoustic—delays to obtain a target bearing. The inherent port or starboard bearing ambiguity was resolved either by deploying a second eel on a different tow or by also using a hull-mounted sensor for crude triangulation. Following its British ally, the U.S. Navy also designed variants of both the K tube and the Electric Eel for use by seaplanes and airships.

One of the more elaborate U.S. Navy listening devices to see World War I service was a hull-mounted system, the MV tube. Based loosely on France's Walser gear, it mounted 12 acoustic diaphragms in an underwater blister on each side of the bow and used a multiplicity of air tubes to combine the individual signals for presentation to a time-delay compensator similar to that described in conjunction with the K tube. Reportedly, this binaural compensator could provide a target bearing to within a few degrees, and the shielding effect of the ship's hull largely eliminated the port or starboard ambiguity. In trials on a 20-knot destroyer in late 1918 it succeeded in tracking a seven-knot submarine at ranges of 500 to 2,000 yards. However, the MV-tube instal-

lation had a very large footprint, weighing two tons with each blister more than 38 feet long, and it soon was supplanted by other technologies after the war, even though an electro-acoustic version had been devised with electrical phase compensation.

The many variants of U.S. and British underwater sound equipment saw increasing operational use in the latter half of the war, largely on patrol craft and subchasers. Destroyers were considered too noisy to be used as acoustic listening platforms and certainly as less amenable to the "sprint-and-drift" tactics required for effective listening. The two navies adopted similar search procedures, generally involving three small ships—trawlers or subchasers—acting as a hunting team, often with a sloop, P-class escort, or destroyer standing by as a "pouncer." The three ships would steam in a line abreast several miles apart and stop every 15 minutes or so, shut down engines and auxiliaries, and listen for indications of a nearby U-boat. The first ship to make contact headed along the indicated bearing line while summoning the others by flag signal or wireless so that they could maneuver to gain detection and collaborate in refining the target's position by repeated triangulation. If and when the team developed sufficient confidence in the enemy's estimated position, the area was saturated with depth charges by all the participants. If the submarine escaped destruction, the process was repeated.

While this approach seemed promising in theory, it was almost entirely fruitless in practice. For example, of the 255 encounters between U-boats and Royal Navy patrol units in 1918, hydrophones played a part in only one-fifth, with the rest resulting from visual sightings, just as in the early days of the war.[23] Only three or possibly four sinkings have been credited to patrol groups using underwater listening devices, all during the last months of the conflict. In July 1918, near Scarborough, the periscope of the *UB-107* was initially seen from a motor launch, and after the submarine had been located by a hydrophone-equipped trawler, she was destroyed in a depth-charge attack by an accompanying destroyer. The next month, the minelaying submarine *UC-49*, damaged by one of her own mines off Plymouth, attempted to escape an alerted patrol group by initially lying on the bottom, but her every attempt to move away was detected by the group's listening devices, and she was eventually depth-charged and sunk. The most interesting success occurred in September 1918, when the British airship *R-29* spotted the *UB-115* off England's east coast near Sunderland, dropped a smoke bomb to mark the U-boat's position, and summoned two nearby destroyers and three trawlers. Subsequent depth charge attacks left the submarine wounded on the sea floor, and as with the *UC-49*, her attempts to creep away were heard clearly on the trawlers' listening gear and countered with renewed depth charge attacks that fatally damaged the boat.[24]

In a pattern similar to what emerged in other areas of ASW, the Germans lagged behind the Allies in developing underwater listening devices. They, too, entered the war with little more than the techniques of the Submarine Signal Company to build on. Although the German Navy had affixed crude hull-mounted hydrophones to its submarines as early as 1915, its subsequent progress in underwater acoustics was minimal in comparison to that of the British and Americans. The first U-boat installations consisted of port and starboard carbon microphones that were effective only with all of the submarine's machinery shut down. An improved version used three pairs of hydrophones in the bow and in the port and starboard ballast tanks, but these were used primarily to listen for distant targets and to avoid patrolling escort vessels—and

only under conditions of complete silence. Admiral David Beatty, at least, believed that the hydrophones installed on German U-boats were a major cause of the ineffectiveness of his hunter-killer groups. On 6 July 1917, he wrote, "It is doubtful whether surface craft can accomplish very much in these open waters. The modern German submarine has excellent powers of diving and has developed the use of the hydrophone to a great extent by means of which it is able to detect the presence of surface craft a long way off; also unless the weather is exceptionally fine, a submarine on the surface can only be seen a short distance away."[25]

The German Navy also developed both over-the-side and towed hydrophones, the latter consisting of little more than buoy-suspended directional microphones linked by cables to patrol craft. Although intended for use at low speeds, these were no more effective than the various Allied techniques that were supposed to allow listening while under way. Unlike the British, the Germans did not establish shore listening stations during the war but relied instead on hydrophones streamed from large anchored buoys and cabled to operators on nearby ships. Because these systems—for defending the approaches to the western Baltic—were both unreliable and largely ineffective, they were abandoned in July 1917.

Subsequent developments soon would prove that World War I naval technologists were on the right track in pursuing underwater acoustics for submarine detection and tracking. In practical terms, however, their early listening equipment made only a minimal contribution to ASW effectiveness, because of technical shortfalls. Although submarines could be detected and even localized by passive listening at ranges of up to several miles, all but a few later acoustic systems required patrolling ships to go dead in the water to ameliorate the effects of own-ship and flow noise at the hydrophones. This limitation—which inevitably imposed a lengthy "time-late" in determining a target's position and track—minimized the usefulness of underwater listening devices in pursuing and attacking enemy U-boats in real time. Even quieting one's own ship could not eliminate the cacophony of ocean background noise that so easily masked submarine sounds, particularly in areas often crowded with shipping. Relatively little was known about the physics of underwater acoustics in the first two decades of the 20th Century, and electronic—that is, vacuum tube—amplification had appeared in only a handful of experimental systems. Thus, almost the entire repertoire of acoustic processing techniques now taken for granted, such as pre-amplification, beam-forming, and frequency-filtering, still lay in the future. And although *active* acoustic detection—echo-ranging by emitting short sound pulses into the water and listening for reflected returns—was being tried in the United States, Britain, and France, it had reached only a rudimentary stage by the end of the war.

Lessons Learned

Because World War I was the first conflict in which submarines played a significant role, it was also the first in which *anti*-submarine warfare became a critical mission. After the Germans commenced unrestricted submarine warfare in early 1917, nearly driving Great Britain out of the conflict by throttling her supply lines, defeating the undersea threat became the number-one priority for the Royal Navy. Although the outbreak of war in 1914 had found both the Allies and the Central Powers totally unprepared to wage an ASW campaign of any kind, both sides improvised, and improvised quickly, by deploying a series of measures—mines, nets, area patrols, explosive sweeps, and the like—to defeat the new menace at sea. Although these early approaches brought a modicum of success, they proved completely inadequate to counter contemporary submarine operations.

Eventually, only the pressure of merchant losses forced the offensively minded Royal Navy to refocus its ASW efforts from killing submarines in a losing war of attrition to concentrating primarily on reducing the ruinous shipping losses experienced in 1917 by a series of defensive measures. Killing submarines was one of these, but far more important were the several means adopted to minimize the number of opportunities given to the U-boats to strike at Allied supply lines. The largest single factor in reversing the mounting toll of shipping losses was the introduction of convoying in mid-1917. In his memoirs many years later, Admiral Karl Dönitz, a German U-boat commander in World War I and the head of the German submarine force in World War II, admitted candidly that "in the First World War, the German U-boat arm achieved great successes; but the introduction of the convoy system in 1917 robbed it of its opportunity to become a decisive factor."[26]

The total Allied merchant tonnage lost to enemy action for each month of the war is portrayed in Figure 4-1. These figures include losses caused by all enemy action, including German surface raiders, but after a flurry of successes in the first six months of the war, the latter were almost entirely eliminated, leaving the U-boats responsible for an overwhelming majority of merchant ship sinkings. The steady increase throughout 1916 was due largely to the growing number of German submarines at sea, while the peak after February 1917 reflects the initial surge of activity following the onset of unrestricted submarine warfare. The rapid drop in merchant losses following the introduction of convoys in June 1917 is readily apparent. Also shown in Figure 4-1 is the number of German U-boats lost by month. Even with the increasing German and Austro-Hungarian submarine losses after mid-1917, the number of operational submarines available for the anti-shipping campaign continued to increase because of Germany's massive construction program, which provided more than 150 new U-boats to the fleet in 1917 and 1918.

The appendix tabulates the causes of submarine losses in World War I. Of particular significance is the percentage of submarines lost not to enemy action but to accidents, scuttling, "friendly" weapons (notably mines), and unknown factors.[27] Sixty-one percent of the Allied submarines sunk were lost to these "other" causes. The corresponding figure for the German and Austrian Navies—28 percent, less than half the Allied number—is indicative largely of the much more intensive Allied ASW campaign.

Focusing on the German numbers, Figure 4-2 depicts two curves of cumulative U-boat losses between August 1914 and November 1918. The upper

curve includes all losses listed in Table 4-1 (except for those boats scuttled near the end of the war), whereas the lower curve, rising to a total of 143 submarines, represents losses due only to Allied ASW efforts. The second of these plots—in conjunction with historical data on the number of operational U-boats at sea—shows the degree to which Allied ASW effectiveness improved toward the end of the war. This lower curve shows that for the first 26 months of the conflict, until October 1916, the cumulative loss is almost linear with time and corresponds to an average loss of one submarine per month. There is then a transitional period with losses curving sharply upward until, after July 1917—just after the introduction of convoying—it rises again in a near-linear fashion at a

Figure 4-1. Allied/Neutral Merchant Ship Tonnage Sunk by German U-Boats During World War I and German U-Boats Sunk, Both by Month

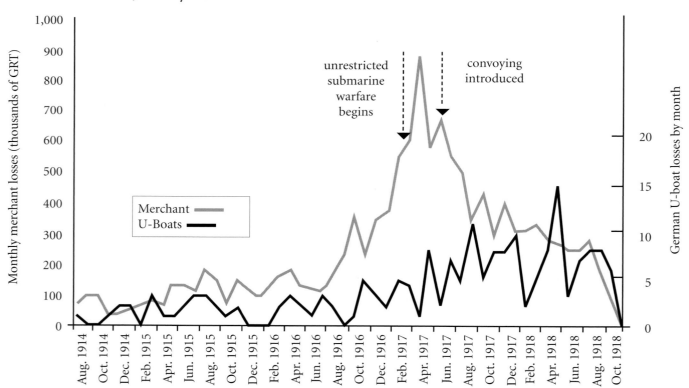

Source: Great War Primary Document Archive, www.gwpda.org; also see J. A. Saker, *Allied Shipping Control* (London: Oxford, 1921); Robert M. Grant, *U-Boat Hunters* (Annapolis, Md.: Naval Institute Press, 2003).

rate of nearly six boats per month until the end of the war. It is tempting to say that this marked increase in the monthly kill rate provides a convincing demonstration of increasing Allied ASW effectiveness, but in fact, two influences are at work. First, Allied ASW capabilities were improving steadily in the last 18 months of the war, but the primary reason for the large increase in the German losses was the much greater number of U-boats the Germans were putting to sea and their ability to replace casualties until the end of the conflict.

For the earlier 26-month period to October 1916 the number of German submarines at sea each month averaged 10 or 11 U-boats. By July 1917—following the onset of unrestricted submarine warfare—this number climbed to nearly 45 and remained near that level for the duration of the war.[28] Comparing the average monthly losses and the average number of submarines at sea until October 1916, the probability that a German submarine would be destroyed by Allied ASW during a month at sea averaged about 10 percent. Then, for the subsequent period from July 1917 until the Armistice, the corresponding figure was approximately 13 percent—a small increase, in light of the enormous amount of resources invested in ASW during the final two years of the war. Looked at another way, if Allied ASW effectiveness—as measured by the average monthly kill probability—had remained at its earlier, lower value during the period following July 1917, the four-fold increase of German submarines at sea alone would have accounted for approximately 68 of the 93 kills (73 percent) that actually occurred.

Moreover, the Germans were able to offset their growing submarine losses with new construction sufficient to maintain the number of operational boats at a near-constant level until the final collapse in October 1918. During the end-game period examined above, the German Navy lost 117 U-boats to all causes except end-of-war scuttling, but during that same time, 126 new submarines joined the fleet. In fact, the number of German U-boats in commission—if not combat ready—actually peaked at 184 in October 1918, less than a month before the end of the war, with another 150 under construction.

In the final 18 months of World War I, as the Germans threw more and more submarines into the fray, the Allies countered with more ASW resources until by October 1918, a rough de facto equilibrium had been reached in which the number of U-boats lost each month was almost exactly balanced by new construction. It is occasionally claimed that "the German U-boats were never defeated at sea," a striking counterpart of the "stab-in-the-back" theory that sought to explain the German Army's collapse on the Western Front. In fact, the U-boats *were* defeated at sea—if not by significant increases in the monthly kill probability achieved by Allied ASW forces, then by the Allied success in thwarting the U-boats' primary post-1916 objective of interdicting Allied supply lines and thereby starving Britain into submission before the United States could enter the war with major ground forces. This Allied ASW success resulted from growing anti-submarine prowess, but it was due even more to the Allies' willingness to commit increasingly more forces to counter the U-boats.

In conjunction with convoying, another major factor in keeping Allied shipping out of harm's way was a growing sophistication in the use of technical intelligence, notably communication intercepts, radio direction-finding, and cryptography, for estimating where hostile submarines were operating and then rerouting convoys away from them. Similarly, increasing numbers of convoy escorts, including airships, put marauding U-boats at greater risk, forcing them to remain

Figure 4-2. Cumulative German U-Boat Losses by Month in World War I

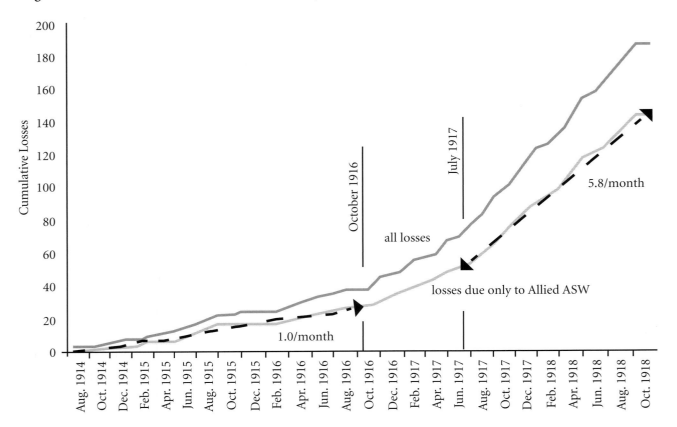

Source: Great War Primary Document Archive, www.gwpda.org; also see J. A. Saker, *Allied Shipping Control* (London: Oxford, 1921); Robert M. Grant, *U-Boat Hunters* (Annapolis, Md.: Naval Institute Press, 2003).

below the surface, hampering their mobility, and further reducing opportunities for attack. The advantage of holding U-boats underwater as much as possible was clearly appreciated early in the war, but until the Allies employed tactics like close convoy escorting and airborne Scarecrow patrols off the eastern coast of England in the last year and a half of the war, the full potential of that strategy was only partially achieved.

However, even as more sophisticated capabilities for detecting, tracking, and destroying submarines evolved, undersea mines remained by far the most effective weapons against submarines, particularly as cumulative experience led to improved designs and clever innovations such as the U.S. galvanic-action firing mechanism. Counting losses on both sides,

mining accounted for 36 percent of submarine kills due to known hostile causes (190 victims). Additionally, 6 percent of total German U-boat losses—11 submarines—were due to "friendly" mines, while, significantly, Allied minefields in several areas forced U-boats to consume valuable patrol time following circuitous routes to reach their operating areas.

Not surprisingly, surface ships emerged as the most potent ASW *platform,* accounting for 47 percent of overall submarine losses, about evenly divided among gunfire, depth charges, and ramming as actual causes of submarines' destruction. Although depth charges scored only 14 percent of the overall surface-ship kills—all but one of those, German U-boats—they were the most significant ASW weapon to emerge from the war. Had they been introduced earlier they would likely have exacted a much higher toll.

Significantly, as late-war tactical experience showed the importance of "pouncing" quickly on U-boat contacts at high speed and saturating target areas with depth charges, destroyers assumed new importance and began to evolve into a primary ASW platform. At the other end of the "warship" spectrum, Q-ships succeeded in sinking 14 U-boats, or about 10 percent of German combat losses, while simultaneously giving rise to a number of stirring "war-at-sea" stories.[29] However, with their own losses estimated at twice that number, the mystery ships' overall effectiveness was questionable, especially after the onset of unrestricted submarine warfare.

Attacks on submarines by opposing submarines scored 26 kills during the war, accounting for 12 percent of German losses (17 boats) to hostile action and 18 percent of British losses (5 boats). In all of these engagements, the victims were torpedoed while on the surface.

Two nascent developments—airborne ASW and underwater acoustics—enjoyed only limited success in World War I, but offered clear promise for the future. As noted earlier, the sinking of only a half-dozen submarines can be attributed unequivocally to aircraft, but for reconnaissance, surveillance, and area patrols, aircraft had come into their own by the end of the war. Their very presence kept submarines submerged over large areas, and only clumsy attack procedures and the lack of effective air-dropped ASW weapons prevented greater success. That would come later.

Although the Allies were experimenting vigorously with active sonar at the end of the war, only passive listening devices were sufficiently well developed to be employed operationally. Moreover,

lacking any kind of electronic amplification or signal processing, these early tactical systems were virtually useless while ASW ships were under way, and that limitation required them to remain stationary to listen for their quarry. While this technique often provided valuable clues to the nearby presence of an enemy, prosecuting the contact from a standing start generally proved impossible. Nonetheless, the enormous potential for using underwater sound as the primary technical means to detect, track, and locate submarines underwater was clear to all and held great portent for the future.

While the effectiveness of anti-submarine methods in the Great War fell well short of necessity, it is extraordinary that so much was accomplished in establishing this new form of naval warfare in so short a time and with the limited technologies available. Faced with a threat that was largely unanticipated, both sides—but especially the Allies—managed to deploy a variety of platforms, weapons, and techniques that by the end of the conflict were beginning to make serious headway against the submarine menace.

Although a vast amount of effort went into developing specialized ASW weapons, the one that caused the most submarine kills in World War I was the relatively unsophisticated and inexpensive sea mine. Nonetheless, it is particularly interesting to note that with a few prominent exceptions—for example, radar, rotary-wing aircraft, space satellites—virtually all the technical and operational innovations that were to prove successful in future ASW conflicts—from towed arrays and intelligence-based cueing to hunter-killer groups, ahead-thrown weapons, and sprint-and-drift tactics—all were conceived of and at least *tried* a century ago during the four eventful years of World War I.

Developing Sonar and Radar

Even with the advances in ASW that appeared by the end of the war, the detection of submerged submarines at tactically useful distances persisted as a stubborn problem, and despite wartime research on underwater sound and rudimentary magnetic-loop systems, the conflict ended without satisfactory solutions.

In particular, passive acoustic detection remained virtually impossible at any speed because of own-ship noise and turbulent flow around ship-mounted or towed hydrophones. Moreover, the submarines themselves had become steadily quieter since 1914, rendering passive listening even more difficult. In seeking to improve detection performance at speed, the Royal Navy tried several approaches to lower the noise output of the anti-submarine ships themselves, including air-bubble screens, hydraulic propulsion, and rudimentary machinery quieting; nothing availed.

Active Sonar—Asdic

By mid-war, the continuing impasse in detecting submerged submarines had already moved the Allied technical community to consider a variety of alternatives to passive listening, most importantly *active* acoustic detection using some form of echo-ranging.[1] (In echo-ranging, or active sonar, a short pulse of sound energy is projected into the water, and the operator listens for a sound signal reflected back from the target in the form of an "echo.")[2] Serendipitously, a rudimentary underwater transmitter was already at hand. In 1913, under the sponsorship of the American-based Submarine Signal Company, Professor Reginald A. Fessenden had developed a signaling device called the Fessenden Oscillator that was intended to facilitate underwater acoustic communication using Morse code. In Fessenden's transmitter the magnetic forces generated by a cylindrical assembly of fixed electric coils excited a steel diaphragm in contact with the water. Driven by an electrical generator at its resonant frequency of 540 Hz, the device could be heard underwater 30 miles away. Unlike earlier underwater sound sources, such as bells or explosives, the Fessenden Oscillator could also be reconfigured for underwater listening. With the electrical source switched off and the drive coils connected to a radio head set, underwater sounds and echoes could be easily discerned. Although Fessenden's invention was intended primarily for ship-to-ship or ship-to-shore communications, its greater potential was revealed in an April 1914 demonstration when echoes were detected from both an iceberg two miles away and, occasionally, from the ocean bottom.

With the coming of World War I, the British bought a number of Fessenden Oscillators for underwater telegraphy, typically between a surface

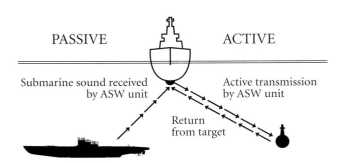

Figure 5-1. Shipboard Sonars. In passive acoustic submarine detection, acoustic sensors on the searching ship are used to listen for characteristic underwater sound emissions generated by the submarine itself. In active detection, a transducer on the searching ship transmits a train of short, high-frequency sound pulses into the water, and the operators listen for echoes returned from the target.

ship and a submerged submarine under tow, and by 1917 both the Royal Navy and the U.S. Navy were experimenting with submarine echo detection using the oscillator as a sound source. Late that year, with an experimental vacuum-tube amplifier to boost the echo level, an American team succeeded in detecting a return from a submerged submarine at 1,000 yards while the transmitting ship was moving at 15 knots. Similar trials in Britain under G. H. Nash (inventor of the Nash Fish) using directional hydrophones without electronic amplification were largely unsuccessful. Moreover, the slow dynamic response of the Fessenden Oscillator (i.e., its long "turn-on/turn-off" time) made it impossible to detect underwater targets closer than 500 yards, and its relatively low frequency of operation precluded any significant directivity.[3]

Simultaneously, the British experimented with a variety of other ASW sound sources, including underwater sirens and impulse generators using both explosives and mixed-gas reactions (in which a mixture of oxygen and hydrogen was detonated), but neither of these approaches nor higher-frequency variants of the Fessenden Oscillator could be made practical. Fortunately, important scientific developments in France revealed an alternative that, although too late to affect ASW in World War I, would revolutionize underwater acoustics between the wars—piezoelectricity and ultrasonics.

First described in the late 19th Century by the brothers Pierre and Jacques Curie, *piezoelectricity* is a property of certain dielectric, crystalline materials, such as quartz or tourmaline, by which a mechanical deformation along one axis of the material generates a small electrical voltage across a pair of opposite faces. Conversely, applying a voltage across those same faces will produce a corresponding mechanical strain. A similar phenomenon, *magnetostriction,* is found in certain ferromagnetic materials, such as steel and nickel alloys, in that, for example, a magnetic field applied parallel to the axis of an iron rod will vary the length of the rod slightly in proportion to the strength of the impressed field. During World War I the French Navy pioneered the application of both of these effects to underwater echo-ranging.

Early in the war, Constantin Chilowsky, a young Russian émigré living in Switzerland, proposed to the French an active echo-ranging system based on a moving-armature magnetic transducer. In 1915, Chilowsky's ideas were passed on to the renowned French physicist Paul Langevin, who was engaged in war work for the Navy. In a brief collaboration, he and Chilowsky concluded that the latter's original idea for a magnetic transducer was infeasible but turned to the investigation of several alternatives, including both piezoelectricity and magnetostriction. Eventually, they fashioned a crude transducer that took the form of an electrical capacitor with a flexible mica sheet as the dielectric and the contiguous seawater as one electrode. When this "capacitor" was driven at 100 kHz by an arc transmitter of the type used in early radio, the alternating attractive forces between the capacitor's effective "plates" vibrated the mica sheet to produce underwater sound. Signals from the device were successfully transmitted across the River Seine to a carbon hydrophone in late 1915, and by the following April, the first underwater echoes from a suspended armor plate had been detected at a range of 200 yards by putting the hydrophone at the focus of a parabolic reflector. This performance was significantly less than Fessenden had achieved with his sonic oscillator several years previously, but it convinced Langevin that further development was feasible, particularly using piezoelectric materials and electronic amplification to increase the returned signal levels. While Chilowsky moved on to other interests, Langevin's subsequent research soon made him the Allies' most respected authority on electro-acoustics and active sonar.

In 1917, Langevin concentrated his efforts on piezoelectric phenomena in quartz crystals and fabricated a receiver by sandwiching a slice of quartz between a mica cover exposed to the sea and, on the other side, an inboard foil electrode. In this arrangement, the undulating pressure of an external sound field would stress the underlying quartz crystal and produce small piezoelectric voltages measurable on the foil. A key factor in the success of this novel device was the introduction of

Dr. Paul Langevin
(B. 1872 D. 1946)

Working initially with Russian émigré scientist Constantin Chilowsky during World War I, French physicist Paul Langevin was primarily responsible for the development of the first successful piezoelectric hydrophone and its application to submarine detection devices.

Born in Paris, Langevin studied physics at the École de Physique et Chimie and the École Normale Supérieure. After graduate work at Cambridge's Cavendish Laboratory under Sir John J. Thomson, he completed his doctoral degree under Pierre Curie at the Sorbonne in 1902. (In 1910, Langevin reputedly had an affair with the widowed Marie Curie, creating a major scandal.)

In 1904, as an early pioneer in understanding physical phenomena in terms of atomic and molecular behavior, Langevin became professor of physics at the Collège de France and in 1908 developed what became known as "Langevin dynamics" and the "Langevin equation" to simplify the modeling of dynamic systems at the molecular level. As a colleague of Albert Einstein, he also was active in gaining acceptance for the theory of relativity in France.

Drawn into war work in underwater acoustics by the submarine threat, he made his key contributions to ultrasonic submarine detection between 1916 and 1919. After the conflict he returned to academic life and his research in molecular physics and subsequently made major contributions to the understanding of paramagnetism and diamagnetism, which he explained as a consequence of electron spin within atoms.

Langevin was fired from his academic position and held under house arrest by the Vichy government for most of World War II because he had been an active anti-fascist in the 1930s. He was restored to his professorship after the liberation in 1944, but died in Paris two years later. He is buried there in the Panthéon.

an electronic amplifier—a French derivative of an earlier American design using the Audion vacuum tube—to boost the tiny output voltages to discernable levels.[4] Combining his earlier mica-dielectric transmitter and the new quartz receiver, Langevin succeeded by November 1917 in signaling underwater for more than three miles.

Encouraged by the success of his piezoelectric receiver, he then exploited the reverse piezoelectric effect—using applied electric voltages to generate mechanical motion—by demonstrating a powerful quartz-based transmitter using a single perfect crystal cut to resonate at 150 kHz. However, because this configuration required large drive voltages and consumed substantial quantities of crystalline quartz, a rare strategic material, he modified his design into the form of a mosaic of thin quartz slices sandwiched between two-inch-thick steel plates. Additionally, he lowered the operating frequency to 40 kHz to achieve longer propagation ranges in water.[5] Sea trials of the new transmitter commenced in February 1918, and almost immediately, echoes from a submerged submarine were detected at a maximum range of nearly a mile and a minimum of 100 yards. Further experimentation revealed that by exploiting the forward and reverse piezoelectric effects in a single transducer, the same device could be used to both transmit and receive. Moreover, by using the relatively new electronic technique of *heterodyning*, the received signals could be made audible to an operator who would use the time delay between the outgoing sound pulse and the arrival of a submarine echo to estimate the range to the target.[6] In related research activities, Langevin became one of the first to consider such key factors in hydroacoustics as the relationship between the size and shape of transducers to their output intensity, beamwidth, and directivity, as well as the effects of frequency,

ocean currents, temperature, and salinity on sound transmission.

In light of Langevin's rapid progress in improving his echo-ranging technique, the French Navy in early summer 1918 impaneled a technical commission to judge the practicality of his concept for ASW. In July the authorities rendered a favorable report, recommending that the equipment be adapted for French warships and that a training center for operators be established at Toulon. The minimum detection range—100 yards—precluded determining the precise time for dropping depth charges, but the passive-acoustic Walser gear was proposed to fill that need. Subsequent plans to fit the Langevin apparatus in seven ASW ships (small destroyers) by early 1919 were overtaken by the end of the war.

Not until after May 1916, when the French invited a British delegation to Toulon to observe Langevin's experiments, did the Royal Navy embark on a similar program of its own. Principally under the direction of R. W. Boyle, of the Board of Invention and Research's facility at Parkeston Quay in Harwich, this early British effort focused on first replicating the French results; it also began its own investigations of piezoelectricity, magnetostriction, and mica dielectric transmitters. By late 1917, Boyle successfully transmitted ultrasonic signals at 75 kHz for nearly a mile using a small quartz slab backed by a single steel plate, and with electronic amplification he was able to hear the audio signature of a steam pinnace at about a half-mile using the same device.

With this initial capability to transmit and receive ultrasonic signals in hand, Boyle next attempted to detect submerged submarines using a "shadow" method that depended on a transiting target blocking the normal sound transmission between a transmitter and receiver separated by some considerable distance. When this failed because of confusing sound reflections from the surface and bottom, Boyle turned to Langevin's echo-ranging approach, and in March 1918, he achieved his first echoes from a submerged submarine, at a distance of 500 yards. Within three months, he had refined his system into a single 20-inch-diameter, non-resonant quartz transducer that functioned as both the transmitter and receiver.[7] Additionally, Boyle began investigating methods of sheltering his active transducer inside a dome external to the ship's hull to facilitate search operations while under way. The first installation was made on the trawler *Ebro II* just after the Armistice in November 1918 and used a retractable canvas dome similar to those used earlier on Royal Navy submarines to protect passive directional hydrophones. Earlier tank experiments had shown that interposing the dome affected sound transmission into the water only negligibly, and in the ensuing sea trials clear target echoes were gained at a range of 600 yards.

As a security measure, the Admiralty coined the term "asdic" as a cover name for its ultrasonic submarine detection program in the middle of 1918. Over the years, there has been considerable confusion about the origin of the word, which many have identified as an acronym for the "Allied Submarine Detection Investigation Committee." But no committee by that name ever existed, and "asdic" may just have appeared as shorthand for the Admiralty's "Anti-Submarine Division," which *did* exist.[8] (The word remained in use in the Royal Navy until the 1950s, when it was phased out in favor of the term "sonar," which had originated in the United States during World War II.)

In June 1918 the Admiralty's Anti-Submarine Division had become so encouraged by Boyle's progress toward fielding a viable asdic system that it ordered 20 ship-sets of equipment to his preliminary design and began preparatory work for

Dr. Robert William Boyle
(B. 1883 D. 1955)

A Canadian physicist, Boyle was the Royal Navy's counterpart to France's Paul Langevin in the development of the earliest asdic systems late in World War I and immediately after. Boyle was born in Carbonear, Newfoundland, and studied at McGill University in Montreal under Nobel Prize–winning physicist Sir Ernest Rutherford. After receiving McGill's first Ph.D. in physics in 1909, he followed Rutherford to the University of Manchester in England to continue work on radioactivity. In 1912, Boyle returned to Canada to head the physics department at the University of Alberta and shifted his research interests to ultrasonics.

With the coming of World War I, Boyle volunteered his services to the Admiralty, returned to England, and—with the aid of Rutherford's influence—was selected to join the Board of Inventions and Research. Subsequently, having been shown Langevin's successes and then collaborating with his team in France, Boyle led the development of Britain's first successful active sonar transducers and their earliest system installations on Royal Navy escorts.

Boyle returned to the University of Alberta in 1919 and served as the dean of the Faculty of Applied Science until 1929. Subsequently, he joined Canada's National Research Council (NRC), where he supervised radar research during World War II. He remained with the NRC until his retirement in 1948, when he moved back to England to spend the remainder of his life.

installations on trawlers, sloops, K-class destroyers, P-boats, and PC-boats. The first of these sets, installed on the patrol craft *P.59* in early 1919, was used for both technical evaluation and tactics development. Its 15-inch-diameter, non-resonant quartz transducer was housed in a retractable canvas dome and could be manually trained and tilted. Driven by a vacuum-tube transmitting set similar to those used in early radio, it was pulsed with a telegrapher's key and operated at frequencies between 20 and 50 kHz. With the operator listening for echoes on a set of headphones and the search craft moving at 15 knots, submarines were successfully detected at ranges between 2,500 and 3,000 yards, clear evidence of how rapidly the acoustics field had advanced under the impetus of the wartime emergency.

Meanwhile, the Americans too had recognized the potential of active acoustic sensors and sought immediately to build on French and British efforts in the area.[9] Following a three-day ASW conference in Washington in June 1917, major research efforts were begun at New York's Columbia University; at the jointly operated experimental facility of the Submarine Signal Company, General Electric, and Western Electric at Nahant, Massachusetts; and at Stanford University and the future California Institute of Technology on the West Coast. By the end of the war the Americans had made significant progress in developing certain advanced *components* needed for ultrasonic detection, but they never equaled the French or British in demonstrating a total system. Two areas in which the Americans made notable contributions were the refinement of advanced high-frequency electronic amplifiers and the fabrication of piezoelectric transducer elements from a more readily available alternative to quartz—synthetic Rochelle salt crystals. The latter, potassium sodium tartrate, could be grown in the laboratory and displayed much higher levels of piezoelectric activity than quartz. Despite Rochelle salt's disadvantages of being soluble in water and relatively fragile, its greater sensitivity made possible more efficient transducers that could be operated at lower voltages, and it quickly found application in hydrophones.

A research team at Columbia also produced a series of large and powerful quartz transmitters based on Paul Langevin's basic design. Only one test of an entire detection system was accomplished before the war ended when a quartz transmitter and Rochelle salt receiver were used at New London, Connecticut, in October and November 1918 to generate and detect echoes from a passing surface ship at 400 to 600 yards. In other experiments, a steel protective dome was tried as a protective cover over a Langevin-type transducer on the USS *Fish Hawk*, a small steamer, but the resulting echo levels were so severely attenuated that the idea was dropped.[10]

Despite good progress during the war—due both to excellent cooperation among American academic and industrial researchers and free interchanges with the French and British—most of the U.S. work in ultrasonic acoustics was cancelled when the conflict ended. A small residuum continued at the naval experimental stations in New London and at Annapolis, Maryland, but not until the founding of the U.S. Naval Research Laboratory in 1923 was a serious U.S. effort on active sonar resumed.

Asdic: Ongoing Development

Genuinely shaken by the experience with the German submarine threat in World War I and convinced that active acoustics was the key to defeating similar dangers in the future, the Royal Navy continued an ambitious ASW research program into the 1920s and 1930s. In particular, the British asdic effort focused on three major areas: improving the effectiveness and reliability of the basic quartz transducer; devising a streamlined dome to facilitate operating the device at speed; and developing a display system to estimate better the range and bearing to a target. During the early 1920s, the wartime acoustics research that had begun at Hawkcraig, Harwich's Parkeston Quay, and on the Gareloch in Scotland was gradually transferred to the new ASW training facility at Portland (denoted HMS Osprey), the Signal School at Portsmouth, and the Admiralty Research Laboratory at Teddington, southwest of London.

The first asdic set adopted for operational use in the Royal Navy was the Type 112, fitted in the ships of the 6th Destroyer Flotilla: eight destroyers and the destroyer leader *Campbell*. The set differed little from Boyle's last wartime prototype in using non-resonant quartz mosaic transducers, but almost immediately, the British developers turned to Langevin's resonant quartz-steel sandwich for subsequent designs. A number of different variants and construction techniques were tried—several using multiple plies of quartz and steel—but by 1928, in the Type 118, the transducer design had stabilized in a basic 15-inch-diameter configuration that remained largely unchanged until after World War II, except for moving from a two-ply to a four-ply sandwich in 1937.

The relative fragility of early canvas transducer covers severely limited the asdic operating speed and necessitated that the domes be made retractable for normal steaming. Thus, the small wartime effort that provided the first rudimentary asdic dome expanded significantly in the 1920s to investigate a variety of configurations and materials for fixed, streamlined fairings that could be permanently mounted beneath the hull to protect the transducer head. This required a sensitive balance among shape, material strength, durability, and sound transmissibility, and a number of steel, aluminum-alloy, composite, and even wooden designs were tested. However, the Navy eventually returned

again to retractable domes to allow destroyers to reach their top speeds of around 35 knots when not engaged in active-acoustic searches.

Prior to World War II, the Royal Navy developed almost two dozen identifiable shipboard asdic systems, with multiple modifications within each type.[11] However, many of these were experimental prototypes or unsuccessful designs that saw only limited production. After the Type 112, the most important of these later variants included the Types 113 and 114, the first submarine and destroyer asdic sets, respectively, which appeared in 1922. Both used retractable canvas domes (later copper or stainless steel) and operated at 21 to 31 kHz. The Type 118, introduced in 1928, became the standard interwar set for submarines, and its counterpart for destroyers, the Type 119, appeared a year later. Optimized for operations under Mediterranean conditions, the latter operated at 14 to 26 kHz and used a fixed, streamlined steel dome. The last important pre–World War II asdic sets were the submarine Type 129 and the surface-ship Type 128, both deployed in 1937. The Type 129 used a permanent, keel-mounted transducer, whereas the Type 128 had a retractable, streamlined dome. As an aid to target tracking, both used the newly available "electrochemical range recorder" that had just appeared as the result of a lengthy research and development effort.

In the earliest asdic sets, the range to the target was estimated by an operator who listened on a headset and used a stopwatch to measure the time delay between the outgoing transmission and any returning echoes. For nominal target ranges up to 3,000 yards, this time delay would be no more than three and a half seconds, and a measurement error of only one-tenth of a second corresponded to a range error of 85 yards. Thus, human reaction time and its repeatability were a major limitation on the range accuracy of the system. To minimize this variability a number of simple fixes were attempted, first by starting the stopwatch automatically when the manual transmitting key was depressed, later by indicating the range on a circular dial with a pointer driven by a constant-speed motor. If the motor was started automatically by the transmitted pulse and stopped manually when the operator heard an echo, the amount of angular rotation clocked off was proportional to the target range. This approach still depended heavily on the operator's aural acuity and reaction time. In an alternate approach a small stylus was mounted on a ballistic galvanometer to provide a visual trace of the returning signal on a moving strip of paper, as in a seismograph. For any echoes whose corresponding deflections were discernable against the background noise, the return time and hence the target range could be measured as a distance along the moving paper. Meanwhile, because even the earliest asdic transducers were designed to be trained in azimuth—analogous to searching with a beam of light—the target's direction could be determined from the bearing on which the transducer was aimed.

To get a more useful display—one that portrayed a time *history* of the changing target range more intuitively—the next step was to build an instrument that traced a horizontal line corresponding to the return from each pulse, so that distance along the line represented time (and thus range), with the echo intensity at any moment shown by a darkening of the trace by an electrical discharge from the moving stylus. By using automatic gain control on the returning signal to suppress the reverberation generated by the large transmitted pulse, a target echo would appear as "tick" on the trace at a distance from the origin corresponding to target range. Each successive transmission added a new trace just below its predecessors, giving a paper graph on which the varying echo range appeared clearly as a function of time. After a laborious engineering effort to adapt the orig-

inal cumbersome design for shipboard use, the resulting instrument, denoted the "A/S3 Electrochemical Range Recorder," entered production in 1932, and by the end of the decade it had been incorporated into a wide variety of asdic sets for both surface ships and submarines. Numerous variants and modifications followed and saw extensive use in World War II and beyond.[12] Additionally, a number of other tactical aids were incorporated into shipboard asdic systems, such as remote loudspeakers and target-bearing indicators on the bridge to assist in conning the ship during search and attack. Also, various analog-computation or graphical adjuncts were added to the range recorder to indicate the optimum time to drop depth charges or, later, to launch ahead-firing weapons.

Along with the engineering development of asdic transducers, domes, and processing and display systems, the Royal Navy also began to study the fundamental behavior of sound in the sea to understand better the performance limitations of active echo-ranging.[13] This work began with a more accurate determination of the sound speed in seawater—found to be approximately 4,950 feet/second—but it soon turned to the effects of temperature and hydrostatic pressure. In 1922, the destroyer *Rocket*, fitted with a Type 114 asdic set, and the submarine *H-32* (to serve as a target) were sent to the Mediterranean, Red, and Black Seas specifically to evaluate detection performance in warmer waters. These experiments were the first to indicate the strong effects of water-temperature gradients on underwater sound propagation, and even though the phenomenology was not clearly understood, the resulting variability in detection range was readily apparent. A similar set of Mediterranean experiments in 1930 with the patrol craft *P.59* using a Type 119 set further explored the effects of ocean temperature and discovered the role of the rapid decrease of water temperature with depth, known as the *thermocline,* in determining detection range.[14] The *P.59* trials were also the first to associate the long asdic ranges often obtained on submarines at periscope depth with the horizontal ducting of sound waves by a temperature gradient in the surface layer of the ocean.

The Mediterranean asdic tests of 1922 and 1930 forced the realization that the Royal Navy required a far more thorough understanding of the behavior of underwater sound to predict and optimize submarine detection under a wide range of oceanographic conditions. In 1933, HMS Osprey described its intended "Sea Research" program in these terms:

> In the past the development of submarine detection by asdics has been directed chiefly toward improvements in the components of the apparatus, and no very fundamental changes in the method of detection have been made. It is considered that development has now reached the stage where further improvement is dependent on discovering new methods of overcoming the limitations imposed by the acoustic properties of the sea. It is unlikely that such improvement can be obtained without a more fundamental knowledge of the causes that account for the very marked differences between the effects observed in practice, and the results expected from existing theories of the transmission of sound in water.[15]

Accordingly, the Royal Navy's efforts in underwater acoustics were broadened to cover all of the phenomena that affected the transmission loss of sound in the sea: spreading, refraction, reflection, scattering, absorption, and the influence of the surface and bottom. The development of a practical in-situ sound velocity meter in 1932 was particularly useful for studying the complex dependence of transmission loss on water temperature variations. Parallel efforts addressed the frequency and temporal character of ocean background noise, as well as the asdic self-noise caused both by own-ship machinery and the flow of water past the hull and over the dome itself. By the late 1930s, understanding and ameliorating these latter effects had raised the maximum asdic operating speed to 25 knots. A limited effort was mounted to characterize the acoustic "signature" of submarines—the frequency spectrum and noise level radiated by the targets themselves—but except for noting that the submarine's "blade rate" (the product of shaft-rotation speed and number of propeller blades) dominated its total signature, the work was downplayed because of the emphasis on active, vice passive, detection.

A major performance limitation on active echo-ranging was imposed by the phenomenon of "reverberation," the sum total of miniscule echoes returned by individual particles, air bubbles, and other inhomogeneities in the water mass traversed by the outgoing sound pulse. Reverberation noise is loudest at short range—immediately after the transmitted pulse—and tails off exponentially as time and range increase. Low-level target echoes may well be concealed by it, notably at the longer ranges. Reverberation was attributed originally to surface and bottom effects—which indeed play a role; the fact that its main source is within the water mass itself was not appreciated until 1925, when a variety of attempts were begun to minimize its effects by shaping the outgoing sound beam. Principal among these were experimental arrays of multiple transmitter elements whose outputs were time-phased by either mechanical or electrical means to narrow and focus the transmitted wave front. Although some initial success was achieved with these measures, the array program was abandoned because of practical difficulties in implementing the concept, and reverberation remained a fundamental problem—and one that just had to be accommodated—for years to come.

One of the most important outcomes of the Royal Navy's early research in underwater acoustics was the realization that lowering the asdic operating frequency would yield better performance in range because of the intrinsically high attenuation of ultrasonic sound in water. Thus, during 1928 to 1932, the frequency spread for destroyer asdic sets was dropped from 21 to 31 kHz to the range of 14 to 26 kHz, with 20 kHz considered optimum. Further reductions were precluded by the louder ocean background noise found at lower frequencies and—given the size of the existing standard transducers—a significant broadening of the beam and less precision in determining target bearing. By the end of the 1930s, operating with the best equipment under "good" asdic conditions yielded reliable detection ranges on the order of 2,000 yards, while with "poor" conditions—due almost entirely to the local oceanography—the range could fall to less than a quarter of that distance.

Sonar Development in the United States

Deprived of its wartime information exchange, the United States lagged well behind Britain in the development of active sonar during the 1920s and 1930s.[16] However, as the newly established Naval Research Laboratory (NRL) in Washington grew in size and assumed a broader scientific purview, a program in underwater acoustics gathered momentum. By picking up where the earlier American efforts had left off, NRL managed to demonstrate a submarine-mounted 16-inch-diameter active transducer called the Type XL—a steel-quartz Langevin "sandwich"—in a 1927 sea test in which surface ships were detected at ranges on the order of 1,500 yards.

Subsequently, NRL designed all U.S. sonar sets fielded during the interwar period, with manu-facturing shared by the Washington Navy Yard and the Submarine Signal Company. The laboratory's scientists next explored a return to passive listening with a 15-inch-diameter, non-resonant Rochelle salt receiver called the Type JK, which went into production in 1929. At rest, the JK could discern typical targets at a range of 6,000 yards with three-degree bearing accuracy, while passive detection ranges of approximately 500 yards were achieved at speeds between five and nine knots. As an interim next step, the XL and JL were combined to produce a passive-active system, and when it was realized that Rochelle salt crystals could also be used effectively as active elements, the Type QB Rochelle salt transducer followed directly. Designed by the Submarine Signal Company and manufactured in quantity after 1933, the non-resonant Type QB could be tuned over a frequency range of 17 to 30 kHz to allow non-interfering sound searches by ships steaming in company.

The Type QB was followed in 1934 by the Type QC sonar, which used the magnetostriction properties of an array of 600 nickel tubes rigidly mounted on a backing plate to generate and receive sound. Between 1937 and 1939, four different models were developed for surface ships and several others for submarines. These U.S. active systems—like their British counterparts—operated at supersonic frequencies in the range of 15 to 25 kHz, but the United States was slower to overcome the problems of operating at high search speeds. The JK and QB sets were limited by flow noise to searching at under five knots, but the later addition of a spherical rubber cover raised the maximum operating speed to ten knots. However, not until the U.S. Navy adopted British-style thin steel domes in 1940–1941 could the operating speed of the QC sonar be increased to 15 knots, albeit still several knots slower than the Royal Navy's earlier standard.

By 1933, 15 U.S. destroyers, 2 cruisers, and 5 submarines had been equipped with active sonar, and in 1934, four destroyers became the first to be equipped with the Type QC, which was adopted across the board in 1938. By the outbreak of World War II in Europe in 1939, 60 U.S. destroyers had been fitted, and sonar schools were flourishing in San Diego, California, and New London.

Under the Versailles Treaty, dictated in 1919 by the Allies to end World War I, the German Navy was restricted to a purely defensive role, and thus it placed its major emphasis in the 1920s and early 1930s on passive underwater listening systems for ship self-defense. Germany became the world leader in developing conformal hull arrays for detecting surface ships, submarines, and incoming torpedoes. These broadband listening sets first used electro-dynamic, then Rochelle salt, and finally magnetostrictive hydrophones. At first, simple six-element, rotatable line arrays were installed on submarines and ASW craft. Subsequently, these evolved into fixed, hull-mounted conformal arrays with as many as 60 elements per side on large surface combatants and 24 per side on submarines, when the latter began to be constructed in Germany in the late 1930s.

This passive system, known as the *Gruppenhorch-gerät* (GHG), used sophisticated electronic phase compensators to scan these arrays in azimuth with a bearing accuracy of one degree. Surface ships steaming at 20 knots could detect noisy targets passively as far as 13 n.miles away; from submerged submarines at four knots, destroyers at a goodly speed could be heard at ranges of 10 to 20 n.miles, and merchant ships at 4 to 8 n.miles. In 1935, when Germany began building U-boats openly, the Navy's research establishment designed an active echo-ranging system for submarines that operated at 15 kHz with a magnetostrictive transducer. This basic design formed the starting point for a new, improved version known as the S-Anlage, which in various forms became the standard German active sonar for both surface ships and submarines in World War II.

In contrast, amid a neglect of ASW in general, the Italian Navy undertook virtually no sonar development between the wars and would later pay a stiff price for this oversight.

Working independently, the Japanese Navy initiated programs for both passive listening and echo-ranging sonar systems in 1930 and 1931, respectively. These efforts culminated principally in the Type 93 sonar, with which it entered World War II.[17] This system used 16-element, elliptical hydrophone arrays port and starboard for passive detection in the frequency range of 500 to 2,500 Hz, with electronic phase compensation for bearing determination. Additionally, the Type 93 incorporated a separate, retractable echo-ranging sensor, similar to but more rudimentary than contemporary British systems, with a 15-inch-diameter quartz transducer operating at 17.5 kHz. In practice, active detection range was limited to approximately 1,000 yards, and only about 20 destroyers had been fitted with the system before the attack on Pearl Harbor.

Similarly, the Soviet Union initiated a program of hydroacoustics research in 1924. Over the next several years, as Soviet historians later noted, "The basic lines of [hydrophone] development within this marine science gradually took shape, the industry was founded, departments were set up within universities, and so on."[18] The initial purpose of this effort was to provide hydrophones for submarines, and its progress benefited significantly from the 1928 salvage of the British submarine *L-55*, which had sunk in the Baltic in 1919. In addition to submarine and surface ship-mounted hydrophones, Soviet scientists tested sea-floor hydrophones as early the summer of 1929 in the Black Sea, out to distances of 1,300 feet offshore. A five-element array was installed in the Gulf of Finland in the fall of 1930 to test that approach for detecting submarine intruders, an early precursor of the U.S. Sound Surveillance System (SOSUS) developed during the Cold War.

These efforts resulted in a series of passive submarine- and ship-mounted sensors known as "Mars" for submarines; "Arktur" for battleships, cruisers, and destroyers; and "Poseidon" for submarine chasers, the first Poseidon being installed in 1934. These sets subsequently were modified and improved for new generations of warships and became standard issue for the coming war. Another new device was the Tamir, an ultrasonic active/passive sonar successfully tested on board the Baltic Fleet submarine chaser *MO-521* in late 1940 after a brief (eight-month) development program. Despite early installations on additional warships, active sonar did not become widespread until after World War II began, with many ships not fitted with active systems until near the end of that conflict.

The Advent of Radar

Whereas asdic had reached a relatively high state of development by the outbreak of World War II in September 1939, radar—the other sensor that would achieve major ASW importance—had attracted serious attention only since the early 1930s and offered only limited capabilities at the beginning of the war.[19] In 1886, Heinrich Hertz had verified the existence of the electromagnetic waves predicted by the earlier physical theories of James Clerk Maxwell and had noted that they could be reflected from both metallic and dielectric bodies. As early as 1904, a German inventor was granted patents for a device that used radio waves to detect ships or obstacles to navigation at a distance of about a mile, but its lim-

ited range precluded active interest by contemporary navies. In an address to the Institute of Radio Engineers in 1922, Guglielmo Marconi, the pioneer of long-wave radio communications, observed:

As was first shown by Hertz, electric waves can be completely reflected by conducting bodies. In some of my tests, I have noticed the effects of reflection and detection of these waves by metallic objects miles away.

It seems to me that it should be possible to design apparatus by means of which a ship could radiate or project a divergent beam of these rays in any desired direction, which rays, if coming across a metallic object, such as another steamer or ship, would be reflected back to a receiver screened from the local transmitter on the sending ship, and thereby, immediately reveal the presence and bearing of the other ship in fog or thick weather.[20]

Within a few years—both by accident and on purpose—radio scientists in several countries had observed these very phenomena, and several national efforts had been initiated to develop the capability for detecting ships and aircraft at useful distances using reflected radio signals.

The first of these systems radiated continuous waves (vice a series of discrete pulses) and determined the presence of a target from the interference patterns produced between the transmitted signal and its reflected returns. At the U.S. Naval Research Laboratory this effect was first noticed in conjunction with radio direction-finding experiments in 1930, when aircraft crossing the path of radio signals beamed to a receiver two miles away were seen to increase the received level. This led to purposeful detection experiments, and within two years aircraft could be "seen" at 50 miles. However, these early continuous-wave radars, operating between 30 and 60 MHz, were useful only for detecting the *presence* of a target, perhaps as a tripwire, but could provide only limited information about target range, bearing, course, and speed.

This limitation led to the development of *pulsed* radars, in which short bursts of electromagnetic energy were emitted in a narrow, directional beam, with the time elapsed before receiving a reflected target echo used to measure the range, and with the direction in which the antenna was pointing to indicate the bearing. However, pulsed radar posed major technical challenges—notably, the need to operate at much higher frequencies, generating short pulses at those frequencies, and measuring very short time intervals to a high degree of accuracy.[21] By April 1936, the NRL had overcome these difficulties and demonstrated a pulsed radar at 28.3 MHz that soon was able to detect an aircraft at 25 n.miles. Encouraged by this success and motivated by the need to reduce the size of the antennas to facilitate shipboard operation, the NRL scientists that summer developed a 200 MHz system, which was installed on the destroyer *Leary* (DD 158) the following year, and after several upgrades—notably increasing the transmitted power to six kilowatts—the set succeeded in detecting aerial targets out to 50 n.miles. This system, with a wavelength of 1.5 meters, was designated the XAF radar, and it was demonstrated successfully on the battleship *New York* (BB 34) in fleet maneuvers in early 1939, when surface targets were detected at 10 to 12 n.miles. By late 1941, 20 XAF radars (known as the CXAM in production) had been installed on six carriers, six battleships, and five heavy cruisers.

Although Britain delayed starting a formal radar program until early 1935, it was driven to a faster-paced effort by the growing threat of war and the nation's vulnerability to air attack from the continent.

Although they too started with continuous-wave radars, British scientists nonetheless demonstrated their first pulsed radar nearly a year earlier than the United States and by September 1935 had detected aircraft at 40 n.miles using a 12 MHz transmitter. Six months later, the frequency was increased to 25 MHz, and the set achieved 90 n.mile detections. This variant became the prototype for the land-based Chain Home system, largely completed in September 1938, that later provided critical early warning during the Battle of Britain. More significant for the future of anti-submarine warfare, however, was the British development in 1939 of a rudimentary *airborne* radar operating at 200 MHz, primarily for intercepting other aircraft. It soon became apparent that this same system was also effective for detecting ships from the air, and it became the forerunner of a long series of airborne radars that would prove invaluable for detecting surfaced submarines during World War II.

Similarly, Germany started a program of radar research in 1933 and within a year had developed a continuous-wave set that had detected a ship at 7 n.miles. By 1936, the Germans had developed the pulsed Seetakt system, primarily as a radar range finder, and installed it for sea trials on the "pocket battleship" *Graf Spee* and the light cruiser *Königsberg*. Later versions were capable of detecting a battleship at 10 n.miles, a destroyer at 8 n.miles, and a motor torpedo boat at 3 n.miles with a bearing accuracy of less than one degree. But of the 12 radar sets available at the beginning of World War II, only the two Seetakt radars were at sea, with the rest installed for coastal defense.

While the American, British, and German Navies began fitting radar to their ships in the late 1930s, by 1941 the only Japanese warships that had radar were the battleships *Ise* and *Hyuga*, which had the

Radar would become a major factor in ASW operations in World War II and beyond. This is the antenna for the prototype XAF radar as fitted in the battleship *New York* (BB 34) in 1938, the second U.S. ship to carry an experimental radar. The XAF was developed by the Naval Research Laboratory, and its successful trials led to similar radars being rapidly fitted in other major warships. *U.S. Navy*

Gô Dentan Mark 2 Model 2 surface search radar.[22] British naval historian Stephen W. Roskill, in writing of the high state of Japanese submarines, carrier aviation, and night tactics at the start of World War II, observed, "Only in radar development did the Japanese lag seriously behind Britain and the USA; and that deficiency was in the long run to offset the advantages of their other developments."[23]

At the end of the 1930s, while France, Italy, and Japan showed little progress in developing radar for military use, the United States, Britain, and Germany were poised for the rapid advances that soon made it a major adjunct to acoustics as the primary method for finding submarines at sea. Both would have a profound effect on the coming naval war.

6

Building ASW Forces

Both Britain and the United States emerged from World War I with large flotillas of destroyers and escort ships that had demonstrated significant potential for anti-submarine warfare during that conflict. However, the financial burden of the war (particularly on Britain), the desire to achieve what later would be called a "peace dividend," and limitations imposed by international naval agreements led to a rapid demobilization of both fleets, including most of the smaller ASW ships in both nations. For example, the Royal Navy ended World War I with more than 400 destroyers and destroyer leaders, plus just over 200 smaller ASW ships, many of them virtually new; by 1932, these numbers had fallen to 150 and 34, respectively.[1]

In mid-1919 the U.S. Navy had 258 destroyers in commission, of which 218 were relatively advanced flush-deck, four-stack types, which were heavily armed (for fleet action) and could attain 35 knots. Another 166 four-stackers were building or under contract, for a total of 424.[2] In addition, there were 331 submarine chasers and 53 Eagle boats flying the Stars and Stripes.[3] In 1932 there were 251 destroyers in commission—still a significant force—as well as 24 subchasers and a dozen Eagle boats, with most of the latter used as training ships for the Naval Reserve.

New ASW Ships

Because of the surfeit of ships left over from World War I, the Royal Navy did not resume significant destroyer construction until 1927, when a series of new classes—designated by successive letters of the alphabet—began to appear at a nominal rate of nine ships each year.[4] As war threatened in the late 1930s, these efforts accelerated, and beginning with the Tribal class of 1937, the Royal Navy laid down a whole series of destroyer classes, most designated by letters of the alphabet and grouped in "flotillas" of eight ships each. All told, a total of 129 destroyers joined the Royal Navy between the wars, but of the most modern ships, only the 32 ships of the Tribal, J, and K classes were completed before conflict broke out September 1939.[5] Since the Royal Navy's strategic and tactical concepts remained grounded on the primacy of the battle fleet, the destroyer's principal role was protecting the battle line and attacking enemy capital ships in future Jutland-like fleet engagements. Anti-submarine requirements had little or no priority in the design and armament of British destroyers in the 1920s and 1930s; typically, these ships were powerfully engined for speeds in excess of 35 knots and armed for surface warfare with four 4.7-inch guns and up to ten torpedo tubes. Their ASW armament was limited to depth-charge racks at the stern, with even the World War I–era depth-charge mortars left out.

Although the United States did not resume destroyer construction until 1933, this same pattern prevailed across the Atlantic.[6] During the decade of the 1930s, 97 new destroyers were authorized, beginning with the 1,365-ton *Farragut* (DD 348) class and continuing through the 1,620-ton *Benson* (DD 421) class. With the impetus of the new war in Europe,

At least 65 four-stack destroyers can be seen in this view of the reserve fleet at San Diego between the world wars. Most of these ships would serve in World War II—under U.S., British, and Soviet colors. And, many would be converted to minelayers, minesweepers, high-speed transports, and seaplane tenders. *U.S. Navy*

another 200 (!) destroyers were ordered in 1940. Like their British counterparts, these ships were intended primarily for fleet actions and were armed with up to eight 5-inch guns and 16 torpedo tubes, although most carried five 5-inch/38-caliber dual-purpose guns and ten torpedo tubes.[7] Their speeds of 35 to 37 knots and large torpedo batteries were testimony to their primary fleet role. As originally completed, the only anti-submarine weapons in these destroyers were a pair of five-round depth charge racks on the fantail. This minimal emphasis on ASW and the scarcity of open deck space precluded Y-guns or similar weapons being mounted on new U.S. destroyers, and these were removed from older ships as well.

Turning to smaller ASW vessels, the Royal Navy in 1927 began replacing the remaining World War I Flower-class sloops, which had been retained postwar primarily for "showing the flag" and patrolling Britain's far-flung empire. Over the next eight years 20 lightly armed sloops of the *Bridgewater* and *Grimsby* classes (1,190 and 990 tons, standard, respectively) joined the fleet, but these were largely intended for service abroad and were fitted for minesweeping. To the degree that the British showed any concern for commerce protection during the late 1920s, it was assumed that surface raiders would be the most significant threat and that the older destroyers, patrol craft, and trawlers would suffice for ASW convoy duty in a future war.

Still, a comprehensive Admiralty ASW study in 1932 concluded that these older ships would be inadequate against a renascent submarine threat and suggested that significant numbers of purpose-designed escort vessels would be needed for both convoy escort and coastal patrol. This concern gave rise to two new classes of small ASW ships that first appeared in the Royal Navy's 1933 fiscal estimates: the 1,220-ton *Bittern*-class "convoy sloops" and the 570-ton *Kingfisher*-class "coastal sloops," or corvettes. The former were armed with four 4.7-inch guns, light anti-aircraft guns, and depth charges; they were capable of a maximum speed of 18 knots, with an endurance of 7,500 n.miles at 12 knots. The nine *Kingfishers*—built between 1935 and 1939—were similar to the P-class patrol boats of World

War I and carried only light guns and depth charges, but they could make 20 knots, with an endurance of 3,500 n.miles at 12 knots. Ultimately, six sloops of the *Bittern* and *Egret* classes were laid down between 1934 and 1937, and these were followed by nine of the first variant of the slightly larger *Black Swan* class, first begun in 1938. At 1,250 tons, these last pre–World War II escorts carried eight 4-inch guns and additional depth charges and could reach 20 knots. Like their destroyer contemporaries, all of these smaller ASW ships eventually were fitted with asdic as it became available in quantity.

These relatively minimal measures were soon overtaken by the rapidly gathering threat of war in the late 1930s, and, alarmed by the growing menace of the German submarine force, the Admiralty finally responded with the Naval Estimates for 1939 that included 20 Hunt-class escort destroyers and 56 Flower-class corvettes, as well as 20 Tree-class trawlers (later increased to 60), useful for both ASW and minesweeping.[8] All were to be equipped with asdic. The first three of the Hunt class were launched in mid-December 1939, and all of the first group were commissioned within a year. Displacing 1,000 tons on a length of 280 feet overall, the Hunts were armed with four 4-inch guns, several anti-aircraft guns, and depth charges, but—significantly—no torpedo tubes. With a top speed of 28 knots, they could steam unrefueled for 3,500 n.miles at 15 knots. Subsequently, 66 more Hunt-class escorts appeared in improved versions, which were larger to increase their sea-keeping ability, range, and ordnance load-out.

The Flower-class corvettes were designed to be mass-produced in smaller British shipyards, and ultimately nearly 20 builders in the United Kingdom and Canada turned them out. Based on a commercial whale catcher, the *Southern Pride*, the Flower-class escorts were simple, single-screw,

no-frills ships, powered by triple-expansion steam engines, whose 2,800 horsepower could drive them at up to 16 knots. At 925 tons displacement and 205 feet in length, they carried a single 4-inch gun, a few anti-aircraft guns, and both racks and throwers for depth charges. Although they were often buffeted by typical North Atlantic conditions, the Flowers were excellent sea boats and enjoyed a range of 3,500 n.miles at 12 knots. Eventually, the Royal Navy accepted 144 of them, plus ten of a larger version; another 130 Flowers served in other Allied navies, including that of the United States. The first was launched in February 1940, and the Flower-class corvettes would prove to be extremely effective ASW platforms, although their crews would have little love for these "lively" ships. In his classic account of the Battle of the Atlantic, *The Cruel Sea,* novelist Nicholas Monsarrat has Chief Engine Room Artificer Watts declaring, upon reporting to the (fictional) *Compass Rose* of the class, "Whoever designed that ship must have been piss-arse drunk."[9]

To supplement the nearly two dozen trawlers of World War I vintage remaining in the mid-1930s, the British had started a modest new-construction program for "Admiralty trawlers," and by late 1939, a total of 50 trawlers of all types were in commission, with approximately 40 more on the ways. The newer ones, such as the Tree class, were based on the prototype, HMS *Bassett,* which had been launched in 1935. The *Bassett* displaced 461 tons on a length of 160 feet and carried a 4-inch gun and multiple depth charges. Like the Flower-class corvettes, she and her successors were powered by triple-expansion steam engines and could make 12 knots full out. In addition, the Admiralty in 1939 requisitioned several hundred trawlers and drifters from their commercial owners, and these—suitably equipped—were used variously for ASW, minesweeping, and inshore patrol throughout the coming war. By June 1939, 200 asdic sets (mostly

Type 123) had been manufactured and stockpiled for installation on ASW "ships of opportunity," mostly trawlers. At the beginning of the war, 20 of these had already been fitted out, joining 100 modern destroyers, 30 sloops, and the 15 "escort destroyers" of the V and W classes that were similarly equipped.

Thus, as the Armageddon of 1939–1940 approached, the Royal Navy belatedly was acquiring a large number of specialized ASW ships. Even these would not be enough to counter the "steel sharks" of the German Navy.

Not until 1937 was interest in small patrol or ASW vessels revived in the United States, where it had been assumed that future ocean escort missions—if required—would be carried out by the significant number of older, flush-deck destroyers laid up in reserve. To relieve these older destroyers from competing coastal duties, the Navy in 1938 promulgated a specification for small patrol craft as a successor to the earlier Eagle boats.[10]

The U.S. Navy initiated two series of submarine chasers. The first comprised the wood-hull *PC 449, PC 450,* and *PC 453.* These were 95-ton, 110-foot craft with twin diesel engines. The three craft differed in detail, with the first two capable of 15 knots and the *PC 453* rated at 21 knots. Before the United States entered World War II, 90 follow-on "repeats" of these prototypes had been ordered. (These wood-hull PCs were reclassified as SCs in 1943, reflecting the World War I–era "splinter fleet" designations.)

The other series considered of larger, steel-hull prototypes simultaneously constructed to competing designs, the *PC 451* and *PC 452.* The first was powered by twin diesel engines, the second by geared turbines; both could make 20 knots. The 165-foot *PC 451* and 173-foot *PC 452* both entered production, with 72 165-footers and 50 of the larger craft being on order by December 1941. All

production SC/PC subchasers would be diesel propelled. This mass production of SCs and PCs took place at relatively small shipyards on both coasts, the Great Lakes, and inland waterways. These yards would produce many hundred such submarine chasers during the war.

Other major navies were also building destroyers between the wars, most notably Japan (completing 118), Italy (120), and France (84).[11] Germany had a later start, beginning in 1934 by laying the keels for the first of 22 destroyers. Although all of the German ships were armed with depth charges, their primary mission—like that of U.S. and British destroyers—was to support big-ship surface operations, and their ASW role was considered secondary at best.

In the middle and late 1930s all of these navies added modest numbers of smaller, multi-mission escort ships and torpedo boats armed with both depth-charge racks and depth-charge throwers. In Italy, these craft included 36 large torpedo boats of the *Partenope, Orsa,* and *Spica* classes, the largest of which displaced 855 tons on a length of 293 feet; in France were four submarine chasers of the *Chantier-Bretagne* type, launched in 1934. Between 1937 and 1939, France authorized an additional 25 subchasers, but none was completed before the war.

Germany launched a homogeneous class of ten 600-ton *Geleiteboote* (escort vessels) in 1935, the *F1* through *F10,* intended for both ASW and minelaying. Japan added only four 860-ton escort vessels of the *Shimushu* class intended for coastal defense and ten small subchasers between 1933 and 1938. Despite the service of a Japanese destroyer force in the Mediterranean in World War I, the need for convoy and coastal escort forces was largely lost on the Japanese Navy.

Thus, between the wars, only the U.S. and British Navies were laying foundations for effective ASW forces with new types of ships—many fitted with acoustic and radar detection devices—although not in the numbers that would be required.

Airborne ASW

Aircraft and airships had a significant, albeit nascent, impact on ASW in World War I. Between the wars the world's navies gave little thought to airborne ASW, with the Royal Navy even having lost its air arm at the time of the establishment of the Royal Air Force (RAF) in 1918. Rather, aircraft developed for overland reconnaissance and bombing missions would also be expected to carry out anti-submarine operations employing that most basic sensor—the "Mark I Eyeball"—and weapon—the depth bomb—used by aircraft in the previous conflict.

Naval aircraft developed in the 1930s, both land-based (mostly flying boats) and ship-based aircraft on board warships (floatplanes) and carriers (wheeled aircraft), were intended to support fleet operations. Significantly, the highly effective, carrier-based Fairey Swordfish developed for the RAF and the Douglas SBD Dauntless developed for the U.S. Navy later served competently as ASW aircraft, as did their common successor—the Grumman TBF/TBM Avenger, which served on board carriers of both the United States and Britain.[12]

All major navies operated flying boats for maritime reconnaissance, and these also would serve in the ASW role. The most effective of these aircraft—and that which was produced in larger numbers than any other military seaplane—was the twin-engine, high-wing, Consolidated PBY Catalina flying boat, which entered U.S. Navy service in late 1936. The early versions had a top speed of 160 knots and boasted a range of 1,860 n.miles, performance that was improved significantly in later variants.[13] The Royal Air Force introduced the much larger Short Sunderland flying boat in 1938. With four nine-cylinder radial engines, it could reach 180 knots with an endurance of more than 13 hours, carrying 2,000 pounds of bombs internally. It would be adapted as a commercial airliner after World War II.

Until 1941 almost all land-based maritime patrol aircraft in various air forces and navies were flying boats. In April 1938, Lockheed proposed a land-based bomber aircraft adapted from the firm's commercial Model 14 Super Electra. The Royal Air Force liked the plane, and in June 1938 the British government placed a contract for 250 aircraft, primarily for coastal patrol (an RAF mission). Eventually some 1,500 of the aircraft—named Hudsons—were procured for British and Australian service. It was later to be the first operational Coastal Command ASW aircraft to be fitted with a surface-search radar. (The first experimental surface-search radar fitted in a Coastal Command aircraft was installed on a trial basis in a twin-engine Avro Anson utility transport. This set, installed in 1938, had a power of only 50 watts; it was the progenitor of the ASV [Air-to-Surface Vessel] Mark I radar later installed in the Hudsons.)

The Lockheed Hudson was an effective ASW aircraft in the early stages of the Battle of the Atlantic. Flown by the Royal Air Force and the U.S. Navy and Army Air Forces, the aircraft was adapted from the commercial Lockheed Model 14 Super Electra. Note the pre–June 1941 markings on this U.S. Navy PBO-1. *U.S. Navy*

A number of additional Hudson bombers ordered by Britain were withheld for use by the U.S. Army Air Corps, with 20 of those being delivered to the U.S. Navy. Designated PBO-1 by the Navy, they were assigned to Patrol Squadron (VP) 82, the first land-based patrol/ASW aircraft to be flown by the Navy. With a top speed of 220 knots and a range of 1,900 n.miles, the aircraft could carry four 325-pound depth charges in an internal bomb bay in addition to several machine guns. Although its naval service lasted only from October 1941 to October 1942, Hudsons flown by VP-82 would sink the first two German U-boats destroyed by U.S. forces; the fourth U-boat sunk by U.S. forces was credited to an Army A-29 Hudson. (The third was destroyed by a Navy PBM Mariner flying boat.)

An unusual aircraft proposed for ASW in the immediate pre–World War II period was the autogiro. This rotary-wing aircraft obtained lift from its horizontal propeller—a rotor—that drew energy from the air stream rather than the aircraft's engine. Although the engine could be connected to the rotor during takeoff or landing, in flight the engine was geared to a conventional propeller for forward motion. It required a takeoff run of about 100 feet.

Several nations experimented with autogiros in this period. The U.S. Navy was the first to evaluate an autogiro at sea, the Pitcairn XOP-1 on board the USS *Langley* (CV 1) in 1931. The British and Italian Navies undertook shipboard autogiro trials later in the 1930s. The U.S. Navy was developing the small escort, or "jeep," carrier concept in the late 1930s, and the Pitcairn autogiro was proposed for use on board such ships in the ASW role. In the event, only conventional aircraft would be used on board U.S. and British escort carriers during World War II. However, the Japanese *Army* did operate a small number of autogiros from escort carriers in that conflict, as will be described later (see Volume 2, chapter 3).

The successor to the autogiro was the helicopter, and in the 1930s Germany was a world leader in helicopter development. The Flettner Fl 184 *gyroplane*—a cross between a helicopter and an autogiro—first flew in 1936 and, before the lone prototype crashed, the German Navy had planned to evaluate it for possible shipboard operation. The firm's Fl 282 Kolibi (humming bird) was probably the most capable helicopter developed during World War II. Following its first flight in 1940, a ship-based variant for ASW was developed with trials conducted on board the cruiser *Köln* during heavy seas in the Baltic.

The German Navy ordered mass production of the two-place helicopter—30 prototypes were to be followed by *one thousand* for the land- and ship-based ASW roles and for Air Force use. Only 32 are believed to have been completed before shifting aircraft priorities stopped production. The production Fl 282 was to search for submarines; it had no attack capabilities, being intended to guide ASW ships to the target. A later, lightweight version was to carry bombs. Reportedly, the Navy used them operationally in the ASW role in the Aegean Sea.

The Fl 282 was the first helicopter to enter military service with any nation.

Priorities, Doctrine, and Tactics

In the climate of austerity that prevailed after World War I, the Royal Navy soon eliminated the ASW Division of the Admiralty staff. Moreover, as early as the Paris Peace Conference in 1919, which led to the Treaty of Versailles later that year, the British strongly advocated outlawing submarines as weapons of war, a position that they argued again at the Washington Naval Conference of 1921 and the London Naval Conference of 1930. Opposed by both the Americans and the French, the British failed to carry this position, although the London Naval Conference did limit undersea craft to 2,000 tons surface displacement, effectively ending—temporarily—the construction of large "cruiser" submarines. At the same time, confidence in asdic as the effective answer to future submarine threats grew steadily in the Royal Navy. Then-Rear-Admiral Ernle Chatfield noted, "We have got to the stage when the hitherto 'undetectable craft' is detectable. . . . [T]he time is coming when we shall have to rebalance our theories as to the practical use of submarines."[14]

Consequently, the Royal Navy instituted a vigorous program of asdic training and tactical development at the ASW school HMS Osprey that had been established in 1924 at Portland.[15] Among other shore-based training aids, Osprey introduced in 1925 the first ASW attack trainer, consisting of the control station of an asdic set and a glass table covered with thin plotting paper.[16] Two independently controlled light spots beamed from underneath represented the attacking ship and a target submarine, and asdic transmissions were simulated by beams of light from the former. If the beam hit the target, a simulated echo was played into the operator's headset, and both the operator and the officer "conning" the ship could practice tracking the target. The initial emphasis at the Osprey attack trainer was to provide operator practice in hunting and screening, and a variety of scenarios could be generated with that goal in mind. Osprey also became the home of the 1st Anti-Submarine Squadron, which served for both at-sea training and trials of new ASW equipment and tactics. The 1st Anti-Submarine Squadron initially consisted of four P-class escorts, two PC-class subchasers, and two converted whale catchers. Establishment of this unit showed a keener appreciation of the intricacies of ASW than that found in any other navy at the time.

The Royal Navy had ended the use of explosive paravanes in 1925, leaving depth charges as its sole ASW weapon throughout the decade before World War II. Although ahead-thrown bombs were revisited as an alternative in the 1920s, it was not until early in World War II that such weapons were fitted to ships.

In the ASW search scenario, the asdic operator would sweep the area ahead of his ship by training the transducer back and forth in five-degree steps over a 120-degree arc forward of the bow.[17] As the ship maneuvered to engage, however, asdic's minimum effective range caused the attacker to "go blind" at 500 yards and obliged it to proceed only by dead reckoning for the crucial, final phase of a depth-charge attack. To overcome this time-late problem, several tactics were devised. In one, a second ASW ship, standing far enough away from the target to maintain active contact, was used to talk the primary "pouncer" into attack position. In another approach, known as the "medium-range constant-speed maneuver," the attacker, continually correcting course in accordance with an estimate of the submarine's speed and direction, would accelerate to maximum speed at about 900 yards and cover the remaining distance to the target as quickly as possible. Still, the overall success probability remained relatively low, particularly when frequent, time-consuming false contacts complicated the process of searching a wide area.

Starting in 1925, the 6th Destroyer Flotilla, the first operational unit to be fitted with asdic, practiced a wide variety of ASW scenarios in exercises with the rest of the fleet. These included screening the flanks of the battle force, protecting outlying battle cruisers, defending ports, and operating with ASW aircraft. Major emphasis was placed on optimizing screen size and formation, devising search and attack tactics, and balancing the role of the escorts between defense and offense. By 1928, 31 of 200 Royal Navy destroyers had been equipped with asdic, and after 1932 all new-construction destroyers had sets installed when completed. Despite the lessons of 1914–1918, however, the Royal Navy paid little attention to the problem of protecting slow merchant convoys with asdic-equipped escorts, and it staged virtually no exercises of that nature between the wars. Thus, while the battle fleet was believed to be reasonably well protected against the submarine threat, merchant shipping remained highly vulnerable. In effect, evasion continued to be the primary means planned for defending convoys against submarine attack.

The U.S. Navy's series of fleet exercise "problems" conducted between 1923 and 1940 are useful for examining the evolving views in the United States of both submarine warfare and ASW. The fleet problems were large, at-sea strategic exercises involving virtually the entire U.S. fleet in loosely scripted scenarios intended to replicate major elements of the spectrum of naval warfare. Participants were divided into friendly and opposing forces, each with its own objectives, and in real-world maneuvers and simulated combat operations, the effectiveness of competing tactical concepts and new technologies was evaluated.

Historically, these fleet problems have been noted for the major role they assumed in the development of operational doctrine for carrier aviation and amphibious warfare. Additionally, 13 of the 23 exercises explored aspects of ASW as a major objective.[18] Indeed, submarines were active participants in the earliest fleet problems, at first tied closely to the opposing forces, but later given freer rein, and protecting the fleet train (auxiliaries) against them was a common feature. The submarine force demonstrated its potential lethality as early as Fleet Problem I (1923), in which the submarine *O-4* (SS 65) penetrated the escorting screen and simulated sinking the new battleship *California* (BB 44). In similar events in Fleet Problems V (1925) and VII (1927), opposing submarines successfully attacked the battleships *California* (again), *Colorado* (BB 45), *Maryland,* (BB 46), *Wyoming* (BB 32), and *West Virginia* (BB 48), as well as the pioneer aircraft carrier *Langley.*

To counter the submarine threat many of the lessons of World War I were restudied and reapplied. In response to the threat posed to his fleet train by the first use of an independent submarine striking force in Fleet Problem V, the Black (enemy) fleet commander established the first formal task organization for a convoy, including zig-zag plans and screening formations. By 1927, aircraft from the carrier *Langley* had been used in a fleet problem to fly convoy escort. They succeeded in detecting periscopes from the air and in mounting simulated attacks on opposing submarines. Subsequently, as larger carriers joined the fleet, carrier-based ASW patrols became routine out to as much as 35 miles from the center of the force. Other elements of naval aviation—land-based flying boats and even airships—were brought into play, and by Fleet Problem XIII (1932) a "combined-arms" approach involving multiple aviation and surface elements had proved highly successful in finding and attacking opposing submarines. Then, during the initial phase of Fleet Problem XVI (1935), in which the White (friendly) fleet faced significant submarine opposition in a transit from the West Coast to Hawaii, a combination of deception and evasive routing avoided submarine contacts entirely.

Apparently the first use of acoustic ASW in a U.S. fleet problem occurred in 1925, when the destroyer *Melvin* (DD 335) detected a submarine passively at a range of approximately 5,000 yards. However, as late as Fleet Problem XVI (1935), none of the participating destroyers had listening devices of any kind, and active sonar was first used only in Fleet Problem XIX (1938). On that occasion nine of 13 destroyers made solid detections despite lack of operator experience and difficult acoustic conditions that resulted in false echoes. Still, ten of the 13 opposing submarines were able to penetrate the screen—three of them undetected—and made 11 attacks on major targets with actual (but unarmed) torpedoes.

Although ASW remained a significant, albeit subsidiary, presence in the U.S. Navy's fleet problems of the 1920s and 1930s, and even though valuable tactical experience was gained, the exercises may well have lulled the U.S. fleet, like its British counterpart, into a false sense of security about the ability to deal with a hostile submarine threat. For example, the convoys formed up in most of the fleet problems consisted entirely of units of the fleet logistics train, under military discipline and operated collectively as an integral element of the total force. Thus, the difficulties of organizing and protecting a much larger formation of merchant ships—habituated to independent steaming and maneuver—were totally underestimated despite the lessons of World War I. Moreover, because most of the fleet problems were conducted in the relatively benign weather and clear waters of the Hawaiian Islands and the Caribbean, where submarines could often be sighted from the air while submerged at shallow depths, aviators became over-optimistic about their own effectiveness in the ASW role. Consequently, U.S. submarine commanders, advised to stay below periscope depth as much as possible and to detect surface targets using passive sonar alone, were severely criticized whenever they were detected from the air in tactical exercises. With even less experience than the British in asdic, the Americans became similarly convinced that their new active sonars would invariably tip the ASW balance in favor of surface ships.

Overall, the U.S. Navy appears to have adopted the view by the late 1930s that submarines were largely a tactical threat that could be managed by the clever application of available ships and aircraft. There was little recognition of the potential threat that submarines could pose by sea denial to stifle commerce and interdict supply lines, particularly under conditions of unrestricted submarine warfare. In the critique of Fleet Problem XVI, the White commander of the second phase, Admiral Harris Laning, claimed—despite having suffered successful submarine attacks on three of his battleships as they sortied from Pearl Harbor—that "in actual war, we can nullify the effectiveness of enemy submarines. . . . [W]e must bring home to [our] submarines that they cannot in war operate as they do in our fleet problems."[19]

The Spanish Interlude

The most significant European conflict between World War I and World War II was the Spanish Civil War, from July 1936 to March 1939, which gave rise to significant naval actions in both the Mediterranean and the Bay of Biscay.[20] By the late summer of 1937, Nationalist forces under General Francisco Franco, rebelling against the elected Republican regime, had seized all of southern and northwestern Spain, leaving the central government with external access to food and war material only through Mediterranean ports between Almeria and the French border. In what was in many respects a dress rehearsal for the weapons and tactics of World War II, German and Italian forces intervened freely on the Nationalist side, while France and the Soviet Union supported the Republican cause with arms, ammunition, and advisors.[21]

Franco requested assistance from Benito Mussolini and the Italian government in interdicting Republican supplies and equipment arriving through Spain's Mediterranean ports. When the conflict began, the Republican Navy included 12 submarines. But the Navy's officers were conservative and opposed to the socialist government and were almost entirely replaced with young, barely qualified officers. As a result, no Republican submarines would sink any ships during the conflict, and five Republican submarines would be lost (see Table 6-1).

In March 1937, Italy transferred two submarines to the Nationalists, but they were immediately put under repair and were not operational for well over a year. Subsequently Italy "loaned" four operational submarines to Franco's forces, and they operated with Italian officers and crews, each with a Nationalist liaison officer embarked. From August 1937 through February 1938, they conducted 13 war patrols, and several Spanish, British, French, and other merchant ships were sunk by the Italians.[22] In his classic account, *The Spanish Civil War*, Hugh Thomas related:

> On August 29 a Spanish steamer was shelled by a submarine off the French coast. A French passenger steamer reported that she was chased by a submarine into the Dardanelles. On the 30th the Russian merchantman *Tuniyaev* was sunk at Algiers, on its way to Port Said. . . . On September 1 the Russian steamer *Blagaev* was sunk by a submarine off Skyros. On September 2 the

British merchantship *Woodford* was sunk near Valencia.[23]

These attacks on merchant ships were described by Winston Churchill, then outside of the government, as "sheer piracy."[24] Representatives of the Mediterranean powers—including Great Britain and Italy—met at Nyon, Switzerland, in September 1937 to address the issue. At that brief session Britain and France agreed to institute ASW patrols in the western Mediterranean to protect shipping, with, wrote Churchill, "orders which left no doubt as to the fate of any submarine encountered. This was acquiesced in by Italy, and the outrages stopped at once."[25] (One more British ship was sunk off Valencia on the last day of January 1938, apparently by an Italian submarine.)

On 31 August 1937, the British destroyer *Havock* was narrowly missed by a torpedo fired by the Italian submarine *Iride*, possibly because of a misidentification by the Italian commanding officer. In the first use of asdic in combat, the *Havock* gained contact on the submarine, but soon lost it. She was joined by several other destroyers, which carried out a systematic search and then depth-charge attacks. While the Italian submarine was not sunk, oil sighted on the surface indicated that she may have been damaged.

Following these ASW operations, Britain's First Sea Lord, Admiral Ernle Chatfield, expressed considerable concern that asdic's unpromising performance in this first real-world encounter would undermine confidence in the Admiralty's ability to control the submarine threat. Additionally, the Royal Navy was moved by the Spanish experience to establish an Operational Intelligence Centre (OIC) similar to World War I's Room 40 to keep track of Italian submarines in the Mediterranean. The OIC establishment began in 1937, and its size, purview, and effectiveness grew steadily as the next war approached. It soon became

Table 6-1. Republican Submarine Losses

Submarine	Date	Cause
B-6	19 Sep 1936	Nationalist destroyer
B-5	12 Oct 1936	Nationalist aircraft
C-3	12 Dec 1936	German submarine *U-34*
C-6	20 Oct 1937	Scuttled after Nationalist air attack
C-1	9 Oct 1938	Nationalist aircraft in port (Barcelona)

Source: Capt. John F. O'Connell, USN (Ret), *Submarine Operational Effectiveness in the 20th Century: Part One 1900–1939* (New York: Universe, 2010), 293.

the nerve center of the Admiralty, being employed to collect, coordinate, analyze, and disseminate information from every source that could provide insight into the intentions and movements of German naval forces. The OIC was housed in one of the subterranean complexes at Whitehall, near the underground Cabinet war rooms.[26]

The Spanish Civil War demonstrated unquestionably that the submarine would be a major factor in future European conflicts. Specific "lessons" would be difficult to apply to future wars, because of the political-personal factors affecting submarine operations in that crisis; however, the transit of relatively small U-boats from Germany to the war zone demonstrated the potential range of these craft, while the predictions that asdic would change the "odds" overwhelmingly in favor of the hunter were now open to question in some quarters.

Nonetheless, as the European conflict loomed in the late 1930s, the submarine threat and anti-submarine warfare attracted relatively little interest. In the gun-oriented Royal Navy of 1935, only 11 of 1,029 lieutenants and 16 of 972 lieutenant-commanders were anti-submarine specialists.[27] Like the Americans, the British considered submarines largely a tactical threat to the fleet and discounted the possibility of unrestricted submarine warfare against seaborne commerce. This view was encouraged by the 1935 Anglo-German naval agreement, in which Germany agreed to restrict its submarine force to just 45 percent of parity with its British counterpart—but insisted on a clause that allowed Germany to build to full parity if unforeseen situations arose. Additionally, the German government agreed to abide in future by the prize rules covering attacks on merchant shipping in the London Naval Treaty of 1930.

The confidence in asdic's effectiveness that still prevailed in much of the Royal Navy had convinced the British government that the prob-lem of detecting and tracking submarines underwater had largely been solved. Even though all new destroyers after 1932 were fitted with asdic, there was no training in using it tactically for the protection of convoys, and no fleet exercises addressed the defense of large, slow merchant convoys.[28] In February 1937 the Admiralty established the Shipping Defence Advisory Committee to study the problems of defending merchant shipping against both submarine and air attack, and that group concluded both that convoying would likely be required in a future war and that large numbers of escorts would be needed for that purpose.[29] As a result, initial planning began for organizing a convoy system along the lines of that adopted in World War I, but it was only on the eve of war that the Royal Navy instituted a "crash" program to acquire small ocean escorts and ASW trawlers in the quantities sufficient to make convoying possible.

Similarly, on the opposite side of the globe, the Japanese Navy, while paying lip service to the need for commerce protection in wartime, failed to take any serious measures to prepare for meeting a submarine threat.[30] This lack of emphasis—some might say lack of interest—in convoy/merchant protection by the Japanese government was astounding. Japan was an "island empire" with major overseas possessions (Korea and Formosa, now Taiwan) and fighting an overseas conflict (in China). By the late 1930s the likelihood of a future conflict with the United States was obvious to perceptive persons on both sides of the Pacific.

While the Japanese practiced ASW for defending the battle force, shipping protection was relegated to little more than an element of coastal defense, which in any event would be guaranteed by the Empire's powerful battle fleet. A 1936 Imperial defense policy document referred to the need for an escort force for Japanese shipping, but peacetime preparations were limited to creating a few core units and ordering further studies. Thus, by the eve of the Pearl Harbor attack, the Japanese had done very little to organize, train, or equip specialized forces for ASW or convoy escort, and initially the latter duty was assigned to the several naval districts in home waters, which had minimal suitable assets.

Similarly, in the Mediterranean, the Italian and French Navies—their nations less dependent on overseas commerce and involved in a battleship-building race—had little time for commerce protection or ASW, despite the fact that their submarine forces were two of the world's largest. The Soviet Union (USSR), still largely an outcast from the world order, smarting from the defeat of its proxy in the Spanish Civil War, and undergoing a massive and bloody purge of its military leadership, evidenced little interest in ASW activities. Paradoxically, when war broke out in Europe in September 1939, the USSR had the world's largest undersea fleet, with 170 boats; when Germany invaded the Soviet Union in June 1941, this force had grown to 225 submarines.

A Navy without Submarines

Among other punitive terms, the Versailles Treaty that followed World War I prohibited Germany from owning submarines. Still, even during the period of the Weimar Republic (1918–1933), the renascent German Navy had begun to circumvent this restriction and to maintain its skills in submarine technology by funding the design and construction of several submarine prototypes by a Krupp front organization—the IVS—in the Netherlands, Spain, and Finland.[31] Additionally, IVS funded a plant for manufacturing torpedoes and torpedo tubes in Spain, and the German Navy staffed a submarine school in Turkey to train the crews of three IVS submarines sold to that country, as well as many German Navy personnel. In the spring of 1935, two years after his Nazi party came to power, Chancellor Adolf Hitler effec-

tively abrogated the Versailles Treaty by announcing his intention to build the German Army to 36 divisions (300,000 men) and to reestablish the prohibited German Air Force. On 29 June 1935, only a week after the terms of the new Anglo-German Naval Treaty were announced, the German Navy (the *Kriegsmarine*) publicly commissioned its first new submarine, the 250-ton *U-1*, which, with five sister ships built to an IVS Finnish design, had been under construction in secret. By the end of the year, amid much international consternation, a total of 14 submarines had been completed.

The head of the German Navy, Admiral Erich Raeder, chose a promising young captain named Karl Dönitz to nurture his new submarine arm.[32] Dönitz, a World War I U-boat commander, was given responsibility for directing the expansion, organization, tactical development, and training of the submarine force. He soon became a strong advocate for submarine warfare to achieve strategic goals, arguing that if Germany had concentrated largely on building U-boats instead of battleships before World War I and had adopted unrestricted submarine warfare at the outset, Britain would have been defeated. Against those who warned of the effectiveness of convoying and the new threats of active sonar and airborne ASW, Dönitz argued that improved submarines, longer-range and wakeless torpedoes, and the coordination of multiple attackers by radio would overpower convoy escorts in an unrestricted submarine campaign. In particular, Dönitz noted that asdic was not only severely range-limited but ineffective against surfaced submarines, which at night were virtually invisible from the surface and air. Thus, he envisioned night surface attacks on convoys, and the creation of coordinated U-boat or "wolf pack" tactics, centrally controlled by a shore command that had access to multiple intelligence sources.

By late 1937, Dönitz began developing his wolf-pack technique in a series of exercises. These culminated in a large Atlantic exercise in May 1939 in

Grossadmiral *Karl Dönitz, German Navy*
(B. 1891 D. 1980)

Commander of the German U-boat force and Adolf Hitler's successor as head of the Third Reich, Dönitz was born in Berlin and began his naval career as a cadet in 1910. During World War I he served in a German light cruiser loaned to the Turkish Navy and then commanded the small submarine *UB-68* in the Mediterranean. While attacking an Allied convoy in October 1918, the *UB-68* was forced to the surface by British escorts and, after scuttling the boat, Dönitz was taken prisoner and held in England until July 1919. After his repatriation he remained in the German Navy (under the Weimar Republic) and distinguished himself in a series of sea and shore positions while gravitating toward National Socialism and the Nazi party.

In 1934 he commanded the light cruiser *Emden,* essentially a training ship, and in July 1935, newly promoted to *kapitän zur see,* he was named to command the newly formed 1st Submarine Flotilla. During the prewar period he was active in expanding the U-boat force while simultaneously developing his innovative wolf-pack tactics. In January 1939, Dönitz was promoted to commodore and *führer der unterseeboote* (commander of submarines).

He led the German U-boat force into World War II, and a month after the conflict began, he was promoted to *konteradmiral.* On 1 September 1940, he was made a *vizeadmiral,* followed by promotion to full admiral in 1942. In January, 1943, when Admiral Erich Raeder resigned as commander-in-chief of the German Navy in a dispute over the future of surface ships,

Hitler appointed Dönitz to head the Navy and promoted him to *grossadmiral.*

In 1943–1945 Dönitz presided over a series of defeats of the German Navy in the Atlantic, Arctic, Baltic, and Black Sea areas. He attempted to continue the U-boat war, but after May 1943 the issue was never in doubt: the British and U.S. Navies had won the Battle of the Atlantic, although there were periodic successes for the U-boats late in the war.

As the Allied armies cut Germany in half in the spring of 1945, Hitler gave Dönitz command of German forces in the northern sector, and on the night of 30 April, Dönitz was informed that Hitler had appointed him as his successor as President of the Third Reich and Supreme Commander of the Armed Forces. Amid the crumbling Reich, Dönitz attempted to continue the war on the Eastern Front to delay the Soviet advance while German troops and civilian refugees fled toward the British and American lines. Finally, he sent his representatives to sign surrender agreements with the Allies between 4 and 9 May 1945.

British troops arrested Dönitz and his cabinet on 23 May, and he was held to be tried at Nuremberg. He was found guilty of war crimes and sentenced to ten years in prison. Released in 1956, he lived quietly for the rest of his life in Schleswig-Holstein in northern Germany, writing his memoirs and occasionally lecturing on the Nazi movement and submarine warfare. Both of Dönitz's sons died in the war, one in a U-boat and the other on a torpedo craft; his daughter's husband also died in a submarine.

which 15 U-boats, organized into several wolf packs, simulated group attacks on a "convoy" of German surface ships. Despite adverse weather and several communication breakdowns, 13 of the 15 submarines successfully converged on and attacked the convoy after its initial detection by one of them, thus lending strong credence to Dönitz s concept. However, even this success was not enough to convince Admiral Raeder—and through him, Hitler—to shift the emphasis in the pre-war German building program from large surface warships to submarines.

On 27 January 1938, Hitler had approved a massive naval program—the "Z Plan"—that was to take precedence over all other military projects, including Army and Air Force expansion. While the German Navy had envisioned completing the building program by 1948, Hitler ordered a six-year deadline. As originally approved, the Z Plan called for a battle fleet consisting of:

4	aircraft carriers (about 20,000 tons standard displacement)
10	large battleships (including the *Bismarck* and *Tirpitz*, and the battle cruisers *Gneisenau* and *Scharnhorst*)
12	smaller battleships (20,000 tons)
3	armored ships (so-called pocket battleships of 10,000 tons)
5	heavy cruisers (10,000 tons)
16	light cruisers (8,000 tons)
6	light cruisers (6,000 tons)
22	scout cruisers (5,000 tons)
68	destroyers
90	torpedo boats
27	long-range submarines
62	short-range submarines.

It is clear from these planned ship totals that Hitler and his high command did not believe that submarines could be a war-winning naval weapon. Even Dönitz later recalled,

After the First World War the British had written and published a great deal about a new British apparatus for the detection of a submerged submarine—the Asdic, which, it was claimed, could locate and pinpoint the position of a submarine at ranges of many thousands of yards. . . . The submarine, therefore, could be regarded, in British official opinion, as a more or less obsolete weapon, and it was not thought by the British that other nations would find it worth while to continue to build them. For these reasons there existed in the German Navy, too, in 1935, considerable doubts about the real value of the new U-boats.[33]

Dönitz had calculated that he would need about 300 ocean-going U-boats to prevail in an anti-shipping campaign against Britain. He argued passionately for increasing the number of submarines to be constructed, but Hitler—and even Admiral Raeder—remained unmoved. Only nine U-boats were completed in 1938 and 18 in 1939. Fifty-seven submarines were in commission when the war came in September 1939, only 46 of those ready for action. Of the combat-ready U-boats, only 22 were large enough for long-range ocean patrols; the others, 250-ton craft, could only be employed in the North Sea.[34] This small undersea force, operating in accordance with Karl Dönitz's strategic views, would soon be put to the test of combat against British anti-submarine forces.

First Confrontations in the Atlantic

On the evening of 17 September 1939, just two weeks after Great Britain and France declared war on Germany in response to the Nazi invasion of Poland, the German submarine *U-29* torpedoed and sank the large aircraft carrier *Courageous* some 350 n.miles west of Land's End, the westernmost tip of England. Converted from a World War I light battle cruiser in the 1920s, the *Courageous* was by 1939 outmoded and minimally effective, but she was the first Royal Navy warship lost in World War II—and one of the largest units in the fleet. Her sinking dealt a profound shock to both the national leadership and the British public.

Ironically, HMS *Courageous* and two other aircraft carriers, the *Ark Royal* and the *Hermes,* had been sent to sea with their accompanying escorts specifically to hunt submarines a week earlier. Faced with a gaggle of merchant traffic in the ocean areas west of the British Isles and a paucity of ASW escorts during the first weeks of the war, the Admiralty had deployed the three carriers as a stop-gap anti-submarine measure until sufficient escorts became available to allow the full introduction of convoying. Thus, on the fateful afternoon of the 17th, in response to the sinking of the British freighter *Kafiristan* by the German *U-53,* the *Courageous* sent a flight of Swordfish biplanes and two of her escorting destroyers to the scene. Meanwhile,

Korvettenkapitän Otto Schuhart, commanding the *U-29,* had spotted the carrier on the horizon and noting only two destroyers in company, attempted to close and attack this tempting target.

Schuhart was thwarted at first by the great disparity between his own speed—submerged—and that of the carrier, but when the *Courageous* turned into the wind to recover aircraft, she headed directly toward the unseen *U-29.* At a range of only 3,000 yards, Schuhart fired a fan of three torpedoes, two of which hit the carrier on the port side. Fifteen minutes later, the *Courageous* rolled over and sank, taking with her 519 of her 1,260-man crew.

Only three days earlier, the *Ark Royal,* Britain's newest carrier, had narrowly escaped a similar fate when the *U-39* happened upon her while she was launching aircraft. After firing three torpedoes, which barely missed—from either bad aim, technical malfunctions, or both—the *U-39* was detected and attacked successfully by three accompanying destroyers, becoming the first U-boat to be sunk in World War II. In view of this incident and the loss of the *Courageous,* the Admiralty quickly withdrew its remaining carriers from ASW missions.

Initial Moves and Counter-moves

World War II began in Europe in the early hours of 1 September 1939, when Hitler unleashed the

Wehrmacht for his long-anticipated attack on Poland. The leadership of the German Navy had hoped to delay the onset of a general war until at least 1945, by which time its planned building programs would have redressed much of the Navy's significant inferiority to the navies of Britain and France of ten to one in major surface ships. In late 1939, the German surface fleet could hope for little more than hit-and-run commerce raiding on the high seas and operations to maintain command of the Baltic to support the Polish campaign and protect shipments of raw materials from Scandinavia. Thus, when Britain and France declared war on 3 September, the brunt of a naval response fell largely on the German submarine force.

Of the 57 submarines in commission at the beginning of the war, 27 were medium-to-large, ocean-going Types IA, VII, VIIB, and IX, and the remainder smaller Types II, IIB, and IIC, known as "ducks" and originally intended for training and coastal missions (see Table 7-1).

In anticipation of the attack on Poland, Navy headquarters on 19 August had ordered the submarine flotilla and the "pocket battleships" *Graf Spee* and *Deutschland* to deploy secretly to their war stations. Initially, *Kapitän* Karl Dönitz, commander of the German submarine force, had planned to retain approximately half of his combat-ready submarines in the Baltic for operations against the Poles and possibly the Russians. However, the signing of the Nazi-Soviet non-aggression pact on 23 August made possible the transfer of most of the Baltic boats westward into the North Sea and North Atlantic just before the conflict began. Thus, Dönitz's initial

Table 7-1. German Submarine Classes, September 1939

	Type IA	Type IIB*	Type VIIA	Type VIIB	Type IXA
In service	2	18**	10	8	7
Operational	Apr 1936	July 1937	Aug 1936	June 1938	Aug 1938
Displacement					
surface	862 tons	279 tons	626 tons	753 tons	1,032 tons
submerged	983 tons	329 tons	745 tons	857 tons	1,153 tons
Length	237½ ft	140 ft	217½ ft	218 ft	251 ft
Shafts	2	2	2	2	2
Range (surface)					
@12 knots	6,700 n.mi	1,800 n.mi	4,300 n.mi	6,500 n.mi	8,100 n.mi
Torpedo tubes	4 B+2 S	3 B	4 B + 1 S	4 B + 1 S	4 B + 2 S
Torpedoes	14	6	11	14	22
Guns	1 x 105-mm	1 x 20-mm	1 x 88-mm	1 x 88-mm	1 x 105-mm
	1 x 20-mm	1 x 20-mm	1 x 20-mm	1 x 37-mm	1 x 20-mm

* The Type IIs were slightly smaller, and the Type IICs slightly larger.
** Additionally, there were six Type IIs and six Type IICs in commission.

Source: The definitive data source for German submarines is Eberhard Rossler, *The U-boat: The evolution and technical history of German submarines* (Annapolis, Md.: Naval Institute Press, 1981); this table is derived from pp. 334–337.

deployment placed 18 ocean-going boats in the North Atlantic west of the British Isles, in the Bay of Biscay, and southward toward Gibraltar. An additional 18 U-boats—17 "ducks" and a Type VII, the *U-36*—were in the North Sea, with two patrolling off the coast of Scotland, five assigned to lay mines in British and French ports, and the remainder in defensive patrols guarding the sea approaches to Germany.[1]

With war approaching rapidly in the last days of August 1939, the British also were completing preparations. On the 26th, a week before the declaration of war on Germany, the Admiralty brought the British merchant marine under naval control, requiring arrivals, departures, and routing to conform to Royal Navy directives. In contrast to the three-year delay in World War I, merchant convoys were instituted immediately at the outbreak of war. As Winston Churchill—newly invited into the government to again serve as First Lord of the Admiralty—later wrote,

> The organization of convoy had been fully prepared, and shipowners had already been brought into regular consultation on matters of defense which affected them. Furthermore, instructions had been prepared for the guidance of shipmasters in the many unfamiliar tasks which would inevitably fall upon them in war, and special signaling as well as other equipment had been provided to enable them to take their place in convoy.[2]

By 8 September, two main routes were in operation: for westbound ships, from Liverpool and from the Thames Estuary, and another route for coastal traffic between the Thames and the Firth of Forth. Other outbound ships were corralled at Plymouth and Milford Haven to await the organization of westbound transatlantic convoys, and by the 14th and 16th, respectively, the first homeward-bound convoys had from departed Freetown, Sierra Leone, and Halifax, Nova Scotia. Additionally, the Admiralty instituted an emergency program to arm merchant ships with deck guns, and in the first three months of the war a thousand ships were fitted out, largely with weapons retained from World War I.

Simultaneously, Admiral Martin Dunbar-Nasmith, a celebrated World War I submarine officer then serving as the Commander-in-Chief, Plymouth, was assigned as Commander-in-Chief, Western Approaches, heading a new operational command with responsibility for the safety of British shipping in the ocean area stretching west from the British Isles as far as the longitude of Iceland. Known informally as the Western Approaches Command, Dunbar-Nasmith's combined operations headquarters, initially at Plymouth, coordinated all convoy movements and the assignment of escorts and air cover, in cooperation with Royal Air Force (RAF) Coastal Command. The primary source of U-boat locating information was the Admiralty's Operational Intelligence Centre (OIC) in London, in which the Axis Submarine Plot (also known as the Submarine Tracking Room) was a key activity. By maintaining an "all-source" picture of the best position estimates of U-boats at sea, based on tactical reporting, high-frequency radio direction-finding, and the latest cryptographic information, the OIC provided the Western Approaches Command with the intelligence needed for the optimal timing and routing of convoys and allocation of ASW resources across the entire western Atlantic.

In another return to earlier practice, the Admiralty reestablished a network of land-based radio direction-finding stations in England and Scotland—initially six at high frequency and four at medium frequency—to detect and locate German submarine transmissions in the waters around the United Kingdom and the eastern Atlantic. A 24-hour watch was begun in July 1939, and under good conditions the network could provide position estimates with 25-mile accuracy.

The greatest challenge created by the introduction of the convoy system was providing enough escort ships of all kinds, both coastal and ocean-going. Although the Royal Navy had more than 180 destroyers in commission in September 1939, most were assigned to the Home, Channel, and Mediterranean Fleets or dispersed among a myriad of foreign stations. A dozen of the latter were ordered home from the Mediterranean and the Far East and arrived within a month. Additionally, in 1938 and early 1939, 15 destroyers of the older V and W classes had been converted to escort ships by removing their torpedo tubes and fitting asdic and additional depth charge capabilities.[3] However, the experience of World War I had shown that destroyers were poorly suited for the escort mission, where their high speed and relatively heavy gun armament found little use; also, their operating and maintenance costs were high. Actually required were large numbers of small, cheap, minimally manned ships, with sufficient weapons, sea-keeping ability, and speed to protect convoys and drive off attacking submarines—and little more. As described above, the Royal Navy had begun addressing this need in the late 1930s, but virtually none of the new escorts were in service by the beginning of the conflict.

The Royal Navy immediately instituted a blockade of Germany when war began, establishing a patrol line of eight old light cruisers from Iceland to the coast of Norway to intercept German merchant ships or neutrals carrying war materials bound for northern German ports. Even earlier, on 23 August,

the RAF Coastal Command—responsible for air operations off the coasts of Great Britain—had begun flying patrols over the North Sea in search of German warships or submarines outbound for the Atlantic. With the declaration of war on 3 September, Coastal Command aircraft began carrying live bombs with orders to attack any U-boat on sight, but they had no effective relationships with the relevant naval commands, no procedures for communicating with ASW ships, no crews adequately trained for open-ocean operations, and no suitable ASW weapons. In the event, the *Graf Spee, Deutschland,* and Dönitz's first submarines had already departed.

Simultaneously, the Admiralty OIC, which had been fully functional for several years and linked closely with both the surface-ship plot and the submarine tracking room, guided the first offensive moves against the U-boats deployed in the eastern Atlantic and the North Sea. These opening gambits included the deployment of aircraft carriers and their escorts as hunter-killer groups, which led to the tragic loss of the *Courageous* and the narrow escape of the *Ark Royal.*

Because he still hoped to avoid all-out war with Britain and France, Hitler had sent his pocket battleships and submarines to sea under tight restrictions.[4] In particular, for both practical and political reasons, he ordered the U-boats to avoid attacking enemy naval units and rather to concentrate on merchant shipping. Moreover, German submarines were to operate in strict accordance with the "stop and search" protocols of the London Naval Conference, which Germany had accepted in 1936. The only ships that could be sunk without warning were troopships, ships in convoy or otherwise escorted, and those taking an active part in enemy actions. These rules were honored in the breach on the very first day of the war.

At 4:30 p.m. on 3 September, *Kapitänleutnant* Fritz Julius Lemp in the *U-30* spotted a lone ship in his patrol area, about 300 miles northwest of Ireland. When Lemp maneuvered for a better view in the failing light, he saw through his periscope a large merchantman that appeared to be blacked out and zig-zagging. He also saw what seemed to be deck guns on board. Concluding that the ship was likely an armed merchant cruiser—and thus a warship that could be attacked without warning—he fired two torpedoes at the target, one of which scored a direct hit.

After diving deep to avoid a possible circular run by his other torpedo, Lemp surfaced near the listing ship, only to discover that he had torpedoed the well-known British passenger liner *Athenia*, headed for Canada with civilian passengers fleeing the war zone. Neither breaking radio silence to report what had happened nor offering assistance to the *Athenia*'s passengers and crew, the *U-30* quickly left the scene. Fortunately, the stricken ship stayed afloat long enough for help to arrive. Still, 118 lives were lost, 28 of them U.S. citizens. Despite significantly less mortality, the torpedoing of the *Athenia* was immediately compared with the sinking of the *Lusitania* in World War I, causing widespread revulsion around the world at what seemed to be the initiation of unrestricted submarine warfare at the very start of the conflict. Meanwhile, Lemp's radio silence denied German headquarters his version of events, and Germany was forced into a series of lies and evasions about the episode, at first denying that any U-boat could possibly have sunk the *Athenia* and later even accusing the *British* of having destroyed the liner in an attempt to inflame world opinion against Germany.

Although Lemp was never disciplined for his error, the *Athenia* incident moved Hitler to tighten his submarine restrictions further by forbidding attacks on *any* passenger ships, even in convoy. The resulting ambiguity in the rules of engagement severely hampered the German submarine campaign for the first several months of the war. Nonetheless, German submarine attacks—and British efforts to thwart them—gathered momentum. Two days after the attack on the *Athenia*, the *U-47*, under *Kapitänleutnant* Günther Prien, encountered the small British freighter *Bosnia* in the North Atlantic, several hundred miles west of Bordeaux. Prien surfaced and attempted to stop the ship with a warning shot from his 88-mm deck gun, but the *Bosnia* turned and tried to escape. After the ship was hit three times by shellfire from the *U-47*, the *Bosnia*'s crew abandoned her, capsizing a lifeboat in the process. Prien rescued the survivors, turned them over to a passing Norwegian merchantman, and sank the *Bosnia* with a single torpedo. She was the first freighter lost in what Churchill would later label the Battle of the Atlantic. Later that same day, 5 September, the *U-48* sank the British freighter *Royal Sceptre*, and subsequently, two British merchant ships were lost on the 6th, one each on the 7th and 8th, and two on the 11th. One of the those lost on 6 September, the *Manaar*, sunk west of Lisbon, was armed with a 100-mm deck gun and before she was torpedoed by the *U-38* became the first British merchantman to fire in self-defense against a U-boat.

On 8 September, *Kapitän* Dönitz ordered home ten of the 18 submarines in the North Atlantic—most of which had deployed on 19 August—to be rearmed and replenished for a second round of sorties. Except for the *U-39*, which had been lost in her unsuccessful attack on the *Ark Royal*, the returning boats arrived in Germany from 15 to 17 September. They had sunk a total of eight ships, but seven of the ten U-boats recalled had been scoreless. The remainder of the 21 ocean-going submarines deployed in Dönitz's "first wave" returned to base from 26 to 30 September. Altogether, Germany's first North Atlantic submarine offensive destroyed 39 ships totaling nearly 190,000 tons, including the *Courageous* and five large tankers. However, a second submarine was lost on 20 September in the northern North Sea when the *U-27* came across a line of Royal Navy destroyers while returning to Germany and attacked them with a salvo of three torpedoes. Two of these exploded prematurely and alerted the destroyer *Fortune,* which turned to engage. In a series of skillfully executed asdic-guided, depth-charge attacks, the *Fortune* forced the *U-27* to the surface, where she was scuttled without loss of life.

During the month of September, the *U-36* and a total of 23 different "ducks," several of them making two patrols, had been "working" the North Sea. Because of the restrictive rules of engagement and the heavy presence of neutral shipping, only two small freighters had been accosted and destroyed in the first three weeks of the month. This led Dönitz and Raeder to appeal to Hitler for a relaxation of the stop-and-search rules, which was granted on 24 September. An earlier prohibition on sinking French merchantmen was also removed, and any ship attempting to radio a submarine sighting could be sunk without inspection. Also, any merchant ship carrying less than 120 passengers was liable to destruction under the auspices of the existing submarine protocols. With these new rules, the North Sea U-boats quickly sank or captured 13 small ships totaling nearly 17,000 tons, and an additional five ships of nearly that same tonnage were destroyed in submarine-laid minefields.

In addition to organizing a convoy system and forming ASW hunter-killer groups around their few aircraft carriers, the British adopted several other defensive measures. In mid-September, with French cooperation, they planted a line of 3,000 moored mines across the English Channel from Dover to Cape Gris-Nez, and by the end of the month, this field had been augmented by an additional 3,600 controlled mines associated with underwater listening arrays.[5] The rationale for the initial mining campaign was the same as in World War I: to deny German submarines easy access to the approaches to British ports from their bases in the Helgoland Bight. The third U-boat casualty of the war—the *U-12*—was snared in the English Channel minefield on 8 October and lost with all hands.

The RAF Coastal Command entered the war with approximately 300 aircraft in 19 squadrons, more than half of which flew the Avro Anson, a twin-engine maritime reconnaissance airplane, already nearing obsolescence.[6] As a step-child within the RAF, the Coastal Command's only up-to-date aircraft were one squadron of Lockheed Hudson reconnaissance bombers and two squadrons of large Short Sunderland flying boats. Additionally, there were four squadrons of older flying boats and two squadrons of Vickers Vildebeest biplane torpedo bombers. Trained crews were available for only half of these aircraft, and they were only minimally practiced in spotting and attacking submarines from the air. "Light-cased" bombs—100, 250, and 500 pounds—were the principal ASW weapons, fitted with both impact and delay fuzes. Because existing RAF bombsights were ineffective against small surface targets, submarines could only be engaged by attacking at low altitude and loosing sticks of bombs largely by eye. Moreover, even the 500-pound bomb was ineffective in holing a U-boat unless it detonated within eight feet of the hull. (Coastal Command also had modified depth charges, but their aerodynamic instability made accurate placement nearly impossible.) Thus, Coastal Command could do little more initially than revert to the "Scarecrow" tactics of World War I.

The Royal Navy's Fleet Air Arm, newly re-established under the Navy in 1937, provided the aircraft for the six operational carriers. It had 25 Blackburn Skua monoplane fighter/dive bombers marginally suitable for ASW missions, plus 150 Fairey Swordfish biplanes—nominally reconnaissance aircraft and torpedo bombers.[7] Because the Navy was so confident in the ability of asdic-equipped destroyers to handle the submarine threat, ASW training in the Fleet Air Arm was minimal. Also, despite a rapid program of engineering development, no operational aircraft in either Coastal Command or the Fleet Air Arm carried air-to-surface radar at the beginning of the war.

In light of these limitations, it was not surprising that the first British air attacks on German submarines bordered on farce. On 5 September, the third day of the war, a Coastal Command Anson sighted a surfaced submarine off the west coast of Scotland and immediately attacked from low level with two 100-pound bombs. The ill-designed bombs skipped off the surface of the water and exploded beneath the aircraft, perforating its fuel tanks. Forced to ditch the aircraft by the resulting loss of fuel, the crew was quickly rescued—only to discover that the submarine they had attacked was HMS *Seahorse,* luckily undamaged. In the war's first air attack on a *real* German U-boat, much the same happened. On 14 September, the *Ark Royal* launched three Skuas in response to a distress call from the freighter *Fanad Head,* which had been stopped by the *U-30* northwest of Ireland. The arrival of the aircraft prompted the submarine to abandon her quarry and crash-dive, but not before the Skuas had loosed salvoes of bombs at the disappearing U-boat. Once again, several bombs ricocheted back into the air and exploded, mortally damaging two of the aircraft, which promptly ditched. The *U-30* returned to the surface, rescued the four British aircrew (making them prisoners of war), completed sinking the *Fanad Head,* and safely departed the area despite subsequent follow-on attacks by *Ark Royal* aircraft. And only a day later a second Anson was damaged by its own bombs after unsuccessfully attacking another U-boat. It would be mid-March 1940 before a British aircraft finally sank a German submarine.

During the uneventful period on land known as the "phony war"—or *Sitzkrieg*—that followed the fall of Poland, the war at sea ramped up steadily. On the night of 13 October the German submarine *U-47,* under Prien, successfully threaded her way through the tortuous approaches to the British fleet anchorage at Scapa Flow, in the Orkney Islands north of Scotland, skillfully avoided a series of blockships and other submarine obstacles, and just before midnight encountered the old battleship *Royal Oak* only 3,500 yards distant. Prien hit the *Royal Oak* with a total of four torpedoes. Within minutes she rolled over and sank with the loss of more than two-thirds of her 1,200-man crew. Prien and the *U-47* escaped back to sea without even being detected by British ASW patrols.

The torpedoing of the *Royal Oak* inside a fleet anchorage hitherto considered impregnable not only shocked and humiliated the Royal Navy but, strategically, forced the Home Fleet commander to order his ships out of Scapa Flow and disperse to more distant bases on the northwest coast of Scotland and in the Shetland Islands, mirroring a similar incident in World War I (see Chapter 2).

Wolf Packs and Convoys

In sending a second wave of U-boats to sea in early October, Dönitz—newly appointed to *Konteradmiral*—made his first "wolf-pack" deployment against Allied convoys. By then the North Atlantic convoy system was fully up and running, with regularly

Hail to the heroes: The *U-47* passes the light cruiser *Emden* as the U-boat returns in triumph to Wilhelmshaven on 17 October 1939, after sinking the British dreadnought *Royal Oak* in Scapa Flow. *Kapitänleutnant* Günther Prien is on the conning tower of the Type VIIB U-boat. *U.S. Navy*

scheduled formations—both "fast" and "slow"—churning both ways between Halifax and the western approaches to the British Isles. The eastbound convoys from Halifax were denoted HX, with westbound counterparts (of ships largely in ballast) designated OA or OB, depending on whether they departed the English Channel or the Irish Sea, respectively.[8] Initially, when the German threat was limited largely to the waters west of Great Britain, convoy escorts and air cover were provided from the British Isles out to 15 degrees west longitude, about 180 n.miles west of Ireland, and down to the middle of the Bay of Biscay (for convoys to and from Gibraltar, denoted OG and HG). Convoys from Halifax were escorted a similar distance eastward by the few units of the Royal Canadian Navy and Air Force. While German surface raiders remained a threat,

important eastbound convoys were at first escorted all the way across the Atlantic by armed merchant cruisers or Royal Navy battleships, aircraft carriers, and cruisers with their destroyer screens. However, assigning major fleet units to escort duty was a huge waste of resources, and moreover, the accompanying destroyers could barely make it across the Atlantic without refueling. Therefore, convoys were more often unescorted for the mid-ocean portion of their journey, approximately 80 percent of the distance between Canada and the British Isles. Arrivals and departures were scheduled to facilitate the same escorts exchanging outbound and inbound convoys at both ends, but often these rendezvous were thwarted by weather and poor navigation.

Notwithstanding these vulnerabilities, Admiral Dönitz had only six U-boats to commit—three

Type VIIBs and three Type IXs. The first five left Germany the first week of October, heading north around Scotland and Ireland. The sixth, the *U-40,* was delayed in departing and to catch up with her sisters chose the English Channel route, where she ran afoul of the cross-Channel minefield and was destroyed on 13 October.[9] That same day, another of the group, the *U-42,* was attacked and sunk by a pair of Royal Navy destroyers that had responded to a call for help from an armed British convoy straggler after the submarine attempted a deck-gun attack.

Unbeknownst to Dönitz, two of his first six "wolves" had already succumbed before engaging a convoy. However, he had good location information on several convoys in the area. The German Navy's codebreaking organization—the Beobachtungsdienst (or B-dienst)—had broken the Royal Navy's non-machine operational code as early as 1935, and it could also read messages sent in the relatively less secure merchant marine code. At the beginning of the war, B-dienst could usually predict the movements of most Royal Navy capital ships and large formations, as well as determining convoy routing and rendezvous points for the escorts. On this basis, Dönitz ordered his wolf pack to attack KJF-3, a large English/French convoy inbound from Kingston, Jamaica. Of the four remaining U-boats, only two found the convoy immediately, and although they sank four ships in a coordinated attack, one of the pair, the *U-45,* was destroyed by escorts. The next morning, after the convoy had dispersed, one of the two other submarines, the *U-37,* sank a merchant straggler, whereas the remaining U-boat never found a target. Subsequently, Dönitz ordered the surviving members to concentrate against a nearby convoy inbound from Gibraltar, and two of the remaining boats succeeded in sinking three ships of that group. All told, however, only seven Allied ships had been sunk at a cost of three U-boats, and one of the Allied losses was the 10,000-ton French liner, *Bretagne,* which should not have been targeted under the existing rules of engagement.

Thus, the first wolf-pack deployment was somewhat less than the success that Dönitz claimed on the basis of initial, fragmentary reports: No more than two submarines had managed to attack together, contact information had been shared only sporadically, and in general, overall coordination had been poor. There were significant lessons that would be put to good use later, but for the immediate future, a shortage of U-boats prevented the wolf-pack idea from being tried again until well into 1940.

By the beginning of that year, after four months of war, 147 Allied and neutral merchant ships, totaling nearly 510,000 gross tons, had been lost to either direct submarine attack or submarine-laid mines.[10] On the other side of the ledger, nine U-boats had been destroyed by enemy action: five by surface combatants, three by mines, and one by the British submarine *Salmon,* which found the *U-36* on the surface during a North Sea patrol and torpedoed her, leaving no survivors, on 4 December 1939.[11] During this same period, the Royal Navy, which started the war with 58 submarines, lost only one, in a fratricide incident on 10 September, when HMS *Oxley* was mistaken for an enemy by her sister submarine *Triton* and torpedoed. She had strayed out of her patrol area off the coast of Norway; there were two survivors. Early in the new year, however, three British boats—the *Undine* and *Seahorse* on 7 January, and the *Starfish* on the 9th—were lost to depth-charge attacks by German minesweepers in the Helgoland Bight.

During the first two months of 1940 the contest at sea devolved into a low-grade war of attrition in

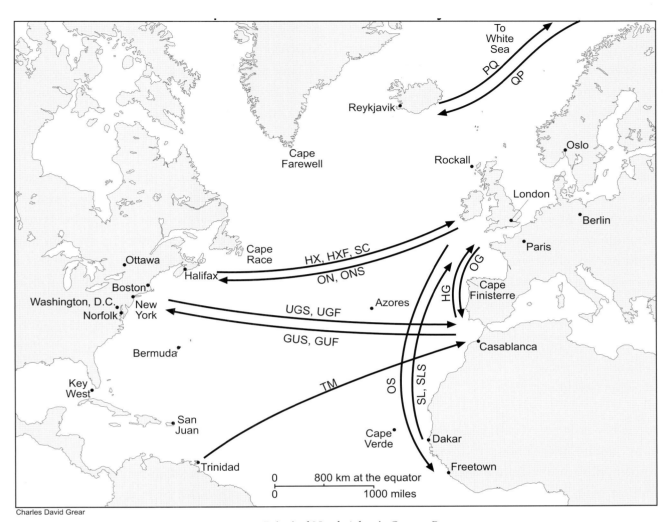

Map 3. Principal North Atlantic Convoy Routes

which neither side obtained a clear advantage. In January and February, now-*Konteradmiral* Dönitz sent 11 of his ocean-going U-boats into the Atlantic and dispatched seven more on mining missions around the British Isles, including forays into Loch Ewe, Falmouth, Portsmouth, the Bristol Channel, Liverpool, and the Firth of Clyde.[12] Of these 18 submarines, five were lost, including the *U-33* in the Clyde on 12 February, after she was detected passively on a hydrophone towed by the minesweeper *Gleaner* and then acquired on asdic for a successful depth charge attack. The submarine was forced to the surface, where she was scuttled. Earlier, on 30

January, the *U-55* had been sunk after an attack on a convoy in the Western Approaches, the victim of a relentless pursuit by a Royal Navy sloop and two destroyers, plus a French destroyer and a Coastal Command Sunderland flying boat, which bombed and strafed the submarine in the end game. This was the first submarine kill in which an Allied aircraft was given partial credit. (Not until mid-March 1940 was a U-boat destroyed entirely from the air—the *U-31*, attacked and sunk by an RAF Bomber Command Blenheim in the Helgoland Bight on the 11th.)

During January and February 1940, U-boat torpedoes and submarine-laid mines sank 103 merchants, totaling just over 345,000 tons of shipping. These were serious losses, but they were more than offset by new construction in British yards and ships bought, captured, or chartered from foreign sources.[13] Nonetheless, British imports fell by a quarter, largely from the inefficiencies of the convoy system. Although this caused deprivation and shortages in some areas, there was, as yet, no imminent threat to Britain's survival from the U-boat campaign. With the German Navy unable to keep on average more than ten ocean-going U-boats at sea during the early months of the war and the Royal Navy's growing proficiency in countering them with asdic and depth charges, there was no clear-cut winner in these early phases of the Battle of the Atlantic. Moreover, German submarine losses through February 1940 totaled 17 U-boats—30 percent of the force—and new construction totaled only eight.

At the beginning of March, Hitler ordered all German submarines withdrawn from the Atlantic anti-shipping campaign to make them available to support his planned invasion of neutral Norway, which took place on 9 April, neatly forestalling a similar British incursion that had already moved beyond the planning stage. In lightning-swift seaborne assaults, German troops seized four Norwegian ports, from Kristiansand in the south to Narvik in the north, and quickly invested the capital of Oslo with a detachment of airborne infantry.[14] Forty-two of the 49 U-boats then in commission were assigned to the operation, both to interdict potential Allied countermoves in the North and Norwegian Seas and to attack British ships responding from Scapa Flow. British-French troops landed at Aandelsnes, Namsos, and Narvik between 14 and 18 April, but the Germans handily defeated both the Norwegian Army and the Allied relief force and soon occupied the entire country except for a small enclave around Narvik, which was evacuated by the French and British on 7 June.

This stunning success was mitigated by grave losses to German surface forces. In the initial attack, the heavy cruiser *Blücher* was sunk near Oslo by shore-fired torpedoes, and subsequently, two light cruisers were lost—the *Königsberg,* to British aircraft near Bergen, and the *Karlsruhe,* torpedoed by the British submarine *Truant* off Kristianstad. In sharp surface actions in the fjords near Narvik, where the British battleship *Warspite* also joined the fray, ten Kriegsmarine destroyers were sunk for a loss of two British. Additionally, British submarines and the Polish submarine *Orzel* sank six merchant ships in the German supply train. In response to these reverses and the threat of Allied landings, Hitler ordered as many U-boats as possible to converge on Narvik, leading to multiple torpedo attacks on British surface ships and ASW counterattacks in the constricted inlets of the Norwegian coastline.

Repeatedly, in these often-confusing melées, the Germans were thwarted by faulty torpedo performance, which had already been suspected in earlier incidents. On 13 April, for example, the *U-48* maneuvered to within point-blank range of the *Warspite* and launched three torpedoes without scoring a hit. A myriad of similar incidents caused growing alarm among the German submariners and their high command. Thus, despite sinking over 32,000 tons of merchant shipping, the only enemy combatant destroyed by a U-boat during the Norwegian campaign was the British submarine *Thistle,* torpedoed by the "duck" *U-4* near Stavanger on 10 April. In contrast, the Germans lost five U-boats—three to destroyers, one to a mine in the Helgoland Bight, and one to bombs from a Swordfish floatplane from the *Warspite* near Narvik, only the second air kill of the war.

All told, the near-total dedication of available U-boats to the Norwegian campaign was a dismal failure, and the meager gains they achieved were heavily outweighed by both their losses and the opportunity costs of suspending the anti-shipping campaign in the North Atlantic. It had become clear that submarines were relatively ineffective against major warships protected by both asdic-equipped destroyers and supporting aircraft, particularly in constricted, coastal waters, and thus that commerce raiding was the most efficient use of the U-boat arm.

Admiral Dönitz and his cohort, in turn, blamed defective torpedoes for the debacle and immediately commenced a crash test program to identify and correct torpedo shortcomings. Ultimately, it would emerge that faulty depth-keeping and design defects in both the contact and magnetic-influence exploders were to blame—eerily prefiguring similar torpedo problems faced by American submariners in the Pacific two years later.

Technology at War

During the first months of the war, the British redoubled their efforts in two areas that would have far-reaching effects on the ASW struggle to come. In 1936 a British team under Dr. Edward Bowen had begun investigating the feasibility of a radar system small enough to be installed in an aircraft.[15] In one of their earliest experiments, an obsolescent bomber was fitted with a modified television receiver to detect reflections from a target aircraft illuminated by radar signals from a ground-based transmitter, in a bi-static geometry. A year later this success was transformed into an airborne radar prototype operating at 240 MHz with a power of one kilowatt. The corresponding wavelength—1.3 meters—allowed the use of half-wave antenna elements on the order of only two feet, quite suitable for installation on aircraft. This rudimentary airborne radar was capable of detecting large ships at a distance of approximately 5 n.miles.

Despite having lower priority than the parallel development of ground-based, early-warning radars, devising antenna arrays for airborne counterparts received significant effort.[16] By early 1939 the program had settled on a configuration that used a radar transmitter in the aircraft nose, directed forward in a fan-shaped beam, with forward-looking receiver arrays under each wing. The direction of a target was determined by turning the aircraft until the received echoes appeared at equal amplitude on the two receivers, and a lateral sweep width of about five miles could be achieved. The November 1939 trials of this system, known as the ASV Mark I (ASV indicating Air-to-Surface-Vessel) included target runs against surfaced submarines, where it was found that from an altitude of 3,000 feet a submarine could be detected at as much as 5 n.miles away but disappeared into the sea clutter at ranges less than 4 n.miles; at a 200-foot altitude, the corresponding maximum and minimum ranges were 3 n.miles and half a n.mile, respectively.[17] Although these results against submarines were little better than what could be obtained with daylight visual observations, the ASV Mark I (or ASV-I) was useful for finding large surface ships and convoys, and as a navigation aid it could "see" a coastline at 20 miles. Thus, the ASV-I entered production immediately, and the Royal Air Force ordered 200 sets. By mid-January 1940, 12 Hudson coastal patrol bombers had been equipped with the device.

The obvious shortcomings of the ASV-I stimulated an emergency program to develop the improved ASV-II, which went into production in spring 1940, with 4,000 sets ordered. Operating at 176 MHz, the ASV-II had a more powerful transmitter, a more sensitive receiver, and an elaborate antenna system that permitted two modes of operation—one looking out alternately to either side, perpendicular to the heading of the aircraft, and the other forward-looking, for homing in on any targets detected by the side-looking array. At 2,000 feet the ASV-II could detect a surfaced submarine broadside at 18 n.miles and bow-on at 11 n.miles; at 1,000 feet, these ranges were roughly halved. In the forward-looking mode, the minimum range was approximately three-quarters of a mile before the target was lost in sea clutter. Thus, compared to the five-mile-wide area searchable by the ASV-I, the later radar could sweep an area up to 40 miles wide. Amid great expectations, the first ASV-II radar sets entered operation in August 1940. By December, in an early pre-war instance of trans-Atlantic technical cooperation, the first radar fitted in a U.S. aircraft was a British ASV-II, installed on a U.S. Navy PBY at the Anacostia Naval Air Station in Washington, D.C.

Building on their World War I experience, the British also accelerated their efforts in cryptanalysis. The focus of this activity was Bletchley Park, a former private estate in Buckinghamshire that served as the successor to the earlier Room 40 and to which the British government assigned a talented staff of engineers, scientists, mathematicians, and linguists.[18]

In the late 1920s all three of the German armed services had adopted a more sophisticated variant of the "Enigma" coding machine as their primary cipher. Similar in appearance to a typewriter, the Enigma had been developed for commercial use. It had an alphabetic keyboard connected to an output array of lighted indicators (one for each letter) through a constantly shifting wiring configuration implemented by interchangeable, electro-mechanical

rotors. Each successive plain-text letter generated a new electrical path from the keyboard to the output array, essentially creating a new codebook for each input. The Enigma machine code was considered highly secure by its German users. However, a small team of Polish cryptographers had begun a concerted attack on the German Enigma codes in late 1932, and with an extraordinary combination of mathematical insight and tedious labor they deduced the internal wiring of the machine.[19] This allowed them to decipher a large number of German messages concurrently until 1938, when changes in German protocols and the introduction of additional rotors ended their access. Subsequently, faced with the imminent German invasion in August 1939, the Polish relinquished everything they had learned about Enigma to British and French intelligence.

With this information, and applying two Polish techniques—one that used an electro-mechanical calculating device known as a "bombe," and the other a large multiplicity of perforated paper sheets that could be overlaid on coded material to reveal hidden patterns—Bletchley Park intensified its own work on Enigma. By December 1939, the British succeeded in breaking the Enigma code for one secondary German communication net for a single day during the preceding October, and after January 1940 they were able to read the messages on the German Air Force's "Red" net quite fluently. Unfortunately, the German Navy's Enigma variant was a much harder nut to crack. Naval communications security was significantly more stringent than that of the other German armed forces, and, additionally, naval code clerks were provided with a set of eight different rotors to select from in setting up their machines. Thus, no significant progress could be made in cracking the naval code until mid-1941, when the British completed a much larger bombe under the direction of the brilliant mathematician Alan Turing.[20]

Radar and codebreaking would become two of the most critical factors in the eventual Allied victory in the Battle of the Atlantic.

France Subdued and ASW Implications

On 10 May 1940, the stalemate on the European continent ended abruptly when Germany unleashed another *blitzkrieg* to defeat France in a single sweeping campaign. Attacking through neutral Belgium and Holland, German armies drove quickly into northwestern France, brushed aside the British Expeditionary Force (deployed in late 1939), and turned south toward Paris. Employing a hastily assembled armada of civilian and military shipping, the British narrowly succeeded in evacuating the bulk of their surviving forces and some French troops through the port of Dunkirk between 26 May and 2 June. A week later, in reaction to the rapid success of the German onslaught—and belatedly honoring the terms of its military alliance with Germany (the "Pact of Steel" of May 1939)—Italy declared war on France and Great Britain and launched a half-hearted attack on southern France from the east. Paris fell to German troops on 14 June, and on the 22nd the French accepted the German surrender terms, leaving three-fifths of France under German occupation, including the north and west of the country and, most significantly, the entire Atlantic coastline.

Even before the fall of France, Admiral Dönitz had renewed the campaign against Allied shipping by deploying four submarines to the Atlantic in May and 16 in June. At the time, he had only two dozen ocean-going U-boats in commission, three less than at the beginning of the war. But with heavy Royal Navy commitments in home waters because of the battle for France, Atlantic convoy escorts were cut back, and the Germans took full advantage of the opportunity. In June alone, 66 Allied and neutral merchant ships were sunk for a total of just over 375,000 tons, at the cost of only one U-boat sunk.

Just as the Germans had been quick to exploit their occupation of Belgium in World War I to establish submarine bases on the North Sea coast, the German Navy seized on the fall of France to establish a chain of similar bases on the Bay of Biscay. Within a week of the armistice, Admiral Dönitz had surveyed port facilities along the western coast of France and chosen five sites as U-boat bases: Brest, Lorient, St. Nazaire, La Pallice (near La Rochelle), and Bordeaux. Almost immediately, equipment, supplies, and personnel were shipped across France from Germany, and the four ocean-going U-boats then operating in the Atlantic were ordered to return not to Germany but to Lorient, with their arrivals scattered between 7 and 21 July. On 13 July, the *U-30* under Fritz Lemp—who had earlier sunk the *Athenia*—became the first German submarine to sortie from a French port (Lorient) directly into the Atlantic, and although equipment problems forced Lemp to abandon his patrol after sinking only one small merchantman, the occasion marked a significant watershed in the German U-boat campaign and the Allied anti-submarine response.

On 24 May 1940, in support of the battle for France, Hitler had agreed to a policy of unrestricted submarine warfare in the waters surrounding Britain and France. Moreover, in July, during the preliminary phases of the Battle of Britain for control of the air over England and Scotland, long-range German aircraft increased their attacks on convoys to the west of Britain.[21] These factors, plus the growing threat posed by the new German bases on the Bay of Biscay, forced the Admiralty to re-route convoys along more northerly routes, away from the western and southwest approaches to Britain, thus lengthening Atlantic transit times. Simultaneously, British air and surface escort coverage was extended to 17 degrees west longitude, nearly 350 n.miles west of the British Isles, with in- and outbound rendezvous points in the vicinity of the Rockall Bank, a remote islet and shoal west of northern Scotland. Although these new routes were roughly equidistant from U-boat bases on the North Sea and those on the French Atlantic coast, submarines from the latter were at least spared the harrowing transit through the North Sea, where they were required to run submerged to avoid daylight attacks. Also, the French bases provided the opportunity for "round-robin" patrols, which departed from either Germany or western France and terminated at the other bases for refit and re-supply. Additional U-boats, including seven of the smaller and shorter-range "ducks," began operating from ports in occupied Norway such as Bergen, Narvik, and Trondheim.

But even before the advantages of French and Norwegian basing began to tell, the U-boats entered into a "happy time" in which Allied sinkings mounted sharply. In June, July, and August 1940, German submarines sank more than 160 merchant ships (including 17 tankers), totaling well over three-quarters of a million tons of shipping, to say nothing of the military value of the cargoes sent to the bottom. Then, in mid-August, Hitler extended unrestricted submarine warfare to 20 degrees west longitude, and Admiral Dönitz redoubled his use of wolf-pack tactics to harry the Allied convoys. Cued by locating information developed by B-dienst, Dönitz positioned his patrolling U-boats to ferret out transiting convoys, with orders to track and report the details of potential quarry, without attacking. With this information, Dönitz was able to radio nearby boats to concentrate on the convoy

for a series of coordinated night attacks. Normally, his submarines would shadow the convoys by day on the surface—where asdic was ineffective—and attack after dark, when their own low silhouettes were virtually invisible, even to those few escorts that carried rudimentary radar. In mid-September, Dönitz directed nine U-boats against convoy HX-72, which lost 11 of 47 ships, including seven sunk in four hours by the *U-100* alone. A month later, seven U-boats attacked convoy SC-7, one of the earliest of the eastbound "slow" convoys from Sydney, Nova Scotia, and destroyed 20 of 36 ships. A day later, nearby convoy HX-79 lost 12 of 49 ships, and in November, OB-244 lost seven of 46, and HX-90, 11 of 35. Admittedly, most convoys suffered less severe attrition, and many were never attacked at all, but Britain could ill afford these growing losses in ships, trained seamen, and cargoes.

In October 1940, the German Navy began a major effort to equip Lorient and La Pallice, and later Brest and St. Nazaire, with heavily reinforced "submarine pens," designed to make the submarine berths impervious to aerial bombing. With steel-and-concrete roofs 12 feet thick, these enclosures permitted uninterrupted U-boat maintenance and replenishment despite Allied air attacks. Although British intelligence had clear evidence that these massive building projects were under way and that they were vulnerable to air attack at the time, the Royal Air Force mounted only a few sporadic raids, because of the higher priority assigned to attacks on Germany. Thus, within a year, four submarine pens capable of housing a total of 80 U-boats had been completed, and subsequent costly air raids proved only that they were essentially invulnerable.

Italy Widens the War

In June 1940, when Italy declared war on Great Britain and France, the Italian submarine force—

The Germans constructed heavily protected "submarine pens" along the coasts of Germany, France, and Norway to harbor U-boats safely while they were maintained and resupplied. Like this pen at Trondheim, Norway, they were invulnerable to Allied air attacks once completed. Their construction was so tough that many survive today, too expensive to demolish. *U.S. Army*

consisting of 115 submarines, based in both Italy and East Africa—also joined the conflict. At the outset, 84 of these were combat-ready, and 54 deployed rapidly to war stations as far afield as the Indian Ocean. The result was a fiasco. In the first 20 days of operations, nine Italian submarines were lost to British and French ASW forces, and one was destroyed in running aground. There were a few successes, principally the sinking of the British cruiser *Calypso* by the Italian submarine *Bagliolini* south of Crete on 12 June and the loss of the destroyer *Escort* to the submarine *Guglielmo Marconi* on 10 July. But the inexperienced Italian sailors and their poor-quality boats proved no match for well-practiced Allied ASW teams with state-of-the-art asdic and improved depth charges.

In late July, Italian dictator Benito Mussolini offered to send 30 of his large, ocean-going submarines into the Atlantic to participate under German command in the war on Allied merchant shipping.

Admiral Dönitz reluctantly agreed, and preparations were begun to base the Italian Atlantic submarine flotilla at Bordeaux by the end of the year.

In the Mediterranean, to counter the new threat of Italian surface forces to their strategic position the British committed substantial naval forces to the area: three aircraft carriers, seven battleships and battle cruisers, numerous cruisers and destroyers, and two dozen submarines. Against the latter, the Italian Navy's ASW capabilities were relatively primitive. As late as 1930, escorts were still using rudimentary mechanical listening devices (stethoscope tubes, et al.), but in the next year, active echo-ranging sets began to be fitted to some units, with detection ranges on the order of 2,000 yards. The principal ASW weapons were depth charges, actuated hydrostatically at variable depths and either rolled from rails or lofted by several variants of a compressed-air thrower. A secondary ASW weapon, similar to the explosive sweeps of World War I, was the towed torpedo, which was streamed at depths ranging from 120 to 300 feet and exploded by either a contact or magnetic fuze. Because half of the British submarines sent to the Mediterranean in mid-1940 were chosen from among the Royal Navy's oldest and least capable classes, even these rudimentary ASW measures proved surprisingly effective, and by the end of 1940, eight British boats had been lost, five to Italian surface forces, two to unknown causes, and HMS *Triad* to the Italian submarine *Enrico Toti* in an unusual night-time surface gunnery action in the Gulf of Taranto on 15 October.[22]

The first Italian submarines deployed to Bordeaux in early September, and by the end of the December there were 27 based at the port. Almost immediately they joined the German Navy in its campaign against Allied shipping, but lack of experience in the adverse sea conditions of the North Atlantic made the Italian submarine force relatively ineffective, and it was never successfully integrated into the German wolf-pack strategy. Instead, at Admiral Dönitz's urging, Italian submarines tended to operate independently and somewhat south of the main U-boat operating areas athwart the approaches to Britain. Even so, in the Atlantic in 1940 they sank 18 merchant ships of just under 70,000 tons for the loss of two of their own boats. Eventually, reinforced-concrete submarine pens were constructed for their use at Bordeaux, and the Italians remained low-level participants in the Battle of the Atlantic until Italy surrendered in September 1943.

British ASW Rejuvenation

As the Germans consolidated their hold on Western Europe and the Battle of the Atlantic intensified, the British worked desperately to overcome their weaknesses in ASW. Because of its strategic position just north of the Atlantic trade routes and to prevent the Germans from establishing a military presence there, a force of Royal Marines seized Iceland on 10 May 1940, only a month after Germany had occupied Denmark, Iceland's mother country. Later in the year, after the Royal Air Force prevailed in the Battle of Britain and the threat of a German invasion of England receded, significant numbers of destroyers were released from anti-invasion duty and reassigned to escorting convoys. Also by that time, the first 20 of the small Hunt-class escort destroyers had been delivered. However, they soon proved disappointing on the North Atlantic convoy routes, being top-heavy—thus unstable in heavy seas—and limited in both range and the number of depth charges they could carry topside (50). The Hunts were quickly relegated to less demanding ASW missions in home waters and the Mediterranean.

Their places were taken in the North Atlantic by the increasing numbers of Flower-class corvettes emerging from British and Canadian shipyards. Despite having been designed for inshore escort work, these corvettes soon became key players in convoy protection on both ends of the Atlantic shuttle, and by the end of 1940, 51 of these ships had been commissioned in the Royal Navy and nine in the Royal Canadian Navy. Although the Flowers were extremely seaworthy, they pitched and rolled heavily in even moderate seas, and their poor sea-keeping, teamed with minimal habitability, made them very uncomfortable ships. Moreover, their top speed of only 16 knots significantly limited their tactical repertoire in ASW engagements, and their greatest value proved to be holding down attacking U-boats with repeated depth-charge attacks while their convoys moved on relatively unscathed. Until better ships and aircraft appeared, the Flower-class ships remained the mainstays of the Allied escort force.[23] The British situation vis-à-vis the U-boats improved slightly in mid-August, when the Royal Navy finally recognized that their convoy codes had been compromised.

They were replaced with new, more rigorous ciphers that generally eluded B-dienst's efforts.

Meanwhile, preoccupied by the Battle of Britain and its bomber raids on Germany, the Royal Air Force continued to treat Coastal Command as a poor relation, and airborne surface-search radar continued to be slighted in favor of air-intercept sets. By the end of 1940 only 49 Coastal Command aircraft had been fitted with the improved ASV-II radar. In the event, the radar went "blind" at close ranges, offering no advantage at localizing the target at night.

Although land-based aircraft showed some value in forcing patrolling U-boats to remain submerged, thus reducing their effectiveness, the Costal Command scored no unassisted submarine kills in all of 1940 and contributed to only one successful surface attack in July. Nevertheless, there had been progress in substituting modified Navy depth charges for the earlier "light-cased" bombs by adding streamlined fairings for better stability and using a hydrostatic pistol to detonate the weapon at a pre-determined depth. Eventually, the 250-pound Mark VIII depth charge, filled with a more energetic explosive called Torpex, was adopted as standard by Coastal Command, and subsequent operations research showed how to optimize placement and depth settings to improve the kill probability.[24]

The key to improving airborne radar performance was to operate at higher frequencies, with shorter wavelengths for enhanced spatial resolution. This would also permit smaller airborne antennas that could "beam" the outgoing energy more narrowly to minimize sea clutter. However, this required generating more output power at radio frequencies more than 15 times higher than those used initially, a goal that hitherto had eluded researchers on both sides of the Atlantic. The breakthrough was found in an electronic device called the "cavity magnetron," discovered by a pair of University of Birmingham scientists in February 1940. Based on an American invention from 1929, the magnetron used a beam of electrons accelerated by a strong magnetic field to create vigorous resonant oscillations in a copper cavity, sized precisely to be commensurate with the output wavelength desired.

In its first manifestation at Birmingham, the device produced 500 watts of output power at a frequency of 3,000 MHz, corresponding to a wavelength of ten centimeters. It led directly to a new class of higher-frequency radars that took the name "centimetric" from their shorter wavelengths. Within a few months, during which the power output of the magnetron was increased by more than an order of magnitude, a ground-based centimetric radar had detected an aircraft at a range of 6 n.miles and a submarine conning tower at 4 n.miles. Even so, the higher priority given to air-intercept radar delayed the first flight of an airborne ASW version until March 1941.

In June 1940, the Royal Navy tested a surface-ship search radar, the Type 286M, operating at the earlier wavelength of 1.5 meters, but since it used a fixed antenna aimed straight ahead, the ship had to be steered to search in azimuth. A ten-centimeter counterpart, the Type 271M—still with a fixed antenna—appeared in early 1941.

Drawing in the United States

In the United States, the war in Europe was viewed with growing alarm, both by isolationists who opposed any American involvement in the conflict and by those who feared the threat of an Axis-dominated Europe and thus anticipated eventual U.S. intervention on the side of the Allies to forestall it. When war began in September 1939, President Franklin Roosevelt directed the Navy to establish a "neutrality patrol" to report and track any belligerent forces approaching the Western Hemisphere.

This was followed in early October 1939 by the "Act of Panama," a collective declaration by the Pan-American nations intended to keep the war out of the region by establishing a maritime "neutral zone" to the east of the littorals of North and South America. Subsequently, the fall of France and the Netherlands in 1940 created jurisdictional questions about those nations' colonies in the Caribbean and their associated military forces. These issues were addressed in a similar "Act of Havana" of 30 June 1940, which stated that the transfer of any regional territory from one non-American power to another would not be tolerated.

From the outset, President Roosevelt's sympathies lay with Britain. He had been in regular correspondence with Winston Churchill since the latter had been appointed First Lord of the Admiralty in September 1939, and their friendship developed further after Churchill became prime minister in May 1940.[25] In supporting Britain, the president was forced to walk a narrow line: he was approaching a difficult re-election campaign for an unprecedented third term in November 1940, and he could ill afford to antagonize the large bloc of isolationist voters who expected him to keep the United States out of a European war. Nonetheless, Roosevelt succeeded in moving the Congress to adopt a number of "short-of-war" measures, including a naval expansion bill for creating a "two-ocean navy" in May 1940 and re-establishment of the draft in October. Additionally, the president agreed to increase the production of merchant ships under the auspices of the U.S. Maritime Commission and saw to the establishment of the National Defense Research Committee to mobilize American science and technology for the defense effort. On these foundations, the rebuilding of U.S. defense capabilities could finally begin after the doldrums of the 1920s and 1930s.

Churchill wrote his first letter as Britain's prime minister to President Roosevelt on 15 May 1940,

when the battle for France and rising merchant losses in the North Atlantic had thrown the "escort crisis" into stark relief. After describing the dire war situation and the Royal Navy's immediate need for more escort ships until its own new-construction programs came on line, Churchill asked Roosevelt for the loan of 50 or 60 older U.S. destroyers that might be used to fill the gap, noting that "the worth of every destroyer that you can spare to us is measured in rubies."[26] Following the identification of the need for a quid pro quo to mollify U.S. public opinion, it was agreed on 2 September 1940, that in return for the loan of 50 World War I–era flush-deck, four-stack destroyers, Britain would grant the United States naval basing rights for 99 years in six of their Caribbean possessions: Antigua, Bahamas, Jamaica, St. Lucia, Trinidad, and British Guiana.[27] The "destroyers-for-bases deal" constituted the first significant material contribution by the United States to the Allied cause, and by early 1941, 42 destroyers had been delivered to the Royal Navy and seven to the Royal Canadian Navy.[28] During that same period, ten Lake-class U.S. Coast Guard cutters, 250 feet long, also were transferred to Britain.

Beginning in September 1940, the U.S. Navy acquired scores of private yachts for coastal patrol and escort duties. The largest of these was the German-built *Orion* of 3,015 tons displacement, launched in 1929, which became the USS *Vixen* (PG 53). The *Vixen*, acquired on 13 November 1940, would serve during the war—mostly at pierside—as the flagship for Commander, Submarines, U.S. Atlantic Fleet. Most acquired yachts were designated PY (patrol yacht) or PYc (coastal patrol yacht) and were armed and employed in coastal and harbor patrol duties.

One of the more unusual ships of this type was the USS *Isabel* (PY 10), a 710-ton yacht that had been taken over by the Navy upon completion in 1917. The 26-knot ship served as a "destroyer" in World

War I, and her commanding officer, Lieutenant Commander Harry E. Shoemaker, received the Navy Cross "for distinguished service . . . engaged in the important, exacting and hazardous duty of transporting and escorting troops and supplies through waters infested with enemy submarines and mines." The *Isabel* later served on the China station, where she came under enemy fire on numerous occasions. When the United States went to war in December 1941 she was near the Philippines and operated as an ASW escort for convoys in the East Indies. Then, based in Australia, she served during the war as a training ship and escort for U.S. submarines going to sea. (She did not return to the United States until October 1945 and soon after was decommissioned and scrapped.)

By mid-1940 it had become apparent to the president and his senior military advisors that the Axis domination of continental Europe and Britain's precarious situation posed a grave threat to America's strategic position in the Atlantic. Accordingly, President Roosevelt authorized the sending of a high-level U.S. military-naval delegation to London both to assess the war situation and to conduct exploratory discussions with the British chiefs of staff. The resulting talks, commencing in August 1940, provided U.S. political and military leaders with a clear understanding of the strengths and weaknesses of the Allied position, as well as early indications of where and how U.S. military and naval power might best be applied in the event of American entry into the war. These initial military and naval contacts would eventually lead to comprehensive, top-level staff talks in Washington in January 1941. A more immediate outcome was an extended visit to the United States by a secret British technical mission under Dr. Henry Tizard in late August and September 1940. Its purpose was to share with U.S. counterparts some of Britain's most closely held scientific

and technical developments. These included the cavity magnetron, the Torpex explosive, the latest depth charges, and advances in asdic, high-frequency radio direction-finding, proximity fuzes, and aircraft engines. These revelations excited extraordinary interest in the U.S. scientific establishment and soon led to parallel cooperative efforts in British-American industry and the university community, most notably in microwave radar development.

Since the beginning of the war, the U.S. Neutrality Acts—strictly construed—had prevented the sale of U.S. war materials or the lending of money to any of the warring powers. However, the desire to accelerate the recovery from the Great Depression then under way soon led to the substitution of the so-called cash-and-carry policy, by which belligerents could buy war goods but were required to pay cash and arrange for their delivery in non-U.S. merchant ships. Because of the British blockade of Germany, cash-and-carry primarily benefited Britain, but during the first year of war Great Britain's financial reserves dwindled so rapidly that cash purchases became increasingly difficult.

Having made a tacit decision to increase support for Britain and her European allies, however, President Roosevelt, fresh from his re-election in November 1940, revealed a new approach at a press conference a month later: Lend-Lease. This envisioned an all-out effort to increase U.S. defense production (including food) by mobilizing both public and private resources, and then lending or leasing as much of the extra output as could be spared to Great Britain. A preliminary agreement with the British on 23 February 1941 was purposely vague about repayment, but despite the embarrassment of a British debt still outstanding from World War I, the first Lend-Lease Act was passed by the Congress with comfortable majorities two weeks later.[29] Henceforth, the United States increasingly would become the "arsenal of democracy."

8

The Conflict Widens

By the end of 1940 the U-boat "happy time" that had commenced in June had dissipated, both because of winter weather in the North Atlantic and a temporary cessation of convoy activity for several weeks after the pocket battleship *Admiral Scheer* broke through the Royal Navy blockade and attacked a convoy in mid-ocean on 5 November. Nonetheless, German submarines bagged almost 530 merchant ships during the year, totaling nearly two and a half million tons, balanced against a loss of 23 U-boats. (Additionally, two of the Bordeaux-based Italian submarines had been sunk.)

New construction in 1940 of both coastal (Type II) and ocean-going boats (Types VII and IX) yielded 50 new U-boats, but with all of the Type IIs and the older Type VIIs relegated to training duty in the Baltic, *Konteradmiral* Dönitz only could muster 31 ocean-going submarines at the beginning of 1941, of which roughly one-third could be kept on patrol at any one time.

During January and February 1941, merchant losses totaled 38 ships. Despite the Royal Navy's growing proficiency in using asdic to prosecute depth charge attacks, no U-boats were killed in December, January, or February. Writing about that period, Royal Navy captain and later historian Donald Macintyre recalled:

Filthy weather plagued escorts and convoys from the North Channel across the wider

sweep to Iceland. Huge, menacing seas rose high above the ships to crash down on creaking, groaning decks; men with red, bleary eyes strained to peer through the curtain of drizzle; and low overhead the dark water-filled clouds threatened fresh misery with every dawn. There was no escape from it. [The escorts] had to stick it out and concentrate harder than ever lest some lurking enemy should slink through their screen and decimate a helpless wallowing convoy.

But the U-boats were not so harassed. When the strain took too heavy a toll on tired nerves, they dived to the peaceful protection of the world below the surface, safe in the knowledge that our asdics were unreliable in the weather "upstairs" and, in any event, operators would have lost their keen sensitivity to the wretchedness of their sodden, heaving surroundings as watch followed watch with never a let-up in the weather.[1]

The significant losses suffered by British convoys in the North Atlantic in mid-1940 and early 1941 were inflicted largely by three German submarine "aces": Gunther Prien, commanding the *U-47*, credited at the time with sinking 245,000 tons, including the battleship *Royal Oak* in Scapa Flow; Joachim Schepke of the *U-100*, 230,000 tons;

and Otto Kretschmer of the *U-99*, with a record 282,000 tons.[2] Captain Macintyre later wrote, "These three 'aces' were the toast of all Germany and the recipients of the highest decorations. On return to harbor they would be greeted by their commander-in-chief in person, bands would play triumphal marches, and their crews would be wafted away to the earthly Valhallas of rest camps or to winter-sports resorts at public expense."[3] A German Army bandmaster even composed a *Kretschmer March*.

The three aces sailed from Lorient in early March 1941, the first occasion that all three would be at sea at the same time—a devastating prospect for the British. In the event, it was not to be.

The first to engage was *Korvettenkäpitan* Prien in the *U-47*. Shortly before dusk on 7 March, in heavy seas some 200 n.miles south of Iceland, he detected westbound convoy OB-293. He had been joined by three other U-boats, including Kretschmer in the *U-99*. Then Prien's boat disappeared—apparently sunk with all 45 men on board. It was long thought that he was engaged and sunk by the British destroyer *Wolverine*, one of several convoy escorts that caught the *U-47* on the surface. Most likely, however, she was sunk by one of her own torpedoes on a circular run or by depth charges from other British ships in the area. (The *Wolverine* had, in fact, attacked and damaged the one-of-a-kind submarine *U-A*.)[4]

By 12 March the weather in the area had eased, although rain squalls were frequent. *Käpitanleutnant* Kretschmer in the *U-99* and *Käpitanleutnant* Schepke in the *U-100*, after sinking several stragglers from an eastbound convoy, joined other submarines in attacking the eastbound convoy HX-112 beginning just before midnight on the 15th. Several merchant ships were torpedoed, and the escorting destroyers, including the *Walker* under Commander Macintyre, who also commanded 5th Escort Group,

were unable to halt the carnage, despite several depth charge attacks on the U-boats.

Then the destroyer *Vanoc* sighted, rammed, and sank the *U-100*, Schepke's boat. The submarine had been detected—for the first time in combat—by the primitive radar on the *Vanoc*. Schepke, on the *U-100*'s conning tower, was apparently deceived by the *Vanoc*'s camouflage paint scheme and thought that the fast-approaching destroyer would pass astern of his boat. He held course. A few moments later the destroyer rammed the submarine, crushing Schepke between the destroyer's bow and his own periscope standards. There were six survivors from his crew of 44 men.

Moments later, the *Walker*'s asdic detected another U-boat at almost the same location. Commander Macintyre, in the *Walker*, ordered all ready depth charges released—a pattern of only six. They were enough. Heavily damaged, the *U-99* broke the surface, and gun crews on both destroyers opened fire with 4-inch guns and lighter weapons. In the tracer-filled darkness, a light from the U-boat flashed, "We are sinking," and the *U-99* plunged to the ocean floor with three of her crew. There were 40 survivors, Kretschmer, the last to climb on board the *Walker*, among them. Exhausted, he was led below to Commander Macintyre's stateroom in the *Walker*, where he promptly fell asleep in a leather armchair. Upon waking, Kretschmer told Macintyre, "Things might have turned out different if I had some torpedoes left." After the war Macintyre and Kretschmer became good friends.[5]

Thus, the U-boat arm was deprived of its three top-scoring aces within a few days in March 1941. Yet the struggle in the Atlantic was still two years away from turning in favor of the Allies.

The new German U-boat bases in the French Atlantic ports had forced the rerouting of convoys from the southwestern to the northwestern approaches to Great Britain. Hence, Prime Minister Churchill recommended moving the headquarters of the Western Approaches Command northward from Plymouth, where it had been established at the beginning of the war. On 7 February 1941, the command was relocated to Derby House in Liverpool and placed under Admiral Sir Percy Noble.

The headquarters of the RAF's Coastal Command were shifted to the same site.

By that time, the Admiralty's Submarine Tracking Room had been placed under the direction of Charles Rodger Winn, a civilian barrister who had volunteered for manual intelligence work just before the conflict and had shown a remarkable aptitude for analyzing and predicting U-boat

Captain Donald Macintyre, Royal Navy
(B. 1904 D. 1981)

Captain Macintyre commanded two of the most effective British ASW groups in the Battle of the Atlantic. He was born in India to British parents and joined the Royal Navy in 1926. After first serving in a destroyer in the Mediterranean, he served for seven years as a pilot with the Fleet Air Arm. A 1935 medical issue left him unfit to fly, and he returned to surface ships, commanding the sloop *Kingfisher* at the ASW school at Portland. He then commanded a succession of destroyers and early in World War II participated in the Norwegian campaign as well as in several ASW operations.

In March 1941, Macintyre took command of the destroyer *Walker* and the 5th Escort Group. During its first convoy operation his group was responsible for sinking the *U-100,* commanded by Joachim Schepke, and the *U-99,* commanded by Otto Kretschmer, the two being Germany's two top-ranking U-boat aces. (The *Walker* herself was responsible for killing the *U-99.*) Promoted to commander in early 1942, Macintyre served briefly as the British liaison officer at the U.S. naval base at Argentia, Newfoundland. In June that year he returned to sea in the destroyer *Hesperus* in command of the B.2 Escort Group,

part of the Mid-Ocean Escort Force. He commanded the B.2 Escort Group for two years, escorting 28 convoys, a total of 1,100 ships, with the loss of only two, while sinking three U-boats.

In April 1944, Macintyre assumed command of the frigate *Bickerton* and the re-constituted 5th Escort Group, then forming at Belfast. Soon after, the 5th took part in the ASW defense of the D-day landings, and on the night of 25 June, the *Bickerton* detected and sank the *U-269* in the English Channel, the last of Macintyre's five U-boat kills. On 22 August in the Barents Sea the *Bickerton* was badly damaged by a German homing torpedo and had to be scuttled.

Subsequently, Macintyre left sea duty, re-qualified as an aviator, and ended the war as the commander of a naval air station. Promoted to captain by the end of 1945, he served in a number of aviation, ASW training, and fleet assignments prior to his retirement in 1955.

In a highly successful second career, Macintyre became a well-known naval historian and author, releasing his autobiography *U-Boat Killer* in 1956 and following with 17 additional books on naval history.

movements on the basis of cryptographic intelligence and recurring operational patterns. Subsequently promoted to captain in the Royal Navy Volunteer Reserve, Winn headed the Submarine Tracking Room for the entire war and was highly decorated at the end for his contribution to winning the anti-submarine campaign.[6]

A major innovation introduced by Admiral Noble in mid-1941 was the organization of permanent escort groups of ships that trained and operated together to enhance their tactical effectiveness. Each escort group consisted of approximately ten ships, a mix of destroyers, corvettes, and sloops, of which six to eight would be in readiness at all times for assignment as an integrated convoy escort team. Additionally, Noble established under Vice-Admiral George O. Stephenson a new escort training command, dubbed "HMS Western Isles," at Tobermory on the Isle of Mull off the western coast of Scotland. Every new escort ship was sent there for a month of working up before her first escort-group assignment.

To give greater focus and direction to the U-boat war, Churchill declared a "Battle of the Atlantic" in early March. This initiative—patterned after his announcement of the "Battle of Britain" during the massive German air attacks of the previous year—may largely have been a propaganda exercise, but it included the establishment of a Battle of the Atlantic Committee (which Churchill chaired) and the identification of a dozen top-priority ASW measures. These included increased emphasis on killing U-boats and bombing their bases, carrying aircraft on escort ships, concentrating Coastal Command operations on the northwest approaches, and reducing the turnaround time of merchant ships in port and under repair.[7]

Simultaneously, the Germans increased their pressure on the North Atlantic convoy routes: Convoy HX-111 lost five of 41 ships to submarine attacks on 16 to 18 March 1941, and although Royal Navy escorts sank five U-boats that month, these losses only motivated Admiral Dönitz to move his wolf packs farther westward to the mid-ocean gap, where, because neither British nor Canadian escorts were then operating there, the convoys were unprotected. As a result, convoy SC-26 lost ten of 22 ships on 3 and 4 April. Forced to conclude by this disaster that the mid-ocean gap was unacceptable, the Admiralty decided to establish an escort base in Iceland and to route convoys back and forth to the British Isles in two stages, with Iceland as the midpoint. Thus, Canadian escorts could accompany eastbound convoys all the way to Iceland, refuel at the new base at Hvalfjordur, about 25 miles from Reykjavik, and return with a westbound convoy to Nova Scotia. Similarly, British escorts could bring outbound convoys all the way to Iceland and return with their inbound counterparts.

At this stage of the war, however, the participation of the Canadian forces was almost counter-productive. ASW group commander Donald Macintyre wrote:

During 1941 the Atlantic along the east coast of Canada and the ports of Newfoundland became populated with a motley collection of warships manned largely by landsmen. . . . Discipline was weird and wonderful, equipment was ill-maintained and training in its use was sadly lacking. These ships were units with which to make a show on the operations room maps, and perhaps to give a semblance of security to convoys which would otherwise have gone unescorted, but they were little more.[8]

The Canadian ships of the time were badly kept, their equipment—including depth charges—often was rusted, and their crews were poorly trained, especially in such vital areas as navigation and signaling, according to Macintyre.

The United States "Short of War"

Meanwhile, the United States was edging closer to the war. Late in 1940, the Chief of Naval Operations, Admiral Harold Stark, had ordered the drafting of preliminary plans for possible U.S. involvement in the European conflict, and by December 1940, the initial version of a convoy escort plan had been prepared. On 11 January 1941, secret staff talks commenced in Washington with senior representatives of the U.S. Army

Sir Charles Rodger Winn
(B. 1903 D. 1972)

An English barrister, Winn joined the Admiralty's Submarine Tracking Room as a civilian analyst at the beginning of World War II. Within little more than a year his uncanny ability to deduce the patterns of German submarine operations and predict future submarine locations led to his being given command of the entire tracking section.

Born in King's Norton, Staffordshire, Winn was partially crippled by polio as a child, a debility that never left him. He took degrees at both Cambridge and Harvard Universities and became a lawyer in 1928. With the outbreak of war in 1939, Winn left his successful practice to volunteer as an interrogator of German prisoners of war, but somehow he was assigned to the Submarine Tracking Room, where— even as a civilian—he soon developed a deep understanding of evolving German submarine tactics. By combining his cumulative knowledge of past operations with skillful interpretation of Ultra codebreaking intercepts, he was frequently able to predict future submarine actions and vector British ASW forces to thwart them. In recognition of this unique ability— while lacking any formal naval training—Winn was commissioned a temporary commander in

the Royal Naval Volunteer Reserve in late 1940 and put in full charge of the Submarine Tracking Room, a position he held until the end of the conflict.

In 1942, after the United States had entered the war, Winn was sent to Washington to convince the U.S. Navy of the importance of instituting convoy operations off the U.S. East Coast, and his Submarine Tracking Room was used as a model for a corresponding facility within U.S. naval intelligence. Winn held perhaps the key tactical intelligence position that supported the ultimate Allied victory in the convoy battles of the North Atlantic, and he also played a major role in planning ASW defenses for the Normandy invasion and providing the day-to-day operational intelligence that kept German U-boats at bay during that operation. He was promoted to temporary captain in January 1944, a year after he had been knighted for his contribution to the war effort, and thereafter he exerted an increasingly powerful influence on Allied ASW operations.

Winn returned to the practice of law after the war, became a judge in 1959, and reached the pinnacle of his legal career six years later when he was named a Lord Justice of Appeal.

and Navy and a delegation representing the British Chiefs of Staff. The result of those deliberations, which ended in late March, was a key strategy document, the "ABC-1 Staff Agreement," which called for collaborative planning, spelled out the U.S. role in the current "short-of-war" situation, and envisioned full military-naval cooperation in the event of U.S. belligerency. It was further agreed that every effort would be made to maintain the uneasy peace in the Pacific by discouraging Japanese aggression. But in the event of a general war, the initial goal of Allied cooperation would be to defeat Hitler in Europe. This would require remaining largely on the defensive against Japan until enough forces could be mustered to take the offensive in the Pacific theater. This "Europe-first" strategy, which would dominate the early phases of the war, was a major outcome of the ABC-1 staff talks.[9]

Because the ABC-1 agreement defined major U.S. responsibilities for convoy escort and ASW in the North Atlantic, the Navy accelerated planning in those areas. Following the British lead, a Convoy and Routing Section was established at Navy headquarters in Washington, and by 1 March a Support Force for escort duty had been created by reassigning ships and aircraft from the Neutrality Patrol. A new U.S. base at Argentia, Newfoundland, under construction since the beginning of the year, was earmarked for the Support Force of three destroyer squadrons and four aircraft patrol squadrons, each of the latter with 12 PBY Catalina or PBM Mariner flying boats.[10] Adding a certain urgency to these preparations, Hitler simultaneously declared the ocean areas off Iceland and Greenland as war zones, in which even neutrals could be sunk without warning.

Tension rose quickly when on 10 April 1941 the new U.S. destroyer *Niblack* (DD 424), on a reconnaissance mission to Iceland, dropped depth charges on what was thought to be a U-boat maneuvering into attack position. Although postwar analysis revealed that she had probably attacked a false sonar contact, this was the first incident in which a U.S. ship resorted to deadly force in self-defense. Only three days earlier, Admiral Stark had ordered the transfer of three battleships, the aircraft carrier *Yorktown* (CV 5), four light cruisers, and two destroyer squadrons from the Pacific to the Atlantic to bolster forces there. Even before these moves were accomplished at the end of May, the first American merchant ship was lost to a submarine, the SS *Robin Moor,* accosted and sunk by the *U-69* in the South Atlantic on 21 May after a mistaken assessment of her neutral status. The survivors spent two weeks in open boats before reaching shore.

The Consolidated PBY Catalina was a highly successful reconnaissance aircraft that was effective in the ASW role. More PBYs were built—in the United States and Canada—than any other military flying boat. This PBY-5A "Cat" has pre–June 1942 markings—a red circle within the U.S. star insignia and red-and-white stripes on the tail fin. *U.S. Navy*

Alarmed by these incidents, the growing losses of Lend-Lease cargoes to U-boat attacks, and the recent breakout of the German battleship *Bismarck* onto the high seas, President Roosevelt delivered a major broadcast on 26 May—the day the *Bismarck* was sunk—declaring an "Unlimited National Emergency" and his determination to prevent any attempt by the Axis to gain a foothold in the Western Hemisphere. In a related decision in mid-June, the United States agreed to assume responsibility for the occupation of Iceland, freeing up significant numbers of British troops. With the grudging agreement of the Icelandic government, a brigade of U.S. Marines arrived on 7 July 1941, and construction of a series of new U.S. bases and facilities soon followed. In an additional move to relieve pressure on the British, the U.S. Navy agreed on 18 July to build Royal Navy escorts in U.S. shipyards under Lend-Lease, and a program to build 100 destroyer escorts, of 1,500 tons, at the rate of ten per month, plus 20 minesweepers and 14 rescue tugs, was started immediately.

At the Atlantic Conference, held aboard ship at Argentia from 10 to 15 August, President Roosevelt, Prime Minister Churchill, and their top military advisors not only agreed on the so-called Atlantic Charter, which declared that a future peace "should enable all men to traverse the high seas and oceans without hindrance," but also settled the details of near-term military and naval cooperation.[11] As one key result, the U.S. Navy—with Canadian assistance—assumed responsibility for convoying merchant vessels from Halifax to either Iceland or a Mid-Ocean Meeting Point (MOMP), where the Royal Navy would take over for the rest of the journey. Thus, in late July, as a first step, U.S. destroyers began escorting convoys to and from Iceland.

Still a non-belligerent, the United States required some justification for its growing role in convoy escort on Britain's behalf. The rationale put forward was that the U.S. Navy was merely escorting U.S. and Icelandic ships supporting the occupation of Iceland and that if ships of other nationalities wanted to join its convoys, they were free to do so. However, this transparent argument left somewhat ambiguous the question of how active encounters with U-boats would be handled. Supposedly, U.S. ships could fire in self-defense or in defense of their convoys, but were forbidden to make unprovoked attacks on German U-boats.

The *Greer* incident in early September brought this issue to a head. The American four-stack destroyer *Greer* (DD 145) was proceeding independently toward Iceland when she was warned by a British patrol aircraft of the submarine *U-652*, sighted some miles ahead of the U.S. warship. The destroyer increased speed, initiated a sonar search, detected the U-boat, and held contact for several hours without attacking. At that point, however, the British aircraft dropped depth charges on the *U-652*, which—thus provoked—attacked the *Greer* with a torpedo, which missed. The *Greer* unsuccessfully counter-attacked with depth charges, dodged another torpedo, lost sonar contact, and ended the engagement. The *U-652* escaped unscathed, but the incident aroused a storm of outrage, with President Roosevelt declaring the submarine's attack an act of "piracy" and declaring, "From now on, if German or Italian vessels of war enter waters the protection of which is necessary for American defense, they do so at their own risk."[12] From that moment an "undeclared naval war" existed in the North Atlantic between the United States and Germany.

HX-150, the first trans-Atlantic convoy assisted by the U.S. Navy, sailed from Halifax on 16 September under a local Canadian escort, which was relieved the next day by a group of five U.S. destroyers south of Argentia. After meeting the British escort at the

MOMP six days later, the U.S. destroyers accompanied the Iceland-bound merchants to their destination, refueled, and began the return trip. No U-boats were encountered, and no ships were lost except for one freighter that caught fire and had to be abandoned. The first westbound convoy escorted by U.S. ships was ON-18, which was picked up south of Iceland on 24 September. No ships were lost, partly because U-boat activity was concentrated elsewhere.

The next month, when the wolf packs again returned to the northern convoy routes, the U.S. Navy suffered its first losses. Slow convoy SC-48 of 50 merchantmen, escorted by a Canadian destroyer and seven corvettes (five Canadian, one British, one Free French), was first attacked on the night of 15 October and lost three ships. Nominally, "slow" convoys traveled at from nine to 12 knots; "fast" convoys moved at from 12 to 15 knots.

Help arrived the next day in the form of five American destroyers and another Free French corvette that took station to augment the original escort. Additional attacks that night and into the following morning claimed seven more ships, and when the U.S. destroyer *Kearny* (DD 432) was silhouetted against the flames of one of the victims, she was torpedoed, suffering grievous damage. Although skillful damage control saved the ship and she was able to steam to Iceland under her own power, 11 men were killed—the first American sailors to die in the Battle of the Atlantic.

At the end of the month, worse was to happen. At dawn on 31 October 1941, the old four-stack destroyer *Reuben James* (DD 245), part of the escort of convoy HX-156, was torpedoed by the *U-552* and blown in half. The ship went down in five minutes, and only 45 of the crew of 160 were saved by other escorts. The *Reuben James* was the first U.S. warship lost in the Atlantic war. Her sinking echoed across America, giving rise to a famous folk ballad by Woody Guthrie and providing the president with additional support for greater belligerency. The next day Hitler authorized U-boat attacks as far west as the Canadian littoral.

Enter the Soviet Union

World War II took on an entirely new dimension when Germany suddenly attacked the Soviet Union on 22 June 1941. Perhaps trusting too much in the Nazi-Soviet Non-Aggression Pact of August 1939 and despite significant intelligence indicators of the impending onslaught, the Soviet government was almost totally unprepared for the outbreak of war. By late fall, in the face of a massive German assault, the Red Army had surrendered the Ukraine and been driven back almost to the gates of Moscow and Leningrad. At sea, both sides carried out extensive minelaying in the Gulf of Finland, intended by the Soviets to discourage potential naval moves against Leningrad, and by the Germans to thwart attacks on their iron-ore shipments from Sweden or incursions into the western Baltic by the 70 Soviet submarines there. In the event, the Soviet undersea arm was largely defenseless, and as the Germans pushed eastward along the southern littoral, they and their putative allies, the Finns, took a significant toll of Soviet submarines early in the campaign. Still, as a precaution, the German Navy relocated submarine training and new-construction U-boat work-ups from the Baltic to several fjords in occupied southern Norway.

With the Soviet Union now an unexpected ally, Prime Minister Churchill committed Britain to providing immediate material assistance to the communist state.[13] Moreover, in the U.S.-British discussions in August 1941 that led to the "Atlantic Charter," President Roosevelt agreed to extend Lend-Lease aid to the Soviets. Thus, in that month were born the infamous Murmansk convoys, which carried war supplies from Iceland and Britain to northern Russia. The first of these, which left on 21 August, was largely symbolic and comprised six merchant ships and an aircraft carrier, the old HMS *Argus,* carrying 24 of a shipment of 39 Hurricane fighters for the Soviets, escorted by a British fleet carrier, two heavy cruisers, and six destroyers. All arrived safely. Subsequently, these northern convoys—the outbound denoted "PQ" and those returning "QP"—sailed at roughly two-week intervals, and by the end of the year, 53 merchant ships had arrived in Russia, with 34 returning. Although severe weather north of the Arctic Circle caused significant damage, no ships or matériel on the "Murmansk run" were lost to German action this early in the war.

The Enigma of Ultra

By mid-1941 the determined British codebreaking effort began to make inroads into the German Navy's Enigma cipher, facilitated by several special operations intended specifically to capture German coding materials. On 4 March, a commando raid on the German-occupied Lofoten Islands off Norway yielded the preceding month's Enigma settings and key tables for the German Navy's home-waters code, Heimisch (known as Dolphin to the British). This enabled Bletchley Park to read the entirety of Heimisch traffic for February, which though limited in tactical value, gave invaluable intelligence on German cryptographic practices and procedures, plus information on recent U-boat operations. On 7 May the seizure of the German weather-reporting trawler *München* southeast of Iceland yielded the Enigma keys for June, but this achievement was largely overshadowed two days later by the Royal Navy's capture of the *U-110* following a wolf-pack attack on convoy OB-318 south of Iceland.

After sinking two freighters, *Korvettenkäpitan* Fritz Lemp, the same Lemp who torpedoed *Athenia* early in the war, had brought the *U-110* to periscope depth for a shot at a tanker when he was attacked by the British corvette *Aubrietia,* which dropped 16 depth charges on a firm asdic contact. Heavily damaged, the *U-110* fought her way back to the surface, where she was surrounded by *Aubrietia* and two other escorts, which immediately took the U-boat under gunfire. Lemp ordered the crew to scuttle the boat and abandon ship, but somehow the scuttling was bungled. The *U-110* stayed afloat long enough for the British to embark a boarding party that slowed the flooding and removed a complete Enigma machine, Heimisch keys for April and June, and much other material of both cryptographic and tactical intelligence value. The submarine was then taken under tow for Iceland, 400 miles distant, only to founder the next morning due to damage. Immediately, the British were able to read the entirety of Heimisch for the coming month of June.

Additionally, Bletchley Park had succeeded in breaking the lower-level, hand-enciphered code Werft, which was used by smaller German vessels in home and Norwegian waters. Since many routine messages were encoded and transmitted in both Werft and Enigma, the ability to read the former frequently provided invaluable clues—known as "cribs"—for breaking into Enigma. The resulting intelligence information, known as "Most Secret Ultra"—or Ultra for short—was highly restricted in its distribution but soon proved to be the most important intelligence source for thwarting Admiral Dönitz's evolving U-boat campaign. Central to maintaining its value, however, was concealment from the Germans that their codes had been compromised. Thus, it was put out that the weather ship *München* had been destroyed, not captured, and a series of subterfuges were created to convince the captive crew of the *U-110* that their boat had sunk before she could be boarded.

Additionally, the tactical uses of Ultra were strictly circumscribed. Instead of using the Ultra intelligence to cue attacks on well-located submarines, which likely would have given away the source, the Admiralty instead used the information—along with increasingly refined High-Frequency Direction-Finding (HF/DF) fixes—to route convoys away from patrolling U-boats. Exceptions were made in cases where plausible alternate explanations, such as U-boat sightings by surveillance aircraft, could be evinced for accurately locating submarines at sea.

Nonetheless, during the latter half of 1941, as his wolf packs found increasing difficulty in intercepting Allied convoys, Admiral Dönitz began to suspect that his communications had been penetrated. These fears were exacerbated by the well-publicized capture on 27 August of the *U-570* south of Iceland after it had been surprised on the surface and depth-charged by a Coastal Command Hudson bomber, which summoned additional aircraft and surface ships to the scene. In fact, the *U-570* yielded no important cryptographic information, but the submarine was refurbished, renamed HMS *Graph*, and thoroughly exploited for technical data and performance characteristics of the Type VII U-boat. Still, Dönitz tightened both radio and reference-grid security, and although assured by B-dienst that his Enigma traffic was impregnable, ordered his communications chief to review the whole issue of communications security. A month later, another incident occurred to raise more doubts about Enigma.

Between February and August 1941, Admiral Dönitz had ordered a total of 20 patrols to the South Atlantic, concentrating on British supply routes off the coast of West Africa. Originally these patrols were supported by clandestine supply ships and a tanker tolerated in the Canary Islands by the sympathetic Spanish government. These sorties earlier had reaped a considerable bag: 85 merchant ships, totaling approximately 461,000 tons, just over 30 percent of total Allied losses for the period. With the Royal Navy gradually sinking the supply ships and demanding stricter Spanish observance of neutrality, the South Atlantic U-boats were forced increasingly into mutual support, such as transferring torpedoes at sea from departing boats to those remaining on station. In one such evolution—planned for late September—the *U-67*, *U-68*, and *U-111* were ordered to rendezvous in remote Tarafal Bay in the Portuguese Cape Verde Islands to transfer torpedoes and personnel. Aware of these arrangements from Enigma intercepts, the British dispatched the large submarine *Clyde* in an attempt to destroy all three U-boats. The *Clyde* entered Tarafal Bay late on 27 September only to blunder into the *U-68* and *U-111,* which had already arrived. During the resulting night-time melée, which included several exchanges of torpedoes, the *U-67* appeared on the scene and collided with the *Clyde,* sustaining serious damage. The engagement ended with all four boats withdrawing hastily, the *U-68* and *U-111* to continue their patrols and the *U-67* to return to France for repair.[14]

Despite the *Clyde*'s failure to surprise the three U-boats at their rendezvous, the unexpected appearance of a British submarine at such a remote location immediately rekindled German suspicions about Enigma's integrity. Admiral Dönitz ordered an emergency modification to Enigma procedures, but it only held off the British codebreakers for two weeks. However, to enhance internal security, he also ordered the immediate establishment of a separate Enigma net denoted "Triton" (later called Shark by the British) specifically for the submarine force. Additionally, planning had already begun for adding a fourth rotor to the existing three-rotor Enigma machine, which would greatly complicate cryptanalysis and vitiate many of the codebreaking successes that his adversaries might already have achieved. But the British, using their existing penetrations, had detected early tests of the four-rotor Enigma code, recognized their implications, and begun the design of a corresponding four-rotor bombe to cope with the new code when it appeared. Moreover, before the Germans could introduce their new coding system after the turn of the year, the Royal Navy used Ultra intelligence to intercept the German raider *Atlantis* at a planned rendezvous with several U-boats in the South Atlantic, sank the *Atlantis* on 22 November, and eliminated the auxiliary supply ship *Python* a week later.

Also in mid-1941, the RAF Coastal Command adopted a new, more offensive strategy that emphasized increased patrolling over the Bay of Biscay in an attempt to interdict the stream of U-boats coming and going from the French Atlantic ports. The command was still severely hampered by a shortage of effective ASW aircraft, with only 210 based in the British Isles in June and July.[15] Moreover, nearly half of these were the relatively limited Lockheed Hudsons, with an effective operational radius of only 450 n.miles and the ability to carry only three or four 250-pound depth charges. The best Coastal Command aircraft were the 30 American-built Catalina I flying boats, with a radius of 900 n.miles and a depth-charge load of 2,000 pounds, but there were only enough of these to equip three squadrons.[16]

The ideal ASW aircraft for Coastal Command was the Consolidated B-24 Liberator, an American four-engine heavy bomber that had begun to arrive in Britain under Lend-Lease in mid-1941. The Liberator had twice the cruising speed of the Catalina (190 knots) and boasted an operational radius of 1,000 n.miles carrying up to 32 depth charges, as well as defensive guns. Although the first nine Lend-Lease Liberators were allocated to Coastal Command, the RAF Bomber Command had priority for these superb aircraft, and even as late as January 1943, Coastal Command had only 17 Liberators. Moreover, to achieve the larger operating radius and time on station required for ASW missions, standard-design Liberators had to be heavily modified by removing the turbo-superchargers, the self-sealing liners in the fuel tanks, most of the armor-plating, and the ventral .50-caliber gun turret. The weight saved permitted adding additional fuel capacity that doubled the aircraft's endurance.

At the time of Coastal Command's new focus on the Bay of Biscay, three-quarters of its front-line aircraft were equipped with the improved ASV-II radar. Initially, they achieved virtually no success against the U-boats. In traversing the Biscay area, German submarines submerged during the day and ran on the surface at night while charging batteries. While they could be detected on the surface by airborne radar, night visual range fell well within the radar's sea-clutter "blind spot" (see Chapter 7) and thus bomb or depth-charge attacks were wholly ineffective, particularly with the U-boat taking evasive action. As a result of this shortcoming and several associated flaws in their search and attack doctrine, Coastal Command aircraft sank no submarines in the entire North Atlantic area in all of 1941 and had only been credited with four "assists" since the beginning of the war.[17]

As one of his first actions after taking charge in June 1941, the new chief of Coastal Command, Air Chief Marshal Philip Joubert de la Ferté, ordered an operations research effort to determine why his aircraft were so ineffective at finding and killing the enemy. Statistical analysis of contact and attack reports soon revealed a host of problems in navigation, training, radar maintenance, weapon employment, and personnel policy. These revelations led to wholesale changes in doctrine and procedures. Key among these were an upper altitude limit of 2,000 feet for radar searches, which recognized the limitations of the ASV-II radar; enhancing the yield of the 250-pound depth charge with Torpex and devising a 25-foot minimum depth setting (vice 50 feet) for depth charges; and increasing the length of the standard "stick" of depth charges by a factor of three. Until more capable aircraft and several new airborne ASW technologies appeared in 1942, however, improvement was slow to arrive.

War in the Mediterranean

With the fall of France and the entry of Italy into the war on the Axis side, the shores of the Mediterranean had become an active theater. In mid-September 1940, three months after Italy's declaration of war, Italian troops advanced eastward from Libya into Egypt with the goal of reaching the Suez Canal but in fact penetrated only 50 miles before halting. Six weeks later the Italians invaded Greece through Albania and similarly achieved only limited gains before being stalemated by a staunch Greek defense. Then in early December, the British counter-attacked in North Africa and not only drove the Italians back across the border but by mid-February 1941 had conquered the entirety of Cyrenaica (eastern Libya) as far west as El Agheila. Simultaneously, the Greeks turned on the Italians and pushed them back into Albania.

Dismayed by these Italian reverses and newly convinced of the strategic importance of the Mediterranean, Hitler hurriedly ordered a small German mechanized force under *Generalleutnant* Erwin Rommel to Libya to support his ally. Although

seriously understrength, Rommel's force seized the initiative at the end of March, and in an audacious riposte pushed the British all the way back to the Egyptian border, where he halted—largely for logistics reasons—in late May. During his lightning drive Rommel bypassed and laid siege to the British fortress at Tobruk on the Mediterranean coast, which then had to be supplied by sea.

Meanwhile, in early April, German troops invaded Greece from the northeast (through Bulgaria, an Axis partner), quickly overwhelmed the Greeks and the British Commonwealth troops who had been sent to their aid, and captured Athens on 27 April. Barely a month later, they attacked Crete and seized the entire island in an unprecedented airborne assault, rendering the east-central Mediterranean a virtual "Axis lake" except for the British island stronghold of Malta, only 50 miles south of Sicily.

At sea, the Royal Navy's Mediterranean Fleet completely dominated the Italian surface forces, particularly after British victories in a carrier-launched air attack on the Italian fleet at Taranto and the surface battle off Cape Matapan in November 1940 and May 1941, respectively. Nonetheless, German and Italian aircraft operating from bases in southern Italy, Sicily, Libya, and now Crete gave the Axis effective control of the air over much of the central and eastern sea. Both sides depended on Mediterranean supply routes: east–west between Gibraltar and Alexandria for the British, north–south between Italy and North Africa for the Germans and Italians. To supply their desert armies, the British could bypass the gauntlet of enemy air attacks by diverting war matériel around the south of Africa and up through the Suez Canal, but this added six weeks to the voyage. Moreover, there were no alternatives for supplying Malta and sustaining Tobruk by ship but to steam through the Mediterranean. With only

300 miles between Sicily and Libya, the Axis faced a less demanding challenge, but British surface forces and submarines posed a constant threat to their cross-Mediterranean convoys, and transport aircraft were forced into a major supply role.

In September 1941, with the desert war temporarily stalemated, Hitler ordered six U-boats to the Mediterranean both to defend Rommel's supply lines and in response to an unwarranted fear that the British were planning an amphibious operation against Algeria. Additionally, Admiral Dönitz was ordered to step up his offensive against the Gibraltar convoys. The first German submarine to enter the Mediterranean, the *U-371,* successfully negotiated the Strait of Gibraltar on 21 September, followed by the other five boats within two weeks. The Italian Navy established bases for them at La Spezia and on an island near Athens. Initially, this first U-boat group concentrated against the small ships supplying besieged Tobruk, but with little success. A second wave of six U-boats was dispatched in November, but alerted by Enigma intercepts, the Royal Navy and RAF redoubled their patrols in the vicinity of the Strait of Gibraltar. Additionally, they mounted a new kind of ruse, a "U-boat trap" consisting of a heavily escorted "dummy" convoy of empty merchant ships intended to draw enemy submarines within attack range. On 16 November, the very day she transited the strait, the *U-433* rose to the bait and in a protracted engagement with the corvette *Marigold* succumbed to mortal depth-charge damage.

The *U-81,* under 26-year-old *Kapitänleutnant* Friedrich Guggenberger, had much better luck. On 13 November, only one day after he entered the Mediterranean, Guggenberger encountered a large British formation returning to Gibraltar from delivering aircraft to Malta and—totally undetected—penetrated the destroyer screen and struck the new aircraft carrier *Ark Royal* with one torpedo of a salvo of four. Heroic damage control efforts at first stemmed the resulting flooding, and the ship regained enough power to steam toward Gibraltar. The next day, however, unseen damage from the torpedo hit led to even more flooding, and the *Ark Royal* rolled over and sank only 25 miles from safety.

Then, on 25 November, less than two weeks later, one of the U-boats from the first wave, the *U-331,* chanced on a column of British battleships near Alexandria and managed to hit HMS *Barham* with three of four torpedoes. As the battleship slowly capsized, a magazine exploded, providing one of the most famous—and spectacular—newsreel sequences of war at sea ever filmed. Half of her crew died. The Royal Navy kept her loss secret for many weeks.[18]

Meanwhile, British and Commonwealth forces had counter-attacked Rommel on 18 November in a major offensive dubbed "Crusader," and by Christmas they had driven the Germans and their Italian allies back as far as Benghazi, 300 miles from the Egyptian border. This setback moved Hitler to declare a "state of emergency" in North Africa, and he ordered the Navy to spare no effort in supporting Rommel. Accordingly, the naval high command hastily prepared plans to deploy a total of 50 U-boats to the theater, 20 to the eastern Mediterranean and 30 to the west, to be drawn largely from the North Atlantic anti-shipping campaign and from the Arctic. At the end of November, ten more U-boats departed for the Mediterranean. The first five entered successfully, but two of these were sunk almost immediately: the *U-95* torpedoed by the Dutch submarine *O-1* (under Royal Navy control) on 28 November, and the *U-557* mistaken on 16 December for a British submarine by the Italian torpedo boat *Orione* and destroyed. The second group of five fared even less well. One was sunk by a British mine off her base at St. Nazaire, a second was forced to turn back with engine trouble, and the remaining three were damaged by air attacks and forced to abort, one in the Bay of Biscay and two at the Strait of Gibraltar. By assigning Swordfish aircraft made homeless by the sinking of the *Ark Royal* to Gibraltar, the British materially improved their ASW capabilities in the theater, but still no unassisted air kills were achieved.

Simultaneous with the deployment of U-boats to the Mediterranean late in the year, the German naval command ordered stepped-up attacks on the convoys to and from Gibraltar and Sierra Leone (in West Africa) to put additional pressure on British supply lines. In addition to several new waves of U-boats, long-range Focke-Wulf Fw 200 Condor bombers based at Bordeaux were sent to attack the Gibraltar convoys while also providing valuable reconnaissance for concentrating the submarine wolf packs.[19]

Earlier in the year—in February 1941—the potential vulnerability of the Gibraltar run had been starkly demonstrated by the experience of the homeward-bound convoy HG-53, which lost three ships of 21 to the *U-37* and five more to air attack by another flight of Condors, four-engine, long-range, reconnaissance bombers. Additionally, the Sierra Leone convoy SLS-64, with which HG-53 was supposed to merge the next day, was discovered by the marauding German heavy cruiser *Admiral Hipper,* which sank eight of the 19 merchantmen. Subsequently, the British assigned significantly more escorts to the Gibraltar convoys, and by the time of the new German threat later in the year they were among the most heavily escorted in the Atlantic.

As a desperate measure to fend off air attacks on convoys, the British devised a rocket-powered catapult for launching a fighter aircraft that could be sent aloft if enemy aircraft appeared. After engaging the enemy, the pilot would either land on nearby friendly territory (if available) or parachute in hopes of being picked up by one of the surface escorts. Fitted to five Royal Navy auxiliaries known as Fighter Catapult Ships (FCS) and to 35 merchant vessels called Catapult Aircraft Merchantmen (CAM) beginning in early 1941, the ships normally carried a specially-modified Hawker Hurricane fighter, although the two-seat Fairey Fulmar was used also early in the program.

First to be deployed were the fighter catapult ships, and HMS *Ariguani* made the first combat launch against a Condor shadowing a North Atlantic convoy on 12 May 1941; the enemy escaped. In July, HMS *Pegasus* became the first FCS to be used on the Gibraltar run when she joined the outbound convoy OG-67. Early in the voyage, she launched a Fulmar against an Fw 200, but after an unsuccessful pursuit, the catapult aircraft and crew were lost in a crash due to navigational error. Subsequently, virtually every Gibraltar or Sierra Leone convoy included either an FCS or a CAM, and the first catapult-ship kill of a German aircraft occurred on 3 August when a Hurricane from HMS *Maplin,* accompanying convoy SL-81, shot down an Fw 200. On several other occasions, aircraft from catapult ships chased German reconnaissance planes away from Gibraltar convoys without shooting them down, but two FCS ships were torpedoed: HMS *Springbank,* sunk on 17 September, and the *Ariguani,* damaged on 26 October and withdrawn from service. Meanwhile the toll exacted by the U-boats remained unacceptably high, with convoy OG-69 losing nine of 28 ships, OG-71 losing ten of 23, and HG-73 ten of 25.

A more enduring solution to the problem of providing air cover for convoys beyond the range of land-based aircraft was the escort carrier, the first of which, HMS *Audacity,* became operational in the late summer of 1941.[20] Converted by the Royal Navy from the captured German merchant ship

Hannover, the *Audacity* displaced 11,000 tons and operated six American-built Grumman F4F-3 Wildcat fighters (called Martlets in British service) from a flight deck 475 feet long. Because no hangar deck was provided, the embarked aircraft were parked and serviced in the open on the flight deck itself. The *Audacity* was assigned to the Gibraltar run and joined her first convoy, the outbound OG-74, on 13 September. Two days later her aircraft strafed a U-boat on the surface, forcing it under, and the sighting of another submarine enabled the convoy to take evasive action. Although five of 24 merchants were eventually torpedoed, the carrier's aircraft shot down an Fw 200 on the 21st after it had bombed the convoy's rescue ship. In early October, the *Audacity* returned without incident to the United Kingdom with convoy HG-74. Later that month, as she was escorting convoy OG-76, her Martlets downed two Fw 200s at a cost of one of their own; the convoy reached Gibraltar without loss.

Accompanying convoy HG-76, which departed Gibraltar on 14 December 1941, the *Audacity* took part—and was lost—in one of the most celebrated convoy battles of the war. HG-76 consisted of 32 merchant ships and 17 escorts, including the two sloops and seven corvettes of Escort Group 36 under Commander F. J. "Johnny" Walker, later to become the Royal Navy's most successful ASW tactician. Alerted by local spies to the convoy's departure, Admiral Dönitz ultimately sent 12 U-boats against it, including two that had been assigned to enter the Mediterranean at approximately the same time. One of these succeeded in sinking the freighter *Empire Barracuda* from a different convoy, but neither was able to attack HG-76. Bordeaux-based Fw 200s began shadowing the convoy on 16 December, but Enigma intercepts had warned the British of the German U-boat concentration, and the next day the *Audacity* was ordered to mount daytime

air patrols around the convoy. That morning, her Martlets spotted two U-boats on the surface tracking the convoy from opposite sides, and an escort group forced one of these, the *U-131,* to the surface, where it was attacked by a Martlet with machine-gun fire. Firing back, the submarine mortally damaged the fighter, which crashed into the sea. This appears to be the first time that an aircraft was destroyed by a submarine, but in turn, the *U-131* was quickly engaged by the surface escorts and so severely damaged that she was scuttled by her crew.

During the next several days a small freighter and the destroyer *Stanley*—a former American four-stacker—were sunk, but the *U-434, U-567,* and *U-574* were also killed, all in a series of sharp engagements orchestrated by Commander Walker. Moreover, Martlets from the *Audacity* destroyed two Fw 200s and damaged a third, while also strafing several U-boats on the surface, forcing them to dive. Late on the night of 21 December another small freighter was sunk, and in the resulting melee the *Audacity,* inadvertently silhouetted by a magnesium flare, was torpedoed by the *U-751.* She sank in ten minutes with the loss of 75 men, thus ending the short career of the world's first escort carrier. Ultimately, HG-76 reached home waters on 28 December, having lost only the *Audacity, Stanley,* and two small merchant ships, and thus demonstrating both the value of the escort carrier in convoy protection and the growing ASW proficiency of the Royal Navy. For their part, the Germans had lost four submarines and two Fw 200s, leaving Admiral Dönitz to conclude that the HG-76 engagement had been a disaster for his U-boat force.[21] In particular, he noted of HMS *Audacity,*

> The worst feature was the presence of the aircraft carrier. Small, fast, maneuverable aircraft circled the convoy continuously, so that

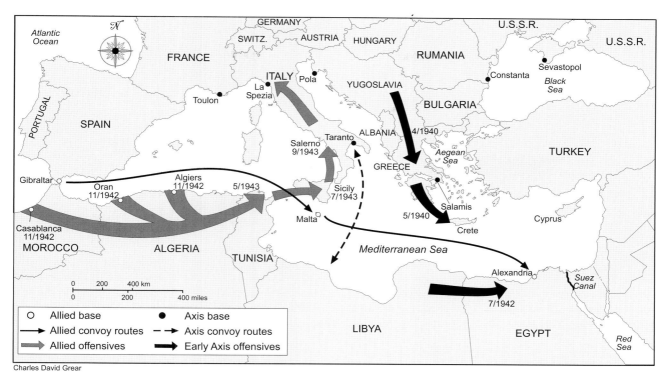

Map 4. The Mediterranean Theater, World War II

when it was sighted, the boats were repeatedly forced to submerge or withdraw. The presence of enemy aircraft also prevented any protracted shadowing or homing procedure by German aircraft. The sinking of the aircraft carrier is therefore of particular importance not only in this case but also in every other convoy action.[22]

At the time that the *Audacity* was sunk, the U.S. Navy already had a major program under way to convert cargo ships to escort carriers—then called aircraft escort vessels (AVGs). These ships, later designated CVEs, would soon be mass-produced by the United States for the U.S. and Royal Navies, with more than 100 such ships built or converted in U.S. shipyards by the end of the war.

Admiral Dönitz's entire effort in support of Hitler's North African campaign to date had come at a heavy cost. Since the spring of 1941, he had lost a half-dozen submarines in attacks on the Gibraltar and Sierra Leone convoys. Of the 26 boats that succeeded in entering the Mediterranean in 1941, five were sunk before the end of the year, in addition to the 11 Italian submarines lost during all of 1941. Four of the 16 Axis boats lost in the Mediterranean were torpedoed by Allied submarines, one was apparently mined, one (the *U-557*) was lost to fratricide, and the remaining ten were killed by surface warships. During this same period, the Royal Navy lost ten submarines in the theater, seven mined or probably mined and three to Italian surface forces. At the end of 1941 a total of 21 German U-boats and about the same number of Italian submarines were still operating in the Mediterranean, and more would arrive in 1942.

In addition to the diversion of German U-boats to the Mediterranean in the latter half of 1941, the naval high command in November ordered eight

The British escort carriers *Biter* (right) and *Avenger* in rough seas. These "jeep" carriers—called "Woolworth" carriers by the British—closed the North Atlantic "air gap," providing aircraft at sea at critical times and in critical locations. The *Avenger* was sunk by the *U-155* near Gibraltar in November 1942; the *Biter* was transferred to France in January 1945. *Imperial War Museum*

submarines to support an Atlantic sortie—later canceled—by the pocket battleship *Admiral Scheer* and six more to act as escorts for surface raiders and their prizes returning to Germany. As a result, the ongoing campaign against the Allied trans-Atlantic convoys was increasingly starved of submarines and came to a virtual halt in November and December 1941. Of the roughly 80 convoys, involving some 3,700 ships that crossed the North Atlantic (both eastward and westward) during the last third of the year, only four came under attack, while the total number of merchant ships lost (including stragglers and independent steamers) fell to only 54. Four escort ships, including the USS *Reuben James,* were lost. During this same period, the Germans lost only two U-boats in attacks on trans-Atlantic convoys (both in September), but for all of 1941, their losses to Allied ASW forces totaled 30 ocean-going submarines (Type VII and Type IX).

By the end of 1941, after 28 months of war, the Germans had deployed 153 ocean-going submarines to the North Atlantic and the Mediterranean, of which 54, or 35 percent, had been lost

in action. During this period, the U-boat force had sunk approximately 1,100 British and neutral ships, including 28 warships, and corresponding to a total loss of 5.3 million gross tons of carrying capacity. Nonetheless, the British were able to replace these losses with a combination of new construction, confiscation, purchase, and lease, so that at the end of 1941 their total gross merchant tonnage had actually *increased* by nearly three million tons since 1939. Moreover, 98 percent of ships inbound for the British Isles since the opening of hostilities reached their destination, although war losses and the inefficiencies of the convoy system reduced imports from 60 million tons in 1939, to 45 million tons in 1940, and to 31 million tons in 1941, causing great domestic hardship.[23]

America Enters the War

Just as the German North Atlantic anti-shipping campaign was languishing in December 1941, extraordinary and largely unanticipated events on the other side of the world dramatically expanded the scope of the war and provided Admiral Dönitz and his U-boats new opportunities to inflict devastation. The Japanese assault on Pearl Harbor on 7 December and the ensuing U.S. declaration of war on Japan took Hitler by surprise but led immediately to his own declaration of war on the United States. This precipitous move was a major strategic blunder. The terms of the Tripartite Pact required Germany to join Japan only if the United States attacked first, and absent the German war declaration—and with all American eyes on the Pacific—it is unlikely that President Roosevelt could have swayed U.S. public opinion to accept entering the war against Germany simultaneously. Hitler's action removed all doubt. In a stroke, the U.S. Navy's "short-of-war" measures in support of the Atlantic convoys transitioned to active belligerency—and Admiral Dönitz immediately ordered a U-boat offensive against American shipping along the U.S. East Coast.

When the United States entered the war in December 1941 the Navy's only viable ASW escorts were 177 destroyers, of which 83 were World War I–era four-stackers; 17 medium-to-large Coast Guard cutters, which had come under Navy control a month earlier; a few dozen small patrol craft and submarine chasers; and the pioneer escort carrier *Long Island*.[24] Of the destroyers, half of them—92—were assigned to the Atlantic Fleet, but 11 of those left for the Pacific in December and January, with the *Long Island* following in May 1942. Most of the remaining Atlantic destroyers were fully occupied with other duties in the battle fleet or escorting troopships, leaving only about 30—the earlier Support Force—available for ASW missions in the North Atlantic. Virtually all had sonar; only a few had radar. Shipboard installations of the CXAF search radar had only begun in October 1941, and just 19 were installed in the entire fleet, most in aircraft carriers, battleships, and cruisers.

The USS *Leary* (DD 158) was typical of the World War I–era four-stack destroyers that were "cut down" (to three funnels) and modified for ASW service in World War II. These "outdated" ships were invaluable to the U.S. and British Navies. Their original gun battery of four 4-inch/50 and one 3-inch/50 often was replaced by various combinations of 5-inch/38 and single and twin 3-inch/50 gun mounts. *U.S. Navy*

The U.S. Navy had none of the smaller ocean escorts typified by the British and Canadian corvettes and no immediate plans for building any. In response to the European war, the U.S. Congress in mid-1940 had authorized a huge new-construction program, including 9 battleships, 11 aircraft carriers, 47 cruisers, and 200 destroyers, but these would be slow coming on line. Early in the program, the Navy's General Board, recognizing a likely future need for numerous, low-cost convoy escorts, had recommended the emergency construction of a variant of the Coast Guard's 327-foot Treasury-class cutters to fill that need, but the proposal was rejected by both President Roosevelt and the Navy. Subsequently, in light of the inadequacies of its Hunt-class escort destroyers and the blue-water limitations of its small corvettes, the Royal Navy had designed a class of larger escorts designated "frigates." At first 20, and later 50, of these ships—1,100 tons, 290 feet long—would be built in the United States for Britain under Lend-Lease. Thus inspired, the U.S. Navy's Bureau of Ships produced a somewhat larger design—1,400 tons and 306 feet long—for what it called a "destroyer escort" (DE) and proposed to Roosevelt that these ships be produced in quantity in response to the General Board's earlier recommendation. In a highly controversial decision, the president agreed to the British request but refused the U.S. Navy's and directed instead a "crash" program to build hundreds of much smaller patrol craft and submarine chasers, which later proved completely unsuited to the ocean escort role. Additionally, Roosevelt's demands for higher priority on the construction of merchant shipping and landing craft delayed the British frigate program significantly, and the first of them—plus the first of the U.S. destroyer escorts—were not completed until mid-1943.

At the time of the U.S. entry into the war, the air reconnaissance capability of the Atlantic Fleet's naval air arm was vested largely in multiple squadrons of flying-boat patrol aircraft. All but one of these units flew the Consolidated PBY Catalina; the other flew the newer Martin PBM Mariner. Additionally, there were a squadron of Vought OS2U Kingfishers (floatplanes normally carried aboard ship for scouting purposes), a squadron of land-based Lockheed PBO-1 Hudson medium patrol bombers, and four blimps.[25] However, a number of these patrol squadrons were immediately transferred to the Pacific after the losses at Pearl Harbor (nearly three squadrons) and elsewhere, and two squadrons had been assigned earlier to Iceland and Argentia for convoy protection.[26] Moreover, the primary mission of the remaining patrol squadrons continued to be long-range reconnaissance and scouting for the battle fleet and patrol of strategic ocean areas, such as the approaches to the Panama Canal. Thus, relatively few Navy aircraft were available initially for ASW missions off the East Coast. These were stationed at bases scattered along the eastern seaboard and the Gulf of Mexico, from the Panama Canal to Maine, with a heavy concentration at Norfolk, Virginia, the principal Atlantic Fleet base.

Although other factors contributed, this serious lack of escort ships and ASW aircraft left the United States largely unprepared for the first German submarine offensive against the U.S. eastern seaboard that commenced in late December 1941. At that time, Admiral Dönitz had 64 U-boats assigned to the North Atlantic, and German yards were completing 16 new submarines per month. (The average for all of 1942 would eventually emerge as 22.2 per month, but half of the boats commissioned in that year would not see action until 1943.) Of Dönitz's 64 submarines, only 20 were the larger and longer-legged Type IXs, adequate for traveling the considerable distance from the French Atlantic bases to the United States, approximately 3,000 n.miles. Although at the end of December, only six of these were available to initiate the new campaign—designated *Paukenschlag* (Drumbeat)—Dönitz augmented the Type IXs with ten Type VIIs sent to Canadian waters to discourage the southerly redeployment of Allied ASW forces.

The first of the Type IXs departed Lorient on 18 December and the last on 27 December, by which time all of the Type VIIs also were under way. One of the former was forced to abort its mission due to a fuel leak, and two of the larger boats operated initially off Canada, but three, the *U-66, U-123,* and *U-125,* were vectored directly to the east coast of the United States with orders to commence hostilities simultaneously on 13 January. Reinhard Hardegen in the *U-123* jumped the gun by torpedoing a British freighter southeast of Nova Scotia on the 12th, but upon reaching Long Island he opened *Paukenschlag* in earnest by sinking two tankers on the 14th and 15th before heading south for the waters off Cape Hatteras, arriving almost simultaneously with the *U-66* on 18–19 January. The *U-125* arrived several days later after a fruitless search off the coast of New Jersey. The density of unprotected coastal shipping off Cape Hatteras provided easy pickings for the three Type IXs, later joined by the *U-130* diverted from Canadian waters. Counting merchants sunk during the outbound and return trips and those torpedoed off the coast of Canada, the five Type IXs sank 23 ships and damaged another—13 in U.S. waters alone. The ten Type VIIs sank 18 ships, for a total bag of 41, roughly 236,000 tons, including 13 tankers.[27] All told, it was a promising beginning for the U-boat campaign in American waters, and in January 1942, 12 more Type IXs and 14 Type VIIs headed west for a repeat performance.

The primary responsibility for the defense of shipping off the East and Gulf Coasts and in the West Indies fell on four Navy "sea frontiers" that had been established on 1 July 1941. These consisted of the Canadian Coastal Zone, the Eastern Sea Frontier (from the Canadian border to Jacksonville, Florida), the Gulf Sea Frontier (from Jacksonville south, including the Gulf of Mexico and part of the Bahamas), and the Caribbean and Panama Sea Frontier, which covered the southern Caribbean Sea and the eastern approaches to the Panama Canal.

The brunt of the initial German submarine campaign fell on the Eastern Sea Frontier, commanded by Vice Admiral Adolphus Andrews. He had few forces under his direct command, but theoretically he could request the assignment of ships and aircraft from the Atlantic Fleet to carry out the mission of protecting coastal traffic and convoys that originated in his area.[28] One of his—and the Navy's—fundamental difficulties was that very few long-range, land-based aircraft fell under naval jurisdiction. In accord with a convention that dated back to 1920, the Army held responsibility for virtually all large land-based aircraft, with the Navy limited largely to flying boats and sea-based aircraft. Thus, unlike the situation in Britain with Coastal Command, the U.S. Navy directly controlled very few land-based ASW aircraft and had to depend on the Army to supply the vital capabilities they provided. Unsurprisingly, the Army had never considered ASW a primary mission and lacked pilots skilled in operating over water or attacking small, moving targets at sea. Nonetheless, Admiral Andrews quickly secured an agreement with the Army to commit nine of its aircraft to two offshore sweeps every 24 hours in areas of interest and ordered defensive minefields be laid off Portland, Boston, New York, Charleston, and the entrances to the Chesapeake and Delaware Bays. Additionally, he ordered coastwise merchant traffic to hug the shoreline as tightly as possible and to use inshore "short cuts," such as the Cape Cod and the

Chesapeake and Delaware Canals, whenever feasible. Unfortunately, none of these measures proved adequate against the gathering onslaught.

Of the 12 Type IX U-boats sent to the Americas in January 1942, five were ordered to make a first foray into the Caribbean to attack merchant shipping in the vicinity of Aruba and Trinidad, key nodes in the supply chain for oil and bauxite from South America northward. The remainder of the Type IXs concentrated on the U.S. East Coast and the Type VIIs on Canadian waters. The British freighter *Oranjestad,* torpedoed at Aruba on 6 February, became the first of an enormous toll of merchant losses in the Caribbean during the next nine months. The five Type IXs of the first wave alone sank 24 ships totaling 119,000 gross tons, and half of them were tankers. All told, the U-boats deployed in January plus five large Italian submarines patrolling just east of the Windward Islands bagged a total of 77 ships, representing more than 430,000 tons of merchant shipping. Of the 14 shorter-range Type VIIs among the January boats, three made the first appearance of that type off the United States, two on "experimental" sorties southward from Canadian waters to the New York area and one that "worked" Cape Hatteras after refueling in the mid-Atlantic from a clandestine surface ship. These three submarines sank a total of eight ships and showed both the value of mid-ocean refueling and the feasibility of using Type VIIs off the East Coast, where—by husbanding their fuel in the trans-Atlantic crossing—they could spend seven to ten days on patrol.

Taking advantage of the unreadiness of U.S. ASW measures and a target-rich environment, Admiral Dönitz was quick to follow up by sending more U-boats to the Americas: 18 in February, 26 in March, and then a peak of 31 in April.[29] Additionally, beginning with the March patrols, he deployed submarine tankers with the attack boats to extend their patrols by refueling at sea.

The *U-459,* the first of the Type XIV submarine tankers, was tasked with refueling 15 of the March boats. Also, the *U-A,* the one-of-a-kind submarine that Germany had been building for the Turkish Navy at the beginning of the war, was deployed to service three more of the attackers. The Type XIVs, known as *Milchkühe* ("milk cows"), displaced 1,900 tons submerged on a length of 220 feet and carried 600 tons of diesel fuel, of which 450 tons was available for refueling others. They could also carry food, miscellaneous supplies, and a limited number of replacement torpedoes in deck canisters. With neither deck guns nor torpedo tubes, the Type XIVs were virtually defenseless, and all ten of those commissioned were lost by mid-1944.

In the meantime, however, refueling at sea made possible the first attacks on merchant traffic in the Gulf of Mexico by two Type IXs and a Type VII of the April group. The main emphasis was on attacking oil tankers from Texas and Louisiana and general shipping at the mouth of the Mississippi River. This first excursion by only three U-boats netted 19 Allied ships, including eight tankers, and in June and July, 25 more ships fell victim to follow-on U-boat patrols in the Gulf area.

The losses continued to rise elsewhere. Within the Eastern, Gulf, and Caribbean Sea Frontiers, a total of 84 merchants of 410,350 gross tons were sunk in May, and 82 were lost in June, representing 438,700 gross tons.[30] Forty-six of these 166 ships were oil tankers.[31] This unprecedented bloodletting on America's doorstep led to a rapid acceleration of ASW measures, beginning in the Eastern Sea Frontier, where the threat had first appeared. In late January, Admiral Ernest J. King, Commander-in-Chief U.S. Fleet since December 1941, ordered a variety of Atlantic Fleet aircraft be made available for ASW in the sea frontiers where they were based. In particular, this gave Admiral Andrews operational control of 44 PBY Catalinas, although their availability was subject to higher

Atlantic Fleet priorities. Additionally, several initiatives were undertaken to enlist amateur yachtsmen (under the Coast Guard Auxiliary) and private pilots (under the Civil Air Patrol) for a system of inshore patrols intended to augment the Navy and Army Air Forces (AAF) efforts already under way. By mid-year, hundreds of small ships and aircraft were participating, and although their military value was questionable, they made occasional U-boat sightings and provided useful service in search and rescue operations. More importantly, after protracted negotiations between the Secretaries of War and Navy to formalize the AAF's new responsibility for land-based airborne ASW and to clarify command relationships, an agreement of 26 March 1942 placed "all Army Air Forces units allocated by defense commanders for operations over the sea, to protect shipping and conduct anti-submarine warfare" under the operational control of the sea frontier commanders. Simultaneously, the Army began assigning additional aircraft to the ASW mission, notably the twin-engine Douglas B-18 Bolo medium bomber, augmented its training program for over-water flying, and created an ASW operations analysis group at Langley Field, Virginia.[32] In October, it established the 1st Anti-Submarine Army Air Command, consisting of two squadrons for the Eastern and Gulf Sea Frontiers, respectively, and co-located their command centers with the corresponding Navy organizations.

These measures—as welcome as they were—largely downplayed fundamental differences between the Army and Navy over ASW tactics, mirroring the same issues that had divided the Royal Navy in two wars. Whereas the Navy—to whose sea frontiers the Army aircraft had been parceled out—emphasized *defensive* patrolling intended to protect shipping lanes and (later) convoys, the Army Air Forces wanted to adopt a more *offense*-oriented approach, using radar-equipped hunter-killer aircraft to track

down and destroy U-boats roughly located by intelligence, "flaming datums," or at-sea contacts.[33] This orientation also implied more central command and direction of air assets, releasing them from the local control of the individual sea frontiers. In the event, these issues were never fully resolved until the dissolution of the 1st Anti-Submarine Army Air Command in September 1943.

Even more angry disagreements emerged over the issue of coastal convoys, urged persistently on the United States by the British government, whose petroleum supplies were seriously threatened by the increasing number of tankers—many of them Commonwealth ships—lost in American waters. But strongly influenced by their perception of the British experience in 1939 and early 1940, U.S. Navy officials maintained that weakly escorted convoys were worse than none at all and hesitated to establish a coastal convoy system until adequate escort forces became available. As noted above, the number of U.S. Navy destroyers available for convoy duty off the East Coast had already been significantly reduced by transfers to the Pacific theater, routine Atlantic Fleet responsibilities, and escort assignments with the trans-Atlantic merchant convoys already functioning. Moreover, by the end of June 1942, some 20 U.S. troop convoys—several carrying British troops—had left North America for destinations in both the Atlantic and Pacific, and since Navy policy gave top priority to escorting troopships, this placed other inescapable demands on the destroyer force.[34] Nonetheless, the Navy's delay in establishing coastal convoys led to significant friction between the U.S. and British high commands and fueled a controversy over the U.S. policy that continues today. Ironically, if the United States had not earlier supplied the British with 50 old destroyers in the "destroyers-for-bases" deal—plus ten Coast Guard cutters under Lend-Lease—

adequate escorts *would* have been available to start the coastal convoys immediately.[35]

Several interim steps were taken by the U.S. Navy to ameliorate the immediate crisis, first by initiating on 1 April a "bucket brigade" system that routed coastal shipping between protected anchorages and minimized night-time sailing off the eastern seaboard, the latter action because of the limited effectiveness of available surface ships and aircraft at night. Thus, southbound ships from Boston or New York, sailing only by day when air patrols were possible, could take refuge successively in the Chesapeake or Delaware Bays, Cape Lookout (North Carolina), Charleston (South Carolina), and finally Jacksonville, and vice versa on the northbound trip. Additionally, in what was called "reverse Lend-Lease," the Royal Navy transferred to the United States 24 ASW trawlers and ten Flower-class corvettes to serve as coastal escorts. By early April all of the former had arrived, with 14 "combat-ready," and the corvettes trickled in over the next year.[36]

More significantly, as a follow-on to the Arcadia strategy conference (December 1941–January 1942) and subsequent negotiations among the American, British, and Canadian Navies, a new, more efficient North Atlantic convoy system was put in place that was expected to free up as many as a dozen U.S. destroyers for East Coast convoy duty. In this new scheme, two rendezvous locations for the Atlantic convoys, the West Ocean Meeting Point (WESTOMP) and an East Ocean Meeting Point (EASTOMP), were defined at longitudes 45 west and 22 west, respectively. The Canadian Navy was given responsibility for escorting convoys between Canada and the WESTOMP and the Royal Navy between the British Isles and the EASTOMP. To cover the 1,800 miles separating the two meeting points a multi-national Mid-Ocean Escort Force (MOEF) was proposed, consisting of 14 close-escort

groups, totaling nearly 150 destroyers and corvettes. Going eastward, these escort groups were expected to steam at their best cruising speed from bases in North America to the WESTOMP, escort convoys to the EASTOMP, and then continue across the Atlantic to bases in Ireland for rest and replenishment before repeating the process in the opposite direction. Provision also was included for shuttling the merchant ships engaged in supplying Russia between Iceland and the main Atlantic convoys.

By the time the "bucket brigade" started at the beginning of April 1942, the slowly increasing forces assigned to Admiral Andrews consisted of roughly 90 small surface ships (including some 65 Coast Guard cutters and the first British trawlers), four blimps, 82 other Navy aircraft, and nearly 100 Army aircraft. These assets could provide a modicum of local escort and area patrol. Meanwhile, in the Canadian Coastal zone, a U.S. Navy PBO-1 Hudson of Patrol Squadron (VP) 82, based at Argentia, scored the first kill of a U-boat in American waters—and the first U.S. submarine kill of the war—when it caught the *U-656* on the surface on 1 May and destroyed it with bombs. Two weeks later, on the 15th, a second Hudson from VP-82 sank the *U-503* on the Grand Banks.

Within a month, on 14 April, the four-stack destroyer *Roper* (DD 147) became the first U.S. Navy surface ship to destroy a U-boat in World War II. The *Roper* gained a night radar contact on the *U-85*, which had surfaced in shallow water just north of Cape Hatteras. After a short surface chase and gun action, the *Roper* drove her under and finished the job with depth charges. There were no German survivors in any of these encounters. Navy and Coast Guard forces destroyed three more submarines before an Army A-29 Hudson based at Cherry Point, North Carolina, achieved the first unassisted submarine kill by the Army Air Forces on 7 July, when during a routine patrol it caught

The British Flower-class corvettes were common sights in the North Atlantic during the Battle of the Atlantic. They were sailed by the British and Canadian Navies during the war—and also by the U.S. Navy. This is the USS *Surprise* (PG 63) in 1944, one of eight Canadian-built Flowers that served in the U.S. Navy under reverse Lend-Lease. *U.S. Navy*

the *U-701* on the surface and sank her with depth charges. Seven German survivors were eventually rescued after being sighted by a Navy blimp.

Although the bucket brigade and a concomitant increase in air and surface coverage had some mitigating effect on shipping losses off the eastern seaboard, the Gulf and Caribbean areas remained relatively unprotected. In fact, Admiral Andrews's initial ASW measures in the Eastern Sea Frontier—notably the larger number of aircraft and ships, which achieved growing effectiveness in keeping the U-boats down—plus the allocation of Atlantic Fleet destroyers, had begun to cut the U-boat success rate there. Accordingly, Admiral Dönitz shifted his emphasis to the Gulf and Caribbean areas. As sinkings in the Eastern Sea Frontier dropped from 23 in April to five in May, those in the Gulf and Caribbean areas rose from 15 to 78, driving total losses in American waters in April and May to 40 and 85 sinkings, respectively—one-third of them tankers.

Tanker attrition became so serious that on 16 April all tankers under American control were ordered to remain in port until further notice, with the British following suit two days later. After another six days, the British directed their tankers to steam from the Caribbean directly across the Atlantic to West Africa to join northbound convoys from Sierra Leone to Great Britain. On the 29th U.S. authorities relaxed their hold on coastwise tanker sailings, but the renewed losses generated even more strident demands from the British for American coastal convoys.

By scraping together ships of virtually every size and description, the Navy finally gained enough escorts to establish a formal system of coastal convoys off the East Coast. Following top-level negotiations among American and British authorities in London, Admiral King directed that the first of these be established by the middle of May. The first segment became operable between Key West and Norfolk on 14 May. It was protected by a mixed force of 45 warships, including U.S. destroyers, submarine chasers, Coast Guard cutters, and British corvettes and trawlers. This route was followed within a week by segments operating between New York and Halifax, between Guantanamo Bay and Halifax, and between Trinidad and Aruba.[37] In August, additional convoys were established between Galveston (Texas), the approaches to the Mississippi, and Key West, while other Gulf and Caribbean routes were added as necessary. To assist in area patrol and convoy cover, the RAF Coastal Command sent a squadron of Lockheed Hudsons to Trinidad, joining a squadron of U.S. Army B-18 Bolos and a detachment of U.S. Navy PBY Catalinas already assigned there.

By the end of August 1942, the first steps had been completed to coordinate the sailing of coastal, Gulf, and Caribbean convoys with the trans-Atlantic convoys coming and going from Halifax. An additional direct route was established between New York and Key West, and eventually New York supplanted Halifax as the principal western terminus for the trans-Atlantic routes. In effect, this created a system of trunks and feeders, known as the "interlocking convoy system," that rationalized the flow of war matériel from the Americas to Britain and minimized delays in organizing and routing convoys and escorts.[38] This whole complex was fully operational by the end of 1942 and operated essentially unchanged until the end of the war.

However belated, convoying in American waters reduced the losses of merchant shipping to the U-boat campaign almost immediately. By July 1942 the monthly toll had been reduced to less than half that of May, and because of their diminishing productivity, Admiral Dönitz withdrew the smaller Type VIIs from independent patrols and significantly curtailed the sailings of the larger Type IXs. Thus, during the last three months of 1942 no merchant ships were sunk in the Eastern, Gulf, and Panama Sea Frontiers, although losses remained appreciable in the Caribbean Sea Frontier.[39] Between 1 July and 7 December 1942 (the first anniversary of Pearl Harbor), only 39 vessels were sunk of the 9,064 participating in the new convoys—a loss rate of less than one-half of 1 percent. By the end of the year, Dönitz had acknowledged this decreasing success by virtually abandoning the American campaign to concentrate his U-boats again on the North Atlantic convoy routes.

Nonetheless, this initial German submarine offensive against the Americas had been one of the most successful of the war. During the 184 war patrols to the Americas mounted in 1942—80 by Type IXs and 104 by Type VIIs—the U-boats sank 609 ships of 3.1 million gross tons. This total represents fully *one-quarter* of the Allied shipping sunk by German submarines in World War II, and it was gained at the loss of only 23 U-boats, of which were 13 killed by U.S. forces. However, these shipping losses—while serious—were rapidly being replaced. In 1942, U.S., British, and Canadian shipyards built a total of 7.1 million gross tons of new shipping, a million tons more than the total lost to U-boats worldwide. Moreover, the total Allied shipping pool amounted to approximately 30 million gross tons, of which the losses in American waters represented only one-tenth. Although 188 tankers were sunk worldwide in the first eight months of 1942 (143 in the Americas), Allied shipyards replaced more than two-thirds of the tanker tonnage lost, and in two Lend-Lease programs denoted "Red Gap" and "Blue Gap," the United States provided the equivalent of 100 tankers to Britain the same year.

In the near term, however, British imports indeed suffered significantly, dropping 18 percent from 1941 to 1942, causing significant shortages of food, fuel, and heating oil, which led to major hardships and widespread rationing of most commodities.[40]

The End of the Beginning

While Admiral Dönitz's U-boat offensive in the Western Hemisphere was reaching its apogee in mid-1942, the substantial Anglo-American effort to supply the beleaguered Soviet Union with war matériel was peaking also. There were three sea routes available to the Allies: across the Pacific to the Russian northeast; around southern Africa to the Persian Gulf and then overland through Iran; and the most direct—and fastest— route from Britain or the United States, north of Norway, to Murmansk or Archangel. Roughly one-quarter of the Russian aid eventually arrived via the "Murmansk run," but that was by far the most dangerous route, with Allied convoys threatened not only by the two dozen U-boats stationed in Norway because of Hitler's fear of a British invasion but also by German Air Force squadrons operating from the North Cape and by major German surface warships, including the battleship *Tirpitz*, lurking in northern Norwegian fjords.

Accordingly, the Anglo-American convoys to northern Russia demanded large and powerful escort forces, capable of defending both outbound (PQ) and returning (QP) convoys against the multiple German threats. Because of difficult winter weather and the Arctic night that prevailed over the region in early 1942, most of the first PQ and QP convoys sailed unmolested. However, when the approach of near-continuous daylight in April provided German submarines and aircraft more opportunities for attack, Allied shipping losses increased. Of the 84 ships that left U.S. ports for Russia via the Murmansk run in April, May, and June, only 44 reached their destination. Twenty-three were lost to enemy action or marine casualties, and 17 were diverted to Scotland pending less threatening conditions.[1] While aggressive Allied escorts discouraged both submarines and attacking aircraft, however, the steadily lengthening day—essentially 24 hours of sunlight as late as September—also disadvantaged the U-boats, which relied on the cover of night for concealment while transiting on the surface. Thus, until the end of May, the Arctic U-boats managed to sink only nine merchant ships for a loss of three of their own. Convoy PQ-16, which arrived in Murmansk on 30 May, lost seven of 34 merchant ships, but six of these were sunk by relentless German air attacks and only one by a U-boat.

The next Russia-bound convoy, PQ-17, however, suffered the worst losses of any Allied convoy in World War II. Departing Iceland on 27 June, the convoy consisted of 35 merchant ships, three rescue ships, two tankers for refueling, and a massive screen that included a close escort force of 21 ships, a covering force of four heavy cruisers and three destroyers, and a distant support force of two battleships, two cruisers, and an aircraft carrier.

The German high command planned to augment heavy submarine and air operations against

The use of convoys to gather in and defend merchant ships dates to the age of sail. It was a basic tactic for the Allies in World Wars I and II. This photo—taken by a German reconnaissance aircraft—shows part of the ill-fated PQ-17 en route to Murmansk, probably taken early in its voyage in July 1942. *U.S. Navy*

PQ-17 with a powerful surface force formed around the battleship *Tirpitz*. The convoy was first sighted by a German submarine on 1 July and, ultimately, 11 U-boats converged for the attack. First blood was drawn by the Air Force on 4 July, when three merchant ships were mortally damaged despite furious anti-aircraft fire from the cruisers of the covering force, which had come up in direct support. (Two of the three losses were finished off by U-boat torpedoes.)

That evening, believing erroneously that the *Tirpitz* battle group was at sea and preparing to attack the convoy before the heavy support force could intervene, the Royal Navy's First Sea Lord, Sir Dudley Pound, ordered the Allied cruisers and destroyers to retreat westward and directed the convoy itself to "scatter," with the merchants to proceed independently on their own, "every man for himself." As the orphaned ships of PQ-17 spread over the Barents Sea without protection, the German Navy and Air Force seized the initiative. The result was a slaughter: 24 merchant ships (65 per-

cent) and their much-needed cargoes were lost—nine to aircraft, seven to submarines, and nine to joint action. No German submarines were sunk, but five aircraft were shot down. The effect of this debacle on the Allied camp was shattering, and the Murmansk convoys were suspended immediately until the change of seasons provided more hours of darkness. In the next attempt, in September 1942, another fierce battle raged around the outgoing convoy PQ-18 and the nearby returning QP-14, but this time, although the Allied losses were still significant, with nine ships sunk by submarines and ten by aircraft (29 percent), three U-boats were lost in the encounter. Fortunately, as the Arctic winter closed in, merchant losses to German action dropped, becoming negligible by the end of the year.

In August 1942, after suspending Type VII patrols to the Americas and gaining an average of 20 U-boats each month from new construction, Admiral Dönitz re-opened his offensive against the North Atlantic shipping lanes, assigning three-quarters of his operational submarines to that theater and concentrating his wolf packs largely in the "air gap" north of the Azores, beyond the reach of Allied land-based aircraft. By deploying north–south patrol lines athwart the usual convoy routes, emphasizing central direction, and using radio beacons from boats in contact, the U-boat command succeeded regularly in concentrating wolf packs of as many as a dozen submarines against Allied convoys. Merchant losses again mounted rapidly.

In September 1942, German submarines began regular attacks on shipping in the Gulf of St. Lawrence, one even penetrating up the St. Lawrence River a distance of some 200 miles. All told, the monthly total of U-boats leaving for North Atlantic patrols rose from ten in June to 30 in August, to nearly 60 at year's end, while Allied losses reached nearly 30 per month by November. During the month of August not one trans-Atlantic merchant convoy escaped submarine attack, and from that month to the end of the year 131 ships, totaling three-quarters of a million gross tons, were lost on the North Atlantic routes. Additionally, as the year drew on, more U-boats moved southward to attack shipping concentrations in the Gulf of Guinea and off the Cape of Good Hope. In October and November, the Allies established new convoy systems (designated UG and GU) across the mid-Atlantic from Norfolk to North Africa and back, in preparation for and support of the Anglo-American landings in Morocco and Algeria—Operation Torch, which commenced on 8 November. These convoys offered even more opportunities for the U-boats. Allied and German sources agree that worldwide losses of Allied shipping to Axis submarines peaked in November 1942, when approximately 130 ships were sunk, for about 800,000 tons.[2] Of these, about 30 were sunk on the North Atlantic run, with the remainder lost in the Mediterranean, the Pacific, and elsewhere.

The increasing German success was abetted by three significant factors. First was Admiral Dönitz's growing use of Type XIV submarine tankers and converted Type X minelayers to refuel and re-supply U-boats at sea, which enabled them to extend the length of their patrols by a factor of two—reaching an average of nine weeks.[3] Moreover, the German Navy's cryptographic organization, B-dienst, had broken into the vulnerable Allied convoy code early in the year and by September 1942 was reading it rapidly enough to supply Dönitz with timely tactical information on convoy schedules and routing. In contrast, when the German submarine command at the end of January 1942 switched to the new Triton code, which added a fourth rotor to the Enigma coding machine, British codebreakers at Bletchley Park abruptly lost their ability to decrypt German submarine communications and did not regain it for the rest of the year. This setback was at least partially offset, however, by increasingly effective Allied use of the land-based HF/DF network to locate U-boats at sea, and this in turn was augmented in mid-1942 by the initial deployment of miniaturized ship-borne HF/DF receivers on convoy escorts.[4] At first, there were only enough sets available to equip a single ship in each convoy, generally the rescue ship. The rescue ships—lacking a potentially interfering radar set and stationed at the rear of the convoy—were in an ideal position to use HF/DF to locate trailing U-boats that were reporting the convoy's movements to other submarines and to U-boat headquarters. By the end of 1942, most convoys had two or three HF/DF-equipped escorts, which often enabled the detection and location of approaching submarines by cross-fixing on the U-boat chatter that had become an important aspect of wolf-pack operations. With British technical assistance, the U.S. Navy that same year developed its own shipboard HF/DF sets, which were first installed on two Coast Guard cutters in October.

The slow convoy SC-107 serves as an example of one of the more spectacular German successes in late 1942. Sailing from New York on 24 October with 20 merchant ships, it was joined by 22 more from Halifax and Sydney (Nova Scotia), a total of 42. The local escort passed the convoy to the Canadian mid-ocean Escort Group C-4, which consisted of the Canadian destroyer *Restigouche* and five corvettes, four Canadian and one British. The *Restigouche* carried the older Type 286 1.5-meter radar; the British corvette was equipped with a more recent Type 271 centimetric set, but it was inoperable at the time. The rescue ship *Stockport* was fitted with an HF/DF receiver, which gave clear warning of the impending attacks. On 29 October, the *U-522*, one of three Type IXC U-boats deploying to the Gulf of St. Lawrence, reported SC-107 near Cape Race. By radio, Admiral Dönitz ordered the two other Type IXCs and attack group *Vielchen*—14 U-boats—to converge on the convoy, and on the night of 1–2 November six boats were in position to attack. By morning eight merchant ships had been lost, including four torpedoed by the *U-402* alone, with partial credit for a fifth.

The relatively inexperienced Canadian escort group was virtually powerless against the marauding submarines and inflicted no damage on any of them. Admiral Dönitz promptly ordered another wolf pack to join the fray, for a total of more than 20 potential attackers. The Allies also brought up reinforcements: three destroyers (two American, one British) and a U.S. Coast Guard cutter from Iceland, all arriving late on the 2nd. Still, over the next two nights seven U-boats attacked the convoy, sinking seven more merchant ships and causing the diversion of the *Stockport* and the two U.S. destroyers to Iceland with 600 survivors. Eight of the remaining merchant ships accompanied them.

On the morning of 5 November, with the remnants of SC-107 now within their range, Liberators and Catalinas from Iceland arrived over the convoy to escort it to the East Ocean Meeting Point, and increasingly harassed by the Allied aircraft, the wolf pack withdrew. SC-107 finally reached Liverpool on 10 November, having lost 15 ships of 42, with eight others diverted to Iceland. Although this was the fourth most successful convoy attack of the war, the Germans lost three U-boats, including two caught on the surface by Allied aircraft from Newfoundland on 30 October before they could join the battle. The third, the Type VII *U-132*, appears to have been destroyed by the nearby explosion of the British ammunition ship *Hatimura* after she had been torpedoed by both the *U-132* herself and the *U-442*.

While "horror stories" like that of SC-107 abound in the first half of the Battle of the Atlantic, a broader perspective reveals a much less dire situation. In fact, as the Allies brought more ASW forces to bear and gained experience in countering the German submarine offensive, the tide was beginning to turn slowly in their favor. German U-boats attacked only six of the 39 North Atlantic convoys that sailed in September and October 1942—a total of 1,700 ships—and sank 57 (3.4 percent).[5] (Fifteen of these losses were from SC-107.) Of the November and December sailings, 11 of 31 convoys were attacked, with losses of only 34 of 1,218 ships, or 2.8 percent.[6] Moreover, only *three* of the 34 ships lost from these 31 convoys were *eastbound,* meaning that the flow of war material to Britain was only minimally affected. In the North Atlantic for all of 1942, a total of 7,558 ships arrived safely at their destinations, against 169 lost (2.2 percent).[7]

Meanwhile, U-boat losses were considerable and mounting. In the last four months of 1942, 24 submarines were destroyed in the North Atlantic and 21 elsewhere. Since the beginning of the war, 153 had been lost. Although approximately 340 new-construction U-boats had become operational since 1939, the many war-hardened and experienced submariners that had been lost to enemy action were much more difficult to replace, and the growing preponderance of relatively inexperienced officers and crews began to show in decreasing "production" per patrol. For example, of the 84 submarines commencing North Atlantic patrols in November and December 1942, 43 returned to port without having destroyed a single merchant ship, and overall the number of merchants sunk per patrol dropped to 0.69.[8] In contrast, during the "happy time" of the campaign off the Americas, from December 1941 through August 1942, 184 war patrols had resulted in 609 Allied sinkings—3.31 ships per patrol—and only six patrols had been fruitless.

A major reason for increasing Allied effectiveness in protecting convoys from even concentrated German U-boat attacks was the growing number of ASW aircraft based around the North Atlantic basin in the United States, Canada, Greenland, Iceland, and Britain. By October approximately 700 aircraft had been assigned to front-line ASW units, and almost 300 of these were the long-range Catalinas, Sunderlands, Halifaxes, Fortresses, and Liberators, the last two mostly Lend-Lease aircraft flown by the British.[9] A growing number of aircraft were equipped with the new centimetric radar, and all carried more destructive, fast-sinking depth charges that could be set to detonate reliably at a depth of 25 feet to catch a crash-diving U-boat.

In contrast to the debacle of convoy SC-107, the experience of fast convoy HX-217, which left New York on 27 November 1942, exemplifies the growing ability of Allied escorts and long-range aircraft to minimize losses on the North Atlantic run. The 35 merchant ships of HX-217 were joined at the WESTOMP by the Royal Navy's Escort Group 6, consisting of a British destroyer and corvette, a Polish destroyer, three Norwegian corvettes, and the British rescue ship *Perth*, the last with HF/DF. All six escorts carried the Type 271 centimetric radar. Because of a howling storm, eight of the merchants were forced into St. John's, Newfoundland.

The remaining 25 ships were sighted by the *U-524* some 300 miles south of Greenland on 7 December. Admiral Dönitz quickly ordered in the other six boats of wolf pack *Panzer,* but an aggressive defense by the convoy escort that night—including a gunnery action—limited HX-217's losses to one tanker. Dönitz then called in another wolf pack, for a total of 22 U-boats, but severe weather and bad communications prevented effective concentration. By the morning of the 8th the weather had moderated, but three Coastal Command Liberators arrived from Iceland to provide air cover, subsequently spotting 13 U-boats on the surface and attacking 11 of them with both depth charges and strafing fire.[10] Although the three aircraft expended all their depth charges without making a kill, they succeeded in keeping the submarines away from the convoy for the rest of the day. In an unusual incident that night, the *U-254* was sunk in a collision with the *U-221* that left only four survivors from the former and forced the *U-221* to withdraw. Subsequently, only two U-boats achieved firing position, one of them blowing up a British ammunition ship. Inclement weather returned on 9 December, precluding Allied air operations, but with skillful use of radar and HF/DF the surface escorts managed to keep the Germans at bay and out of position to attack the following night. Good flying weather on 10 December produced a swarm of Flying Fortresses, Liberators, Sunderlands, Catalinas, and Hudsons from Iceland, and a British Liberator sank the *U-611* that afternoon. At that point, Dönitz called off his U-boats, having sacrificed two of them—one by accident—to sink only two merchant ships. Convoy HX-217 arrived in Liverpool on 14 December.

The accelerating Anglo-American success in countering the U-boat offensive in late 1942 was due to a synergistic combination of factors: greater ASW resources, better tactics, and key technical advances in sensors, weapons, and cryptography. However, one of the most notable achievements in the latter area—regaining the ground lost when the Germans adopted their new Triton code—was not fully accomplished until late 1943. Evidence of the impending code change with its addition of a fourth Enigma rotor had first appeared in early October 1941, when several test transmissions were detected. Accommodating the fourth rotor required the Allies to design and build much larger and faster bombes capable of sorting through possible key settings that now numbered several orders of magnitude more than what the earlier machines could handle. This was a formidable engineering task that would take many months to complete.

In mid-1942 the British overcame their last hesitancy about revealing the details of Enigma decryption to the United States, and the latter became a full partner in attacking the four-rotor Enigma code, both by joining the analysis team and by exploiting the larger industrial infrastructure and more advanced electronic technology available in America. In September the Navy Department contracted with the National Cash Register Company in Dayton, Ohio, to build more than a hundred four-rotor bombes, and by May 1943 two cranky prototypes dubbed "Adam" and "Eve" were

completed. After the design was refined for production, 104 more were ordered.

Earlier, in October 1942, another cryptographic windfall had occurred. On the 30th a radar-equipped RAF Sunderland detected the Type VIIC *U-559* in the eastern Mediterranean, northeast of Port Said, and called in five destroyers, which re-detected the submarine and forced her to the surface after a relentless series of depth-charge attacks.[11] With their boat pummeled by surface gunfire, the German crew scuttled the boat and abandoned ship, without, however, jettisoning their code books. The British destroyer *Petard* managed to get a hawser on the sinking *U-559*, keeping her afloat long enough to allow a boarding party to go below and retrieve crucial Enigma coding materials. Two of the boarding party lost their lives when the submarine suddenly plunged to the bottom, but their heroic action provided the keys that within two months allowed Bletchley Park to read much of the Triton traffic that had been sent between late November and early December. Although these decryptions occurred after the fact, their intelligence and technical value represented a major breakthrough. By September 1943, 17 four-rotor bombes were operating in Washington, increasing to 84 by the end of that year, and more and more German traffic could be decoded in near-real time. Although the British eventually produced 69 four-rotor bombes of their own, the superior performance of the American machines led to the U.S. Navy's taking over the processing of virtually all of the German Navy Enigma traffic, and by April 1944, the Allies were reading essentially all encrypted radio communications between the U-boat command and their submarines at sea.

The Battle of the Bay

As increasing Ultra decryptions enabled the Allies to vector more and more aircraft toward confirmed submarine operating areas, airborne ASW soon emerged as a major factor in killing U-boats, particularly on the submarine transit routes through the Bay of Biscay. Eventual success was relatively slow in coming, however. Although radar-equipped Coastal Command aircraft based in southern England had flown regular patrols over the Bay of Biscay for much of 1941, the German practice of transiting on the surface only at night had deprived the aircraft of so much as a single kill that year. Even if a submarine was detected on radar, the lack of spatial resolution and the short-range "dead zone" of the early instruments made it impossible to attack surface targets reliably in the dark. The first Allied breakthrough in the see-saw "Battle of the Bay" that ensued was the so-called Leigh Light, first put forward by Squadron Leader Humphrey de Verde Leigh in October 1940 as the result of a call for innovative tactical suggestions by the higher command.

Leigh proposed a powerful airborne searchlight that could be directed along the path of an ASW aircraft during its final, radar-directed attack, thus providing illumination to drop depth charges accurately at night. After overcoming a series of bureaucratic hurdles and the objections of the "official" aircraft-development establishment, by March 1941 he was testing his searchlight in a Wellington bomber, at first in isolation and then in conjunction with the ASV-II radar. Despite demonstrating several successful simulated night attacks in May, it was not until August 1941 that the design was "frozen" and production engineering approved. The final version used a standard Royal Navy 24-inch searchlight mounted in a retractable pod under the center of the fuselage and powered by batteries that were trickle-charged by an auxiliary generator. The light could be steered in azimuth and elevation, and tactical doctrine called for lining up on

the target using radar, approaching at precisely 250 feet altitude, and activating the spotlight one mile before expected weapon release. Because of additional delays in production and aircraft modification, the first five Wellingtons equipped with Leigh Lights became operational only in June 1942, but demonstrated their value immediately.[12]

Early on the 4th of that month, in the southwest corner of the Bay of Biscay, an RAF Wellington made a night radar contact on a surfaced submarine and made the first Leigh Light–guided attack on the Italian submarine *Luigi Torelli*, outbound from Bordeaux for a patrol in the Caribbean. In a second pass the Wellington dropped four depth charges that so damaged the Italian boat that she was forced to head on the surface for the nearest port (in Spain), where she ran aground. (After being bombed again while attempting to leave Spain after a brief stay, she would eventually be interned there.) Those first five Leigh-Light Wellingtons made 11 submarine sightings and six attacks during July and August. In addition to working over the *Luigi Torelli,* they sank the *U-502* on 5 July and seriously damaged the *U-159* on the 12th. Accordingly, Coastal Command immediately started a crash program to fit as many ASW aircraft as possible with the searchlight.

Admiral Dönitz reacted immediately to the Leigh Light attacks. On 16 July 1942, he reversed his earlier direction and ordered U-boats in the Bay of Biscay to transit on the surface during the day, when they could at least make visual sightings of approaching aircraft. As daytime U-boat contacts increased markedly and Allied aircraft sank three more that summer, Dönitz demanded a longer-term solution. A British ASV radar having been captured a year earlier, German scientists were familiar with its characteristics and quickly designed a radar warning receiver capable of detecting the 1.5-meter ASV signals up to

30 miles away. Manufactured by a firm in occupied France, the resulting Metox receiver incorporated a crude but effective wood-framed antenna that could be affixed to a U-boat conning tower while surfaced to provide early warning of searching aircraft well beyond their radar range.

By September, Allied airborne radar contacts in the Bay of Biscay dropped to nil, along with the temporary advantage conveyed by the Leigh Light. That same month, Dönitz prevailed on the German Air Force to mount long-range fighter patrols over the bay, and a total 30 Ju 88C twin-engine fighters based in western France began taking a regular toll of the lumbering ASW aircraft. In response, the RAF began sending long-range Beaufighters and Mosquitoes to protect the ASW aircraft. Meanwhile, the engineering development of shorter wavelength (10-centimeter) air-to-surface radars had proceeded rapidly in both America and Britain, and by July 1942 the U.S. production version, known as the SCR-517, was being installed in long-range ASW aircraft of the Army Air Forces. This same radar was included in Lend-Lease Liberators supplied to the RAF Coastal Command later that year and operational by December. The parallel British radar program brought two more versions to fruition at the end of 1942: the H2S for radar-guided precision bombing and the ASV Mark III for ASW aircraft. Wanting to conceal the existence of the latter from the German submarine command as long as possible, the naval authorities urged the British government to delay deploying the H2S in the strategic bomber force for fear of its being compromised when aircraft were shot down over Europe. Ultimately, Prime Minister Winston Churchill himself ruled that the H2S should be fielded immediately, and by early February 1943— just when the first ASV-IIIs became operational in Coastal Command—the Germans retrieved an H2S set from a downed Stirling bomber near Rotterdam.

Hitherto convinced on technical grounds that centimetric radar was not possible, the German technical community was both dismayed and alarmed by this unwelcome evidence of Allied prowess and began development of a corresponding U-boat warning receiver called "Naxos." However, the "other shoe" had already "dropped" in the Bay of Biscay.

Beginning in February 1943, Coastal Command's 19 Group initiated a series of intensive ASW patrols over the main U-boat transit lanes in the bay. Initially, U.S. Army Air Forces B-24 Liberators also participated before they were transferred to Morocco in March, but the brunt of the effort was borne by British Wellingtons equipped with both ASV-III radar and Leigh Lights.[13] By March, 32 of these aircraft were available, and a month later, about 70 of 19 Group's aircraft—Wellingtons, Liberators, and Halifaxes—carried centimetric radar. On 5 March, when the outbound *U-333* was illuminated and attacked without warning by a Leigh-Light Wellington, which she nonetheless succeeded in shooting down, the German Navy got its first indication that the new radar had become operational.

Initially, however, Coastal Command's stepped-up Biscay campaign found little success. In its first three operations—denoted "Gondola," "Enclose," and "Enclose II"—the last of which ended in mid-April, Allied patrol aircraft detected 56 U-boats and attacked about half of them, but for the first four months of 1943 the aircraft managed only four conclusive kills. (Two other German boats disappeared in the bay without explanation, in January and in April.) However, German losses rose rapidly to unacceptable levels in May when Coastal Command's concentrated ASW effort in the Bay of Biscay hit its stride.

Airborne ASW Sensors and Weapons

Four important technical innovations that would play a major role in airborne ASW came to fruition in late 1942 and early 1943: Magnetic Anomaly Detection (MAD), sonobuoys, anti-submarine rockets, and the homing torpedo.

The first of these sought to exploit the small localized changes caused in the earth's magnetic field by the presence of a large ferrous mass, such as a steel submarine hull. Geomagnetic measurements had been suggested for use in prospecting for iron ore as far back as the mid-19th Century and had become quite useful for that purpose by the 1920s. Although U.S. scientists had proposed the use of the phenomenon for submarine detection before the war, the necessary technology only became available in late 1940, with the invention in the United States of the fluxgate magnetometer by a research-and-development subsidiary of the Gulf Oil Company. The fluxgate combined small sensor size with enough sensitivity to measure a change in the earth's field of only a few hundredths of a percent, which is what would be observable from a low-flying aircraft directly above a submarine submerged at a depth of 100 feet.[14] In early 1941, the U.S. National Defense Research Committee took over sponsorship of the program and by October had flown a crude MAD detector on a Catalina to demonstrate the feasibility of the concept. A joint effort by the Western Electric Company and the Airborne Instruments Laboratory developed an operational version for trials in spring 1942, and late that year installations of the MAD system began on blimps and patrol aircraft.[15]

Beyond the engineering challenge of detecting such a small signal against a fluctuating noise background, it was necessary to ensure strict isolation of the fluxgate from the ferrous parts of the aircraft structure by using non-magnetic materials and locating the sensor away from the fuselage in a tail boom or on a wing-tip. Moreover, because the magnitude of a submarine's MAD signature diminishes in proportion to the inverse third power of the range—lessening by a factor of eight with each doubling of distance—MAD detections were only possible at very short stand-offs, usually with the aircraft directly overhead. Thus, magnetics were essentially useless for wide-area search but could be valuable for fine localization after the approximate position of a target had been determined by some other means.

For use in an actual attack, MAD had another serious drawback. Since most detections occurred directly over the target, the forward motion of the aircraft ensured that any weapons dropped from that point would surely miss by a considerable margin. This was overcome by devising a system of under-wing "retro-bombs," with small rockets that drove the weapons *backward* off the launching rails, thus canceling their initial forward velocity and essentially dropping them straight down. In the standard installation devised for the Catalina flying boat, 24 contact-fused, 35-pound retro-bombs were carried under the wings and released in three salvoes of eight, a half-second apart. It worked!

Another innovation was the sonobuoy—a contraction of "sono-radio-buoy"—which provided ASW aircraft the capability for initial localization using acoustics. In June 1940, the U.S. Navy Department directed the Naval Research Laboratory to begin investigating the design of an air-dropped surface float that could deploy a hydrophone to listen for nearby submarines and radio its detections to a circling aircraft. A crude, hand-emplaced test model was tried on Long Island Sound in August 1940 and, reportedly, detected a submarine ten miles away.[16] The development proceeded apace with participation by the Radio Corporation of America and the Airborne Instrument Laboratory, and in March 1942, another hand-emplaced prototype successfully radioed submarine noises to an overhead blimp. In July the first full-speed aircraft drops—at 110 knots—took place, and by autumn 1942, the final sonobuoy design, designated CRT-42, had entered production at the Emerson Radio and Phonograph Corporation. The resulting device was a four-inch-diameter cylinder, 45 inches long, weighing 14 pounds. Its descent was slowed by a small parachute. The water impact of the buoy released a magnetostrictive hydrophone on the end of a 24-foot cable and activated the electronics, including a small FM transmitter for sending sound signals to patrolling aircraft. The first model provided no directivity, but subsequent versions incorporated a rotating sensor to determine target bearing. These first sonobuoys were only sensitive enough to detect the propellers of a submarine at relatively high speed. Typically, they could hear a seven-knot submarine submerged to 60 feet in calm seas at three and a half miles; under adverse conditions—three knots at 250 feet in rough seas—range dropped to only 90 yards. The U.S. Navy supplied the first operational sonobuoys and their associated radio receivers to blimps and ASW aircraft in late spring 1943, and hundreds of thousands eventually were manufactured for U.S. and British use.

Two new air-to-surface ASW weapons also appeared at this time. Both were intended to improve on the relatively low kill probability of approximately 9 percent observed in attacks using conventional air-dropped bombs and depth charges. In 1942 the British adapted an existing solid-fuel, anti-tank rocket for use by ASW aircraft against surfaced submarines. Several inches in diameter and weighing 66 pounds—including a 25-pound, solid-steel warhead—the rockets were carried in launchers under the wings, four on each side, and were aimed to impact the water at a shallow angle just short of the target. The shaped nose of the weapon created an upwardly curving underwater trajectory intended to impact

and punch through the U-boat's pressure hull. The weapon was introduced to British ASW aircraft in the spring of 1943 and scored its first kill on 23 May, when a Swordfish from the escort carrier *Archer* sank the *U-752* some 700 n.miles west of Ireland. Subsequently, the United States developed a similar ASW missile, the 3.5-inch Forward Firing Aircraft Rocket (FFAR), which entered service in late 1943.

The most revolutionary of the new airborne ASW weapons to reach the final phases of development in late 1942 was the Mark 24 "Mine," the world's first homing torpedo to see combat use.[17] Named "Fido" by its developers, the Mark 24 was proposed in November 1941 by Captain Louis McKeehan of the U.S. Navy's Bureau of Ordnance, who had inquired whether acoustic homing control might be applied to an air-dropped, torpedo-like weapon.[18] This approach would solve the problem of the limited effectiveness of depth charges dropped—largely blind—against submarines that had recently submerged. The Navy convened a series of meetings to discuss the feasibility of the idea in December and January, meetings that included representatives from the Harvard Underwater Sound Laboratory, Bell Telephone Laboratories, General Electric, and the Navy's David Taylor Model Basin. The notional specifications called for a device of size and weight compatible with existing aircraft and droppable from an altitude of 200 to 300 feet at approximately 120 knots. The weapon was to have an in-water speed of 12 knots for five to 15 minutes and carry a 100-pound high-explosive warhead. A formal development program began in mid-January 1942, with Bell Telephone Laboratories and the Harvard Underwater Sound Laboratory each developing a prototype in a competitive yet collaborative effort.

The Mark 24 torpedo—nicknamed Fido—was the first Allied acoustic homing torpedo. Launched from aircraft, it proved highly effective against German and Japanese submarines. Few photos of the Mark 24 were taken, because of wartime secrecy. This Mark 24 torpedo is being installed on a Navy airship in 1949. The protective "collar" dropped away upon striking the water. *U.S. Navy, courtesy William F. Althoff*

Considering the technical complexity of the requirement and the innovative nature of the concept, Fido's engineering development proceeded with startling rapidity, and in-water tests were begun in April. In October 1942, only ten months after the start of the project, the design was frozen and a contract issued to Western Electric to manufacture 5,200 torpedoes. The weapon that emerged was 84 inches long and 19 inches in diameter, weighing 680 pounds with a 92-pound warhead. A 48-volt, lead-acid battery powered a five-and-a-half-horsepower electric motor, and four hydrophones spaced evenly around the circumference of the cylindrical body provided guidance inputs. Because each hydrophone was shadowed by the torpedo body from sound coming from the other side, the difference in sound level between diametrically opposite sensors indicated the left-right and up-down direction of a sound source. The torpedo's electronics processed these acoustic signals in a frequency band centered on 24 kHz to provide steering commands for the four paired rudders, whose angles were set proportional to the azimuthal and vertical offsets of the target bearing. In operation, the Mark 24 dove to a depth of 125 feet and started a circular search until its hydrophones detected a submarine signal, at which time directional homing commenced. Total endurance at 12 knots was, as specified, as much as 15 minutes.

The first Fido production models appeared in March 1943, and by May 500 torpedoes had been delivered to both U.S. and British ASW forces. Because of its profoundly game-changing potential, rigid security measures accompanied the Mark

24's introduction, and the weapon could not be employed if there was any chance of its running up on shore or being observed by other enemy units. A British Liberator on a convoy protection mission from Northern Ireland scored Fido's first success on 12 May 1943, when it so badly damaged the *U-456* that it was driven to the surface until approaching destroyers forced it to submerge again. It sank the next day from the damage inflicted by the Mark 24. Two days later, an American Catalina from Iceland dropped a Fido on the *U-640* and sank her outright—the first unequivocal kill by an air-dropped homing torpedo in history. By the end of the war in mid-1945, U.S. and British aircraft had dropped 340 Fido torpedoes in 264 encounters, of which 204 were actually with submarines. These attacks scored kills on 37 submarines—including five Japanese boats—and damaged 18 others, for an overall kill probability of 18 percent, twice that achieved with air-dropped depth charges.[19]

Destroyers and Destroyer Escorts

As noted above, both Britain and the United States increased the production of destroyers in the late 1930s, but relatively few ships of the new classes had entered service when war came in September 1939. The Royal Navy's pre-war Tribal, J, and K (32 ships) classes were followed by the L, M, and N classes (24 ships) in the first two years of the conflict. Thirteen "War Emergency Flotillas" of eight ships each (the O, P, Q, R, S, T, U, V, W, Z, and three C classes—a total of 104 additional ships) followed in quick succession.

As the war continued, lessons learned in combat caused a steady evolution of the characteristics of Royal Navy destroyers, but typically, they displaced between 1,700 and 1,900 tons standard on a length of approximately 360 feet and were armed with four or six 4.7-inch dual-purpose guns (in twin mountings) and eight torpedo tubes. Virtually all were powered by geared turbines and could make 36 knots, as befitted their role as "fleet" destroyers. Relatively few of these 160 ships were assigned to ASW missions per se or to convoy duty in the Atlantic. During 1940 and 1942, five new *King George V*–class battleships entered Royal Navy service, and between 1937 and 1942, 15 fleet aircraft carriers had been laid down. Thus, the new destroyer flotillas were intended largely as fleet escorts, with primary missions to protect capital ships against surface and air threats. As before the war, ASW remained a secondary mission, and although most of the new destroyers were fitted with asdic and depth-charge racks (generally two) and throwers (four), these capabilities were there largely for fleet self-protection. Thus, as early as 1939, Churchill—then First Lord of the Admiralty—had argued for smaller ASW ships by noting, "The destroyer is the chief weapon against the U-boat, but as it becomes larger it becomes a worthwhile target. The line is passed where the hunter becomes the hunted. We could not have too many destroyers, but their perpetual improvement and growth imposed severe limitations on the numbers the yards could build, and deadly delay in completion."[20]

Initially, few such doubts appeared on the other side of the Atlantic. Between 1937 and 1941, the U.S. Navy ordered 64 *Gleaves/Livermore*-class destroyers and 32 of the virtually identical *Benson* class, with the first of these, the USS *Gleaves* (DD 423), commissioned in June 1940. With standard displacement of 1,620 tons on a length of 348$\frac{1}{6}$ feet, the *Benson*s carried five 5-inch guns in single mounts and ten torpedo tubes in quintuple mounts. Lacking plans for small, ocean-going ASW escorts such as the British corvettes, the United States fitted on even pre-war destroyers two depth-charge racks (with five rounds each) and a centerline Y-gun depth-charge thrower. Subsequently, the deck-edge K-gun was devised to free up centerline space, and the Y-gun was phased out. The following *Fletcher* (DD 445) class of 175 ships—the first of which, the USS *Nicholas* (DD 449), commissioned in June 1942—were somewhat larger, with displacement of 2,050 tons standard and a length of 376½ feet. Although they carried the same anti-ship armament as their predecessors, they added additional anti-aircraft guns and four to six K-guns for ASW. All of these destroyer classes were powered by geared steam turbines driving twin screws, and their top speeds exceeded 35 knots. By necessity, the United States pressed more of its destroyers into ASW service than did Britain, but given its own massive construction programs for capital ships, most of these destroyers would go to the Pacific.

In view of the demonstrated inadequacy of the myriad of small subchasers and patrol craft then under construction for deep-ocean ASW, the U.S. Navy belatedly accepted the concept of the "destroyer escort," which had been discarded earlier in favor of building PCs, SCs, and follow-on versions of the *Benson*-class destroyers. In mid-January 1942, six weeks after Pearl Harbor, President Roosevelt proposed the "1799 Program," which called for building that number of ships and small craft for Great Britain—including 250 ASW escorts of British design—with the proviso that if needed some might be taken over for the U.S. Navy. In the event, with the continuing shortage of ocean escorts in the Atlantic and with the demands of the Pacific war mounting rapidly, fully 195 of the initial 250 became U.S. warships and were designated destroyer escorts (DE) in U.S. service. Eventually, 270 more were completed, and by the end of the war, 420 had been commissioned, including 47 as high-speed transports (APDs).[21]

The initial DE production schedule suffered from low priority, and not until late February 1942 were the first two ships, *Brennan* (DE 13) and *Doherty* (DE 14), laid down. Only on 20 January 1943 were the first two commissioned, the *Brennan* and *Baynton* (DE 1), with the latter sent to the Royal Navy. Only 53 more entered service during the first half of 1943, and of the total, seven went to Britain, five to the training schools, and 21 to the Pacific as convoy escorts, leaving just 22 for ASW in the Atlantic, and then not until June.[22]

With so many ships and such a long production run—the last DE was laid down in June 1944—there were many variants within the overall DE category, with a wide variety of hull forms, armament, and propulsion plants—diesel-electric, diesels with reduction gears, turbo-electric, and geared steam turbines.[23] Few of the shipyards to which these ships were assigned had previously built warships, and at least initially, diesel engines were the preferred propulsion, because they were easier to manufacture than steam turbines, with their reduction gears and boilers. The earliest and least capable ships were those of the "short-hull" *Evarts* (DE 5) class, essentially the original British design, 289 feet long and 1,050 tons standard displacement, with twin-shaft diesel-electric power for 20 knots. Their endurance at 12 knots was 6,600 miles, and they were armed with three 3-inch dual-purpose guns, depth charge racks, and eight K-guns. The most advanced of the DEs were the "long-hull" *John C. Butler* (DE 339) class, 306 feet long, 1,275 tons standard displacement, and steam-turbine powered. Armed with two 5-inch dual-purpose guns, three torpedo tubes, and the same ASW weapons, they could make 24 knots. The Royal Navy designated their U.S.-built destroyer escorts as "frigates" and assigned them to the Captain class (named after famous British naval captains). There were two variants—32 ships essentially identical to the U.S. *Evarts*-class DEs, and 46 of the follow-on *Buckley* class. A total of 78 American-built DEs ultimately went to the Royal Navy.

Considerably less successful U.S. escorts were the *Asheville* (PF 1) and *Tacoma* (PF 3) classes, based on the British River class and built to mercantile (i.e., non-naval) standards. Named after small towns and cities, they were 304 feet long, displaced 1,100 tons standard, and were powered by two triple-compound reciprocating steam engines for speeds up to 19 knots. They carried three 3-inch guns, plus depth-charge racks and four K-guns, but by the time they entered service, the submarine threat was waning rapidly. Ninety-six were completed in 1944, of which 21 were turned over to the Royal Navy, where they were known as the Colony class.

At the beginning of the war the Royal Navy dramatically increased its own production of ASW escorts, resulting in a huge increase in numbers by early 1943. The 64 frigates of the River class, later replicated in the American *Asheville*s, displaced 1,370 tons on a length of 301 feet and carried two 4-inch guns plus ASW armament. Like the earlier Flower-class corvettes, they had vertical triple-expansion engines driving two shafts, because of limited production capacity for steam turbines and the higher priority for diesel engines for landing craft and submarines. Nonetheless, the River-class ships could steam at 20 knots. The first was completed in January 1942 and the last in October 1943, but subsequently, the Royal Australian Navy built 18 and the Royal Canadian Navy more than 70 in their own yards.

Somewhat more heavily armed than the Royal Navy's frigates were the nine "sloops" of the pre-war *Black Swan* class, the first of which were laid down in mid-1938. The last took the water in November 1942, following the launch of the first of 22 Modified *Black Swan*s in July. Turbine-powered for a speed of 20 knots, the latter displaced 1,300 tons on a length of 283 feet and carried, in addition to an evolving array of ASW weapons, a powerful battery of six 4-inch dual-purpose guns (plus multiple 2-pounders or 20-mm guns), which made them very useful for ASW in the Bay of Biscay, with its dangerous German air threat.

Additionally, in late 1942, the Royal Navy laid down the first of 48 Castle-class corvettes, a larger follow-on to the earlier Flower class intended to address many of the shortcomings in endurance, armament, and sea-keeping of the earlier ships. Displacing 1,010 tons compared to the earlier ships' 925 tons, and at 252 feet overall, some 50 feet longer, the Castle class was much better suited to North Atlantic conditions. Although only marginally faster—16.5 knots—they carried twice as much fuel (which doubled their endurance to 7,800 miles at 12 knots), stowed more depth charges, and were fitted with the new ahead-throwing ASW weapons just coming into service. The first of the new class, *Hadleigh Castle,* was commissioned in September 1943 and the last, *Hedingham Castle,* in May 1945.

New Surface Weapons

Meanwhile, an intensive Royal Navy development program dating from the beginning of the war had finally brought to fruition a revolutionary new surface ASW weapon: the hedgehog. ASW experience in World War I had already demonstrated that a major shortcoming of conventional depth-charge tactics was the necessity of conning an attacking ship over the anticipated position of the U-boat before releasing the weapons. Even in asdic-guided approaches the target disappeared from "view" at short range, because of both reverberation and the downwardly directed sound beam, this provided the submarine quarry time for evasive action. Additionally, a close estimate of the target depth was needed for optimal setting of the hydrostatic pistols on the depth charges, and early asdic sets were unable to provide this information directly.

Early attempts to solve this problem included the heavier Mark VII fast-sinking depth charge, which descended at approximately 16 feet per second, vice ten for the previous weapon, and the giant Mark X 1,000-pound depth charge, which was fired from a torpedo tube. Required was a method of projecting a pattern of depth charges to the target's estimated position from a stand-off range before sonar contact was lost. Ahead-throwing depth-charge mortars had been tried in World War I, but their subsequent development fell victim to post-war austerity, and interest was revived only in 1939. There followed a lively technical debate on the size and number of individual charges needed for effectiveness—several large depth bombs versus many small ones—but eventually, the concept proposed by the Admiralty's Directorate of Miscellaneous Weapons Development emerged as the hedgehog.[24]

Based on a British Army anti-tank spigot mortar known as the Blacker Bombard, each hedgehog mount ripple-fired a pattern of 24 projectiles from slanted steel rods, or spigots, in six rows, to form a circular impact pattern about 130 feet in diameter, approximately 250 yards ahead of the ship. Each projectile was contact-fuzed and weighed 65 pounds, of which 30 pounds were high explosive, a charge deemed sufficient to breach the pressure hull of a submarine if detonated against the outer casing. The spacing between charges was chosen to be somewhat less than the beam of a typical submarine and this, combined with a sinking speed of 22 feet per second, yielded a high probability of at least one projectile hitting the target. All the rest fell harmlessly to the bottom. Because no underwater explosions resulted unless a target had actually been hit, the hedgehog offered the additional advantage of not causing the wholesale deterioration of asdic listening conditions caused by the detonation of a pattern of conventional depth charges.

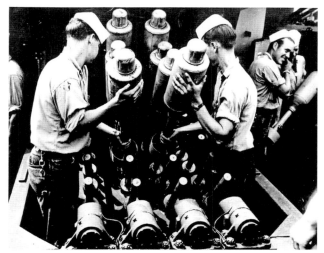

Sailors load a hedgehog on board a U.S. destroyer escort during the war. The ahead-firing weapon was more effective than depth charges, and, because the 24 spigot bombs did not detonate unless they struck a submarine, they did not interfere with sonar. *U.S. Navy*

This permitted much faster re-attacks. The earliest hedgehog projectors were fixed to the deck, but later models were steerable plus or minus 20 degrees in azimuth and incorporated ship-roll compensation.

Once the basic concept was decided, development, testing, and production proceeded rapidly. The first field trials took place in May 1941 on the destroyer *Westcott,* and the system entered production six months later, with ship installations beginning in the late spring of 1942. One hundred Royal Navy ships had been fitted by the end of that year. The first known use of hedgehog in combat occurred on 23 August 1942, when the destroyer *Viscount,* escorting convoy ONS-122 south of Iceland, fired a salvo—unsuccessfully—against the submarine *U-135.* In the event, the initial deployment of hedgehog was hugely disappointing, and in its first year at sea scored only one kill and three probable, many fewer than had been predicted statistically.[25] Even what appears to be the weapon's earliest success remains somewhat equivocal: the forced scuttling of the *U-660* in the Mediterranean near Oran on 12 November 1942 following a long engagement with the Flower-class corvettes *Lotus* and *Starwort*. The *Lotus* fired her hedgehog at the *U-660* only after she had run out of depth charges and apparently scored a hit that forced the U-boat to the surface.

This early lack of success was due largely to poor management and logistics. Because of hedgehog's high security classification, it was often foisted on escort crews with little preparation and limited understanding of the tactical concept. Installations were rushed, training was minimal, and maintenance neglected. Most ship captains opted to use their "tried and true" depth charges in prosecuting an attack rather than trusting in this new and unknown quantity. In desperation, the Admiralty *ordered* the use of hedgehog in preference to conventional depth charges, but it was only in early 1944, after a commission was impaneled to investigate its poor performance, that the weapon began fulfilling its potential.

Another key factor in increasing the lethality of both hedgehog and conventional depth charges was the Royal Navy's introduction of the depth-determining sonar, at first as a device called the "Q attachment" for existing asdic sets. This was a separate transducer for producing a downward-angled sound beam, and it quickly evolved into the Type 147 asdic, which formed a "stack" of thin, fan-shaped beams that could be tilted down to 45 degrees below the horizontal. Operating at 60 kHz, the Type 147 made possible the determination of the target's depth well beyond the stand-off needed for launching hedgehog and subsequent ahead-thrown weapons. The prototype passed its sea trials in May 1943 and was in production three months later.

New Directions

A month after Pearl Harbor, the chief of staff of the U.S. Navy Support Group in Argentia, New-foundland, suggested the establishment of a fleet analysis activity to collect and analyze tactical data from anti-submarine and convoy-escort operations in the North Atlantic and thus to draw lessons to be learned from the growing experience of the ASW escort and air forces. Accordingly, on 2 March 1942, the Atlantic Fleet Anti-Submarine Warfare Unit was commissioned in Boston under Captain Wilder D. Baker, who held command until mid-April, when he was tapped to set up a new ASW section under Admiral King, the Commander-in-Chief, U.S. Fleet, in Washington. Baker was relieved by Commander Thomas L. Lewis, an experienced destroyer officer. Although the primary function of the ASW Unit was to collate and analyze the statistics of attack information to measure the effectiveness of weapons and tactics, it was the only U.S. activity to provide training for the instructors of the sound and subchaser schools and to formulate ASW tactical doctrine. The unit issued its first manual of standardized procedures in May 1942, and the following November, the Navy promulgated a general manual on anti-submarine warfare largely derived from it.

A closely related—and ultimately better known—organization was the ASW Operations Research Group (ASWORG), stood up only a month after the Boston ASW Unit, following a proposal by Captain Baker to the head of the National Defense Research Committee that a civilian operations research organization be created to deal with emerging ASW issues. Organized and led by Professor Philip M. Morse of the Massachusetts Institute of Technology, the ASWORG consisted of university and industry scientists skilled in applying quantitative methods to analyzing operational data. They would derive optimum tactics and procedures for search, attack, and regaining contact, and they determined the most effective ways to use existing and developmental weapons and sensors for protecting convoys and killing submarines. Eventually headquartered in Washington, the ASWORG soon established satellite groups at major fleet bases around the world, and for the rest of the war its scientists and engineers worked closely with local operating forces to put the practice of ASW on a more rigorous scientific footing.[26]

Early in 1943—entering the fourth year of the European war—the belligerents made significant changes in their strategies and direction. In Germany, in an angry tirade directed against Admiral Raeder about the impotence of the German surface fleet, Hitler ordered the retirement of its larger ships to free up men and material for other uses. This precipitated Raeder's resignation—actually a sacking—and he was replaced by Admiral Dönitz as commander-in-chief on 30 January. Dönitz promptly moved his headquarters from Paris to Berlin and assigned command of the U-boat arm to Admiral Hans-Georg von Friedenburg in nearby Charlottenburg. Nonetheless, Dönitz retained de facto direction of the submarine campaign and, despite convincing Hitler to reverse his decision to decommission the battleships and heavy cruisers, secured agreement to increase both submarine production and Air Force support of naval operations in the Atlantic.

On the Allied side, one of the most important events of early 1943 was the conference in Casablanca, Morocco, at which American president Roosevelt and British prime minister Churchill met to concert their joint strategy for the remainder of the war. (The Soviet premier, Josef Stalin, also was invited, but the press of the ongoing battle for Stalingrad apparently prevented his attendance.) Convened from 14 to 24 January, the Casablanca Conference dealt largely with strategy at the global level—for example, the balance of manpower and shipping between the European and Pacific theaters and the decision to invade Sicily and Italy later in the year. The future of the ASW campaign was also a major topic of discussion. In particular, the protection of shipping and defeat of the U-boats were assigned top priority in the allocation of Allied resources, and broad direction was given for the reorganization of the convoy system, accelerated construction of destroyer escorts, and an increased allocation of long-range aircraft to both ASW directly and to the bombing of German submarine bases and building yards.

The implementation of these new measures was hammered out at an Allied Atlantic Convoy Conference held in Washington during the first half of March 1943. The decisions reached there during 12 days of inter-Allied and inter-service deliberations largely determined the course of the ASW campaign for the rest of the war. A key issue for the British—already raised at Casablanca—was their desire for a single Allied ASW commander for the entire Atlantic, likely Admiral Max Horton, recently appointed Commander-in-Chief Western Approaches, at Liverpool. This proposal was firmly rejected by the Americans, although in its place a more definitive allocation of responsibilities and more efficient protocols for Allied cooperation were instantiated. Notably, the British and Canadian Navies would thenceforth assume full responsibility for convoy escort in the North Atlantic, with virtually no U.S. participation. Similarly, the U.S. Navy would assume all responsibility for escorting the growing amount of convoy traffic across the *mid*-Atlantic, between the U.S. eastern seaboard, Gibraltar, and Africa, largely to supply military material for the Mediterranean theater and oil for Britain. Detailed plans also were promulgated for the allocation and deployment of land-based, long-range ASW aircraft, which at the time of the conference were playing an increasing role in the North Atlantic, with 516 long-range and very-long-range bombers and patrol aircraft stationed around the periphery of the region, from the United States and Canada through Iceland, and Britain, and extending as far south as Gibraltar and Morocco.[27] By the end of the year, the total had increased to nearly 750 aircraft. In

Dr. Philip McCord Morse
(B. 1903 D. 1985)

A long-time professor of physics at the Massachusetts Institute of Technology (MIT), Morse became one of the early pioneers of military operations research during his leadership of the ASW Operations Research Group (ASWORG) in World War II.

Born in Shreveport, Louisiana, Morse graduated from Cleveland's Case School of Engineering in 1926 with a degree in physics. After earning his Ph.D. from Princeton University several years later, he did postdoctoral research in Munich and Cambridge and joined the MIT faculty in 1931. Although he was trained as a nuclear physicist, Morse's first assignment was to develop and teach a course in acoustics, and his theoretical background soon led to new applications of wave theory to describe acoustical phenomena.

As World War II approached, Morse was drawn into several research programs sponsored by the Navy and the National Defense Research Committee, including the devising of countermeasures for German acoustic mines and the control of ambient noise within land combat vehicles. After the United States joined the conflict the Navy established an operations research group in Washington in mid-1942 to optimize ASW tactics and weapons. Morse was an obvious choice to assume the leadership of that effort, and he served in that capacity until the end of the war. During his tenure, the ASWORG developed many of the basic techniques of ASW operations research for optimizing resource allocation and search-and-track procedures, evaluating effectiveness, and deploying weapons for maximum kill probability. This effort represented one of the earliest attempts to base the development of ASW tactics and system design on solid scientific and mathematical principles, and it led after the war to rapid acceptance of operations research as a valid and useful discipline. Other outcomes were Morse's ground-breaking text *Methods of Operations Research* (with G. E. Kimball) and his election in 1952 to become the first president of the Operations Research Society of America.

After the war Morse served for two years as the first director of the Brookhaven National Laboratory and then as the director of research for the Weapons Systems Evaluation Group of the Joint Chiefs of Staff. He returned to the faculty of MIT in 1950, later establishing the Institute's Operations Research Center, which he directed until 1968. He was also the first director of the MIT Computation Center and, in addition to *Methods of Operations Research*, wrote several highly regarded textbooks, most notably *Vibration and Sound* and *Methods of Theoretical Physics* (with Herman Feshbach). Morse retired from MIT in 1968.

particular, the number of B-24s assigned to ASW in the North Atlantic exceeded 200 by the beginning of 1944, although less than one-half of these had been modified to the very-long-range ASW configuration.

In addition, two major tactical innovations were confirmed at the Casablanca and Atlantic Convoy Conferences. Both had been in the planning stages since mid-1942. The first was the introduction of independent surface support groups that could be vectored to exploit submarine position intelligence and to augment the escort of hard-pressed convoys. The second—closely related—was the use of escort aircraft carriers as the nuclei of many of these support groups, thus providing on-scene air cover in areas beyond the reach of land-based ASW aircraft. Neither the support groups nor the carriers, however, were intended for random search and offensive patrols; rather, they were to be adjuncts to the regular escort forces in areas where U-boats were likely to be—that is, along convoy routes or where all-source intelligence, especially Ultra, predicted their presence.

As early as February 1943, the U.S. Navy had formed a hunter-killer group of four destroyers in support of the mid-Atlantic convoy UC-1, and Admiral Percy Noble, before his relief by Admiral Horton as CinC Western Approaches, had begun planning for similar formations, made up of from three to five destroyers, corvettes, frigates, and sloops. Encouraged by the huge number of new-construction escorts entering service in 1943, the Atlantic Convoy Conference called for the Royal Navy and the Canadian Navy together to form five support groups for the North Atlantic convoys, while directing the U.S. Navy to form five of its own—of four to five destroyers each—to support the mid-Atlantic convoy routes. Both the British/Canadian and U.S. Navy support groups would be augmented by escort carriers as they became available, and several of these hunter-killer groups were already in action by April and May.

Enter the Escort Carriers

Escort carriers—later CVEs, in U.S. nomenclature—were not a new idea.[28] As described above, the first of the type, the Royal Navy's ill-fated *Audacity,* entered service in June 1941, following conversion that had started in January from a merchant ship. That same January, the U.S. Navy began converting two C3-type merchant ships into escort carriers; these emerged as the USS *Long Island,* mentioned above, and HMS *Archer,* transferred to the Royal Navy under Lend-Lease in November 1941. At about the same time, the United States undertook four more C3 escort carrier conversions for the Royal Navy, all diesel-powered with a single shaft: HMS *Avenger, Biter, Charger,* and *Dasher,* although the *Charger* ultimately was retained for the U.S. Navy as the CVE 30.

After Pearl Harbor the U.S. Navy ordered 24 more CVEs for itself and one for the British, also to be built on C3 merchant hulls but steam-turbine powered for additional speed, from 17 to 19 knots. Because a sufficient number of steam-powered C3s was lacking, however, four of the new ships were converted from the 19-knot fleet oilers *Chenango, Sangamon, Suwannee,* and *Santee,* and ultimately ten of the newly ordered escort carriers went to the British.[29] On average, the later C3 conversions displaced 9,800 tons on a length of 496 feet (with a 442-foot flight deck), carried 30 aircraft, and were fitted with a catapult and two elevators. They were rated for a top speed of 19 knots.[30]

The first of the new CVEs to see action was HMS *Avenger,* which joined the escort of the Murmansk convoy PQ-18 in late August 1942. During that operation her Sea Hurricane fighters shot down five enemy counterparts and vectored accompanying surface escorts to kill two submarines spotted from the air. Subsequently, the *Avenger* joined her sisters *Biter, Dasher,* and *Archer,* along with the U.S. escort carriers *Chenango* (CVE 28), *San-* *gamon* (CVE 26), *Suwannee* (CVE 27), and *Santee* (CVE 29), in support of the invasion of North Africa (Operation Torch) in November. They provided aircraft ferry services, ground air support, and ASW cover. In the last role, on 11 November,

Admiral Sir Max Kennedy Horton, Royal Navy
(B. 1883 D. 1951)

As commander-in-chief of the Western Approaches during the second half of World War II, Horton was largely responsible for directing the British anti-submarine campaign in the western Atlantic from late 1942.

Born in Anglesey, Horton entered the Royal Navy in 1898 as a naval cadet and after commissioning served mostly in submarines. During World War I he earned a fearsome reputation as a marauding submarine skipper, sinking the German light cruiser *Hela* in the second month of the war and three weeks later bagging a German destroyer. In October 1914, Horton threaded his submarine *E-9* through the narrow Danish and Swedish Straits into the Baltic Sea and, operating from Reval (in Estonia) under the tactical command of the Russian Navy, waged an anti-shipping campaign against German iron-ore carriers from Sweden. Before he left the Baltic in December 1915, he had sunk another destroyer and a large number of merchant ships, plus damaging the German armored cruiser *Prince Adalbert.* Given command of the larger submarine *J-6,* Horton carried out a series of war patrols in the North Sea before being assigned to supervise the completion and command of the submarine monitor *M-1,* which—most unusually—was armed with a single 12-inch gun.

During the 1920s and early 1930s, Horton alternated between at-sea and staff assignments, including as commanding officer of the light cruiser *Conquest* (a submarine flotilla flagship) and the battleship *Resolution,* as second in command of the Home Fleet, and as commander of the 1st Cruiser Squadron. In 1937, as a vice-admiral, he was named commander of the Reserve Fleet.

With the coming of World War II, Horton was put in charge of the Northern Patrol, which enforced a "distant blockade" of Germany in the North Sea, but in early 1940 he was assigned as Flag Officer Submarines and in January 1941 was raised to full admiral. In November 1942, Horton relieved Admiral Sir Percy Noble as Commander-in-Chief, Western Approaches Command and held that position for the duration of the conflict. During his tenure he dramatically improved convoy protection and anti-U-boat operations by vigorously adopting the use of support groups, escort carriers, long-range patrol aircraft, and "all-source" intelligence. Within six months of his taking command the tide in the Battle of the Atlantic had begun to change in favor of the Allies, and the final victory owed a great deal to his energy and initiative.

At the end of the war in August 1945, Horton requested that his name be placed on the retired list to facilitate the promotion of younger officers.

aircraft from the *Suwannee* sank the (Vichy) French submarine *Sidi-Ferruch* off Casablanca, the first submarine kill by a U.S. escort carrier. Only four days later, however, the German submarine *U-155* torpedoed the *Avenger* south of Portugal and sent her to the bottom, leaving only 12 survivors.

Commissioned on 26 September 1942, the *Bogue* (CVE 9) was the first U.S. CVE to see escort duty with the North Atlantic convoys. Following a lengthy working-up and training period, she first joined convoys HX-228, SC-123, and HX-235 but saw relatively little action. Escorted by four old four-stack destroyers and bearing nine Wildcat fighters and 12 Avenger torpedo bombers, the *Bogue* left Argentia to join HX-228 on 3 March but was forced to return only five days later because of sea conditions unfavorable for launching and recovering aircraft, plus several aircraft matériel problems.[31] Subsequently, HX-228 lost four merchant ships, but the convoy's surface escorts sank two submarines in return, the *U-432* and *U-444*. Similarly, heavy weather later that same month forced the *Bogue* group to turn back from supporting convoy SC-123 and to put into Boston for two weeks of storm repairs. In mid-April, however, the *Bogue* and her escorts—known as American Support Group 6—provided scouting and air cover for convoy HX-235, which made it to England without loss. One of *Bogue*'s Avengers spotted and depth-charged a U-boat without achieving a kill. Once in Britain, Support Group 6 spent two weeks in ASW training in Liverpool and Northern Ireland, and the *Bogue* was fitted with an HF/DF set.

Also entering North Atlantic service in March 1943 were three of the Royal Navy's new escort carriers—the *Archer, Biter,* and *Dasher*—flying Wildcats (Martlets) and Swordfish biplane torpedo bombers. The first kill by an escort carrier on the North Atlantic convoy routes—actually an assist—was scored by the *Biter* on 25 April while escorting convoy ONS-4. Flying out an HF/DF bearing provided by one of the surface escorts, a Swordfish from the carrier surprised the *U-203* on the surface, dropped two depth charges on the diving submarine, and summoned the destroyer *Pathfinder* to the scene. The *Pathfinder*'s subsequent asdic-guided, depth-charge attack added to damage already inflicted by the Swordfish and forced the U-boat to the surface, where she was scuttled by her crew. *Biter* aircraft also shared credit with surface escorts for the second North Atlantic U-boat sunk with carrier assistance: the *U-89* on 10 May during an attack on convoy HX-237. The *Bogue*'s first "air kill" occurred on 22 May while escorting convoy ON-184 when a *Bogue* Avenger discovered the *U-569* on the surface just 20 miles from the carrier and dropped four depth charges close aboard. The submarine crash-dived but was forced by damage to surface again, just in time to be bombed by a second Avenger, which drove the submarine back under, only to have to surface again and be scuttled by her crew. Additionally, *Bogue* aircraft inflicted significant damage on the *U-231, U-468,* and *U-305,* and convoy ON-184 reached port unscathed. A day later, aircraft from the *Archer,* escorting HX-239, destroyed her first victim, the *U-752,* with anti-submarine rockets fired from a Swordfish. This was both the Royal Navy's first unassisted kill by carrier aircraft and, as noted earlier, the first successful use of this new weapon. However, these early escort carrier successes were offset by the tragic loss of the *Dasher* in the Firth of Clyde on 27 March due to an aviation gasoline explosion. Of 528 crew members on board, 379 lost their lives. For morale reasons the government initially suppressed the news of the sinking. Nonetheless, the escort carriers quickly proved their worth at sea, and eventually, a total of 105 were built or converted in the United States, with 38 going to the British. Shipyards in Britain built or converted an additional five escort carriers.

Another air ASW effort that began in this period was the helicopter. The German Navy led the way (see Chapter 6), followed closely by the U.S. Navy—or actually the U.S. Coast Guard, which was subordinated to the Navy during the war. Under the aegis of the Coast Guard and the Army, aviation genius Igor Sikorsky pursued his longtime dream of a practical rotary-wing aircraft. His VS-300 helicopter test bed flew in 1940, followed by the militarized version that first took off on 13 January 1942. With the Army designation R-4 and as the Navy/Coast Guard HNS-1, it quickly was ordered into production.

The Army flew tests of an XR-4 from a platform on the tanker *Bunker Hill* on 6–7 May 1943 and more XR-4 trials from the transport *James Parker* on 6–7 July 1943. Subsequently more rigorous R-4 trials were flown from the British merchant ship *Daghestan* and from the U.S. Coast Guard cutter *Cobb* (WPG 181) during a trans-Atlantic crossing with two helicopters on board. Navy and Coast Guard pilots flew Army helicopters before the sea services received their first of 23 HNS-1s in October 1943. These were fitted with wheels or pontoons, the latter suitable for shipboard, water, and ice operations.

While looked at primarily as a rescue platform by Navy/Coast Guard leadership, the ASW potential was considered. As a portent of the future, tests were conducted of lowering "dipping" sonar from a helicopter in the hover mode.

The Dark before the Dawn

The RAF Bomber Command had continued its sporadic bombing of the German submarine bases on the Bay of Biscay into 1942, and on the eve of Operation Torch in November, these attacks and RAF raids on submarine construction facilities in Germany were redoubled in an attempt to hinder U-boat operations against the Torch convoys. The U.S. Eighth Air Force, established in Britain in June, also joined the attacks on Lorient, St. Nazaire, Brest, and La Pallice, striking first at Lorient on 21 October with 90 heavy bombers (including diversionary aircraft), of which only 15 reached the target, inflicting no appreciable damage. Three aircraft were shot down. During November and December, the Eighth Air Force flew eight more raids (a total of 488 sorties) against the submarine "pens," but again only a small percentage actually bombed the target areas, and 15 aircraft were lost. Not only were the French submarine ports heavily defended by German fighters and anti-aircraft artillery, but the reinforced concrete roofs of the submarine pens themselves proved impregnable to even 2,000-pound bombs, the largest then in the Allied inventory.

Still, the bombing campaign continued into 1943. From January through May, the British and Americans flew 31 raids—each with up to 437 aircraft and totaling nearly 4,000 individual sorties—and lost more than 100 heavy bombers. Although the towns of Lorient and St. Nazaire were largely obliterated, none of the submarine pens themselves sustained appreciable damage, and U-boat operations continued unimpeded. Meanwhile, the RAF attacks on submarine-related facilities in Wilhelmshaven, Hamburg, Bremen, and Emden—later augmented by a series of Eighth Air Force bomber raids—failed to damage the German new-construction effort seriously. The British decision in 1940 not to mount a vigorous bombing campaign against the Germans' Biscay bases while they were still under construction thus emerged as one of the major blunders of the European war.

The monthly average number of German U-boats at sea worldwide peaked at approximately 115 from

February through May 1943, and the assault on the Atlantic shipping lanes intensified correspondingly. The Allies had already suffered a serious blow in January, when convoy TM-1, the first of a new series for shipping oil directly from Trinidad to the Mediterranean theater, was set upon by a ten-boat wolf pack. The convoy, which consisted of nine large, fast tankers escorted by a British destroyer and three corvettes, was restricted to a speed of only eight knots by the limited endurance of the latter and fell easy prey to the Germans. The U-boats sank seven of the nine tankers with no losses of their own. Despite this devastating loss—percentage-wise the highest in the war by far—the next two TM convoys were unscathed, largely because their destroyer-only escorts could sustain a speed of 12 knots, and the convoys could outrun the U-boats.

From January through April 1943, a total of 59 convoys of approximately 2,400 merchant ships plied the various North Atlantic convoy routes in both directions. Of these, 111 ships—about 5 percent—were sunk by the U-boats, with a particularly worrying spike in March, when eastbound convoys HX-228, HX-229, SC-121, and SC-122 together lost 39 merchants (20 percent of those involved), plus the British destroyer *Harvester*.[32] In contrast, the associated ASW forces sank only four attacking U-boats (of 17 submarine losses in March). Worldwide, 110 Allied merchant ships went under, up from 67 in February. Writing after the war with unrestricted access to Admiralty archives and records, British naval historian Captain Stephen W. Roskill wrote:

> Nor can one look back on that month [March 1943] without feeling something approaching horror over the losses we suffered. In the first ten days in all waters, we lost forty-one ships; in the second ten days fifty-six. More than a half a million tons of

shipping was sunk in those twenty days; and what made the losses so much more serious than the bare figures indicate, was that nearly two-thirds of the ships sunk during the month were sunk in convoy. "It appeared possible," wrote the Naval Staff after the crisis had passed, "that we should not be able to continue [to regard] convoy as an effective system of defense. . . ."

Where could the Admiralty turn if the convoy system had lost its effectiveness? They did not know; but they must have felt, though no one admitted it, that defeat stared them in the face.[33]

However, in his *Hitler's U-Boat War,* historian Clay Blair argues that this Allied sense of crisis was somewhat overblown. While indeed 5 percent of the ships convoyed from January through April were lost, the other 95 percent *got through,* and even during the March bloodletting, 11 convoys crossed without incident, with a twelfth losing only one ship.[34] Moreover, during that same four-month period, U.S. shipyards produced 546 new merchants totaling 3,520,000 gross tons, double the number lost at sea. Even more ominous for the Germans, the 256 U-boats which departed on North Atlantic patrols from January through April averaged only 0.58 sinkings per sortie, and 63 percent scored no kills at all. Sixty-five of these boats—one-quarter—were sunk by Allied forces, yielding an exchange ratio (on the North Atlantic convoy routes) of approximately 2.27 merchant ships lost per submarine sunk. Given both the size and the replacement rate of the Allied merchant fleet, German hopes for throttling the trans-Atlantic supply routes were badly misplaced.

But there was another side to the "statistics war." The need for massive amounts of food, fuel, bombs, and other cargo to keep Britain "alive" and to continue the RAF bombing of German-held Europe was compounded by the need to support large-scale Allied combat operations in the Mediterranean after November 1942, especially the invasion of Sicily in July and the buildup for invading the Italian mainland in September. In addition, there were hundreds of thousands of Americans in Britain by 1943, flying and maintaining Eighth Air Force bombers and other aviation commands, and there was the buildup in preparation for the massive invasion of Western Europe then planned for the spring of 1944. All these "Yanks" preparing for the assault on German-held Europe also needed food, fuel, aviation gas, bombs, bullets, and other material, as well as tens of thousands of guns, tanks, trucks, and the omnipresent jeeps.

With war shipments continuing to the besieged Soviet Union and the United States fighting a major conflict across the broad Pacific Ocean, *every merchant hull was vital to the Allied war effort.*

Typical of the large North Atlantic convoy battles fought during this period of diminishing German fortunes—and even before the full effect of the escort carriers was felt—was the struggle of ONS-5, a large, slow, westbound convoy consisting mostly of freighters in ballast.[35] ONS-5 left the Clyde on 22 April 1943 with 40 merchant ships, escorted by two destroyers, a frigate, four Flower-class corvettes, and two armed trawlers as rescue ships. Four days later, it was joined by three more merchants and a destroyer from Iceland. The escort was under Commander P. W. Gretton, in the destroyer *Duncan*. On 28 April, the convoy was sighted about 250 miles southwest of Iceland by the German submarine group *Star* (starling), which had established a north–south patrol line at approximately longitude 30 west. The *U-650* summoned up the rest of the *Star* group, but shipboard HF/DF detection of their periodic patrol reports alerted the escort to the German presence. Commander Gretton was able to fend off the U-boats by detaching individual ships to search down the HF/DF bearing lines, thus forcing the submarines to submerge before they could approach the convoy. During the night of 28–29 April, several German sorties were similarly thwarted by aggressive counterattacks that damaged a number of the U-boats, but at dawn the *U-258* managed to slip through the screen and torpedo an American freighter in the center of the formation. At this point, increasing gale winds thwarted both sides, though sporadic air cover could still be provided by Iceland-based Catalinas and Liberators. One of the former so damaged the *U-258* on the 30th that she had to abort and withdraw to France, and on that same day, the convoy came within range of Allied aircraft from Greenland as well. Faced with this increasing air threat and the rapidly deteriorating weather, Admiral Dönitz called off Group *Star,* which by then was engaged in a futile stern chase.

Meanwhile, 250 miles to the south, the German command had deployed two additional attack groups, *Fink* (Finch) and *Amsel* (Blackbird), a total of 53 submarines, across the paths of two lucrative eastbound convoys, SC-128 and HX-236. Allied codebreakers, because they had "lost" Enigma for an entire week starting 28 April, had no precise locating information for *Fink* and *Amsel* beyond clear indications of a rising level of submarine activity in the area. This was sufficient, however, to cause the Allies to reroute the two eastbound convoys along a more southerly track and to redouble their air activity south of Greenland. The latter effort got its first success on 4 May, when a Canadian Catalina found Group *Fink*'s *U-209* on the surface and sank her with a single depth-charge attack. These Allied defensive measures and the prevailing weather conditions combined to enable SC-128 and HX-236 to slip through the area without encountering a single U-boat.

But simultaneously, ONS-5—already disorganized by the earlier storms—was heading directly into the waiting German wolf packs, thus precipitating another of the most violent convoy engagements of the war. The ensuing defense of ONS-5 benefited both from the newly augmented air cover and the early deployment of two surface support groups only recently established. On the afternoon of 2 May, Support Group 3—four British destroyers from Newfoundland and one from Iceland—arrived to reinforce ONS-5, which permitted several of the original escorts, including the destroyer *Duncan,* and Gretton with her, to detach for refueling. But by the afternoon of 4 May, following several additional departures for fuel, the screen consisted of only seven ships as 40 U-boats of the *Fink* and *Amsel* groups gathered to attack ONS-5 and several stragglers that were lagging behind.

For the next 48 hours, a running battle raged amid fog and floating ice. At first, the advantage fell to the Germans. During the night of 4–5 May the U-boats sank seven merchantmen, including three by the *U-264* alone, which fired two salvoes into the center of the convoy. On the afternoon of 5 May five more merchants succumbed, three torpedoed by the *U-266.* The escorts fought back fiercely, and the *U-192* was fatally holed by hedgehog attacks from the corvette *Loosstrife.* During the night of 5–6 May the wolf pack concentrated to attack again but succeeded only in losing four more of its own to a combination of hedgehog and depth charge engagements by the destroyer *Vidette* (which killed two) and the corvette *Sunflower,* plus a ramming attack on the *U-125* by the destroyer *Oribi.* Early on the morning of 6 May, Support Group 1—the British sloop *Pelican,* three frigates, and a former U.S. Coast

Guard cutter—arrived from Newfoundland to reinforce the escort, and the *Pelican* promptly sank the *U-438* with multiple hedgehog attacks. With the arrival of these additional ships, two destroyers of Support Group 3 were detached for much-needed refueling, and as the convoy neared the West Ocean Meeting Point on 7 May the battle flamed out.

Although the Germans eventually deployed 53 U-boats in three groups against ONS-5, only 13 of 43 merchant ships were destroyed, with only eight individual submarines scoring kills. In the convoy engagement, Allied ASW forces killed seven U-boats from the *Star, Fink,* and *Amsel* groups, and two more—for a total of nine—were sunk on the voyage home. A further 12 had been badly damaged. Despite the heavy loss of merchantmen—most of them in ballast—the successful defense of ONS-5 against the largest concentration of U-boats ever assembled was hailed as a major victory in Allied circles. Meanwhile, the U-boat losses raised alarm and dismay within the German submarine command, which blamed Allied shipboard and airborne radar for the escorts' success in driving off even massive wolf-pack attacks.

Much worse was soon to come for the U-boat force. Despite maintaining more than 90 U-boats on patrol in the North Atlantic at the beginning of May, the German anti-shipping campaign continued to lose ground. Between the 9th and the 23rd, B-dienst's locating information was accurate enough to bring the wolf packs into contact with six of the seven convoys at sea, but only six merchantmen were sunk, totaling 35,000 tons. Moreover, 15 more submarines were lost to land-based aircraft (seven), surface escorts (five), carrier-based aircraft (two), and combined surface and air action (one).[36] Another eight U-boats were so seriously damaged that they were forced to abort their missions. Counting the submarines destroyed in attacks on convoy ONS-5 and those killed in other areas, the German submarine force lost 40 boats during May, just under 10 percent of the total number in commission—and manned by some 2,000 men. Additionally, the Italian Navy lost four submarines that same month.

These were unsustainable U-boat losses, particularly in view of the dwindling percentage of Allied shipping that was being interdicted. Thus, on 24 May, Admiral Dönitz—in great frustration—ordered the withdrawal of his wolf packs from the North Atlantic convoy routes pending the installation of better anti-aircraft protection and the appearance of newer and faster submarines, an acoustic torpedo, and a microwave radar–jamming device. In an attempt to mask his retreat, Dönitz left 13 submarines at sea to broadcast dummy radio messages simulating a continuing high level of activity. Enigma intercepts quickly detected this ruse, however, and three of the decoy U-boats were promptly tracked down and destroyed. On the same day that he ordered this rapid and unexpected stand-down, Dönitz radioed a strong appeal for steadfastness to all his U-boat officers:

> You alone can, at the moment, make an offensive attack against the enemy and beat him.

The U-boat must, by continuous sinking of ships with war matériel and the necessary supplies for the British Isles, force the enemy to continual losses which must slowly but steadily sap the strength of the strongest force. The German people have long felt that our boats constitute the keenest and most decisive weapon and that the outcome of the war depends on the success or failure of the Battle of the Atlantic. . . . The time will come in which you will be superior to the enemy with new and stronger weapons and will be able to triumph over your worst enem[ies]— the aircraft and the destroyer.[37]

But this was only "whistling in the dark." After nearly four years of war—and with striking suddenness since the preceding fall—the anti-submarine campaign in the North Atlantic had finally turned in favor of the Allies. There would be some future German U-boat successes, but the trends were unmistakable, and the Allies' growing superiority in ships, aircraft, advanced ASW weapons, and experienced commanders would soon overwhelm the hard-pressed German submariners.

Appendix

World War I Submarine Losses

Nation	Mines	Depth Charges	Ramming	Gunfire	Q-Ships	Explosive Sweeps	Submarine Torpedoes	Aircraft	Accidents (Note 1)	Scuttling	Unknown	Totals
Great Britain	12	1	1(1)	4	0(1)	--	5	2(1) (Note 2)	14	8 (Note 3)	7	54(3)
France	2	--	1	2	--	--	2	1	5	--	1	14
Italy	2	--	--	1(1)	--	--	2(1)	--	3	--	--	8(2)
Russia	1	--	--	1	--	1	--	--	1	13	11	28
United States	--	--	--	--	--	--	--	--	1	--	--	1
Germany	48(11)	26	23	9	14 (Note 4)	3	17(1)	3 (Note 5)	12	13	19	187(12)
Austria-Hungary	3	--	--	1	--	1	1	--	1	1	1	9
Totals	68(11)	27	25(1)	18(1)	14(1)	5	27(2)	6(1)	37	35	39	301(17)

← Surface Ship Total: 89(3) →

(Figures in parentheses denote additional losses due to friendly forces or own mines.)

Notes:

1. "Accidents" include strandings, explosions, etc., but not losses to "friendly" mines.
2. Counts C-25 as a loss.
3. Includes C-3, used as a demolition ship at Zeebrugge.
4. Includes two submarines lost to the Royal Navy's trawler/submarine ruse.
5. Includes the U-39, which was interned in Spain after severe damage from an aircraft attack.

Notes

Perspective

1. Winston S. Churchill, *Their Finest Hour* (Boston: Houghton Mifflin, 1949), 598.
2. Winston S. Churchill, *The Hinge of Fate* (Boston: Houghton Mifflin, 1950), 125.

Chapter 1. Early Undersea Warfare

1. Quoted in Brayton Harris, *The Navy Times Book of Submarines* (New York: Berkley, 1997), 31.
2. Considerably more detailed technical descriptions of Bushnell's *Turtle,* with several drawings, can be found in Paul Bowers, *The Garrett Enigma and the Early Submarine Pioneers* (Shrewsbury, England: Airlife, 1999), chap. 4; Alex Roland, *Underwater Warfare in the Age of Sail* (Bloomington: Indiana University Press, 1978), chap. 6; and Harris, *Navy Times Book of Submarines,* chap. 3.
3. Several later sources erroneously conclude that Lee's attack on the *Eagle* was thwarted by copper sheathing installed on the ship's bottom to defend against the teredo, or shipworm, but correspondence by both Lee and Bushnell indicate that it was the rudder fittings that prevented the auger from penetrating. Moreover, Royal Navy records show that the *Eagle*'s bottom was coppered for the first time only in 1782.
4. Detailed accounts of early submarine history can be found in the references cited in conjunction with Bushnell's *Turtle,* as well as from Jeffrey Tall, *Submarines and Deep-Sea Vehicles* (Leicester, England: Silverdale Books, 2002).
5. The most comprehensive treatment of undersea vehicles in the American Civil War is found in Mark K. Ragan, *Union and Confederate Submarine Warfare in the Civil War* (Cambridge, Mass.: Da Capo, 2001). See also Bowers, *The Garrett Enigma and the Early Submarine Pioneers,* chap. 10.
6. A large portion of the Confederate archives was destroyed in the burning of Richmond in April 1865, and comprehensive and authoritative accounts are lacking for many of the South's underwater ventures.
7. The entire dispatch, with interesting technical details, is quoted in Ragan, *Union and Confederate Submarine Warfare in the Civil War,* 17.
8. Ibid., 23–24.
9. Until the recovery of the sunken *Hunley* in 2000, it was universally accepted on the basis of early drawings and firsthand accounts that the craft had a crew of nine: a captain and eight men to crank the propulsion system. However, the internal configuration of the actual hulk reveals that there were seats for only seven crank-turners, and only eight sets of human remains were discovered inside.
10. The Confederate Navy built several of these wooden, low-slung spar-torpedo boats, known generically as "Davids." Approximately 50 feet long and powered by a small steam engine, they could make as much as seven knots, even when ballasted down so that little more than the funnel appeared above the surface.
11. Quoted in Ragan, *Union and Confederate Submarine Warfare in the Civil War,* 176–177.
12. Ibid., 204.
13. A recovery team carefully brought the *Hunley* back to the surface in August 2000, and after the hull had been gingerly dewatered, the remains of the eight crew members were found inside and given ceremonial burials. The hulk itself underwent an intensive preservation and restoration effort. A comprehensive account of the discovery and raising of the *Hunley* is found in Brian Hicks and Schuyler Kropf, *Raising the Hunley: The Remarkable History and Recovery of the Lost Confederate Submarine* (New York: Ballantine Books, 2002).
14. Bowers, *The Garrett Enigma and the Early Submarine Pioneers,* provides a comprehensive survey of late 19th-Century European submarine development, with excellent technical drawings.
15. Because early submarines operated at near-neutral static buoyancy, they were unusually sensitive to the fore-and-aft distribution of weight and were quick to tip down toward the heavier end if trim was lost. Ballast tanks only added to the problem. If these were only partially filled and the boat inclined toward one end or the other, the ballast water would tend to slosh toward that lower end, unbalancing the submarine even more.
16. The *Resurgam* was lost at sea in February 1879 while attempting a 500-mile transit from Birkenhead to Portsmouth, where the craft was to have been demonstrated to the Royal Navy. The hulk of the *Resurgam* was discovered off Great Orme's Head in 1995.
17. A comprehensive technical summary of early torpedo development is found in E. W. Jolie, *A Brief History of U.S. Navy Torpedo Development,* NUSC Technical Document 5436 (Newport, R.I.: Naval Underwater Systems Center, 15 September 1978). See also Thomas Wildenberg and Norman Polmar, *Ship Killer: A History of the American Torpedo* (Annapolis, Md.: Naval Institute Press, 2010), chaps. 1 and 2.

18. Simon Lake (1866–1945) was an American inventor and entrepreneur who tested his first submarine, the *Argonaut Junior,* in 1894. Subsequently, he became John Holland's primary competitor in supplying submarines to the U.S. Navy, for which he eventually built 33 boats between 1909 and 1922. Earlier, he had contracted to build 11 submarines for Russia and two for Austria-Hungary. Lake is sometimes credited with inventing double-hull submarine construction and pioneering the use of the periscope, but these claims are often disputed. See John J. Poluhowich, *Argonaut: The Submarine Legacy of Simon Lake* (College Station: Texas A&M University Press, 1999), or Edward C. Whitman, "The Submarine Heritage of Simon Lake," *Undersea Warfare* (Fall 2002), 22–26, 32. For an outline of the influence of Jules Verne's 1870 novel *Twenty Thousand Leagues Under the Sea* on the early submarine pioneers, see Whitman, "The Submarine Technology of Jules Verne," *Undersea Warfare* (Winter 2004), 24–28, 30–31.

19. The most comprehensive biography of John Holland is Richard Knowles Morris, *John P. Holland—1841–1914—Inventor of the Modern Submarine* (Columbia: University of South Carolina Press, 1998). A shorter account of his life and accomplishments is found in Whitman, "John Holland, Father of the Modern Submarine," *Undersea Warfare* (Summer 2003), 21–31.

20. Holland used stored compressed air as a source of oxygen for the engine and expelled the exhaust into the surrounding water.

21. Holland's previous five submersibles had been his first attempt in 1878, the *Fenian Ram,* a 16-foot advanced model of the latter, the Zalinsky boat, and the *Plunger.*

22. The dynamite gun was a short-lived, late 19th-Century, projectile-firing weapon that used the relatively "soft" impulse of compressed air to launch powerful dynamite warheads that would likely detonate prematurely if fired from a conventional powder gun.

23. Despite the key role of his innovations in the rapid success of the Electric Boat Company, John Holland was soon marginalized within the management of the new organization, and he left the firm in frustration in early 1904. He attempted to establish a competitor, John P. Holland's Submarine Boat Company, but since he had assigned his original patents to Electric Boat, the latter was able to tie him up in litigation that even attempted to deny him the use of his *name* for commercial purposes and destroyed any hope of viability. After his fledgling company folded in 1907, he lived a quiet life in New Jersey, dying just two weeks after the outbreak of World War I in 1914.

24. Quoted in Ragan, *Union and Confederate Submarine Warfare in the Civil War,* 137.

25. An earlier British objection to the adoption of undersea craft was voiced by the Earl St. Vincent, First Lord of the Admiralty from 1801 to 1805, when he heard that the prime minister, Sir William Pitt (1759–1806), had expressed mild interest: "Pitt was the greatest fool that ever existed to encourage a mode of warfare which those who commanded the sea did not want and if successful, would deprive them of it."

26. For a valuable discussion of the evolution of British attitudes toward the submarine before World War I, see Arthur J. Marder, *From the Dreadnought to Scapa Flow,* vol. 1, *The Road to War, 1904–1914* (London: Oxford, 1961), 328–336.

27. Quoted in ibid., 333.

28. Admiralty, Naval Staff, "Anti-Submarine Development and Experiments prior to December 1916," *Technical History of the Navy,* TH 40 (September 1920), quoted in Willem Hackmann, *Seek & Strike: Sonar, Anti-submarine Warfare and the Royal Navy 1914–1954* (London: Her Majesty's Stationery Office, 1984), 9.

29. Quoted in Marder, *Road to War,* 335. Following their rudimentary use in the American Civil War and particularly during the evolution of the self-propelled torpedo, anti-torpedo nets were adopted by many European navies. Intended for defense against surface-launched torpedoes and generally for ships at anchor, these heavy, steel-mesh nets could be deployed on booms pivoted out from the sides of the hull. Ships could steam with their torpedo nets streamed, but the resulting drag limited their speed to less than ten knots. By the beginning of World War I, torpedo nets had been discarded by all but the British and German Navies, and after the Battle of Jutland, they disappeared entirely. It is of interest to note that early in the Gallipoli campaign in the spring of 1915, three British battleships *(Goliath, Triumph,* and *Majestic)* were sunk by torpedoes while anchored for shore bombardment—even though their torpedo nets were extended.

30. "Declaration concerning the Laws of Naval War," 208 Consol. T.S. 338 (London, February 26, 1909), chap. 4, art. 50.

31. Curiously, of the major powers that participated in the deliberations resulting in the 1909 Declaration of London, only Great Britain—which had convened the conference—refused to sign the convention. The British government did, however, agree to abide by its provisions.

32. The 1911 Agadir crisis occurred when the German government sent a warship to the port of Agadir, Morocco, to force the withdrawal of a French military expedition to the inland city of Fez. The two short Balkan wars were fought among Greece, Bulgaria, Serbia, Montenegro, Romania, and Turkey for possession of the European territories of the deteriorating Ottoman (Turkish) Empire.

Chapter 2. The First ASW Challenge

1. Compiled from Fred T. Jane, *Jane's Fighting Ships 1905/06* (London: Sampson Lowe Marston, 1905).

2. April 20, 1904; Arthur J. Marder, *Fear God and Dread Nought: The Correspondence of Admiral of the Fleet Lord Fisher of Kilverstone* (London: Cape, 1952–1959), vol. 2, 309; cited in Arthur J. Marder, *Road to War*, 332.

3. For example, the Royal Navy's A-class submarines of 1904–1905 had a surface endurance of 310 n.miles at seven knots, but the E-class boats of the 1910–1911 program were capable of 3,000 n.miles at ten knots. Moreover, the submerged endurance of the A-class was three hours, whereas that of the E-class was ten times that long.

4. Probably by the War Staff, Admiralty MSS; cited in Marder, *Road to War*, 364.

5. The *E-9* was commanded by Lt.-Cdr. Max Horton, who was to become one of Britain's most successful submariners in World War I and, later, as Adm. Sir Max Horton, to serve as Flag Officer, Submarines and in World War II as Commander-in-Chief, Western Approaches.

6. Jellicoe to Churchill, 30 September 1914, Jellicoe MSS, quoted in Arthur J. Marder, *The War Years: To the Eve of Jutland, 1914–1916* (London: Oxford University Press, 1965), 67.

7. Lt.-Cdr. Kenneth Edwards, *We Dive at Dawn* (London: Rich & Cowan, 1939), 369, quoted in Marder, *To the Eve of Jutland*, 349.

8. In perhaps the most famous such incident, HMS *Dreadnought*, the prototype of the modern battleship, rammed and sank the German *U-24* in March 1915 near Moray Firth, killing *Kapitänleutnant* Otto Weddigen, who, as the commander of the *U-9*, had earlier sunk the cruisers *Aboukir, Cressy,* and *Hogue.*

9. Gregory K. Hartmann, *Weapons That Wait* (Annapolis, Md.: Naval Institute Press, 1979), 40.

10. A valuable description of early ASW technologies is found in Dwight R. Messimer, *Find and Destroy: Antisubmarine Warfare in World War I* (Annapolis, Md.: Naval Institute Press, 2001), chaps. 5–6 and 9–10.

11. Marder, *To the Eve of Jutland*, 352–353.

12. Messimer, *Find and Destroy*, 55–56.

13. Marder, *To the Eve of Jutland*, 356.

14. Cdr. (later Adm.) Campbell left a lively account of his Q-ship experiences in *My Mystery Ships* (Garden City, N.Y.: Doubleday, 1929). Also see E. Kebble Chatterton, *Q-Ships and Their Story* (Annapolis, Md.: Naval Institute Press, 1972).

15. Rear Adm. William Sowden Sims, *The Victory at Sea* (Garden City, N.Y.: Doubleday, Page, 1920), 196–197.

16. Paul G. Halpern, *A Naval History of World War I* (Annapolis, Md.: Naval Institute Press, 1994), 294.

17. Quoted in Arthur J. Marder, *1917: Year of Crisis* (London: Oxford University Press, 1969), 50.

18. Another *casus belli* was the publication of the secret Zimmerman telegram sent by German foreign minister Arthur Zimmermann to Germany's U.S. ambassador in January 1917. It revealed a suggestion to the Mexican government that the southwestern United States could be restored to Mexico if that country were to ally itself with Germany in a victorious war. The message was intercepted by the British, decoded, and by a convoluted route passed to the American government.

19. Julian S. Corbett and Henry Newbolt, *History of the Great War: Naval Operations* (London: Longmans-Green, 1920–1931), vol. 4, 385, quoted in Marder, *1917*, 99.

20. Quoted in Marder, *1917*, 70.

21. In discussing the evolution of the depth charge and depth charge throwers, the authors relied heavily on Messimer, *Find and Destroy*, 76–81 and chap. 18. See also Marder, *1917*, 71–73.

22. The Royal Navy fielded a number of light naval guns, classified by the approximate weight of their projectiles: the 12-pounder was a 3-inch quick-firing piece that used fixed ammunition; the 3-pounder had a caliber of 1.85 inches.

23. Late in the war, the British also developed a crude magnetic bottom mine known as the "M-sinker," which used an assembly of pivoting bar magnets to detect the relatively rapid changes in the local magnetic field caused by the passing of a nearby ship. See Hartmann, *Weapons That Wait*, 43–44. Although this weapon was largely experimental, Robert M. Grant, *U-Boat Hunters* (Annapolis, Md.: Naval Institute Press, 2003), 24–25, notes that the Royal Navy laid a field of 234 M-sinkers north of Zeebrugge in August 1918. It apparently claimed as victims a German destroyer, a torpedo boat, and a trawler but no U-boats.

24. Hartmann, *Weapons That Wait*, 49–51.

25. Grant, *U-Boat Hunters*, 30.

26. A particularly concise but thorough account of Room 40's genesis and subsequent activities is found in David Kahn, *The Codebreakers* (New York: Macmillan, 1967), chap. 9. Also see Donald McLachlan, *Room 39: A Study in Naval Intelligence* (New York: Atheneum, 1968).

27. A *superenciphered* message is one coded twice in succession. First, the plaintext is converted into code groups using some initial coding technique, and then the code groups themselves are enciphered using a second, generally different code. In the case of the German naval messages, the superencipherment was accomplished with the simplest of all possible codes—a mono-alphabetic substitution—which made it relatively easy to decipher, even with frequent changes.

28. Grant, *U-Boat Hunters,* provides a detailed description of these various diving operations.

29. Halpern, *Naval History of World War I,* 340–341.

30. Adm. David Beatty, letter to his wife, 7 July 1917, quoted in Halpern, *Naval History of World War I,* 367.

31. Operations Division, Admiralty War Staff, "Remarks on Submarine Warfare, 1917"; Technical History Monograph TH14 (1919), *The Atlantic Convoy System, 1917–1918;* quoted in Marder, *1917,* 121–122.

32. Admiral Jellicoe's acquiescence was also partly motivated by the entry of the United States into the war, which seemed to promise the availability of large numbers of U.S. Navy destroyers for escort duty.

33. Although the raider threat was relatively minimal at this point in the war, the last active German surface raider, the full-rigged sailing ship *Seeadler,* was wrecked in a storm in August 1917.

34. Quoted in Sims, *Victory at Sea,* 58.

35. Halpern, *Naval History of World War I,* 365, provides a concise discussion of the extent to which shipping losses decreased after the onset of convoying.

36. Quoted in Marder, *1917,* 288.

37. Halpern, *Naval History of World War I,* 365.

38. David Lloyd George, *The War Memoirs of David Lloyd George* (London: Nicholson & Watson, 1933–1936), quoted in Marder, *1917,* 256.

Chapter 3. ASW in Other Areas

1. For a more detailed account of the submarine and anti-submarine campaigns in the Mediterranean Sea, see Halpern, *Naval History of World War I,* chaps. 3, 6, and 12. For similar accounts of the campaigns in the Baltic and Black Seas, see Halpern's chaps. 7 and 8, respectively.

2. *Standard,* London, 29 May 1912, quoted in Marder, *Road to War,* 290.

3. See Peter Shankland and Anthony Hunter, *Dardanelles Patrol* (New York: Scribner's, 1964).

4. The *U-5* was commanded by *Linienschiffsleutnant* Georg Ritter von Trapp, later the founder of the Trapp Family Singers, in which role he was portrayed in the musical *The Sound of Music.*

5. Adm. Sir Henry Oliver, "Question of a Naval Conference between France, Italy, and Great Britain," 29 December 1916, Admiralty MSS, quoted in Marder, *1917,* 93–94.

6. Marder, *To the Eve of Jutland,* 336.

7. Halpern, *Naval History of World War I,* 393.

8. Sims, *Victory at Sea,* 228–239.

9. The other British submarine lost in the Mediterranean was the *B-10,* destroyed in an Austro-Hungarian air raid on the Arsenal of Venice in August 1916.

10. Messimer, *Find and Destroy,* part 6, provides a comprehensive discussion of the ASW systems and tactics adopted by the Central Powers, such as they were.

11. Monitors were large, shallow-draft, shore-bombardment platforms, generally mounting a pair of large-caliber naval rifles. The three *Lord Clive*–class monitors employed at Zeebrugge and Ostend were each armed with a 12-inch twin turret removed from the Royal Navy's old *Majestic*-class battleships.

12. The second cargo submarine of this design, the *Bremen,* departed the city of that name en route to the United States in September 1916. She disappeared at sea with all hands. British war records indicate no action against a U-boat that could have been the *Bremen.* See Dwight R. Messimer, *The Merchant U-boat: Adventures of the* Deutschland, *1916–1918* (Annapolis, Md.: Naval Institute Press, 1988), and Paul König, *Voyage of the* Deutschland: *The First Merchant Submarine* (Annapolis, Md.: Naval Institute Press, 2001 [originally published 1917]).

13. Two of the German losses, both in mid-1915, were due to the trawler/towed-submarine ruse described earlier.

14. Sims, *Victory at Sea,* 272–273.

Chapter 4. Lessons Learned, New Platforms, and New Technologies

1. Winston Churchill, "The U-Boat War," in *Thoughts and Adventures* (London: Thornton Butterworth, 1932).

2. Quoted in Marder, *1917,* 3.

3. A *dirigible* is any lighter-than-air craft or airship that can be directed or guided. A *rigid airship,* such as a Zeppelin, has an outer framework that contains a series of gas bags, or cells, that provide the lifting force. Thus, even if the gas cells are emptied, a rigid airship maintains its shape. A *non-rigid airship,* often called a "blimp," has no external structure, and only the pressure of the lifting gas inside an inflatable envelope maintains its shape.

4. Sources for the evolution of airborne ASW in World War I include Alfred Price, *Aircraft versus Submarines: The Evolution of Anti-submarine Aircraft 1912–1945,* 3rd ed. (Annapolis, Md.: Naval Institute Press, 2004); Marder, *1917,* chap. 1; and Messimer, *Find and Destroy,* chap. 15.

5. One explanation for the origin of the word "blimp" traces it to a purported World War I classification system for airships: Class-A Rigid and Class-B Limp. Unfortunately, no such nomenclature seems to have been used at the time, and the accepted origin of the term now appears to be an incident on 5 December 1915 at the Royal Navy's Cappel Airship Station, when, in the process of inspecting the airship *SS-12,* Lt. A. D. Cunningham gave the belly of the gas bag a flip of his thumb. The taut bag gave off the odd

sound "blimp," which at once Cunningham imitated. The incident was quickly repeated. And "the rest is history."

6. Col. L. H. Strain, "Aircraft v. Submarines," *The Aeronautical Journal* (London) (April 1921), 203.

7. The designation Short Type 184 was derived from the name of the manufacturer and the serial number allocated to the first aircraft. Later the aircraft was known as the "225," which was the horsepower of its Sunbeam engine; subsequently, more powerful engines were fitted to the aircraft.

8. For a detailed account of the *UC-6* sinking by aircraft see, for example, Sqdn.-Ldr. T. D. Hallam, *The Spider Web: The Romance of a Flying-Boat Flight in the First World War* (London: Arms and Armour, 1979; first published in 1919), 156–162.

9. Halpern, *Naval History of World War I,* 425.

10. For the role of U.S. naval aviation during World War I, see Sims, *Victory at Sea,* chap. XI.

11. As a result of damage sustained in a French air attack on 18 May 1918, the German submarine *U-39* was interned at Cartagena, Spain, and at the end of the war was turned over to the French Navy.

12. Two much-modified Flower-class sloops—the former HMS *Chrysanthemum* and the former HMS *Saxifrage*— are still moored in the Thames at London, where they served until 1987 as drill ships for the Royal Navy Volunteer Reserve.

13. The Royal Navy deployed two other classes of small patrol ships toward the end of the war, neither of them particularly successful. Curiously, they were both designed purposely to appear symmetrical in outline fore and aft, so that from a distance it was difficult to tell which way they were heading, particularly when dazzle-painted. These were the 1,320-ton, 276-foot "24" class, of which 22 were eventually built, and the patrol gunboats of the Kil class (*Kilberry, Kilbride,* etc.), 890 tons on a length of 182 feet. Eighty-five of the latter were ordered, and the first were delivered at the end of 1917. Both classes were quickly paid off and disposed of after the war.

14. Two of the *Clemson* class carried eight 4-inch guns, and four of the class had four 5-inch weapons.

15. After World War I several flush-deck destroyers were converted for various research roles (redesignated AG and IX), and the USS *Noa* was fitted to carry a floatplane. Another eight ships were converted to light minelayers (DM), 18 to high-speed minesweepers (DMS), 36 to high-speed transports (APD), and 14 to seaplane tenders (AVD). At the end of World War II there still were 34 of the flush-deck, four-pipe ships in service as destroyers (DD).

16. Hackmann, *Seek & Strike,* 19–20. See also Marder, *1917,* 78–79.

17. Marder, *To the Eve of Jutland,* 353–354. However, in describing this same incident, Hackmann, *Seek & Strike,* 67–68, implies that only acoustic sensors were involved.

18. The following account of the early development of underwater acoustic systems draws heavily on Hackmann, *Seek & Strike,* chaps. 1 and 3.

19. A carbon button microphone consists of a small pellet of loosely packed carbon grains in contact with a small diaphragm and serving as a variable resistance in a battery-powered electrical circuit. The vibrations of the diaphragm cause the packing density of the carbon grains to vary in step with the impressed sound waves, and the resulting changes in electrical resistance cause corresponding fluctuations in the electrical current flowing through the device. A magnetophone receiver uses the varying magnetic field generated by an electrical signal in a small coil to vibrate an associated diaphragm (often fitted with a small permanent magnet) and reproduce the original sound. Reversing the process, *external* sound waves will generate small electrical currents and cause the assembly to function as a microphone.

20. A detailed account of the difficult relationship that developed between Captain Ryan and the Board of Invention and Research, leading to the latter's disestablishment in early 1918, is found in Hackmann, *Seek & Strike,* chap. 2.

21. See Sims, *Victory at Sea,* chap. VI, for a near-contemporary description of the development of U.S. Navy listening devices and their tactical employment by U.S. subchasers.

22. Confusingly, even after the U.S. Navy turned to electro-acoustic (i.e., microphone-based) listening devices, it continued to call its successive systems "tubes."

23. Hackmann, *Seek & Strike,* 69.

24. In a fourth incident, on 28 October 1918 northeast of the Dogger Bank, the *U-78* was torpedoed by the British submarine *G-3,* which appears to have been part of a patrol group equipped with listening equipment.

25. "Submarine Screening of Fleet Units," Admiralty Papers, Public Records Office, London, 186/376, quoted in Hackmann, *Seek & Strike,* 63–64.

26. Admiral Karl Doenitz, *Memoirs: Ten Years and Twenty Days* (London: Weidenfeld & Nicholson, 1959), quoted in Arthur J. Marder, *From the Dreadnought to Scapa Flow,* vol. 5, *Victory and Aftermath, 1918–1919* (London: Oxford, 1965), 77.

27. The authors have relied largely on the "Revised List of German Submarines Sunk or Interned" in Robert M. Grant, *U-Boat Hunters* (Annapolis, Md.: Naval Institute Press, 2003), with occasional reference to the table of "German Submarine Losses 1914–1918" in the "Maritime War" section of the online *Great War Primary Document Archive* (www.gwpda.org).

28. These monthly numbers are drawn from Marder, *Victory and Aftermath,* chap. IV, Appendix F, "U-boat Statistics," and corroborated by comparison with several other sources. However, the reader is cautioned that these figures are indeed *averages* over tens of months and that significant month-to-month variability was always present. For example, Marder reports that in October 1917, the Germans had 70 U-boats at sea, their maximum for the entire war. Corresponding monthly maxima for 1914, 1915, 1916, and 1918 were 13, 19, 49, and 60, respectively. Similarly, the monthly loss rates (due to Allied ASW) quoted in the text are also averages; actual losses to Allied action ranged from zero to three for the earlier 26-month period and from two to 13 for the period following mid-1917.

29. The several books and films in this vein include the classic British film *Q-Ships* (1928).

Chapter 5. Developing Sonar and Radar

1. Hackmann, *Seek & Strike,* especially chaps. IV through VII, provides the most comprehensive and accurate published source for the Royal Navy's development of active sonar between the wars.

2. Another advantage of active sonar is that since the transmitted signal is normally centered around a particular frequency, narrow-band frequency filtering can be used to eliminate much of the ambient background noise, which is relatively broadband in character.

3. As a general rule, sound waves can be focused in a narrow direction only when the physical dimensions of the transmitter are large compared to the wavelength of the sound signal itself. The wavelength of the Fessenden Oscillator's 540 Hz output in water was approximately nine and a half feet, significantly more than the two-foot diameter of the transmitting diaphragm. Thus, the device was essentially omnidirectional.

4. Early in World War I, French military authorities had become familiar with Fessenden's low-frequency, three-stage amplifier using American inventor Lee De Forest's Audion valves. Originally intending to adapt Audion amplifiers to wireless telegraphy, the French soon developed an improved version of the three-electrode Audion valve itself and by the end of the war were producing 1,400 per day for applications that included active sonar.

5. For several reasons, including lower inherent power losses from molecular motion and wavelength-dependent transmission phenomena, the lower the frequency of underwater sound signals, the more efficiently they will propagate outward from a source.

6. "Heterodyning" is an electronic signal-processing technique that shifts the frequency spread of a signal to a higher or lower band. The frequency of early active sonars was in the supersonic range—imperceptible to the human ear. Heterodyning the returning echoes downward in frequency made them audible to an operator.

7. A non-resonant transducer produces roughly equal output over a wide range of driving frequencies. A resonant transducer—more efficient in converting electrical input energy into sound—is "tuned" to operate in a narrow frequency band centered on a natural, or self-resonant, frequency associated with the transducer's size and physical configuration.

8. During the early years of its active sonar development, the Royal Navy was so secretive about the project that any mention of quartz—a common material—was cloaked beneath the code word "asdivite." See Hackmann, *Seek & Strike,* xxv.

9. Ibid., 89–95; see also Captain L. S. Howeth, USN (Ret.), *History of Communications-Electronics in the United States Navy* (Washington, D.C.: Bureau of Ships, 1963), 471–478; and Vice-Admiral Sir Arthur Hezlet, *Electronics and Sea Power* (New York: Stein and Day, 1975), 167–168.

10. The *Fish Hawk* was a screw steamer built originally for the Bureau of Fisheries in 1879. She was taken over by the Navy for patrol duty in both the Spanish-American War and World War I and then used in early sonar research at New London. She was returned to the Bureau of Fisheries in July 1919 and finally laid up in 1926.

11. Hackmann, *Seek & Strike,* 197–221 and Appendixes and 5.

12. Ibid., Appendix 3, lists the sequence of range recorders developed between the wars.

13. Ibid., 139–146.

14. Generally, in warmer waters near the ocean surface, sound speed is relatively high. At greater depths, where the water is increasingly cooler, sound velocity decreases toward a minimum. This transition zone in depth is known as the *thermocline,* and it has a complicating influence on the propagation of sound "rays," causing both "shadow zones" and regions of varying transmission loss.

15. Quoted in Hackmann, *Seek & Strike,* 144.

16. Ibid., 195–197. See also Hezlet, *Electronics and Sea Power,* 180; and Elias Klein, *Notes on Underwater Sound Research and Applications before 1939,* ONR Report ACR-135 (Washington, D.C.: Office of Naval Research, September 1967).

17. U.S. Technical Mission to Japan, *Japanese Sonar and Asdic,* Report E-10 (n.p.: December 1945). See also David C. Evans and Mark R. Peattie, *Kaigun: Strategy, Tactics, and Technology in the Imperial Japanese Navy, 1887–1941* (Annapolis, Md.: Naval Institute Press, 1997), 440–441.

18. Yu. F. Tarasyuk and V. F. Martynyuk, "50 Years of Soviet Hydroacoustics," *Sudostroyeniye* no. 5 (1984), 66.

19. Useful accounts of the early development of radar are found in Hezlet, *Electronics and Sea Power*, 168–175; and Merrill I. Skolnik, *Introduction to Radar Systems* (New York: McGraw-Hill, 1962), Section 1.5.

20. Senatore Guglielmo Marconi, "Radio Telegraphy," *Proceedings of the Institute for Radio Engineers* 10, no. 4 (1922), 237.

21. In a pulsed radar, shorter wavelengths are desirable for achieving the spatial resolution needed to measure target range and bearing accurately. Since the radar wavelength is inversely proportional to the operating frequency, smaller wavelengths require higher frequencies. There are two principal reasons for wanting shorter wavelengths. First, radar signals are reflected more efficiently from a target when the wavelength is small in comparison to the dimensions of the target. Moreover, and second, only by moving to shorter wavelengths can the physical dimensions of the antennas be reduced to sizes compatible with installation on ships and aircraft. As a rule of thumb, the beamwidth—or angular spread in degrees—of radiation from a circular antenna is roughly 60 times the ratio of the radar wavelength and the antenna diameter. Therefore, to get a relatively narrow beamwidth—necessary for localizing the target in azimuth by pointing the antenna—the wavelength must be very small compared to the size of the antenna, and the operating frequency commensurately higher. For example, to achieve a beamwidth of ten degrees, a circular antenna would have to be approximately 120 feet in diameter at 50 MHz but only 12 feet in diameter at 500 MHz. Additionally, minimizing range errors in a pulsed radar demands extreme accuracy in measuring the time duration between transmitting a pulse and receiving a target return from that same pulse. Because the speed of light is so high—nearly a billion feet per second—an error of only one millionth of a second (a microsecond) in measuring this interval will cause a range error of 500 feet. Moreover, the time duration of the transmitted pulse itself must also be on the order of microseconds to achieve that same precision in range.

22. U.S. Naval Technical Mission to Japan, *Electronic Targets: Japanese Submarine and Shipboard Radar,* Report E-01 (25 December 1945), 8. The Japanese term for radar was *dempa tanshingi* (electronic wave search device).

23. Capt. Stephen Roskill, RN, *Naval Policy between the Wars,* vol. II, *The Period of Reluctant Rearmament 1930–1939* (Annapolis, Md.: Naval Institute Press, 1976), 181.

Chapter 6. Building ASW Forces

1. Post–World War I force levels are deduced from Surgeon-Lt. Oscar Parkes, RN, and Maurice Prendergast, eds., *Jane's Fighting Ships 1919* (London: Sampson Lowe Marston, 1919) and corroborated by several other sources. Counted as smaller ASW ships are the P-, PC-, "24," Flower, and Kil- classes of sloops and escort vessels but none of the smallest ASW craft, such as trawlers and motor launches. Also see Capt. Stephen Roskill, *Naval Policy between the Wars,* vol. I, *The Period of Anglo-American Naval Antagonism 1919–1929* (London: Walker, 1968), Appendix B, Table I.

2. Parkes and Prendergast, *Jane's Fighting Ships 1919,* 206.

3. Ibid., 224–225.

4. The two early A-class prototypes, *Amazon* and *Ambuscade,* were included in the 1924 estimates.

5. Roskill, *Period of Anglo-American Naval Antagonism 1919–1929,* Appendix C; and Francis E. McMurtrie, ed., *Jane's Fighting Ships 1939* (London: Sampson Lowe Marston, 1939). The 129-destroyer total includes only members of the newer A through K classes.

6. Data for U.S. Navy ships and craft of the World War II era are derived from Bureau of Ships, *Ships' Data U.S. Naval Vessels,* NAVSHIPS 250–010 (Washington, D.C.: Navy Department, 15 April 1945); and James C. Fahey, *The Ships and Aircraft of the U.S. Fleet,* 1st through 5th eds. (privately published, 1939–1945).

7. The eight-gun ships were the *Porter* (DD 356) class of "heavy destroyers," or "leaders." These 13 ships had four twin 5-inch gun mounts and a standard displacement of 1,850 tons. They carried three quad 21-inch torpedo mounts on the centerline, giving them the world's heaviest torpedo salvo. The later USS *Benson,* completed in 1940, provided the basic design for the 271 ships of the *Benson, Livermore* (DD 429), and *Fletcher* (DD 445) classes completed through 1944; they had five 5-inch dual-purpose guns, ten 21-inch torpedo tubes, and depth charges.

8. As their popular names suggest, the Hunt-class destroyers were named after traditional English foxhunting venues, the Flower-class corvettes for indigenous flowers, and the Tree-class trawlers for trees.

9. Nicholas Monsarrat, *The Cruel Sea* (New York: Alfred A. Knopf, 1951), 19.

10. Nine of the original 60 Eagle boats remained on the Navy List at the time; all were assigned to the Naval Reserve as training ships. Fourteen veterans of the "splinter fleet" of World War I—designated in the SC series—also remained.

11. Roskill, *Period of Anglo-American Naval Antagonism 1919–1929,* Appendix C; and McMurtrie, *Jane's Fighting Ships 1939.*

12. During World War II the U.S. Navy directed the Grumman firm to concentrate on production of the F6F Hellcat carrier fighter. Thus, production of the firm's F4F Wildcat fighter and TBF Avenger torpedo plane were transferred to General Motors Corporation's Eastern Aircraft Division, with the planes entering service as the FM and TBM series, respectively.

13. A total of 3,290 of these aircraft would be built in the United States and Canada, with additional aircraft also built in the USSR. The U.S. Navy used the designations PBY for planes built by Consolidated, PBN for those built by the Naval Aircraft Factory, and PBY for those built by Vickers in Canada; the U.S. Army Air Forces flew the aircraft with the designation OA-10.

14. ADM 1/8609, Admiralty minutes dated 20 June 1920 and 27 June 1921, quoted in Hackmann, *Seek & Strike,* 127. Admiral of the Fleet Alfred Ernle Montacute Chatfield, 1st Baron Chatfield, later served as First Sea Lord from 1933 to 1938 and as Minister for Coordination of Defence between 1939 and 1940.

15. The original ASW school, HMS Sarepta, was established at Portland in 1917, but it was subsumed into a new training organization, HMS Gibraltar, in October 1920. In turn, Gibraltar's responsibilities were transferred to HMS Osprey in April 1924, and in 1927 all ASW research and development were also consolidated there. See Hackmann, *Seek & Strike,* 127.

16. Ibid., 187–189.

17. Several attempts to devise a transducer with a broad, 120-degree beam that could search the entire forward sector with a single pulse ended in failure.

18. Craig C. Felker, *Testing American Sea Power: U.S. Navy Strategic Exercises, 1923–1940* (College Station: Texas A&M University Press, 2007).

19. Quoted in ibid., 72. Laning was Commander, Battle Force, U.S. Fleet.

20. See Roskill, *Period of Reluctant Rearmament 1930–1939,* Chap. XII, for a detailed description of the Royal Navy's role in the Spanish Civil War.

21. The Soviet advisors included Nikolai G. Kuznetsov, who was in Spain in 1936–1937. Later Admiral of the Fleet of the Soviet Union, he served as head of the Soviet Navy from April 1939 (at age 34) to February 1947, and again from July 1951 to December 1955.

22. See Brian R. Sullivan, "Fascist Italy's Military Involvement in the Spanish Civil War," *Journal of Military History* (October 1995), 697–727.

23. Hugh Thomas, *The Spanish Civil War* (New York: Harper Colophon, 1961), 475.

24. Winston Churchill, *The Second World War,* vol. 1, *The Gathering Storm* (Boston: Houghton Mifflin, 1948), 215.

25. Ibid., 246.

26. The story of OIC is told in Patrick Beesly, *Very Special Intelligence: The Story of the Admiralty's Operational Intelligence Centre 1939–1945* (London: Hamish Hamilton, 1977; reprinted by Greenhill Books, 2000). Beesly served in OIC from 1940 to 1945. Also see F. H. Hinsley et al., *British Intelligence in World War II: Its Influence on Strategy and Operations* (London: Her Majesty's Stationery Office, 1979), vol. 1, 12–13. The OIC played prominently in the classic film *Sink the Bismarck!* (1960).

27. Ronald H. Spector, *At War at Sea: Sailors and Naval Combat in the Twentieth Century* (New York: Viking, 2001), 228.

28. Roskill, *Period of Reluctant Rearmament 1930–1939,* 226–228.

29. Ibid., 335–337.

30. Evans and Peattie, *Kaigun,* 434–437.

31. IVS stood for *Ingenieurskantoor voor Scheepsbouw,* Dutch for "engineer office for shipbuilding."

32. See his autobiography, Doenitz, *Memoirs.*

33. Ibid., 12.

34. Ibid., 31, 46.

Chapter 7. First Confrontations in the Atlantic

1. Clay Blair, *Hitler's U-Boat War,* vol. 1, *The Hunters: 1939–1942* (New York: Random House, 1996), 53–57.

2. Churchill, *Gathering Storm,* 425. Churchill had served as First Lord of the Admiralty during the World War I era, from 1911 to 1915.

3. A total of 40 V- and W-class destroyers were launched between 1917 and 1919. Displacing between 1,090 and 1,140 tons on a length of 312 feet, they were armed originally with four 4.0- or 4.7-inch guns and either five or six torpedo tubes. Their top speed was 34 knots.

4. Blair, *Hunters,* 64–65.

5. Controlled mines are detonated by a command from shore, generally in response to the detection of an intruding submarine by fixed acoustic or magnetic sensors.

6. Price, *Aircraft versus Submarines,* 31–37. The Avro Anson was a twin-engine maritime reconnaissance aircraft designed in the mid-1930s and introduced in 1936. Maximum speed was 165 knots, range was 700 n.miles. At the outbreak of the war, Coastal Command had ten squadrons of Ansons.

7. The two-sear Blackburn Skua was the Fleet Air Arm's first carrier-based monoplane. Introduced in late 1938, it could carry a 500-pound bomb load a range of 700 n.miles. However, its top speed of 200 knots was immediately outclassed by that of its German opponents, and it was withdrawn from front-line service in 1941. The Fairey Swordfish, a biplane torpedo bomber, entered service in 1936 and despite its modest capabilities was still in action at the end of the war. Maximum speed was only 120 knots, with a range of 480 miles, but it could carry 1,600 pounds of ordnance and was highly valued for its robust construction and excellent flying qualities.

8. Later, the middle letter *N* was added for convoys taking the northern latitude route, e.g., HNX. Also, after the Germans occupied the coast of France in July 1940, the OA convoys were phased out.

9. The *U-40* settled to the bottom in 115 feet of water with nine survivors in the unflooded aft end of the boat. All nine managed to escape the submarine and reach the surface using breathing apparatus—the first successful escape from a sunken U-boat—but only three survived to be picked up by the Royal Navy.

10. Blair, *Hunters,* Appendix 18. We have accepted Blair's summary numbers as authoritative, but other sources differ markedly, often because of divergent rules of inclusion for counting merchant victims, e.g., based on size.

11. Nine days later, *Salmon,* commanded by Cdr. E. O. Bickford, torpedoed and heavily damaged the German light cruisers *Leipzig* and *Nürnberg,* also in the North Sea.

12. During this period, one of the Atlantic U-boats, operating near Gibraltar, made use for the first time of clandestine arrangements with Franco's Fascist Spain for replenishing fuel and supplies from the German merchant ship *Thalia,* stationed in the "neutral" port of Cadiz.

13. Blair, *Hunters,* 143–144.

14. Sir Basil Liddell Hart, *History of the Second World War* (New York: G. P. Putnam's Sons, 1971), chap. 6 and 145–157, provides a concise account of the Norwegian campaign.

15. Price, *Aircraft versus Submarines,* 31–34.

16. Ibid., 49–53.

17. "Sea clutter" arises from that portion of the transmitted radar pulse that is returned to the receiver—or "backscattered"—from the rough and undulating surface of the sea. It is a separate return signal that interferes with detecting a target echo and is more pronounced at more vertical angles of incidence.

18. Much has been written about Allied success in breaking the Enigma codes. See David Kahn, *Seizing the Enigma: The Race to Break the German U-Boat Codes, 1939–1943,* rev. ed. (Annapolis, Md.: Naval Institute Press, 2012); Blair, *Hunters,* 129–135, 239–244; and Simon Singh, *The Code Book: The Evolution of Secrecy from Mary, Queen of Scots to Quantum Cryptography* (New York: Doubleday, 1999), 127–142, chap. 4.

19. The Polish success in analyzing the Enigma machine was aided significantly by information provided by a German spy, Hans-Thilo Schmidt, working for the French authorities, who shared his material with the Poles. See David Kahn, "The Spy Who Most Affected World War II," in *Kahn on Codes: The Secrets of the New Cryptology* (New York: Macmillan, 1983), 76–88.

20. British mathematician and computer theorist Alan Turing (1912–1954) was born in London and studied at Cambridge, later receiving his PhD at Princeton. He made his first great discovery in the area of mathematical "computability and solvability," where he showed that automatic computation cannot solve all mathematical problems. During World War II, Turing played a major role in the cryptological work at Bletchley Park that eventually led to the breaking of the German Enigma code, and afterward he turned to problems of machine computation, becoming one of the founders of both modern computer science and artificial intelligence. Sadly, he was driven to suicide in 1954 by relentless government prosecution for homosexuality, persecution that included the judicial administration of estrogen injections intended to "cure" him.

21. According to Blair, *Hunters,* 176, German aircraft sank 33 ships for a total of 70,000 tons during July alone.

22. HMS *Rainbow* is thought to have been sunk in an inadvertent collision with the Italian merchant ship *Antonietta Costa* on 4 October 1940. In early December, HMS *Regulus* disappeared without a trace in the Strait of Otranto and is believed to have been mined.

23. Monsarrat's *The Cruel Sea,* quoted earlier, the most celebrated novel about British escorts in the Battle of the Atlantic, provides vivid descriptions of life on board a fictitious Flower-class corvette, the *Compass Rose.*

24. Torpex combined RDX (an earlier British military explosive), trinitrotoluene (TNT), and powdered aluminum to produce a mixture that was 50 percent more powerful pound for pound than TNT.

25. Churchill's earlier tenure as First Lord of the Admiralty had overlapped with that of Roosevelt as Assistant Secretary of the Navy, from March 1913 to August 1920.

26. Churchill, *Gathering Storm,* 405.

27. At the same time, additional basing rights were granted separately in Bermuda and Argentia, Newfoundland, but not as part of the "destroyers-for-bases" deal. For additional detail, see Blair, *Hunters,* 187–88; and Samuel Eliot Morison, *History of United States Naval Operations in World War II,* vol. I, *The Battle of the Atlantic—1939–1943* (Boston: Little, Brown, 1964), 33–36.

28. In the Royal Navy, the U.S. destroyers were renamed after towns common to both the United Kingdom and the United States, for example, Newport, Richmond, Mansfield; hence they were called the "Town" class. In the Royal Canadian Navy they were named after rivers.

29. Morison, *Battle of the Atlantic,* 36–38.

Chapter 8. The Conflict Widens

1. Capt. Donald Macintyre, *U-Boat Killer* (Annapolis, Md.: Naval Institute Press, 1976), 42.

2. Postwar analyses accorded the three aces with:

Kretschmer *U-99:* 16 patrols 46 ships of 273,043 GRT plus one destroyer

Prien *U-47:* 10 patrols 30 ships of 162,769 GRT plus one battleship

Schepke *U-100:* 14 patrols 37 ships of 155,882 GRT.

3. Macintyre, *U-Boat Killer,* 41.

4. The large cruiser submarine *U-A,* originally named *Batiray,* had been under construction in Germany for the Turkish Navy at the beginning of the war but was confiscated for use by the Germans.

5. Otto Kretschmer letter to Cdr. R. A. Clarkson, 20 April 1997, *The Navy* (British Navy League) files, London.

6. For an account of Winn's contribution, see Beesly, *Very Special Intelligence.*

7. Winston S. Churchill, *The Second World War,* vol. 3, *The Grand Alliance* (Boston: Houghton Mifflin, 1948), 122–126.

8. Macintyre, *U-Boat Killer,* 86–87.

9. Morison, *Battle of the Atlantic,* 45–49.

10. First entering service in September 1940, four years after the somewhat smaller PBY Catalina, the twin-engine Martin PBM Mariner flying boat could reach 180 knots and had an effective range of 2,600 n.miles. A total of 1,235 were built.

11. Morison, *Battle of the Atlantic,* 69–73.

12. Ibid., 80.

13. A lifelong anti-communist, Churchill justified his position by remarking at the time, "If Hitler invaded Hell, I would make at least a favourable reference to the Devil in the House of Commons" (Churchill, *Grand Alliance,* 370).

14. On 4 October, however, the *U-111* was detected, depth-charged, and then destroyed in a surface gunnery duel by the armed trawler *Lady Shirley* west of the Canary Islands.

15. Blair, *Hunters,* Plate 8, 317.

16. The RAF Catalina I was the U.S. Navy PBY-5 variant.

17. These "assists," all in engagements where surface warships received primary credit, were the sinkings of the *U-55* on 30 January 1940 and the *U-452* on 25 August 1941, the scuttling of the *U-26* on 1 July 1940, and the capture of the *U-570* on 27 August 1941. The three U-boat sinkings by *unassisted* aircraft in 1939–1941 were all credited to Bomber Command and Fleet Air Arm units. However, during this same period, Royal Air Force aircraft participated in the destruction of four Italian submarines in the Mediterranean, two of them unassisted.

18. Another serious blow was struck against British naval power in the Mediterranean on the night of 19 December 1941, when Italian "frogmen" infiltrated the naval base at Alexandria and mined the battleships *Queen Elizabeth* and *Valiant,* putting them out of action for several months.

19. Designed originally as a passenger aircraft in the mid-1930s, the four-engine Fw 200 Condor was adapted as a maritime patrol aircraft and heavy bomber capable of carrying nearly 4,600 pounds of bombs to a range of 2,000 n.miles. In addition to ocean reconnaissance, it was regularly employed against Allied convoys early in the war as a bomber.

20. See Norman Polmar, *Aircraft Carriers: A History of Carrier Aviation and Its Influence on World Events,* vol. 1, *1909–1945* (Washington, D.C.: Potomac Books, 2006), 136–140.

21. In fact, a fifth submarine, the *U-127,* had been sunk by the Australian destroyer *Nestor* on 16 December in a nearby but separate encounter outside of the Strait of Gibraltar.

22. Quoted in Ministry of Defence (Navy), *German Naval History: The U-boat in the Atlantic, 1939–1945* (London: Her Majesty's Stationery Office, 1989), vol. III, 91.

23. Blair, *Hunters,* 418–427.

24. Summaries of U.S. ASW force levels in December 1941 are found in ibid., 447–452, and Morison, *Battle of the Atlantic,* 233–237. The *Long Island* (AVG 1, later CVE 1), was laid down as a freighter in 1939, but was acquired by the Navy for conversion to its first escort carrier in March 1941 and commissioned the following June. Displacing 7,886 tons standard on a length of 492 feet, she could carry 21 aircraft.

25. Some aircraft of the original British order for Hudsons were withheld for use by the U.S. Army Air Corps and the Navy, and the latter began flying the Hudson in October 1941 with the designation PBO-1. The first PBO squadron VP-82 operated initially from Quonset Point, Rhode Island, and then Argentia, Newfoundland.

26. After the shift of maritime patrol squadrons to the Pacific at the start of the war, the Navy was left with the following in the Atlantic:

    11 VP squadrons with PBY Catalinas
    1   VP squadron with PBYs and PBM Mariners
    1   VP squadron with PBM Mariners
    3   VS (shipboard scouting) squadrons with OS2U Kingfishers
    1   VP squadron with PBO Hudsons.

27. Simultaneously, nearly ten Japanese submarines, operating off the *west* coast of the United States, sank two American tankers, damaged five others and two freighters, and shelled an oil field near Santa Barbara. See Chap. 3 of *Hunters and Killers,* Vol. 2.

28. At the outset, Adm. Andrews had approximately 20 small craft under his direct control: seven Coast Guard cutters, seven pre-war SCs and Eagle boats, two gunboats, and four large yachts.

29. Dönitz had planned to send 26 U-boats to the Americas in February, but eight Type VIIs were diverted by the naval command to operations west of Norway, and many of the remainder were delayed in attacking two Atlantic convoys encountered by chance. See Blair, *Hunters,* 509–513.

30. These figures are drawn from Morison, *Battle of the Atlantic*, Appendix I.

31. Derived from Blair, *Hunters*, Appendix 17.

32. Developed from the Douglas DC-2 commercial airliner, the twin-engine B-18 first flew in 1935, and 350 were built in several variants. Capable of a top speed of 190 knots with a range of 1,060 n.miles, the B-18 Bolo could carry up to 6,500 pounds of bombs internally. Although obsolete when first employed for ASW, these aircraft continued in that role until mid-1943, when they were superceded by the B-24 Liberator.

33. A "flaming datum" is a torpedoed and sinking ship whose position is used as a reference point for locating a submarine presumed to be in the immediate vicinity.

34. Derived from Blair, *Hunters*, Appendix 16. Significantly, no U.S. troopship was sunk during the war.

35. For a detailed discussion that defends the American position, see Blair, *Hunters*, 521–525.

36. Additionally, eight Canadian-built Flower-class corvettes were transferred to the United States, and were assigned gunboat (PG) designations.

37. Initially, the "bucket brigade" system was maintained for shipping between New York and Norfolk. Also the Guantanamo-to-Halifax ocean route was reserved for Canadian oil imports. For details of the initial convoy arrangements, see Blair, *Hunters*, 532–533, and Morison, *Battle of the Atlantic*, chap. X, sec. 6, 252.

38. For details on the interlocking convoy system, see Morison, *Battle of the Atlantic*, 260–265.

39. Ibid., 264 and Appendix I, sec. 4.

40. A detailed assessment is given in Blair, *Hunters*, 691–700.

Chapter 9. The End of the Beginning

1. Morison, *Battle of the Atlantic*, 164–165.

2. Clay Blair, *Hitler's U-Boat War*, vol. 2, *The Hunted: 1942–1945* (New York: Random House, 1998), 120. See also Blair's accompanying footnote for a discussion of conflicting sources.

3. Morison, *Battle of the Atlantic*, 314, footnote.

4. Ibid., 226–228. See also Kathleen Broome Williams, *Secret Weapon: U.S. High-Frequency Direction Finding in the Battle of the Atlantic* (Annapolis, Md.: Naval Institute Press, 1996).

5. Blair, *Hunted*, 47.

6. Ibid., 134.

7. Ibid., Plate 11, 712.

8. Ibid., 135.

9. Under Lend-Lease an initial 20 B-17C Fortresses were transferred to the RAF, but proved unsuccessful as bombers.

In October 1942, the surviving aircraft were transferred to RAF Coastal Command and used there until superceded in 1943 by the much improved B-17E.

10. These RAF Liberators were among the first to be equipped with 10-centimeter wavelength radar sets.

11. Blair, *Hunted*, 83–87.

12. A comprehensive account of the development and first tactical successes of the Leigh Light is found in Price, *Aircraft versus Submarines*, 53–60, 80–86.

13. These AAF B-24 Liberators were among the first to be equipped with the SCR-517, the American equivalent of the H2S centimetric radar.

14. In units of magnetic flux density, the average value of the earth's magnetic field is roughly 50,000 gamma (γ). The change in this value due to a submarine at a range of 400 feet is about 10 gamma, or only 0.02 percent. Moreover, the local earth's field varies erratically in both time and space, further obscuring the target signal.

15. Price, *Aircraft versus Submarines*, 98–102.

16. Capt. Christian L. Engleman, USN (Ret.), "Prewar Development of the Sonobuoy," *Shipmate* (September 1987).

17. Fido was designated a "mine," vice a torpedo, for security reasons.

18. On Fido development, see Robert Gannon, *Hellions of the Deep: The Development of American Torpedoes in World War II* (University Park: Pennsylvania State University Press, 1996), 99–130; Wildenberg and Polmar, *Ship Killer*, 141–44; and Frederick J. Milford, "WWII Development of Homing Torpedoes," *Submarine Review* (April 1997), 64–79.

19. U.S. Navy, Operations Evaluation Group Study No. 289, 12 August 1946.

20. Churchill, *Gathering Storm*, 465.

21. Samuel Eliot Morison, *History of United States Naval Operations in World War II*, vol. X, *The Atlantic Battle Won: May 1943–May 1945* (Boston: Little, Brown, 1964), 34–36.

22. Blair, *Hunted*, 163, and Appendix 14, 809–810.

23. Norman Friedman, *U.S. Destroyers: An Illustrated Design History* (Annapolis, Md.: Naval Institute Press, 2004), chap. 7.

24. For complementary accounts of the development of the hedgehog, see Hackmann, *Seek & Strike*, 303–310; David Owen, *Anti-Submarine Warfare: An Illustrated History* (Annapolis, Md.: Naval Institute Press, 2007), 143–147; and Gerald Pawle, *Secret Weapons of World War II* (New York: Ballantine Books, 1967), 147–166.

25. Pawle, *Secret Weapons of World War II*, 166.

26. See Morison, *Battle of the Atlantic*, 218–224, for the organization and functions of the ASW Unit and ASWORG.

27. Very-long-range aircraft, almost exclusively modified B-24 Liberator bombers, had a cruising range exceeding 2,000 n.miles and could remain on station for four hours at a distance of 1,000 miles from base. Long-range ASW aircraft, for example, Catalinas, Sunderlands, B-17 Fortresses, and British Halifax bombers, had a cruising range of 1,200 to 2,000 n.miles and thus operating radiuses on the order of 400 to 600 miles.

28. U.S. escort carriers originally were designated "aircraft escort vessels" (AVG, or BAVG for ships ordered for Britain); on 20 August 1942, they were reclassified as auxiliary aircraft carriers (ACV) until 15 July 1943, when changed to escort aircraft carriers (CVE).

29. See Polmar, *Aircraft Carriers*, vol. 1, 268–270, 273–277.

30. The *Chenango, Sangamon, Suwannee,* and *Santee* displaced 7,192 tons on a length of 552 feet and, unlike the C3 conversions, had twin shafts.

31. The Grumman F4F Wildcat was a carrier-based fighter first introduced in December 1940. With a loaded weight of 7,000 pounds (including two 100-pound bombs), it could achieve a top speed of 320 m.p.h. The Grumman TBF Avenger was a three-seat torpedo bomber introduced in mid-1942. Its loaded weight of nearly 18,000 pounds included either 2,000 pounds of bombs or a Mark 13 torpedo; top speed was 275 m.p.h.

32. Blair, *Hunted,* 167.

33. Capt. S. W. Roskill, RN, *The War at Sea 1939–1945,* vol. II, *The Period of Balance* (London: Her Majesty's Stationery Office, 1956), 367–368.

34. Blair, *Hunted,* 164–169.

35. For comprehensive accounts, see Morison, *Atlantic Battle Won,* 64–76; and Blair, *Hunted,* 288–294.

36. Blair, *Hunted,* 338–339.

37. Quoted in Morison, *Atlantic Battle Won,* 83–84.

General Index

A

Admiralty Research Laboratory, 90

Adriatic Sea, 49–51. *See also* Otranto, Strait of

Agadir Crisis (1911), 15

airborne ASW, between the wars, 102–103

airborne ASW, World War I, 61–66

airborne ASW, World War II. *See* Biscay, Bay of; Catapult Aircraft Merchantman; Civil Air Patrol (U.S.); escort carriers, Royal Navy; escort carriers, U.S. Navy; Fido (Mark 24 homing torpedo); Fighter Catapult Ship; individual aircraft; Leigh light; magnetic anomaly detection; radar, British; radar, centimetric; rockets, anti-submarine; Royal Air Force, Coastal Command; sonobuoys; submarine campaigns, German, World War II; U.S. Army Air Forces

aircraft, Austro-Hungarian: Lohner Type L, 65

aircraft, British: *America*, 63; Anson 102, 118; BE-2, 62; Beaufighter, 164; Blenheim, 121; Catalina, 142, 160–162, 180; Felixstowe F-2A, 63; Fortress, 161–162; Fulmar, 145; Halifax, 161; Hudson, 102–103, 117, 141–142, 156, 162; Hurricane, 140–145; Kangaroo, 64; *Large America*, 63–64, 75; Liberator, 142, 160–162, 164, 180; Martlet (Wildcat), 146, 177; Mosquito, 164; Short Type 184, 63; Skua, 118; Stirling, 164; Sunderland, 102, 117, 161–162; Swordfish, 102, 112, 118, 122, 145, 166, 177; Vildebeest, 117; Wellington, 163–164; Wildcat (Martlet), 146, 177

aircraft, German: Fl 184 (gyroplane), 103; Fl 282 Kolibi (helicopter), 103; Fw 200 Condor, 145–146; Ju 88, 164; W.29, 65; W.33, 65

aircraft, United States: A-29 Hudson, 103, 154; B-18 Bolo, 156; B-24 Liberator, 142, 164, 175; Curtiss H.12, 64; F4F/FM Wildcat, 177; HNS-1 (helicopter), 178; OS2U Kingfisher, 150; PBM Mariner, 103, 137, 150; PBO Hudson, 102–103, 150, 154; PBY Catalina, 102, 124, 137, 150, 152, 156, 161, 165; R-4 (helicopter), 178; SBD Dauntless, 102; TBF/TBM Avenger, 102, 177; XOP-1 (autogiro), 103

airships, British: Coastal, 62; Coastal Star, 62; listening devices on, 75; Submarine Scout, 62–63; Zero, 62

airships, German, 61–62; *L-5*, 62; *L-9*, 62; Zeppelins, 61–62

airships, United States, 105, 150, 154–155, 165–167

Allied Atlantic Convoy Conference (1943), 173, 175

Andrews, Adolphus, 151–152, 154–155

Anglo-German Naval Treaty (1935), 108

Anti-Submarine Division (Brit.), 33, 43, 88

Arcadia Conference (1941–1942), 154

asdic, definition of, 89. *See also* sonar, British

Atlantic Charter (1941), 138–139

Atlantic Conference (1941), 138

Atlantic Trade Convoy Committee, 42

B

Bacon, Reginald, 23

Baker, George, 9, 11

Baker, Wilder D., 172

Balkan Wars (1912–1913), 16

Baltic operations, World War I: British, 47, 54; German, 24–25, 54; Russian, 25, 47, 53–54

Baltic operations, World War II, 113, 139

"Battle of the Atlantic," 116, 135

"Battle of the Bay." *See* Biscay, Bay of, World War II

Bauer, Herman, 31

Bayly, Sir Louis, 24, 30

Beatty, Sir David, 41, 78

Bell Telephone Laboratories, 166

Bethmann-Hollweg, Theobald von, 31

Biscay, Bay of, World War II: airborne radar in, 163–164; Coastal Command patrols, 142, 163–164; early ASW operations, 114; Enclose (operation), 164; Enclose II (operation), 164; Gondola (operation), 164; Leigh light in, 163–164; transit strategy, German, 163; U-boat defenses, 163–164

Black Sea, World War I, 47, 49–50

Blacker Bombard, 170

Blair, Clay, Jr., 179

blimps, 62–63, 75, 150, 154–155, 165–166

blockade, British, against Germany: World War I, 18–19, 31–32, 56; World War II, 115, 131, 176

Board of Invention and Research, 72–73, 87

Bonaparte, Napoleon, 3

Bowen, Edward, 123

Boyle, R. W., 87–88, 90

Bragg, W. H., 70

British Expeditionary Force: World War I, 23, 55; World War II, 125

Bushnell, David, 1–3

C

camouflage, 44

Campbell, Gordon, 29–30, 34

Canadian Navy, World War II: convoy operations, 119, 128, 130, 135–136, 138–139, 154, 160, 163, 173, 175; Donald Macintyre views of, 135; readiness issues, 135–136, 160

Casablanca Conference (1943), 173, 175

Catapult Aircraft Merchantman (CAM), 145

Chatfield, Ernle, 104, 107

Cheeney, William, 4

Chilowsky, Constantine, 85–86

Churchill, Winston, 107; World War I, 21, 28, 61; World War II, 114, 116, 130, 134–135, 138–139, 164, 168, 173

Civil Air Patrol (U.S.), 153

Civil War, American, 3–8, 24; ASW measures, 6; Confederate undersea craft, 3–8; *Hunley* sinks *Housatonic*, 6–7; Union undersea craft, 8

codes and codebreaking, British, World War I: diver recovery of coding materials, 39; intelligence liaison, 40; *Magdeburg* signal books, 39; Room 40, 38–40, 107, 124; tactical exploitation, 39–41, 81; Zimmermann telegram, 38

codes and codebreaking, British, World War II: Bletchley Park, 124, 140, 159, 162; "bombe," 124, 142, 162; Enigma decryption, 124–125, 140–142, 162, 180; Polish contributions, 124; pre-war activities, 124; tactical exploitation, 141–142, 144, 175, 182; *U-310* capture and exploitation, 140; ultimate capability, 162; Ultra, 140–142, 175; U.S. cooperation, 162

codes and codebreaking, German, World War I, 41

codes and codebreaking, German, World War II: Beobachtungsdienst (B-dienst), 120, 126, 141, 159, 181; Enigma machine, 124, 142; security concerns, 141; successes against Allies, 120, 159, 181; Triton code, 141, 159, 162

Committee on Air Organisation and Home Defense Against Air Raids, 61

Confederate States of America, 3–8

Convoy and Routing Section, 137

Convoy Section (Brit.), 42

convoys, World War II, individual: HG-53, 145; HG-73, 145; HG-74, 146; HG-76, 146; HX-72, 126; HX-79, 126; HX-90, 126; HX-111, 135; HX-150, 138; HX-156, 139; HX-217, 161–162; HX-228, 177, 179; HX-229, 179; HX-235, 177; HX-236, 180–181; HX-237, 177; HX-239, 177; KIF-3, 120; OB-244, 126; OB-318, 140; OG-67, 145; OG-69, 145; OG-71, 145; OG-74, 146; OG-76, 146; ON-18, 139; ON-184, 177; ONS-4, 177; ONS-5, 180; ONS-122, 171; PQ-16, 157; PQ-17, 157–158; PQ-18, 158, 175; QP-14, 158; SC-7, 126; SC-26, 135; SC-48, 139; SC-107, 160–161; SC-121, 179; SC-122, 179; SC-123, 177; SC-128, 180–181; SL-81, 145; SLS-64, 145; TM-1, 179

convoys and convoying, World War I: early use, 41; effectiveness, 79; first trans-Atlantic convoys, 42–44; formal convoy system, 44; French coal convoys, 41–42; Henderson role, 42–43; Mediterranean convoys, 52; North Sea convoys, 41–42; objections to, 42

convoys and convoying, World War II: Allied Atlantic Convoy Conference, 173, 175; coastal convoys (U.S.), 136; Convoy and Routing Section (U.S.), 137; early convoys, 114; effectiveness summary, 179; escort procedures, 119, 135, 138, 154; escorts, Royal Navy, 115, 128; Gibraltar convoys, 143, 145–147; interlocking convoy system, 156; mid-Atlantic convoys, 173; Murmansk convoys (PQ and QP), 140, 157–158; TM convoys, 179; trans-Atlantic system, 118–119, 121, 154; UG and GU convoys, 159

Cruel Sea, The (novel), 100

Curie, Jacques and Pierre, 85–86

Cussler, Clive, 7

D

Dahlgren, John A., 5–6, 13

Dardanelles campaign, World War I, 47–49

de Luppis, Giovanni, 19

Declaration of London (1909), 15, 17, 19, 20, 29, 51

depth charge throwers, British, 35–36. *See also* hedgehog

depth charge throwers, U.S., 35, 99, 169

depth charges, 127, 161; air-dropped, 64, 117, 129, 143; British, 33–36, 129, 171; effectiveness of, 35, 82–83; French, 34; German, 54; U.S., 34–35

destroyer escorts, U.S. Navy, 138, 150, 168–169, 173; British Lend-Lease orders, 138; design evolution, 169; multiple types, 169

destroyers, evolution of, 22

Director of Miscellaneous Weapons Development, 171

Director of Naval Intelligence (Brit.), 38–39

Dixon, George, 5, 7

Dogger Bank, Battle of the (1915), 39

Dönitz, Karl: early career, 79, 110; heads German Navy, 173; heads German submarine force, 109; tactical concepts, 109–111; war crimes trial, 110; World War II, 113–121, 123, 125–128, 135, 140–141, 144, 146–149, 156–158, 160–161, 163, 173, 180, 182

Dover, Strait of: World War I, 22–24, 26, 36–37; World War II, 117

Dover Patrol (Brit.), 23–24, 55

Drzewieki, Stefan, 9

Duff, Sir Alexander, 33, 43

Dunbar-Nasmith, Martin, 49, 114

Dupuy de Lôme, Henri, 9

E

East Ocean Meeting Point (EASTOMP), 154, 160

Edwards, Kenneth, 22

Einstein, Albert, 86

escort carriers, Royal Navy: introduction, 145–147; later operations, 148, 175, 176–178

escort carriers, U.S. Navy: conversion programs, 147, 175; first Atlantic deployments, 177; hunter-killer groups, 177; Operation Torch, 176–177

escort ships, between the wars, 99–101

Ewing, Sir James Alfred, 38–39

explosive sweeps, 25–26

F

Feldkirchner, Johannes, 17

Fenian Brotherhood, 11

Ferdinand, Archduke Franz 16

Fessenden, Reginald, 84, 86

Fessenden Oscillator, 84–85

Fido (Mark 24 homing torpedo), 166–168

Fighter Catapult Ship (FCS), 145

Fisher, Sir John, 19

Flanders, World War I: German submarine bases, 23, 36, 55–56. *See also* Zeebrugge-Ostend raid

Flanders Flotilla (Ger.), 23, 55–56, 59

fleet exercise problems, Royal Navy, 108

fleet exercise problems, U.S. Navy, 105–106

France, fall of, 125–126

France, German submarine bases in, 125–126, 128, 178

Franco, Francisco, 106–107

Franco-Prussian War (1870–1871), 15

Friedenburg, Hans-Georg von, 173

Fulton, Robert, 3, 13

G

Garrett, George, 8

Geddes, Sir Eric, 45

German Navy, between the wars, 109–111

German-Soviet non-aggression pact, 113, 139

Goldsborough, Louis M., 4

Goubet, Claude, 9

Greer incident, 138

Gretton, P. W., 180

Guggenberger, Friedrich, 144

Guthrie, Woody, 139

H

Hague Peace Conference, Second (1907), 15

Hall, Sir William, 39–40

Harvard Underwater Sound Laboratory, 166

Havana, Act of (1940), 130

Hawkcraig Admiralty Experimental Station, 72, 90

hedgehog, 170–172, 181

Heinkel, Ernst, 65

helicopter development, 103, 178

Henderson, Reginald Guy, 42–43

Hertz, Heinrich, 95

heterodyning, 87

High Seas Fleet (Ger.), 60

high-frequency direction-finding, World War I, 38–39, 81

high-frequency direction-finding, World War II, 114–115, 141, 159–161, 177

Hitler, Adolf, 109, 111–112, 115–117, 122, 125, 137, 139, 143–144, 147, 149, 173

Hitler's U-Boat War, 179

Holland, John, 9–14, 19; design principles, 11; early submarine experiments, 10–11

Holzendorf, Henning von, 32

Horton, Sir Max Kennedy, 54, 173, 176

Howe, Richard, 2

Hunley, Horace L., 4–6, 13

Hunt, Horace, 23

I

Iceland: air operations, 150, 160–162, 168, 180; British occupation, 128; convoy role, 135, 138; U.S. occupation, 138

imports, British, World War I, 19, 33

imports, British, World War II, 122, 148, 156, 180

indicator nets, 26–27

Ingenieurskantoor voor Scheepsbouw (IVS), 109

Italy, World War I, 22, 48–49, 51–52, 54

Italy, World War II, 125, 127–128

J

Japanese Navy: pre–World War II ASW views, 101, 108–109; World War I, Mediterranean role, 52

Jellicoe, Sir John, 20–21, 32, 42

Joubert de la Ferté, Philip, 142

Jutland, Battle of (1916), 33, 43

K

Keyes, Sir Roger, 55–56

King, Ernest J., 152, 172

kite balloons, 63

Kretschmer, Otto, 133–134

L

Lake, Simon, 10–11

lance bombs, 27–28

Langevin, Paul: acoustics experiments, 85–88; development of quartz transducers, 86–87; early career, 86; Langevin "sandwich," 87, 90, 93

Laning, Harris, 106

Laubeuf, Maxime, 9

Lee, Ezra, 2

Leigh, Humphrey de Verde, 163

Leigh light, 163–164

Lemp, Fritz Julius, 116, 125, 140

lessons learned, Spanish Civil War, 107–108

lessons learned, World War I, 79–83

Lewis, Thomas L., 172

Lloyd George, David, 43, 46

London Naval Conference (1930), 103, 108, 115

losses, cumulative, shipping: World War I, 32, 41, 45, 79; World War II, 120, 148, 156, 160, 179

losses, cumulative, submarines: World War I, 48, 53, 80–81; World War II, 120, 147–148, 156, 160, 179, 181–182

M

Macintyre, Donald, 132–135

Malta, 143

Magnetic Anomaly Detection (MAD), 165

magnetostriction, 85, 93–94

Marconi, Guglielmo, 95

Marder, Arthur, 51

Max, Prince of Baden, 59

Maxwell, James Clerk, 95

McClintock, James, 4

McEvoy, C. A., 14

McKehan, Louis, 166

Mediterranean theater, World War I: Allied convoys, 52; Allied shipping losses, 50–53; Allied submarine operations, 47; German submarine operations, 47–48, 50, 53; initial Allied defenses, 51–52; Japanese Navy escorts, 52; submarine losses, 50, 53. *See also* Adriatic Sea; Dardanelles campaign; Otranto, Strait of

Mediterranean theater, World War II, 180; Allied naval operations, 143–144; German submarine operations, 144–145; Italian ground offensives, 143; North African campaigns, 143–144; submarine losses, 144

Mid-Ocean Escort Force, 134, 154

Mid-Ocean Meeting Point (MOMP), 138–139

Milchkühe ("milk cows"), 152, 159

mines and mining, World War I: effectiveness, 82; Electro Contact (Brit.), 27; galvanic firing mechanism, 37, 82; Mark 6 (U.S.), 37; mine nets, 27; minefields, British, 23–24, 31, 36–37, 70, 73; minefields, German, 24–25; minefields, Russian, 25; minefields, Strait of Otranto, 50–51; mines, British, 24, 35–36; mines, German, 36; mines, U.S., 37; Northern Mine Barrage, 37, 56; Type H-2 (Brit.), 36–37; Type H-4 (Brit.), 36

mines and mining, World War II: Baltic, 139; minefields, British, 117, 120; minefields, German, 121, 139; U.S., defensive, 151

Monsarrat, Nicholas, 100

Morris, J. T. McGregor, 73

Morse, Philip M., 172, 174

Mussolini, Benito, 106, 127

N

Nahant acoustic research facility, 75, 89

Nash, G. H., 74, 85

National Defense Research Committee, 130, 165, 174

Naval Experimental Station, 75

Naval Research Laboratory, 89, 93, 95–97, 165

Naval Underwater Sound Laboratory, 75

Nazi-Soviet Non-Aggression Pact (1939), 113, 139

nets, defensive, 23, 25, 50

Newbolt, Sir Henry, 33

Noble, Sir Percy, 134–135, 176

Nordenfeldt, Thorsten, 8–9

Norway, 139; German conquest, 122–123; German submarine bases in, 126

O

Oliver, Henry F., 38–39, 51

Operational Intelligence Centre (Brit.), 107–108, 114

operations research: ASW Operations Research Group (ASWORG), 172–174; Atlantic Fleet Anti-Submarine Warfare Unit, Boston, 172; Navy Support Group, Argentia,172; Royal Navy, 129, 142–143; U.S. Navy, 172–174

Osprey, HMS: 1st Anti-Submarine Squadron, 104; attack trainer, 104; establishment of, 90; research and training programs, 92, 104; tactics development, 104

Otranto, Strait of, World War I, 49–51; anti-submarine barrier, 50–51, 53; U.S. subchasers, 53

P

"Pact of Steel" (1939), 125

Panama, Act of (1939), 1940

Parkeston Quay, 87, 90

Patrol Squadron (VP) 82 (U.S.), 103, 154

piezoelectricity, 85

Plan Z (Ger.), 111

Porte, John C., 63

Pound, Sir Dudley, 158

Prien, Gunter, 116, 118–119, 132–134; death, 132; sinks *Royal Oak*, 118

Princip, Gavrilo, 16

Prize Regulations, 15, 17, 23, 29, 31–32, 56

Q

Q-ships, 28–31, 34–35, 42, 57, 66; effectiveness, 31, 83; tactical concept, 28; U.S. Navy, 31

R

radar, British: airborne, 123–124; ASV Mark II, 123–124, 129, 142–143, 163; ASV Mark III, 164; ASV-I, 102, 123–124; Chain Home system, 97; early experimentation, 96–97; H2S, 164; introduced in aircraft, 96, 102, 123–124, 129, 164; introduced in surface ships, 97, 129; Type 271, 129, 160–161; Type 286, 129, 160

radar, centimetric: cavity magnetron, 129; development, 129, 164; first deployments, 160–161, 164; need for, 129

radar, German, 96

radar, Japanese, 96–97

radar, U.S.: CXAF, 149; CXAM, 96, 149; development of, 95–97; introduced in aircraft, 124, 164; introduced in surface ships, 96–97; SCR-517, 164; XAF, 96–97

radar warning receivers, German, 163–164

radio direction finding. *See* high-frequency direction-finding

Raeder, Erich, 109–111, 117, 173

retro-bombs, 165

Revolutionary War, American, 1–3

Rice, Isaac, 12

Rochelle salt crystals, 89, 93–94

rockets, anti-submarine, 166

Romazotti, M., 9

Rommel, Erwin, 143–144

Roosevelt, Franklin D., 129–131, 138–139, 149–150, 169, 173

Roskill, Stephen W., 97, 179

Royal Air Force, Bomber Command, 121, 126, 142, 178

Royal Air Force, Coastal Command, 114–115, 151, 156, 161–164; 19 Group, 164; early ASW weapons, 117; first operations, 115, 117; force levels, 117, 142; initial ineffectiveness, 118, 129, 142; pre–World War II, 102; weapon upgrades, 129, 143

Royal Navy, between the wars: asdic, development of, 87–93; commerce protection, neglect of, 104–105; escort construction, 99–101; force levels, postwar, 98; Sixth Destroyer Flotilla, 90; tactics development, 104; views on ASW, 103, 108

Royal Navy, pre–World War I, 1–3; first submarines, 13; rudimentary ASW, 14–15, 69–70

Royal Navy, World War I, 18–30, 33–45, 48–52, 54, 56, 58–59, 63–75, 77–78; ASW preparations, 21–23; Auxiliary Patrol, 22, 26, 35, 42; surface craft, 66–68

Royal Navy, World War II, 112, 128, 130, 134, 143, 145–147, 160–162, 168, 180–181; ASW preparations, 114–115, 117–119; Fleet Air Arm, 118; war construction, ASW ships, 176

Russo-Japanese War (1904–1905), 13, 19, 24

Ryan, C. P., 72–73

S

Santos Dumont, Alberto, 61

Scapa Flow: World War I, 21, 23, 70, 73; World War II, 118, 122, 132

Scheer, Reinhold, 31, 59

Schepke, Joachim, 132–133

Schuhart, Otto, 112

Scott, Sir Percy, 14

Shipping Defense Advisory Committee, 108

Shoemaker, Harry E., 131

Shuldham, Molyneux, 1, 2

Sikorsky, Igor, 178

Sims, William S., 58

Smith, William, 4

snorkel, 5

sonar, British: active sonar (asdic), development of, 84–93; displays, sonar, 90–91; domes, sonar, 88–90; first asdic installations, 88, 89, 104; first asdic use in combat, 107–108; Nash Fish, 74, 85; passive sonar, development of, 70–74; Portable Directional Hydrophone (PDH), Mk I, 73–74; Portable Directional Hydrophone (PDH) Mark II, 74, 76; Portable General Service (PGS) hydrophone, 72–73; Q attachment (depth finding), 172; Rubber Eel, 74; Type 112, 90; Type 113, 90; Type 114, 90–91; Type 118, 90; Type 119, 90; Type 123, 100–101; Type 128, 90; Type 129, 90; Type 147, 172

sonar, French, 74–75, 85–88

sonar, general: active vs. passive, 79, 84–85; early development, 71–78; early limitations, 79, 83–84; hydrophones, 70, 73–77; initial promise, 83; sea floor systems, 73; on seaplanes and blimps, 75; search tactics, World War I, 77–78

sonar, German, 78, 94

sonar, Japanese, 93–94

sonar, Soviet Union, 94–95

sonar, U.S.: active sonar development, 89, 105; C tube, 75–76; domes, sonar, 89, 93; Electric Eel, 77; first ship installations, 89, 94; fleet exercise experience, 105–106; JL, 93; JK, 93; K tube, 76–77; MB tube, 76; MV tube, 77; passive sonar development, 75–77; QB, 93; QC, 93; SC tube, 76; World War II initial systems, 149; XL, 93

sonobuoys, 165–166

Soviet Union: Allied assistance to, 139, 157–158; enters World War II, 139; Murmansk convoys, 140, 157–158; submarine force 1939, 109, 139

Spanish Civil War, 106–108

spar torpedoes, 5, 6

Special Vessel Service (Brit.), 28–29

Stalin, Josef, 173

Stark, Harold, 136–137

Stephenson, George O., 135

strategy and tactics, ASW: active acoustic search, 104; area saturation (suppression), 22, 81–82; area search, 41; decoying (e.g., Q-ships), 28–31, 57, 144; early, 14–15; gunnery, 23; hunter-killer groups, 41, 112, 115, 117, 175; passive acoustic search, 77–78; "scarecrow" tactics, 64, 82, 118; Spider Web patrols, 64; submarine vs. submarine, 28–29, 49, 57–59, 83, 120, 122, 128, 124; zone defense, 51

Sturdee, Sir Doveton, 15

Submarine Attack Committee (Brit.), 25

submarine campaigns, German, World War I: final failure, 59; force levels, 113, 132; initial phases, 17–18; later operations, 31–32; Mediterranean, 47–48, 50, 53; merchant losses, 32, 41, 45, 54, 56, 79, 132; rationale, 19; rules of engagement, 17, 31–32; submarine losses, 41, 46, 79–81, 132; surrender, 60; unrestricted submarine warfare, 32; U.S. East Coast, 56–58

submarine campaigns, German, World War II: diminishing effectiveness, 161, 181; Gulf and Caribbean, 152, 155; initial phases, 113, 115–116, 119–120; Mediterranean, 144–147; merchant losses, 116–117, 120–122, 125–126, 137, 141, 148, 152, 156–160, 179; against Murmansk convoys, 157–158; North Atlantic, 113–114, 115–117, 118–122, 125–126, 135, 158–162, 178–182; retreat from North Atlantic in May 1943, 182; rules of engagement, 115, 117, 125, 137, 139; South Atlantic, 141, 159; submarine losses, 120–122, 144–145, 147–148, 161, 181; U.S. East Coast (*Paukenschlag*—"Drumbeat"), 150–152, 155–156; wolf packs, 119–120, 126, 139, 158–161, 180–181

Submarine Committee (Brit.), 14

submarine pens, 126–127, 178

Submarine Signal Company, 70–72, 75, 78, 84, 93

Submarine Tracking Room (Brit.), 114–115, 134–136

submarine vs. submarine, 28–29, 49, 58–59, 83, 120, 122, 128, 144

submarines, general: development and evolution, 8–9; employment concepts, 19–20, 109–110; initial attitudes toward, 13–14, 19–20

submarines, German, World War I. *See* submarine campaigns, German, World War I

submarines, German, World War II. *See* submarine campaigns, German, World War II

submarines, Italian, World War II, 126–128, 163

support/escort groups, Allied, World War II, 175; 5th Escort Group, 132; 6th Escort Group, 161; 36th Escort Group, 146; C-4 Escort Group, 160; Support Group 1, 181; Support Group 3, 181; Support Group 6, 177

Sykes, A. J., 73

T

Tausig, Joseph K., 45

Thomas, Hugh, 107

Tirpitz, Alfred von, 31

Tizard, Henry, 131

Tobruk, siege of (1941), 143

Torch, Operation (1942), 176, 178

torpedo development, 8–9, 13

torpedoes, German, problems, 122–123

Torpex (explosive), 129, 131, 143

Tripartite Pact (1940), 149

Tryon, Sir William, 1

Tuck, J. H. L., 9

Turing, Alan, 125

U

underwater acoustics, 87, 91–93

underwater detection systems, rudimentary: birds, 69; electromagnetic indicator loops, 70; sea lions, 28, 69–70

United States, pre–World War II: ABC-1 staff agreement, 132; "cash and carry" policy, 131; convoy escort, 136, 138–139; "destroyers-for-bases" deal, 130, 153; Lend-Lease, 131, 138–139, 153, 161, 175; National Defense Research Committee, 130, 165, 174; naval and merchant marine expansion, 130; Neutrality Patrol, 129, 137; occupation of Iceland, 138; Pearl Harbor attack and war declaration, 149; small craft acquired, 130–131; staff talks with British, 131–132; Support Force established, 137; "undeclared naval war," 138

United States, World War I, 31, 32. *See also* U.S. Navy, World War I

U.S. Army Air Forces, World War II: 1st Anti-Submarine Command, 153; ASW operations, 151, 153, 154, 164; attacks on submarine pens, 178; Bay of Biscay operations, 164; disagreements with Navy, 153; helicopters, 178; sea frontier role, 151, 153

U.S. Navy, between the world wars: destroyer construction, 98–99; escort construction, 101; fleet exercise problems, submarines and ASW in, 105–106; force levels, post–World War I, 98; views on ASW, 106

U.S. Navy, World War I, 56–57; convoy role, 44–45; destroyer construction, 68–69; Eagle boats and subchasers, 66–67; subchasers in the Mediterranean, 53; submarine vs. submarine, 57–58

U.S. Navy, World War II: aircraft available at outset, 150; "bucket brigade" system, 154–155; coastal convoys, 153–155; convoy escort, mid-Atlantic, 173, 175; convoy escort, North Atlantic, 154, 156, 159, 177; East Coast defenses, 150–154; first submarine kills, 154–155; initial force levels and dispositions, 149–150, 154; interlocking convoy system, 156; sea frontiers, 151–152; ship construction programs, 168–170

V

Verne, Jules, 10

Versailles Treaty (1919), 94, 103

W

Walker, F. J. (Johnny), 146

Walser, Georges, 74

Walser gear, 74–75, 77, 87

Washington, George, 2

Washington Naval Conference (1921), 103

Watson, Baxter, 4, 7

West Ocean Meeting Point (WESTOMP), 154, 161

Western Approaches Command, World War I, 24

Western Approaches Command, World War II, 173, 176; establishment of, 114; move to Liverpool, 134; permanent escort groups, 135; training program, 135

Western Isles, HMS, 135

Whitehead, Robert, 9, 13

Wilhelm II, Kaiser, 31–32

Wilson, Sir Arthur, 13

Wilson, Woodrow, 56, 59

Winn, Sir Charles Rodger, 134–135

Y

yachts, 130–131

Z

Zalinsky, Edmund, 11

Zede, Gustav, 9

Zeebrugge-Ostend raid (1918), 55–56

Zeppelin, Count Ferdinand von, 61

Zimmermann telegram, 40

Z-plan (Ger. Navy), 111

Ship Name and Class Index

Ship designations are found on page xii.

British-English

Aboukir (ACR), 20, 21

Admiralty V class (DD), 68

Archer (CVE), 166, 175–177

Argus (CV), 140

Ariguani (fighter catapult ship), 145

Ark Royal (CV), 112, 115, 116, 118, 144–145

Arun (DD), 30

Athenia (passenger liner), 116, 125, 140

Aubrietia (corvette), 140

Audacity (CVE), 145–147, 175

Avenger (CVE), 148, 175–177

Barham (BB), 144

Bassett (armed trawler), 100

Bickerton (frigate), 134

Birmingham (CL), 23

Biter (CVE), 148, 175–177

Bittern (DD), 30

Bittern class (sloops), 99–100

Black Swan (sloop), 100, 170

Bosnia (merchant), 116

Bridgewater (sloop), 99

Britannia (training), 40

C classes (DD), 168

Calypso (CL), 127

Campbell (DD), 90

Captain class (DE), 169

Castle class (corvettes), 170

Cobb (Coast Guard cutter), 178

Collingwood (BB), 72

Colony class (frigates), 170

Conquest (CL), 176

Cornwall (training), 40

Courageous (CV), 112, 115

Cressy (ACR), 20, 21

Cumberland (ACR), 30

Daghestan (merchant), 178

Dasher (CVE), 175–177

Dublin (CL), 49–50

Duncan (DD), 180–181

Dunraven (Q-ship), 30

Eagle (ship-of-the-line), 2

Ebro II (trawler), 88

Egret class (sloops), 100

Erin (BB), 43

Escort (DD), 127

Euryalus (ACR), 72

Fanad Head (merchant), 118

Farnborough (Q-ship), 29, 30, 34

Flora (2nd class cruiser), 30

Flower class (corvettes), 100, 128, 154, 155, 170, 172, 180

Flower class (sloops), 66, 99

Formidable (BB), 20

Furious (CV), 43

Gleaner (minesweeper), 121

Glitra (merchant), 17

Grimsby (sloop), 99

Hadleigh Castle (corvette), 170

Harvester (DD), 179

Hatimura (merchant), 160

Havock (DD), 107

Hedingham Castle (corvette), 170

Hermes (CV), 112

Hesperus (DD), 134

Hogue (ACR), 20, 21

Hunt class (escort destroyers), 100, 128, 150

Impregnable (training), 30

Iverlyon (armed smack), 28

J class (DD), 98, 168

K class (DD), 89, 98, 168

Kafiristan (merchant), 112

King Alfred (ACR), 30

King George V (BB), 168

Kingfisher class (sloops), 99, 134

L class (DD), 168

Loderer (collier), 30

Loostrife (corvette), 181

Lotus (corvette), 172

Lusitania (passenger liner), 31, 116

M class (DD, 1914), 22

M class (DD, 1940), 168

Majestic (BB), 48

Manaar (merchant), 116

Maplin (fighter catapult ship), 145

Marigold (corvette), 144

Mauretania (passenger liner), 44

N class (DD), 168

Natal (ACR), 40

O class (DD), 168

Oranjestad (merchant), 152

Oribi (DD), 181

P class (DD), 168

P class (escorts), 66, 67, 77, 89, 99–100, 104

P.59 (escort), 89, 91–92

PC class (submarine chasers), 89, 104

Pargust (Q-ship), 29, 30

Pathfinder (ACR), 20

Pathfinder (DD), 177

Patrol (CL), 30

Pegasus (fighter catapult ship), 145

Pelican (sloop), 181

Petard (DD), 162

Prince Charles (Q-ship), 28

Prince George (BB), 30

Q class (DD), 168

Queen Mary (CB), 40

R class (DD), 168

R class (frigates), 170

Ranger (DD), 30

Rentoul (Q-ship), 29

Resolution (BB), 176

Rocket (DD), 91

Royal Edward (transport), 48

Royal Oak (BB), 118–119, 132

Royal Sceptre (merchant), 116

S class (DD), 168

Southern Pride (whale catcher), 100

Springbank (fighter catapult ship), 145

Stanley (DD), 146

Starwort (corvette), 172

Stock Force (Q-ship), 29, 31

Stockport (merchant), 160

Sunflower (corvette), 181

T class (DD), 168

Taranaki (armed trawler), 28

Tiger (CB), 30

Tree class (armed trawlers), 100

Tribal class (DD), 98

Triumph (BB), 48

U class (DD), 168

V class (DD), 68, 115, 168

Vanoc (DD), 133

Vidette (DD), 181

Viscount (DD), 171

W class (DD), 115, 168

Walker (DD), 133–134

Warspite (BB), 122

Westcott (DD), 171

Woodford (merchant), 107

Z class (DD), 168

Zealous (DD), 72

Canadian

Restigouche (DD), 160

French

Bretagne (passenger liner), 120

Chantier-Bretagne class (SC), 101

Jean Bart (BB), 49

Le'on Gambetta (ACR), 49

Provence (transport), 51

German

Admiral Hipper (CA), 145

Admiral Scheer (pocket BB), 132, 148

Atlantis (raider), 142

Bismarck (BB), 111, 138

Blücher (CA), 122

Deutschland (pocket BB), 113, 115

Emden (Ger. CL), 110, 119

F1 to *F10* (escort), 101

Gneisenau (CB), 111

Graf Spee (pocket BB), 96, 113, 115

Hannover (merchant), 146

Hela (CL), 20, 176

Karlsruhe (CL), 122

Königsberg (CL), 96, 122

Magdeburg (CL), 39

München (trawler), 140

Prince Adalbert (ACR), 176

Python (supply ship), 142

Scharnhorst (CB), 111

Tirpitz (BB), 111, 157–158

Italian

Amalfi (ACR), 49

Orione (torpedo boat), 144

Orsa class (torpedo boats), 101

Partenope class (torpedo boats), 101

Spica class (torpedo boats), 101

Japanese

Akashi (ACR), 52

Hyuga (BB), 96

Idzumo (ACR), 52

Ise (BB), 96

Sakaki (DD), 52
Shimushu class (escorts), 101

Soviet
Blagaev (merchant), 107
MO-521 (SC), 95
Tuniyaev (merchant), 107

Turkish
Messoudieh (BB), 48

United States
Arabia (schooner), 57
Asheville (PF 1), 170
Baynton (DE 1), 169
Benson (DD 421), 98
Bogue (CVE 9), 177
Brennan (DE 13), 169
Buckley (DE 51), 169
Bunker Hill (merchant), 178
Caldwell (DD 69), 68
California (BB 44), 105
Charger (CVE 30), 175
Chenango (CVE 28), 175–176
Clemson (DD 186), 68
Colorado (BB 45), 105
Congress (frigate), 4
Doherty (DE 14), 169
Eagle type, 67, 98, 101; *PE 56*, 67
Evarts (DE 5), 169
Fanning (DD 37), 34
Farragut (DD 348), 98
Fish Hawk (steamer), 89
Fletcher (DD 445), 169
Gleaves (DD 423), 168
Graham (DD 192), 69
Greer (DD 145), 138
Housatonic (sloop-of-war), 6–7
Isabel (PY 10), 130–131
James Parker (transport), 178

James Whittemore (schooner), 57
John C. Butler (DE 339), 169
Kearny (DD 432), 139
Lake class (Coast Guard cutters), 130
Langley (CV 1), 103, 105
Leary (DD 158), 96, 149
Livermore (DD 429), 168
Long Island (AVG 1/CVE 1), 149, 175
Maryland (BB 46), 105
Melvin (DD 335), 105
Merrimack (frigate), 4
Minnesota (BB 22), 56
Minnesota (frigate), 4
Monitor (monitor), 4
New Ironsides (ironclad), 5–6, 13
New York (BB 34), 97
Niblack (DD 424), 137
Nicholas (DD 449), 169
Orion (yacht), 130
PC 449 to *PC 453*, 101
Reuben James (DD 245), 139, 148
Robert H. McCurdy (schooner), 57
Robin Moor (merchant), 137
Roper (DD 147), 154
San Diego (ACR 6), 56
Sangamon (CVE 26), 175–176
Santee (CVE 29), 175–176
Santee (Q-ship), 31
SC type, 67, 101
Stringham (DD 83), 57
Surprise (PG 63), 155
Suwannee (CVE), 175–176, 177
Tacoma (PF 3), 170
Treasury class (Coast Guard cutters), 150
Virginia (ironclad), 4
Vixen (PG 53), 130
West Virginia (BB 48), 105
Wickes (DD 75), 68
Wyoming (BB 32), 105
Yorktown (CV 5), 137

Submarine Name and Class Index

Australian
AE-2, 49

Austro-Hungarian
U-4, 49
U-5, 49
U-6, 51

British-English
B-10, 65
B-11, 48
C-4, 28
C-25, 65
Clyde, 141
D-3, 65
E-6, 25
E-9, 20, 176
E-11, 62
E-14, 49
E-35, 41
Graph (ex-*U-570*), 141
H-32, 91
Holland I, 13
J-1, 41
J-6, 176
L-55, 94
M-1, 176
Oxley, 120
R class, 58–59
R-4, 59
R-8, 59
Resurgam (Garrett), 8
Salmon, 120
Seahorse, 118, 120
Starfish, 120
Thistle, 122
Triad, 128
Triton, 120
Truant, 122
Undine, 120

Confederate States of America
David (semi-submersible), 5–6, 13
H. L. Hunley, 4–7, 13
Pioneer, 4
Pioneer II, 4

Dutch
O-1, 144

French
Curie, 49
Foucault, 65
Le Plongeur, 8
Narval, 9
Sidi-Ferruch, 177

German, World War I
Deutschland, 56
U-1, 13
U-5, 24
U-6, 53
U-7, 58
U-8, 26, 27
U-9, 20
U-11, 24
U-12, 49
U-15, 22–23
U-16, 17
U-17, 17
U-18, 21, 23
U-20, 31
U-21, 18, 20, 48, 49, 50
U-22, 58
U-24, 18, 20
U-26, 25
U-27, 52
U-31, 24
U-34, 107
U-35, 30, 51
U-36, 28
U-40, 28
U-53, 56
U-58, 34
U-68, 34
U-69, 63
U-83, 30
U-117, 57
U-140, 57
U-151 to *U-157*, 56
U-153, 40–41
U-154, 40–41

UB type transported to Austria,
   47–48
UB-4, 28
UB-14, 48, 49
UB-15, 49
UB-26, 27
UB-32, 64
UB-53, 53
UB-56, 37
UB-68, 110
UB-83, 63
UB-107, 78
UB-109, 73
UB-115, 78
UB-116, 70, 73
UC-6, 64
UC-7, 27, 30
UC-49, 78
UC-70, 64
UC-71, 30

German, World War II
"ducks," 113, 114, 117, 122, 126. *See also*
   Type II
Milchkühe, 152. *See also* Type XIV
Type I, 113
Type II, 113, 132
Type VII, 113, 114, 120, 132, 141, 148,
   151–152, 156, 158, 160, 162
Type VIII, 113
Type IX, 113, 120, 132, 148, 150–152,
   156, 160
Type X, 159
Type XIV, 152, 159
U-1, 109
U-4, 122
U-12, 117
U-27, 117
U-29, 112
U-30, 116, 118, 125
U-31, 121
U-33, 121
U-36, 114, 117, 120
U-37, 120, 145
U-39, 112, 116

U-40, 120
U-42, 120
U-45, 120
U-47, 118–119, 132–133
U-48, 116, 122
U-53, 112
U-55, 121
U-66, 151
U-67, 141
U-68, 141
U-69, 137
U-81, 144
U-85, 154
U-89, 177
U-95, 144
U-99, 133–134
U-100, 126, 132–134, 140–141
U-110, 140–141
U-111, 141
U-123, 151
U-125, 151, 181
U-130, 151
U-131, 146
U-132, 160
U-135, 171
U-155, 148, 177
U-159, 163
U-192, 181
U-203, 177
U-209, 180
U-221, 161
U-231, 177
U-254, 161
U-258, 180

U-264, 181
U-266, 181
U-269, 134
U-305, 177
U-331, 144
U-333, 164
U-371, 144
U-432, 177
U-433, 144
U-434, 146
U-438, 181
U-442, 160
U-444, 177
U-456, 168
U-459, 152
U-468, 177
U-502, 163
U-503, 154
U-522, 160
U-524, 161
U-552, 139
U-557, 144, 147
U-559, 162
U-567, 146
U-569, 177
U-570, 141
U-574, 146
U-611, 162
U-640, 168
U-650, 180
U-652, 138
U-656, 154
U-660, 171–172
U-701, 155

U-751, 146
U-752, 166, 177
U-A, 133, 152

Italian
Bagliolini, 127
Enrico Toti, 128
Guglielmo Marconi, 127
H-5, 58
Iride, 107
Luigi Torelli, 163
Medusa, 49

Polish
Orzel, 122

Spanish
B-5, 107
B-6, 107
C-1, 107
C-3, 107
C-6, 107

United States
Fenian Ram (Holland), 11
H-5 (SS 148), 76
Holland (SS 1), 10
Holland VI, 12
Intelligent Whale, 8
O-4 (SS 65), 105
Peacemaker (Tuck), 9
Plunger (Holland), 11–12
Turtle (Bushnell), 1–3

About the Authors

Norman Polmar is an analyst, consultant, and author specializing in naval, aviation, and science and technology issues. He has been a consultant or advisor on naval-related issues to three U.S. senators, the Speaker of the House, and the deputy counselor to the president, as well as to the director of the Los Alamos National Laboratory. He has testified on several occasions before congressional committees on Soviet naval developments, U.S. naval programs, and related maritime issues.

He has directed several studies for U.S. and foreign shipbuilding and aerospace firms and also has been a consultant to the leadership of the Australian, Chinese, and Israeli Navies. Prior to 1980, Mr. Polmar was an analyst and then corporate executive with firms performing studies in the naval, science and technology, and aviation areas.

From 1982 to 1986 and from December 2002 until June 2008, Mr. Polmar served as a member of the Secretary of the Navy's Research Advisory Committee (NRAC). He chaired the NRAC panel established in 2005 to determine science and technology requirements for supporting the Navy and Marine Corps in the period 2015–2020. He also served on a sub-panel of the Defense Science Board's study of transition to and from hostilities (2004) and was a member of a DARPA advisory panel looking at future warfare requirements (2007).

In early 2007 he was appointed to reestablish and to chair the Science and Technology Advisory Committee of the Department of Homeland Security. He served as chair until 1 August 2009; he remained a member of the committee until its existing charter expired in 2011.

Mr. Polmar has written or coauthored more than fifty published books and numerous articles on naval, aviation, technology, and intelligence subjects.

Edward Whitman studied electrical engineering at the Massachusetts Institute of Technology and later earned a PhD in that subject from the University of Maryland. His Navy civilian career lasted nearly forty years and included senior management positions with the U.S. Sixth Fleet, the Defense Advanced Research Projects Agency, the Office of the Chief of Naval Operations, the Navy Secretariat, and the Office of the Oceanographer of the Navy. Following his Navy retirement in 1998, Dr. Whitman was for five years the senior editor of the U.S. submarine community's magazine *Undersea Warfare*.

The **Naval Institute Press** is the book-publishing arm of the U.S. Naval Institute, a private, nonprofit, membership society for sea service professionals and others who share an interest in naval and maritime affairs. Established in 1873 at the U.S. Naval Academy in Annapolis, Maryland, where its offices remain today, the Naval Institute has members worldwide.

Members of the Naval Institute support the education programs of the society and receive the influential monthly magazine *Proceedings* or the colorful bimonthly magazine *Naval History* and discounts on fine nautical prints and on ship and aircraft photos. They also have access to the transcripts of the Institute's Oral History Program and get discounted admission to any of the Institute-sponsored seminars offered around the country.

The Naval Institute's book-publishing program, begun in 1898 with basic guides to naval practices, has broadened its scope to include books of more general interest. Now the Naval Institute Press publishes about seventy titles each year, ranging from how-to books on boating and navigation to battle histories, biographies, ship and aircraft guides, and novels. Institute members receive significant discounts on the Press's more than eight hundred books in print.

Full-time students are eligible for special half-price membership rates. Life memberships are also available.

For a free catalog describing Naval Institute Press books currently available, and for further information about joining the U.S. Naval Institute, please write to:

Member Services
U.S. Naval Institute
291 Wood Road
Annapolis, MD 21402-5034
Telephone: (800) 233-8764
Fax: (410) 571-1703
Web address: www.usni.org